KU-734-034

WHERE IN ST. PETERSBURG

Paul E. Richardson, ed.

Стахановцев 5, кв39
Минаев Петр Владимирович.
221-96-84

Кефир
ацедофилин

The ultimate directory, including maps, telephone listings, and essential goods and services.

EDITION 2

Russian Information Services, Inc.
Montpelier, VT

Русская Информационная Служба
Москва & Санкт-Петербург, Россия

Copyright © 1994 by Russian Information Services, Inc.

All rights reserved. No part of this guide may be reproduced or transmitted in any form, by any means mechanical or electronic, including photocopying, recording, or any information and storage retrieval system now known or to be invented, without the expressed written permission of the publishers.

Every attempt has been made to make this guide the most up-to-date collection of business information available. Given the swift rate of change in Russia and the new Commonwealth, mistakes in phone numbers, addresses, and on other points of fact are inevitable. The authors, editors and publishers accept no liability for any consequences which may arise from the use of information in this guide.

First edition: September 1992
Second edition: March 1994

Published by:
Russian Information Services
89 Main Street, Suite 2
Montpelier, VT 05602 USA
ph. 802-223-4955
fax 802-223-6105

in cooperation with:
Russkaya Informatsionnaya Sluzhba
B. Kondratyevskiy per. 4, kor. 2, kv. 168
Moscow, USSR 125056
ph./fax 095-254-9275

Cover design by:
Marketing Arts
Bridge Street Marketplace
Waitsfield, VT 05673, USA

St. Petersburg City Street Map by:
Northern Cartographic, Inc.
4050 Williston Rd.
South Burlington, VT 05403

Quotes on page four as translated in The Heritage of Russian Verse, *Dimitri Obolensky, ed. (Indiana University Press, 1965) and* Moscow, a Traveler's Companion, *by Lawrence Kelly (Atheneum, 1984).*

Russian Information Services, Montpelier, VT USA

Library of Congress Catalog Card Number: 93-83110
ISBN 1-880100-13-4

Where in St. Petersburg

Where in St. Petersburg, renowned as the first and best travel and business guide to the New St. Petersburg, is published with the independent traveler in mind. Its unique combination of yellow pages, white pages and full-color city street map brings together, in one concise, easy-to-use volume, all the essential tools for making your trip to St. Petersburg a success. For historical information on tourist sites, look elsewhere. For the most current, accessible information on where to eat, send a fax, get a suit dry cleaned or spend a night out, look no further.

Where in St. Petersburg has been **totally updated** and **significantly expanded** in this new second edition. Each bit of information was reverified just prior to publication. ***All new to this edition is our color city street map of St. Petersburg*** – the first map of this city ever published by a US company. You won't find it anywhere else (except in our stand-alone, fold-out version, of course).

Among the fine members of the RIS team responsible for bringing this book to completion are Stephanie Ratmeyer, S. Todd Weinberg, Bella Gubnitskaya, Yuri Pankratov, Alexander Fall-Jones, Olga Apukhtina, Pasha Apukhtin, Jennifer Krebs, Clare Kimmel, Scott D. McDonald, Patrick Ryan, Glenn Holstein, Galina Levina, Katya Alekseyeva, and Irina Petrova.

Corrections and comments are enthusiastically encouraged. If you would like your company to be listed in the next edition of this guide, simply send your information to either of our addresses given on the page facing.

Where in St. Petersburg is just one of a series of publications of Russian Information Services on doing business in Russia and the Commonwealth, including:

Where in Moscow (4th edition)
Russia Survival Guide: Business & Travel (5th edition)
Russian Travel Monthly
Business Russian
The New Moscow: City Map and Guide (2nd edition)
The New St. Petersburg: City Map and Guide (1st edition)

Ask at your local bookseller or see the back of this guide for ordering information.

The Publisher
March 1994

"I love you, Peter's creation, I love your severe, graceful appearance, the Neva's majestic current, the granite of her banks, the tracery of your cast-iron railings, the transparent twilight, the moonless gleam of your still nights..."

– *Alexander Pushkin*

"There life is empty, silent, stern and grey,
Like the flat foreshore of the Finnish Bay."

– *Mikhail Lermontov*

St. Petersburg Business Telephone Directory

City Codes Within the CIS

To direct-dial long distance within the Commonwealth of Independent States, dial 8, wait for a dial tone, then dial the city code as listed below and then the local number. You will need to add zeroes or twos between the city code and the local number to make a total of 10 digits if the number of digits does not already equal ten.

City	Code
Almaty	327
Arkhangelsk	818
Ashkabad	363
Astrakhan	85100
Baku	8922
Barnaul	3952
Bishkek	331
Blagoveshensk	41622
Borodino	39168
Bratsk	39531
Brest	01622
Bryansk	08322
Bukhara	365
Cheboksari	8350
Chelyabinsk	351
Cherkassy	0472
Chita	30222
Dagomys	8620
Dnepropetrovsk	0562
Donetsk	0622
Dushanbe	3772
Fergana	373
Gomel	02322
Grozny	8712
Irkutsk	3952
Ivanovo	09322
Izhevsk	3412
Kaliningrad	01122
Kaluga	08422
Karaganda	3210
Kaunas	0127
Kazan	8432
Kemerovo	38422
Khabarovsk	4210
Kharkov	0572
Kiev	044
Kirov	833
Kostroma	09422
Krasnodar	8612
Krasnoyarsk	3912
Kuybyshev	8462
Kurgan	35222
Kursk	07100
Lipetsk	0740
Lvov	0322
Magadan	41300
Magnitogorsk	35137
Minsk	0172
Moscow	095
Mozhaisk	238
Murmansk	815
Nikolaev	0510
Nizhny Novgorod	8312
Noginsk	251
Novgorod	8160
Novosibirsk	3832
Odessa	048
Omsk	38122
Orel	0860
Orenburg	35300
Pavlodar	3182
Penza	8412
Perm	3422
Petropavlovsk	3150
Petrozavodsk	81400
Pinsk	01653
Poltava	05322
Pskov	81122
Rostov	08536
Rostov-on-Don	8632
Rovno	0360
Ryazan	0912
St. Petersburg	812
Samarkand	366
Saransk	8342
Saratov	8452
Semipalatinsk	3222
Sergeyev Posad	254
Sevastopol	0690
Simferopol	06522
Smolensk	08100
Sochi	8620
Stavropol	86522
Sukhumi	88122
Sumgait	89264
Suzdal	09231
Syktyvkar	82122
Taganrog	86344
Tambov	07522
Tashkent	3712
Tbilisi	8832
Termez	37622
Tomsk	38222
Tula	0872
Tver	08222
Tyumen	3452
Ufa	3472
Ulan-Ude	30122
Ulyanovsk	84222
Uralsk	31122
Vitebsk	02122
Vladimir	09222
Volgograd	8442
Vologda	81722
Volokolamsk	236
Voronezh	0732
Vyborg	278
Yakutsk	41122
Yalta	0600
Yaroslavl	0852
Yekaterinburg	3432
Yerevan	8852
Zaporozhe	0612
Zhitomir	041

☑ **For other cities, or if you have difficulties with dialing, or if you want the number for directory assistance for a certain city (some are listed in Chapter 4), call 07.**

☑ **Note that Moldova, Estonia, Lithuania and Latvia now have their own country dialing codes (see chart on page 76).**

	Phone	Fax	Telex
AB, Kamenoostrovskiy prosp. 26/28	560-6187		
ABC Law Firm, ul. Sadovaya 55/57	310-8436		
ABINSET Bank, Zakharyevskaya ul. 35	275-6636		
ABS Business Safety Assoc., Moskovskiy prosp. 212	293-1266	291-8135	
Absolut & K Co., Zagorodny prosp. 27/21 kom. 65	164-8655	113-5569	
Absolut St. Petersburg, Kosmonavtov prosp. 54	264-6527	264-6527	
Academy of Sciences			
Geographical Society, p. Grivtsova 10	315-8535		
Institute of Ocean Technology, V. O., 26 Liniya 9	217-0419	217-0693	
Acater JV (Finland), Lomonosov, ul. Feduninskovo 3	422-5065	423-1711	
ACCEPT, ul. Borovaya 19	164-7683	164-7410	
Accis, ul. Shota Rustavelli 31a	538-6781	239-9819	
ACD AutoJV (USA), ul. Kalinina 59a	186-0000	186-3679	
Address Bureau, Liteyny prosp. 6	278-3119		
Addresses of St. Petersburg Residents	009		
Adidas, P.S., Bolshoy prosp. 51	232-2092		
Admiral Makarov Sea Engineers' Academy, V. O., Kosaya liniya 15a	217-5064	217-0782	
Admiralteyskiy Restaurant, ul. B. Morskaya 27	314-4514		
Admiralteystvo Restaurant, Yekaterinskiy park, ul. Komsomolskaya 7	465-3549		
Adonis Pharmacy, Svechnoy p. 7	315-8487		
Adra JV (USA), nab. reki Pryazhki 3/1	219-5180	219-7531	
Advertising Agency, Yurii Gagarin prosp. 28, k. 1	299-3982	299-3982	
Aero-Balt Service, Pilotov ul. 38	104-1875	104-1836	
Aerocommuter Center for Aviation Technological Creativity, ul. Syezzhinskaya 4	233-6035	233-1257	
Aerocourier JV (Germany), ul. Vzletnaya 7/1, Pulkovo Airport	104-3496	104-3512	121172
Aeroflot Airlines, Pulkovo Airport	104-3822		
International Flight Information	104-3444		
Aviagorodok Warehouse ul. Pilotov	104-3411		
Aeromed Firm, ul. Novolitovskaya 15	245-2554	245-5105	
Aeroprit Travel PTI Ltd. JV Singapore, 5 Predportoviy pr. 8 korpus 5	122-6366	108-4158	
Afisha, Rubinshteyna ul. 8	314-3978		
Agency for Apartment Cleaning, Zakharevskaya ul. 14	273-3851		
Agency for International Projects, Klenovaya ul. 2	210-4764	314-9272	
Agency of Independet Inspektions, ul. Parashyutnaya 6	301-2222	301-2222	
Agfa Salon, Nevskiy prosp. 20	311-9974	311-9923	
Agra, Engelsa prosp. 111, kor. 1, kv. 46			
Agrarny Universitet, Pushkin, Leningradskoye sh. 2	470-0422	465-0505	

☑ **All numbers and addresses in the Telephone Directory were individually verified prior to printing and are therefore judged to be the best available at the time of publication. Given the swift nature of change in Russia, it is expected that some numbers will not be correct even soon after printing. If you have corrections or additions to suggest to the Telephone Directory, please call Russian Information Services at (St. Petersburg) 292-7420 or (US) 802-223-4955; fax (802) 223-6105.**

	Phone	Fax	Telex
Agricultural Library, ul. B. Morskaya 42	314-4914		
Agro, Utkin prosp. 13/6	528-6959		
Agropromizdat, Nevskiy prosp. 28	312-4219		
Aguaservice, ul. Kolomenskaya 10 kv. 65	164-5806		
Ahlers Lines, Suvorovskiy prosp. 2	277-2006		
Aibolit, Kolomenskaya ul. 45	164-6211		
Air France Airlines, Pulkovo II Airport	104-3433	104-3433	
Aircraft Arrivals and Departures, Information	297-2509		
Aist, Raznochinnaya B. ul. 6, kv. 28		315-1701	
Aiyu, Voronezhskaya ul. 33	166-0320		
Akater JV (Finland), Lomonosov, ul. Feduninskovo 3	422-4094	423-1711	
Akimova Comedy Theater, Nevskiy prosp. 56	312-4555		
Akkumulator Faktory, ul. Kalinina 50	186-3219	186-9719	
Akkumulator Institut, ul. Dalya 10	234-4695	234-9026	
Akonit Publishers, Yuriya Gagarina prosp. 1, kor. 343	297-8768		
Akos JV (USA), ul. Sergeya Tyulenina 3/25	311-7495	311-3448	
Aksel V, ul. Savushkina 15	538-6781	239-9819	
Aktsioner, Shpalernaya ul. 52, kv. 19	272-9676	275-7611	
Akvamarin, Novosmolenskaya nab. 1	352-0766		
Alak, ul. Pilotov 8	178-2725	178-2771	
Alba JV (US), V. O., 3 Liniya 52	213-3058	218-3935	121329
Albatros Cooperative, Kronshtadt, ul. Manulskovo 2	236-9269		
Alcatel Business Systems, ul. B. Morskaya 16	315-8938	315-9474	
Alcor Technologies Inc. Ltd, ul. Stepana Razina 8/50	310-2687	310-4470	
Aldi Firm, Malookhtinskiy prosp. 68	528-9566	528-8400	
Aleksander Print, nab. reki Fontanki 18	279-0259	272-1552	
Aleksandr Nevskiy Abbey, pl. Aleksandra Nevskovo	274-0409		
Alenkiy Tsvetochek, Prosveshcheniya prosp. 46	597-2694		
Ales, Basseynaya ul. 20, Box 261	294-0455		
Alex Detective Services, ul. Kapitanskaya 3	352-5754		
Alfa (Appraisers), Saltykova-Schchedrina ul. 43	279-3913	279-3913	
Alfa Express	234-3968		
Alfa-700, Gorokhovaya ul. 25			
Alga, V. O., Bolshoy prosp. 8	213-6342	218-5530	
Algo, V. O., 18 Liniya 7 flat 11	217-4246		
Alice Trade House Ltd, V. O., 6 Liniya 35, korpus B	218-3433	213-1777	
Alinda, Mayakovskovo ul. 19	272-8358		
Alinter JV (FRG), ul. Nalichnaya 6	356-6262	356-2414	121434
Alisa, Zanevskiy prosp. 6	221-7441	223-5526	
Alivekt Central Office, ul. Popova 22	234-0232	234-9096	
Lanskoe sh. 27	246-1515		
Liteyny prosp. 59	272-3301		
nab. reki Moyki 40	315-7302	234-9096	
Nevskiy prosp. 112	275-0107		
Nevskiy prosp. 2/24	315-5978		
Nevskiy prosp. 23	311-4645		
P.S., Bolshoy prosp. 82	232-0283		
ul. B. Pushkarskaya 34	230-4740		
ul. Michurinskaya 11	233-8297		
Alkatel BSR, Varshavskaya ul. 11	296-3978	296-7078	
Alkonic-Lakomka Firm, Manezhny p. 8	273-0112	273-0112	
All Petersburg, ul. Sadovaya, #46	210-4879		

	Phone	Fax	Telex
All-Russian Society of Handicapped Persons,			
Krasnogvardeyskiy p. 8	245-2779		
All-Union Geological Library, V. O., Sredniy prosp. 74	218-9228		
All-Union Society of the Deaf,			
Pavlovsk, ul. Kommunarov 16	470-6244	470-6166	121771
Alliance Ltd., Lermontovskiy prosp. 43/1	259-3442	251-8890	
Almaz, Petrovskiy prosp. 26	235-4890	235-7069	
Sredneokhtinskiy 5	224-2048		
Almaz Jewellery, prosp. Veteranov 87	150-4401		
Alpia JV (Austria), ul. Baikonurskaya 19, k. 3	393-1179	552-3652	
Alternativa Sinicy, ul. Dostoevskovo 6	164-4787		
Aluma System-Monolitstroy Corp. JV (Canada),			
ul. Ryleyeva 29	273-2646	272-7930	121266
Alyans Ltd, Millionnaya ul. 29	110-6544		
Amal Charitable Islamic Fund, Dvortsovaya nab. 18	311-5101	311-5101	
Amateur Hand-Weaving Organization,			
ul. Galernaya 33	311-4311		
Ambulance	03		
AMC, See American Medical Center			
Amela, Vladimirskiy prosp. 3	113-2284	301-5913	
American Express,			
in Grand Hotel Europe, Mikhailovskaya ul. 1/7	119-6009	119-6011	
American Medical Center, nab. reki Fontanki 77	310-9611	119-6120	
American Telephone & Telegraph (AT&T),			
Liflyandskaya ul. 4	186-7537	252-1252	
American-Russian Commercial Alliance (ARKA),			
ul. Khlopina 10	535-5459	534-1284	
Americar (Chrysler), Piskarevskiy prosp. 39	544-0590	544-5824	
Americom Business Center, Nevskiy Palace Hotel	275-2001	113-1470	121279
Americs International JV (USA),			
Kamenoostrovskiy prosp. 37	233-8731	232-4413	
Ameros business Company, Ligovskiy prosp. 87	164-1285	112-1844	
Amethyst Jewelry Store,			
Petrogradskaya Storona, Bolshoy prosp. 64	232-0102		
Amixt JV (German,France),			
ul. Sofiyskaya 48 k. i kv. 260	105-6856	105-6856	
Anata, Izmaylovskiy prosp. 14	112-6678		
Ancher-Auto, prosp. Prosvoshcheniya 80	540-8746	530-9761	
Andreyev i Synovya, Ordzhonikidze ul. 5	127-7949	126-6741	
Andreyevskiy Dom, V. O., 8 Liniya 43	218-0614		
Angleterre Bar, Hotel Astoria	210-5838		
Anichkov Most, Nevskiy prosp. 81	279-4641		
Ankor, 6 Krasnoarmeyskaya ul. 17	292-0475		
Anna Akhmatova Museum,			
Liteyny prosp. 53,or nab. Fontanki 34	272-1811		
Anna Laine Ltd, ul. Lenina 1a	291-2546		
Anomaliya, p. Grivtsova 5,kom. 506,508	315-3018		
Antanta Supermarket, V. O., Tuchkov p. 11/5	213-2047	350-5777	
Antanta 2, Novoizmailovskiy prosp. 46	295-0165		
Antanta 3, Moskovskiy prosp. 161	298-7496		
Antanta 4, prosp. Stachek 46	186-8255		
Antik Store, Narvskiy prosp. 18	252-0058		
Antikvarnaya Lavka, ul. Pochtamtskaya 5	311-2643		

	Phone	Fax	Telex
Antikvarno-Bukinisticheskaya Kniga, Nevskiy prosp. 18	315-5078		
Antique Shop, B. Konyushennaya 13	312-3505		
Antiques, Nalichnaya ul. 21	217-1010		
Antraks Hotel, Vyasemskiy p. 5	234-0700	234-0722	
Antwerpen Restaurant JV (Belgium), Kronverkskiy prosp. 13/2	233-9746	233-8482	
Anvi Ltd, ul. Sadovaya 2 (Inzhenerny Zamok)	210-4375	210-4786	
Aphrodite Restaurant, Nevskiy prosp. 86	275-7620		
Apit, prosp. Kima 28	119-6130	350-5548	
Apogey, Gospitalny p. 3	274-0310		
Apollo Agency, ul. Sevastyanova 3	294-8082	294-8082	
Apraksin Dvor Second Hand Shop, Sadovaya ul. 32	310-7350		
Aqua Excurs, nab. reki Moyki 8	314-5645		
Aquaelektronika JV, Konnogvardeyskiy bulvar 4, kv. 16	311-3024	315-4700	
Aquamarine Jewellery, Novosmolenskaya nab. 1	352-0766		
Aragvi Restaurant, ul. Tukhachevskovo 41	225-0082		
Ararat Factory, ul. Sofiyskaya 93	173-6862	172-5331	
Arc JV (FRG), ul. Borovaya 14	164-2313	164-6898	121315
Architect's Union, RSFSR, ul. B. Morskaya 52	311-2729		
Arctic & Antarctic Marine Shipping Company, nab. reki Fontanki 34	273-3725	272-3333	
Arctic Road, Boytsova p. 4	314-1992	314-1992	
Arctis Ltd, ul. Promyshlennaya 7	252-9587	186-2830	
Argos Association for Young Business Persons, Gatchinskaya ul. 11/56	232-7123		
Argumenty i Fakty Petersburg, ul. Zverinskaya 1/3 kv. 22	110-4973	232-5564	
Ariadna, Profsoyuzov bul. 11, #17	311-6997	315-1701	
Arian Consulting, ul. Chekhova 11 kv. 24	275-3171		
ARK Co., Razyeschaya ul. 5	113-3329	112-4134	
Army Sports Club, Inzhenernaya ul. 13	219-2967		
Swimming Pool, Litovskaya ul. 3	542-0162		
Arnika Prima, Aptekarskiy prosp. 10	234-2018	234-2118	
ARS, Leninskiy prosp. 121	254-7611	255-1467	
ARS Publishers, Lermontovskiy prosp. 7/12	219-5787	114-4822	
Art Boutique, Nevskiy prosp. 51	113-1495		
Art Paint Manufacturing Plant, ul. Serdobolskaya 68	245-5028	245-1540	
Art Rest JV (Finland), Nevskiy prosp. 86	275-7640		
Art Shop Varyag, V. O., Sredny prosp. 88	356-6139		
Art Sreda Design Studio, Fontanka 118	251-1541	145-7712	
Art-Motors, Kubinskaya ul. 81	122-5418	122-2415	
Art-Peterhof Gallery, ul. 4 Sovetskaya	427-5450		
ArtAG, Kubinskaya ul. 86	122-2072	122-5423	
Artar-Innery, Belgradskaya ul. 40	260-1888		
Arthur Andersen, V. O., Bolshoy prosp. 10	350-4984	213-7874	
Artis Association, ul. Shirokaya 53	230-3176	230-3175	
Artists' Union, ul. B. Morskaya 38	314-7736		
Ascod, Fontanka 6	275-5813		
Asea Brown Boveri, V. O., Bolshoy prosp. 10a	213-7871	350-2911	121507
Asian and African Literature Book Repository, Liteyny prosp. 49	272-5776		
ASKO-Petersburg, Yuriya Gagarina prosp. 1	297-8500	297-8906	

St. Petersburg Press

Saint Petersburg's
English-language
weekly.

Pick yours up at one of
600 locations in St. Petersburg

Now available internationally
by subscription

Phone: 7(812) 119-6080
Fax: 7(812) 314-2120

Russia has never been this accessible!

This **essential guide** to doing business in the new Russia is the current version of the most widely-read book on doing business in the new Russia. This guide includes valuable information like: how to get a visa, customs regulations, rubles and what you can do with them, dealing with transportation, accommodations and telecommunications, including up-to-date contact information for travel and business in Russia's 77 largest cities, hotel prices and ratings, how to make contacts, business etiquette and customs, and a complete review of investment, trade and enterprise legislation, including import/export, currency and taxation laws.
ISBN 1-880100-18-5
March 1994, 232 p., $18.50

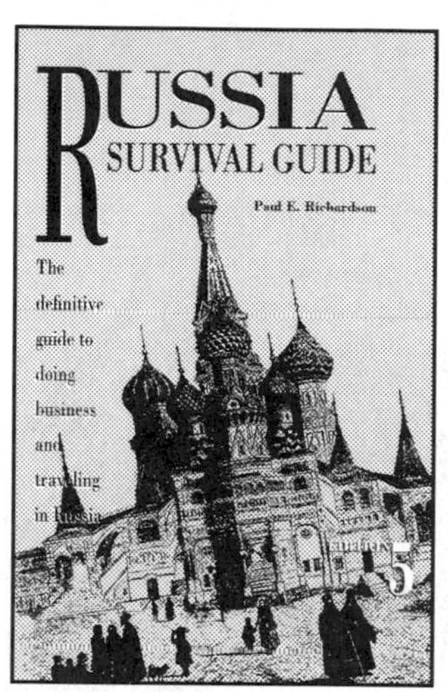

...and Moscow has never been this easy!

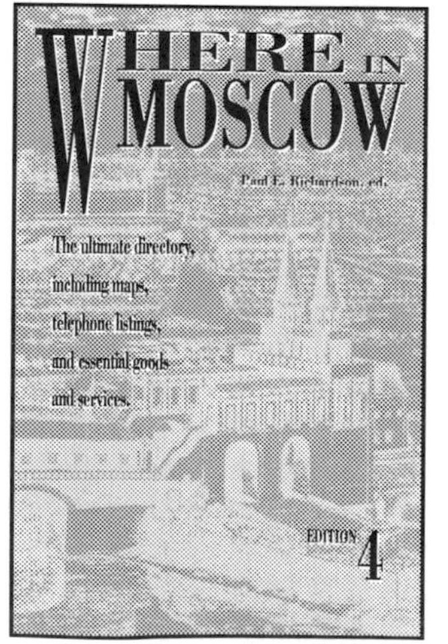

This companion guide to ***Where in St. Petersburg*** is widely-recognized as the most complete and accurate guide to the Russian capital. All-new in the 4th edition of ***Where in Moscow*** is our completely-updated, full-color city street map. This, plus the city's best English language yellow pages and only white pages business directory. Whether you are going to Moscow for business, study or pleasure, you can't afford to go without this all-in-one guide!
ISBN 1-880100-19-3
March 1994, 258 p., $13.50

***Ask at your local bookseller, or see last page of book for ordering information.**

	Phone	Fax	Telex
Askod, ul. Sovetskaya 3	110-7401	275-6385	
AsLANTIS, Box 398	298-9007	298-9007	
Assambleya, ul. B. Konyushennaya 13	314-1537		
Assoc. for Foreign Economic Coop. of St. Petersburg Enter, See AVEKS Association			
Association for Eastern and Central European Businesspeople, ul. M. Morskaya 14	312-8097	315-0954	
Association of Commercial Banks, ul. Plekhanova 36	319-9249	319-9249	
Association of Joint Ventures, ul. Plekhanova 36	312-7954	315-9470	
Association of Representatives of Consumer Cooperatives, nab. reki Fontanki 130a	251-0300	251-0455	122035
Association of Sea Ports, Gapsalskaya 4	186-6822	251-1492	121501
Association Scientifik-Produktion, ul. Zhukova 7a	540-3509	540-3518	
Asta JV (Holland), Ligovskiy prosp. 256	296-0537	315-8687	
Asta-Information, P.S., Bolshoy prosp. 82, kv. 17	230-7898	232-7535	
Asta-Press Ltd., Boytsova p. 4	260-6494		
Aster, Kuybysheva ul. 4	233-7300	233-7168	
Astoria Hotel, ul. B. Morskaya 39	210-5020	315-9668	
Angleterre Bar & Restaurant	210-5838		
Astoria Restaurant	210-5906		
Rent-A-Car	210-5858	542-8798	
Retur Business Center	311-7362	311-7362	121304
World Class Gym, 4th floor	210-5869		
Zimny Sad Restaurant	210-5838		
Astoria-Service, Borovaya ul. 11/13	112-1583		
Astrelle JV (UK), ul. Volkova 146, k. 3	268-6125	312-5280	121326
Astrobank, Nevskiy prosp. 58	311-3600	311-0825	121221
Kuibyshevskiy Branch, ul. Dostoyevskovo 5	164-0278	311-0825	
ATD Ltd, Kolomyazhskiy prosp. 4	511-7087		
Atlant, Yuriya Gagarina prosp. 1	297-8194		
Atlantic Investment, Ryleyeva ul. 18	275-8590	275-8590	
Atlas Firm, ul. B. Morskaya 35	110-6550	319-9709	
Atlas JV (USA), 14 Liniya 39	218-0887	218-0887	
Atmosfera Cooperative, ul. Karbysheva 7	245-9330	247-8661	122612
Audit Firm, ul. Gorokhovaya 30	310-4805	310-4805	
Audit S. P. S., M. Pasadskaya 23 k. 3	233-4142		
Auditing & Management International Centre, Canal Griboedova 34,rm. 210	110-5720	110-5751	
Auditor, ul. Dumskaya 1/3, 3rd flr.	110-5999	312-2136	
Aurora Art Shop, ul. Kuybysheva 33/8	233-4168		
Aurora Cinema, Nevskiy prosp. 60	315-5254		
Aurora Cruiser Ship, Petrovskaya nab. 4	230-5202		
Aurora Kafe, Nevskiy prosp. 60	314-3038		
Aurora Magazine, Millionnaya ul. 4	312-1323		
Aurora Publishers, Nevskiy prosp. 7/9	312-3347	312-5460	
Austeria Restaurant, Peter and Paul Fortress, Ioannovskiy Ravelin	238-4262		
Austrian Airlines, Nevskiy Palace Hotel	314-5086	164-7873	
Auto Star, prosp. Energetikov 65	226-9980	226-1034	
Auto-Vo Firm, prosp. Stachek 106	158-5777		
Autobaltservice, Nakhimova ul. 5, kor. 1	356-7701	355-0440	
Autograph, ul. Lomonosova 5	310-2602		
Autohaus St. Petersburg, ul. Rubinshteyna 6-8	113-1895	314-0597	

	Phone	Fax	Telex
Autohouse, nab. reki Moyki 56	312-9045	312-9045	
Autokhim, prosp. Stachek 106	158-3598		
Automarket, ul. Sevastyanova 13	298-7611		
Autoservice, Oktyabrskaya nab. 40-42	587-7249		
Avalanche Ltd, Vladimirskiy prosp. 2	113-1384		
Avangard Hotel, Metallistov prosp. 115	540-4815		
Avangard Scientific-Production Assn., Kondratyevskiy prosp. 72	544-6901	540-1844	121431
Avant JV (Swiss), ul. Kolontay 30	583-8159	580-8571	
AVEKS Association, 3 Krasnoarmeyskaya 12	292-4837	292-1453	121361
Aviation Instruments Institute, ul. B. Morskaya 67	311-1522	315-7778	
Avicenna JV (Syria), ul. Professora Popova 15/17	234-5028	234-2937	
Avis Rent-a-Car, Konnogvardeyskiy bul. 4	312-6318	312-7292	
AVN Company, Ligovskiy prosp. 56	117-0129	117-0129	
Avto, ul. Kalinina 59-a	186-0000	186-3679	
Avto-Motors (Opel), Novoizmailovski 4	296-5587	296-5592	
Avtobaltservice JV (Sweden), ul. Nakhimova 5, kor. 1	356-4525	355-0440	
Avtodvor, ul. Rustaveli 7	249-1370		
Avtogazstroy Assn, Kingiseppskoye sh. 47	132-4719	132-2304	121660
Avtokolonna 1106, nab. reki Volkovki 13	166-6216	166-1465	321092
Avtomobili, prosp. Stachek 106	157-0459		
Avtomobilist Coop, Lodeynopolskaya ul. 7	235-2817		
Avtoremont, Moskovskiy prosp. 181	293-3373		
Avtosalon, ul. Marshala Zakharova 21	142-5527		
Avtotekhobsluzhivanie, Bogatyrskiy prosp. 12	395-3095	395-3696	
Avtotour JV (Sweden), prosp. Energetikov 65	226-1437	226-2678	
Avtotur Hotel, Klyuchevaya ul. 32	544-7728		
AvtoVAZbank, 2 Sovetskaya ul. 3/7	274-4948	277-3111	
AvtoVAZtekhobsluzhivaniye, Kingiseppskoye sh. 50	132-4789	132-8347	321375
Avtozapchasti, Kubinskaya ul. 76	290-4833		
Ayaks, Krasnoputilovskaya ul. 69	184-6073		
Ayaks Restaurant, ul. Rubinshteyna 25	314-9733		
Aytra JV(British), Sverdlovskaya nab. 52 k. 1	224-1081	224-0597	
AZ Law Firm, ul. Mayakovskovo 50	272-4132	272-9049	
Azalia, B. Sampsonievskiy prosp. 70	245-4619		
Azbuka JV (Finland), ul. Gangutskaya 4	272-5860	272-5860	
Azimut International Ltd, ul. M. Pasadskaya 30	238-7802	232-2581	

B

	Phone	Fax	Telex
Babush JV (Finland), pl. Lenina 5	542-2736	542-2736	
Babylon General Office, ul. Shpalernaya 24	279-6349	275-1414	
Babylon Shops			
Liteyny prosp. 61	273-4212		
Liteyny prosp. 63	273-5254		
Nevskiy prosp. 69	314-6237		
Nevskiy prosp. 130	277-0730		
Bolshoy prosp. 94	234-9068		
Bolshoy prosp. 65	232-0466		
Bolshoy prosp. 25	235-6400		
Bolshoy prosp. 38	232-5243		
Sadovaya ul. 26	310-1815		

	Phone	Fax	Telex
Babylon Supershop, P.S., Maly prosp. 54/56	230-8095		
Baccara, P.S., Bolshoy prosp. 86	232-8407		
Badische Anilin, V. O., Bolshoy prosp. 10a	350-7256	119-6040	
Bahlsen Kafe, Nevskiy prosp. 142	271-2811	271-3060	
Baker & McKenzie, nab. kanala Griboyedova 36	310-5446	310-5944	612151
Baku Restaurant, Sadovaya ul. 12	315-0752		
Balkan Airlines, ul. B. Morskaya 36	315-5030	315-4752	
Balkan Holidays, ul. Artileriyskaya 1	279-6138	279-6144	
Balkankarros Ltd, ul. Ryleyeva 27	273-7284	273-7577	121565
Balkantourist, ul. B. Morskaya 36	315-5030		121565
Balkany Cinema, Budapeshtskaya ul. 102	108-1553		
Balkany Restaurant, Nevskiy prosp. 27	315-4748		
Baltcontainer JV (FRG), Doroga na Turukhtannie Ostrova 17	259-0407	183-7821	
Baltex Ass., ul. Blagodatnaya 55	294-1023	294-1028	
Baltic Communications Ltd., Marata ul. 6	314-5548	164-7653	
Baltic Consulting Group, See Hill International			
Baltic Customs, Mezhevoy kanal 5	113-9945	113-9940	
Baltic Sea Shipping, Mezhevoy kanal 5	114-9001	186-8544	121501
Baltic Sputnik, Litovskaya ul. 10	245-2160		
Baltik Petroleum, ul. Zakharyevskaya 31,bldg 3a	275-4676	275-4677	
Baltika, Kolpino, prosp. Saperny	484-4318	484-3080	321683
Baltika Cinema, V. O., 7 Liniya 34	213-1182		
Baltika Ltd, sh. Revolyutsii 48	226-7520		
Baltika Sports Center, Petrovskiy prosp. 16	235-5164		
Baltika-1 Association, Konnogvardeyskiy bulvar 4, pod. 6	314-1287	311-6315	
Baltika-St. Petersburg, Box 48	543-6211		
Balting Ltd JV(Estoniya), Liteyny prosp. 74	273-3178	279-5648	
Baltink Ltd., nab. reki Fontanki 40	279-7463	279-7298	
Baltinvest, Goncharnaya ul. 25	271-8153		
Baltiya Firm, ul. Shkapina 10	252-1062	252-1062	
Baltiyskiy Bank, ul. Sadovaya 34	310-0580	310-9274	121334
Baltiyskiy Train Station, nab. Obvodnovo kanala 120	168-2972		
Baltiyskiy Zavod, Kosaya liniya 16	217-9580	217-2296	
Baltiyskiy Zavod Shipyard Library, V. O., Bolshoy prosp. 78	217-9406		
Baltiyskoye Strakhovoye Obshchestvo, Ligovskiy prosp. 44, kv. 571	164-0635	165-0635	
Baltperl Company JV (Poland), Khimicheskiy p. 1	186-3776	2527478	
Baltrans Transport Enterprises Assn., ul. Dvinskaya 3	315-8986	314-1823	121501
Bamkredit, prosp. Yuriya Gagarina 1	294-8536	294-8538	321203
Baptist Church, B. Ozernoy ul. 29a	553-4578		
Barrikada Cinema, Nevskiy prosp. 15	315-4028		
Barvas, 8 Sovetskaya ul. 4	271-2069		
Baskin-Robbins, Aleksandrovskiy Park 4	232-9159		
Nevskiy prosp. 79	164-6456		
Bast, prosp. Rayevskovo 16	247-7412	552-3936	
Bavaria Restaurant, Hotel Sovetskaya	259-2454		
Bazis Cooperative, ul. Moskovskaya-Sortirovochnaya 19	554-1616		
BCL, Konnogvardeyskiy Bulvar 4	311-8800	314-8660	

	Phone	Fax	Telex
BDB-Profit, Pochtamtskaya ul. 5, kv. 30	315-4774	315-4774	
Beer Garden, Nevskiy prosp. 86	275-7620		
Begemot, Shpalernaya ul. 60/1	278-5968		
Belaya Loshad Cafe, Chkalovskiy prosp. 16	235-1113		
Belinskiy Central District Library, Grazhdanskiy prosp. 83, kor. 1	217-2923		
Beliye Nochi Hotel, Narodnaya ul. 93, kor. 1	263-2104		
Beliye Nochi Restaurant, Voznesenskiy prosp. 41	319-9660		
Bella Liona Restaurant, Vladimirskiy prosp. 9	113-1670	113-1673	
Belochka Candy Shop, V. O., Sredniy prosp. 28	213-1763		
Benetton, Nevskiy prosp. 147	277-1732		
Benson & Company, ul. Rimskovo-Korsakova 8, kv. 4	311-7097	311-7097	
Bereg Company, Admiralteyskiy prosp. 6, kom. 401	315-9368	315-5059	
Beriozka, Karelia Hotel	226-3237		
Malookhtinskiy prosp. 6	528-6316		
Morskaya nab. 15	355-1875		
Morskaya nab. 9	356-5598		
Nevskiy prosp. 7/9	315-5873		
Sovietskaya Hotel	251-6772		
ul. B. Morskaya 26	315-4647		
Beta, Marinesko ul. 1	184-1383		
Beton JV (German), ul. Inzhenernaya 6	273-6621		
Bibliopolis, Bronnitskaya ul. 17	110-1448	112-6030	
Bikar, Cheliyeva p. 16	586-9528	585-9206	
Biofizpribor Firm, ul. Sabirovskaya 37	239-6650		
Biokompleks Ltd, ul. Pochtamtskaya 14	312-7840	312-7840	
Biokorm-Farm, prosp. Morskoy Slavy 1	567-4092		
Biont, Furmanova ul. 25, kv. 8	275-8757		
Biont Corp., ul. Energetikov 2/60	226-4456	226-9100	
Biotekhnomed Firm, V. O., 6 Liniya 13	350-4311		
Biryuza Jewellery Store, Nevskiy prosp. 69	312-2176		
Birzha, Dostoyevskovo ul. 6	113-3067	113-3068	
Birzha Truda, Podyezdnoy p. 13	164-8456		
Bive, Konnogvardeyskiy Bulvar 4, kv. 20	312-7835	315-3951	
Blaze Productions, Inc., nab. kanala Griboyedova 97	311-0459	311-0459	
Blik Firm, Kanal Griboedova 119	114-6576	114-5538	
Blok Central Library Art Gallery, Nevskiy prosp. 20	311-7777		
Blok Central Library, Nevskiy prosp. 20	311-0106	311-2249	
Blok House Museum, ul. Dekabristov 57	113-8633		
Blue Dolphin Restaurant, See Goluboy Delfin Restaurant			

Less *is* more.

Our philosophy in compiling *Where in St. Petersburg* is that less advertising means more information. In this sense, *Where in St. Petersburg*'s content is driven by its users, not its advertisors. As a result, *Where in St. Petersburg*, now in its third year, enjoys a reputation for concise, easy-to-access and objectively-presented information. With *Where in St. Petersburg*, you don't have to fish through ads to get the phone number or address you need. And you get more phone numbers and addresses than any other guide!

	Phone	Fax	Telex
Blue Drawing Room, See Golubaya Gostinaya			
BMP Reklama A/O, Mezhevoy kan. 5	114-9541	186-8344	121501
Bogoslovskovo Cemetery, Laboratornaya ul. 4	544-7524		
Bolsheokhtinskovo Cemetery, prosp. Metallistov 5	224-2729		
Bolshevichka Clothing, Ligovskiy prosp. 107	164-9310		
Bolshevichka Sewing Production Enterprise Ltd, ul. Tyushina 11	164-5622	164-3388	122706
Bolshoy Dramatic Theater (Gorkiy Theater), nab. reki Fontanki 65	310-0401		
Bolshoy Puppet Theater, ul. Nekrasova 10	273-6672		
Bon-Servis, V. O., Bolshoy prosp. 63	217-3137		
Booz-Allen & Hamilton, Nevskiy prosp. 77, kv. 3	164-5289	164-5289	
Borey Art Gallery, The, Liteyny prosp. 58	273-3693	273-5276	
Bosch, Apraksin dvor korp. 1, kom. 50	226-9539		
Bosko JV(USA), Nevskiy prosp. 8	219-1855	219-1854	
Bosnev JV(Chekhiya), ul. Ochakovskaya 7	255-9562	255-9961	
Bosy, 1 Krasnoarmeyskaya ul. 11	292-1595		
Botanical Garden of the Academy of Sciences, ul. Professora Popova 2	234-1764		
Botanical Gardens Museum, ul. Professora Popova 2	234-0673		
Botanical Gardens of St. Petersburg State University, Universitetskaya nab. 7/9	218-9721		
Brigantina Restaurant, Dvinskaya ul. 3	259-0815		
Brisk-Show JV, prosp. Yuri Gagarina 8	298-2164	298-0107	
Bristol Restaurant, Nevskiy prosp. 22/24	311-7490		
British Airways, Nevskiy Palace Hotel	119-6222		
Briz Kafe, Kolokolnaya ul. 8	110-6225		
Brodskiy House Museum, ul. Mkhailovskaya 3	314-3658		
Brok, Dnepropetrovskaya ul. 31	164-0133		
Bronzoviy Lew JV (USA), ul. Sadovaya 51	314-7292	314-7292	
Buddhist Temple, Primorskiy prosp. 91	239-0341	239-0341	
Budimex, nab. Robespyera 8/46, kv. 93	279-6931	279-6831	121336
Buff Plus Cabaret and Bar, ul. Narodnaya 1	266-4356		
Bukinist, Liteyny prosp. 59	273-2504		
Bumar, Yakornaya ul. 9	528-8490	528-8490	
Burda Moden Peterburg, Kuybysheva ul. 34	232-0276	232-0160	
Bure, Nevskiy prosp. 23	312-2759		
Burevestnik Book Store, Nevskiy prosp. 141	277-1522		
Burevestnik Cinema, Podvoiskovo ul. 38	583-1155		
Burevestnik Scientific-Production Assn., Malookhtinskiy prosp. 68	528-7272	528-6633	121590
Burrows Paper Corporation, nab. reki Fontanki 23, 5th flr.	314-5148	314-5148	
Bushe Restaurant, ul. Ryleyeva 23	272-0168		
Business Center, Nevskiy prosp. 87/2	279-4376	277-4073	
Nevskiy prosp. 30	312-1490	315-5948	
Suvorovskiy prosp. 47	275-6136	312-9385	
Business Center T. A. M., Nevskiy prosp. 16	312-7214	312-7214	
Business Tour, ul. Gorokhovaya 57	113-4676	310-5330	
BusinessLink, V. O., 13 Liniya 14	218-6900	218-7940	
Businessshans, Fontanka 59	210-8069	314-7168	

	Phone	Fax	Telex

C

	Phone	Fax	Telex
C. Itoh & Co., Ltd., Blagoveshchenskaya pl. 2, kom. 41-43	311-8678	311-7745	121171
C. V. C. Firm, prosp. Stachek 18	292-9518		
Cafe 01, ul. Karavannaya 5	312-1136		
Cairos Travel Agency, Teatralnaya pl. 4	312-2517	113-8973	
Cameo Diamond, ul. Kolomenskaya 3	112-4841		
Capricorn, Lesnoy prosp. 19a	542-5588	542-0989	
Car-Service, Bukharetskaya ul. 1	166-9267	166-6768	
Cars Auto Parts Store, prosp. Energetikov 65	226-1922		
Cars Master, ul. Aprelakaya 5	225-2560	225-6273	
Cartas, Dibunovskaya ul. 37	239-4728		
Casino na Sadovoy, sadovaya u. 25	310-0404		
Catalog Express, Sadovaya ul. 34			
Caterpillar, ul. Millionaya 21/60	311-5644	311-9557	
Cathedral of Prince Vladimir. ul. Blokhina 26	232-7625		
Cathedral of St. Nicholas & the Epiphany, Nikolskaya pl. 1/3	114-0862		
Cathedral of the Holy Trinity, Alexander Nevskiy Monastery, nab. Reki Monastyrki 1	274-0409		
Cathedral of the Transfiguration of Our Saviour, pl. Radishcheva 1	272-3662		
Catholic Church, See Church of Our Lady of Lourdes			
Center for Cinematographic Arts, Karavannaya ul. 12	315-5567		
Center for Citizen Initiatives, V. O., 4th Galernaya Liniya, room 418	271-0467		
Center for Creative Initiatives, ul. Komsomola 25	542-4579	542-8719	121378
Center for Humanitarian and Business Cooperation, nab. reki Moyki 59	315-6028		
Center for International Cooperation, prosp. Morisa Toreza 89	553-3269	553-6020	
Center for Lazer Technology JV (FRG), ul. Politekhnicheskaya 29	535-5247	552-0100	121463
Center for Scientific Culture, Zhdanovskaya ul. 8	235-4242	230-7413	
Center of Innovation for Instiutes and Enterprises, ul. Professora Popova 5	234-8486	234-2758	321057
Central Air Transportation Agensy, Nevskiy prosp. 7/9	314-6950	311-5321	
Central Archives of the Navy, ul. Millionnaya 36	315-9054		
Central Bank of Russia, St. Petersburg Branch, nab. reki Fontanki 70/72	312-3940	315-8327	
Central Exhibition Hall, See Manege Central Exhibition Hall			
Central Marine Research and Design Institute, Kavalergardskaya ul. 6	271-1283	274-3864	
Central Naval Library, Sadovaya ul. 2	210-4365		
Central Park of Culture and Leisure named for S. M., See Kirov Park of Culture and Leisure			
Central Post Office, ul. Pochtamtskaya 9	312-8302		
Central State Historical Archives, nab. Krasnovo Flota 4	311-0926		

	Phone	Fax	Telex
Central Telegraph and Telephone, ul. Gertsena 3/5	311-7001		
Telegraph assistance, Sinopskaya nab. 14	274-3982		
Central Yacht Club, Petrovskaya Kosa 7	235-7217	235-7076	
Centre Publik Lectures, Liteyny prosp. 42	273-2049		
CGTT Lepertours, Konnogvardeyskiy Bulvar 4	110-6496	312-7292	
Chaika Cinema, Kupchinskaya ul. 1/5	172-3682		
Chaika Hotel, Serebristy bulvar 38	301-7969		
Chaika Restaurant, nab. kanala Griboyedova 14	312-4631	311-3983	
Champagne and Dessert Wine Factory, Sverdlovskaya nab. 34	225-0741	225-1552	122013
Charitable Society Nevskiy Angel, Gorokhovaya ul. 5	312-5892		
Chas Pik Newspaper, Nevskiy prosp. 81	279-2270		
Chasa Newspaper, 24, ul. Rimskovo-Korsakovo 9	310-6375	314-4596	
Chemistry and Pharmaceutical Institute, ul. Professora Popova 14	234-5729	234-6044	
Cherkasov Institute of Theater, Music and Cinematography, Mokhovaya ul. 34	273-1581	272-1789	
Chernavin, Basseynaya ul. 33/1	122-4789		
Chernyshevskiy Library, prosp. Kima 4	350-1200		
4 Kolesa, Irinovskiy prosp. 2	222-4216		
Chigorin City Chess Club, B. Konyushennaya ul. 25	314-7561		
Children's Fund, Kamenoostrovskiy prosp. 60	234-0439	234-0826	
Chop Sticks, Grand Hotel Europe	119-6000		
Choreographic Miniatures State Ballet, ul. Mayakovskovo 15	273-1997		
Christ Church, ul. Prof. Popova 47	110-1870		
Christian Lutheran Evangelical Society, Sredny prosp. 18	184-9111		
Christina Creative Coiffure, Hotelship Peterhof	213-6321	213-3158	
Church of Our Lady of Lourdes, Kovenskiy p. 7	272-5002		
Church of Saint Seraphim of Sarovo, Serafimovskoye Cemetery, Serebryakov pere. 1	239-1432		
Church of St. Nicholas, prosp. Metallistov 5	224-2708		
Church of the Apostle & Evangelist St. John the Divi, nab. Obvodnovo kanala 17	277-3350		
Church of the Holy Prophet Job, Kamchatskaya ul. 6	166-2544		
Church of the Smolensk Cemetery, Kamskaya ul. 24	213-5414		
Church of the Trinity (Kulich v Paskhe), prosp. Obukhovskoy Oborony 235	262-1387		
Cinema Engineers Institute, ul. Pravdy 13	315-7285	315-0172	
Cinema Workers Union, Karavannaya ul. 12	315-5567		
Citizens' Democracy Corps, Inc., ul. Sadovaya 38	315-7393		
City Architectural and Building Committee, Lomonosova pl. 2	315-5216	110-4825	
Civil Aviation Academy, Pilotov ul. 38	122-3781		
Civil Aviation Technical College, Liteyny prosp. 48/50	273-4657	272-5082	
Cleaning Services Losk, Shpalernaya ul. 30	272-9141		
ClearWater, V. O., 6 Liniya 37	213-5733	213-5733	
Clinical Center of New Medical Technology, prosp. Severny 1	511-0961	511-8102	
Coca-Cola Export Corp., pl. Proletarskoy Diktatury 6	278-1053	274-2678	
Coemar est, Nevskiy prosp. 39	314-9998	310-0907	

	Phone	Fax	Telex
Cole Financial of Russia, pab. Reki Fontanki 70	311-3453	311-7903	
Collectors' Society, prosp. Rimskovo-Korsakova 53	114-3341		
Commark Ltd., ul. Sablinskaya 7	233-3008	233-3008	
Commercial Center, Liteyny prosp. 57	275-0209	272-2677	
Committee for For. Econ. Relations, Petroispolkom, p. Antonenko 6	312-7181	319-9102	
Committee on the Administration of City Property (KUGI), Smolny, 6th entrance	278-1557	274-1026	
Commodore Hotel, prosp. Morskoy Slavy 1	119-6666	119-6667	
Business Center	119-6666	119-6667	
Las Vegas Show Lounge	119-6666		
Los Angeles Restaurant	119-6666		
New York Restaurant	119-6666		
Night Club Restaurant	119-6666		
Sky Club Restaurant	119-6666		
Communications Museum, See Popov Museum			
Company Rimilen JV (Italy), ul. Korablestroiteley 21	352-1432	352-2054	
Composer Publishers, B. Morskaya ul. 45	314-5054	311-5811	
Computerland, Sverdlovskaya nab. 64	224-0243	224-0932	
Computers Shop, Nevskiy prosp. 150	277-3145		
Concord Agency, ul. Rubinshteyna 3	315-1834	315-0659	
Congress Business Center, Galerny Pr. 3	352-0869	352-0377	
Connolly International, Ltd.	122-3033	122-3033	
Construction & Engineering Licensing Services, Manezhnaya pl. 4	315-8043	311-9419	
Consulate of			
Bulgaria, ul. Ryleyeva 27	273-7347	272-5718	
China, V. O., 3 Liniya, 12	218-1721	218-3492	
Cuba, ul. Ryleyeva 37	272-5303	272-7506	
Czechoslovakia, Tverskaya ul. 5	271-0459		
Denmark, Kamenny ostrov B. alleya 13	234-3755		
Estonia, ul. B. Manetnaya 14	233-5548		
Finland, ul. Chaykovskovo 71	273-7321	272-1421	121536
France, nab. reki Moyki 15	314-1443		
Germany, Furshtadtskaya ul. 39	273-5598	279-3242	121529
Great Britain, pl. Diktatury	119-6036	116-0676	
Hungary, ul. Marata 15	312-6458	312-6432	
India, ul. Ryleyeva 35	272-1988	2722473	
Italy, Teatralnaya pl. 10	312-3217	312-2896	121568
Japan, nab. reki Moyki 29	314-1418	311-4891	
Latvia, ul. Galernaya 69	315-1774		
Mongolia, Laninskiy prosp. 115	153-8051		
Netherlands, prosp. Engelsa 101	554-4900		
Norway, V. O., 21 Liniya 8a	213-9295		
Poland, 5 Sovetskaya ul. 12-14	274-4331	274-4318	
Sweden, V. O., 10 Liniya 11	218-3526	213-7198	121550
U. A. R., prosp. Morisa Tereza 118	553-1742		
United States, Furshtadtskaya ul. 15	275-1701	110-7022	121527
Commercial Office, Hotelship Peterhof	213-6537	119-6045	
Conti Casino, Kondratyevskiy prosp. 44	540-0122		
Restaurant	540-8130		
Continental Publishers, Vasenko ul. 3	540-5047	540-1954	
Contur-M Publishers, Liteyny prosp. 29	275-5350		

	Phone	Fax	Telex
Cooperative Computer, Perekupnoy p. 12	274-7160		
Coopers & Lybrand, Astoria Hotel, room 528	210-5528	210-5528	
Costa Inc. JV (USA), Tavricheskaya ul. 39, kv. 353	271-4110	271-4110	
Crazy Bert, prosp. Kultiry 26 k. 1	559-3044		
Creat, ul. Plekhanova 49	314-3081	312-4312	
Credit Lyonnais Russie, Nevskiy prosp. 12, box 139	210-3100	210-3390	
Credobank, ul. Mokhovaya 26	275-0333	272-8688	622588
Cross Roads Business Center, Poltavskaya ul. 10	277-4197	273-4304	121060
Cultural Initiative, ul. Chaykovskovo 29	273-5538	273-1128	
Customs Administration, Pulkovo II Airport	104-3401	104-3294	
Czechoslovak Airlines, ul. B. Morskaya 36	315-5259	315-5264	
Pulkovo II Airport	104-3430		

D

	Phone	Fax	Telex
D & A Design, ul. Morisa Toreza 98, k. 1	553-9747	275-4666	
D. A. B. International JV, prosp. Obukhovskoy Oborony 295	100-5257		
Daddy's Steak Room and Pizza, Moskovskiy prosp. 73	252-7744		
Dalnyaya Svyaz NPO, Petrogradskaya nab. 34	233-5502	233-4327	121573
Damian Pharmacy, Moskovskiy prosp. 22	110-1744	292-5939	
Daugava Restaurant, Hotel Pribaltiyskaya	356-4409		
Decorative Design Center, prosp. Rimskovo-Korsakova 24/135	114-3766		
Defis Publishers, nab. reki Fontanki 117	168-8196	314-2573	
Dekon, Tovarishcheskiy prosp. 3, kor. 1	527-3442		
Delak JV(Belgium), B. Sampsonievskiy prosp. 29b	542-8590	542-8611	
Delikato JV (Finland), pl. Truda 2	311-8922	311-7543	
Delivery Systems International, ul. Dobrolyubov 14	238-9457	238-8989	
Deloitte & Touche, Petropavlovskiy krepost 11	238-4408	238-4408	
Delovoy Peterburg, Malookhtinskiy prosp. 68	528-9555		
Delta, Plovdivskaya ul. 9	108-1917		
Delta Airlines, ul. B. Morskaya 36	311-5819		121586
Pulkovo II	104-3438		121586
Delta Consulting, KIMa prosp. 22, kv. 501-511	350-7961	350-7961	
Delta JV (Finland), Konnogvardeyskiy bulvar 4, office 20	315-3851		
Delta Telecom, ul. Chekhova 18	275-4149	275-0130	
Showroom, ul. B. Morskaya 22	314-6126	314-8837	
Delta-Baltika Firm, Nevskiy prosp. 38	110-4900	310-4537	
Demion Art Gallery, Nevskiy prosp. 3	312-6118		
Demo, p. Klimova 9, kv. 50	114-7724	114-7724	
Demyanova Ukha Restaurant, Kronverkskiy prosp. 53	232-8090		
Deon, Suvorovskiy prosp. 62	271-2868		
Deposit, Ligovskiy prosp. 230	166-5583		
Deserthoil, ul. Belinskovo 5	273-2952		
Deska-Imex, Smolny prosp. 7 kv. 1	164-4861	112-0001	
Deskor JV (FRG), ul. Tsvetochnaya 6	298-7235	294-1615	
Deson Hotel, Shaumyana prosp. 26	528-5628	528-5236	
Deti Blokady-900, ul. Saltykova-Shchedrina 32/34	273-1109		
Detskaya Literatura Liceum, nab. Kutuzova 6	273-4824	273-6004	

	Phone	Fax	Telex
Deutsche Bank, nab. kanala Griboyedova 101	315-0216	315-0655	
Deymos, Smolny prosp. 11	110-0267		121041
DHL, nab. kanala Griboyedova 5, office 325	311-2649	314-6473	
Express Center, Nevskiy Palace Hotel	119-6110		
Dialog Invest Group, Inc., ul. Dostoyevskovo 19/21	164-8747	164-9392	
Dialog JV Filial (USA), nab. reki Fontanki 92	164-7247	164-2707	
Diana, Gavanskaya u. 19	217-0222		
Sadovaya ul. 56	310-3332		
Diant Publishing Center, Box 264	106-0440	106-0440	
Diesel Jeans & Sportwear, Kamenoostrovskiy prosp. 37	233-8581	233-4720	
Digital Equipment Corporation, Moskovskiy prosp. 108	298-2370	298-0748	
Dilar-6, ul. Komsomola 33	541-8372		
Dinamo Sports Center, prosp. Dinamo 44	235-0170		
Dinamo Swimming Pool, prosp. Dinamo 44	235-6606		
Dinas, Ligovskiy prosp. 249	166-1155	167-0528	
DINAT'F, prosp. Entuziastov 18/3	315-6794	315-6794	
Directorate of Petersburg City Hotels, Ligovskiy prosp. 10	315-4259	277-6127	121362
Directory Assistance	09		
DisCo Plus, Bukharestskaya ul. 6, kor. 3	269-9324	269-9324	
DixiJV, Liteyny prosp. 31	272-2035		
DLT, B. Konyushennaya ul. 21/23	314-1654	113-5246	
Dokuchayev Museum of Soil Science, Birzhevoy pr. 6	218-5501		
Dolg Soldiers & Reserve Corps Club, V. O., 1 Liniya 20	213-8037		
Dom Architectora Restaurant, ul. B. Morskaya 52	311-0531		
Dom Knigi, Nevskiy prosp. 28	219-9422		
Dom Leningradskoy Torgovli (DLT), B. Konyushennaya ul. 21/23	312-2627		
Dom Modeley Prichosok 'Studia M', prosp. Morisa Toreza 30	552-6981		
Dom Muzyki i Radio, Grazhdanskiy prosp. 15, block 1	534-4218		
Dom Natali Publishers, ul. Dekabristov 4	311-7460	311-7460	
Dom Nemetskoy Ekonomiki, V. O., Bolshoy prosp. 10	350-4806	350-5622	
Dom Plus, Kanal Griboyedova 3	312-8873	312-8351	
ul. Karavannaya 4	117-2181	312-8351	
Dom Stroitelnoy Knigi, Bolsheokhtinskiy prosp. 1	224-1575		
Dom Voyennoy Knigi, Nevskiy prosp. 20	311-5792		
Domostroy Cooperative, ul. Rubinshteyna 3	311-2060		
Doroga, prosp. Narodnovo Opolcheniya 201-a	155-9150		
Dostoevskiy House Museum, Kuznechny p. 5/2	164-6950		
Double-K Casino, Hotel Sputnik	552-7991		
Dresden, prosp. Morisa Toreza 40	552-2808		
Dresdner Bank, Isakievskaya pl. 11	312-2100	312-6167	
Driver, Leninskiy prosp. 146	255-9097		
Druzhba Cinema, Moskovskiy prosp. 202	293-3061		
Druzhba Hotel, ul. Chapygina 4	234-1844		122556
Druzhba Restaurant	234-4556		
Duncan Travel Firm, Millionaya ul. 23	275-1337	275-1336	
Duty Free — Pulkovo II, See Lenrianta			
DvaTri Publishers, Nevskiy prosp. 44	311-6262	110-4010	
20 Vek Agency, Vladimirskiy prosp. 9	113-1676		
Dvorets Tvorchestva Yunikh, Nevskiy prosp. 39	314-7281	310-1414	

	Phone	Fax	Telex

E

	Phone	Fax	Telex
East Market Ltd, ul. B. Konyushennaya 27,kom. 510	312-8839	315-8738	
East Media Advertising GmbH, Chapygina ul. 6	234-8358	234-3728	
East Way/Lappeenrannan Rautakauppa Oy JV (Finland), ul. Sofiyskaya 6	268-5719	268-5719	
Economic Literature & Business Press, ul. Razyezhaya 16/18	312-9500	312-4128	
Economic Reform Commission of Mayor's Office, ul. Mayorova 16	319-9146		
Ecopolis, Zanevskiy prosp. 32, k. 2, kv. 3	528-2666	528-2666	
Editions de L'espace Europeen, Universitetskaya nab. 3	218-1672	218-0811	
EEE (Energy, Ecology, Engineering) JV (Finland), ul. Atamanskaya 3/6	277-4256	277-4256	121404
EFO, Omskaya ul. 21	246-9242	246-9247	
Ehlehs JV (Hungary), V. O., 17 Liniya, 54 PO Ehkskalator	213-0138	218-0869	
EKO Stahl AG, V. O., Bolshoy prosp. 10a	350-4806	218-1784	
Ekobalt, Voznesenskiy prosp. 36 kv. 11	310-2731		
Ekon Firm, ul. Myasnaya 19	184-6861		
Ekonombank, Nevskiy prosp. 78-19	275-5845	275-5845	
Ekonomicheskaya Shkola, Prazhskaya ul. 30	268-4686		
Ekonomika i Zhizn, ul. Lomonosova 22	315-3148		
Ekoparts JV (Finland), Bolsheokhtinskiy prosp. 19	239-3930	235-4519	
Ekran Cinema, P.S., Bolshoy prosp. 30	230-7151		
Ekran NPO, Sofiyskaya ul. 52	106-1198	106-1214	
EKS JV Filial (Laiks), Nevskiy prosp. 147	277-1590	277-4018	121345
Ekzot, Professora Popova ul. 2	234-8448		
Ekzotika, Leninskiy prosp. 119	254-7591		
Elbi, ul. 4 Sovetskaya 20	274-8642		
Eldorado Discotec, Hotel Karelia, ul. Tukhachevskovo 27, korpus 2	226-3110		
Electrolux, Robespera nab. 16	275-5512	275-0052	
ul. Zakharievskaya 31	275-3685		
Electron Cinema, Karpinskovo ul. 38	249-9340		
Electronics Store, Pulkovo 1 Airport	123-8778	104-3487	
ElectroTechnical Communications Institute, nab. reki Moyki 61	315-3227	315-9586	
Elefant, prosp. Kosygina 7, kor. 1			
Elegant, P.S., Bolshoy prosp. 55	232-8601		
Elegant Furs, ul. Salova 33	166-7249	166-2695	
Elegant Logic, Inc., nab. reki Fontanki 46	311-1064	311-0452	
Elektrik Factory, prosp. Medikov 10	234-1580	234-1679	121598
Elektroapparat Productive Assn., V. O., 24 Liniya 3/7	217-8300	217-1914	
Elektrofizika NPO, Sovetskiy prosp. 1	265-5633	463-9812	
Elektron NPO, prosp. Morisa Toreza 68	552-3600	552-3197	
Elektronika Bekas, Mytninskaya ul. 1	274-4291	274-4291	
Elektronika Gallery and Shop, prosp. Yuri Gagarina 12, korp. 1	299-3849		
Elektronnye Systemy JV(Italy), Petergofskoye sh. 73	130-1592	116-0104	

	Phone	Fax	Telex
Elektronpribor, Levashovskiy prosp. 12	235-7098		122202
Elektropult Factory, ul. Khimikov 26	527-6638	527-3890	
Elektrosila, Moskovskiy prosp. 156	294-3688		
Elektrosila Sports Club, Moskovskiy prosp. 139	298-2075	298-9510	121588
Elektrotekhnicheskiy Institut Svyazi, See ElectroTechnical Communications Institute			
Elektrotekhnicheskiy Institut imeni V. I. Ulyanova, See Ulyanov ElectroTechnological Institute			
Elen, Moskovskiy prosp. 7	310-9537		
Elena, Kolomenskaya ul. 29	312-7072		
Morskaya nab. 15	356-0313		
Elf Cafe, Stremyannaya ul. 11	311-2217		
Eli Lilly & Elanco	550-3026	299-7030	
Eliseevskiy Food Store, Nevskiy prosp. 56	311-9323		
Elita Pet Shop, Stachek prosp. 67, kor. 1	184-5698		
Elkap Ltd, Ligovskiy prosp. 195	166-1253	166-2726	
Elkom, Sotsialisticheskaya ul. 16	112-5906		
Elma, Lesnoy prosp. 73	245-4588		
Eltex JV (Swiss), ul. Odoevskovo 24 k. 1	351-8714	352-2403	
Emergency Medical Assistance	278-0025		
Emperor Paul I Residence, Pavlovsk, ul. Revolyutsii 20	470-2156		
EMS Garantpost, Konnogvardeyskiy bul. 4	311-1120		
Energetik Cooperative, ul. Krasnovo Elektrika 3/6	277-9537	584-1042	121490
Energia, Moskovskiy prosp. 189	293-0147		
Energoatomizdat Publishers, Aptekarskiy p. 1	315-3391		
Energomash, ul. Karavannaya 1	315-7655	315-7655	
Energomash Joint Stock Bank, ul. Karavannaya 1	314-9954	315-9927	
Energomashzhilstroy Architectural-Construction Assn, prosp. Suslova 21, #4	156-0866	156-0866	121328
Energosofin JV (Finland), Serebristy bulvar 38, kv. 152	301-7952	301-6709	
Engineering Business Company, See AVEKS Association			
Ennek, Malookhtinskiy prosp. 68	528-0225	528-1389	
Entuziast Cooperative, Kanonerskiy Ostrov 5	210-9028	314-8267	
ERA, Ligovskiy prosp. 42b	164-3081	164-5602	
Ernst and Young, ul. M. Morskaya 11	312-9911	312-5320	
ERVI Publishers, nab. reki Moyki 20, kv. 33	311-8854	312-6705	
Estafeta Cinema, Petergofskoye sh. 3	155-3351		
Estrada Theater, ul. Zhelyabova 27	314-6661		
Etal, B. Morskaya ul. 53	312-3382	315-5054	
Ethnographic Museum of the Peoples of Russia, Inzhenernaya ul. 4/1	219-1174		
Etude Fraternity of Artists, Zagorodny prosp. 14, pom. 77	315-4318		
Euremade JV(Finland), ul. B. Posadskaya 1/10	233-9615	233-7447	
Euroconsel, p. Bankovskiy 3	310-6543	310-6485	
EuroDonat JV (Belgian), ul. Yakornaya 17	224-1144	224-0620	121118
Europa-Asia Airlines, Rizhskiy prosp. 3	251-4341	251-6055	
Europe Business Center, Grand Hotel Europe, Mikhaylovskaya ul. 1/7	312-0072		
Evangelical Christian Church, Slavyanskaya ul. 13	100-4092		
Evelansh, Izmailovskiy prosp. 14	112-6510		
Vladimirskiy prosp. 2	113-1384	311-8549	

	Phone	Fax	Telex
Everything for Dogs and Cats, Ltd., See Sobakovod Pet Shop			
EVM-Fredriksson JV (Finland), ul. Tyushina 3	164-6185	166-8275	
Evradonat, Olgi Forsh ul. 5	558-9820		
Evrika, Piskaryovskiy prosp. 52	249-0950		
Evrika Firm, Suvorovskiy prosp. 15	277-5041		
Evropa Plus Radio Station, ul. Prof. Popova 47	234-4080	234-9860	
Dance Hall, Kamennoostrovskiy prosp. 68			
Exhibition Center of the			
Association of Artists, ul. B. Morskaya 38	314-6432		
Artists' Union, Sverdlovskaya nab. 64	224-0633		
ul. B. Morskaya 38	314-4734	314-6432	
Experimental Shipyards, Petrovskaya Kosa 7	235-7398	235-4130	
Expo-Center, nab. Obvodnovo kanala 93a	210-1820		
Expoconsta JV (Finland), V. O., Bolshoy prosp. 103	355-1991	355-5840	121532
Express Cooperative, Lipovaya Alleya 15a	510-5230		
Express Mail, Konnogvardeyskiy bul. 4	311-9671	311-9288	
Express Market, Moskovskiy prosp. 73	252-4144		
Stary Nevskiy prosp. 113	277-7771		
Express Media, Manezhny p. 19, kv. 39	273-1748	275-8466	
Express Printing, Konnogvardeyskiy bulv. 4	311-2346	311-2346	
Express-Print, Pushkinskaya ul. 20	113-1808		
ExpressFoto, Zagorodny prosp. 9	314-1914		

F

	Phone	Fax	Telex
Faberge by Ananov Collection, Grand Hotel Europe	119-6008	119-6008	
Faberge Salon, See Yakhont Jewelery Store			
Faeton, Poklonnogorskaya ul. 14	292-3038	292-3038	
prosp. Stachek 55	184-5108		
Fail, Dostoyevskovo ul. 6	113-3066	113-3068	
Fairn & Swanson, Nevskiy prosp. 96	275-5385	275-5386	
Fakel Cinema, Sofiyskaya ul. 44	269-1583		
Fakt, Khimicheskiy p. 6	252-0738		
Fantekh JV (Finland), ul. Dnepropetrovskaya 8	112-0109	112-0109	
Farmadom Pharmacy, Zagorodny prosp. 21	113-3340	113-3340	
Farmaservice Pharmacy, nab. Kutuzova 14	279-0660		
Fast Firm, Nevskiy prosp. 60	311-5328	311-5404	
Favorit, Saperny p. 15			
Fax Service, ul. B. Morskaya 3/5	314-0140	315-1701	
Federal Express, ul. Mayakovskaya 2	279-1287	273-2139	
Fedorov Trans Express, ul. Shturmanskaya 32	104-3449	234-5192	
Feniks, Yaroslava Gasheka ul. 9	176-9602		
Ferguson Hollis, Nevskiy prosp. 30	312-1490	315-5948	
Festival Cinema, Prosveshcheniya prosp. 47	598-3434		
Feximo Oy, Nevskiy prosp. 40	275-7510	275-5096	
Feya-2, Moskovskiy prosp. 124			
Fialka, Stachek prosp. 96	183-2287		
Fiesta, Zverinskaya ul. 42	232-7813		
Filko JV (Finland), Admiralteyskiy prosp. 6	312-3487	312-8610	
Film Consulting, Kronverkskiy prosp. 10	233-9747	233-2174	121534
Filosofskaya Akademiya Library, nab. reki Fontanki 20	273-9484		

	Phone	Fax	Telex
Finkomfort, ul. Sadovaya 15	311-7642	312-8735	
Finlenfilytr JV (Finland), Zanyevskiy prosp. 29a	221-1624	221-1624	
Finlyandskiy Train Station, pl. Lenina 6	168-7685		
Finnair Airlines, ul. Gogolya 19	314-3646	312-0459	121533
Cargo, Pulkovo Airport, Terminal 2	104-3439	104-3439	121533
Finnish-Russian Chamber of Commerce, 4 Krasnoarmeyskaya ul. 4a	292-1641	112-7252	121566
Finnord JV, Italianskaya ul. 37	314-8951	314-7058	121496
Finnrefit Ltd, nab. reki Moyki 3A	312-9998		
Finservis, ul. Engelsa 51	554-3755	554-4929	
Fiodorovskiy Gorodok Hotel, Akademicheskiy prosp. 14	476-3600		
Fire	01		
Fishing Industry Production Assn., ul. Elevatornaya ploshchadka 10	183-5504	183-3335	121587
Fisika i Tekhnika Poluprovodnikov, Politekhnicheskaya ul. 26	247-9106		
Five Corners for Children and Elders, nab. reki Fontanki 59	310-4111	315-6283	
Flora, ul. Shpalernaya 44b	271-1161		
Florman Information Systems, Kamenoostrovskiy prosp. 14b	233-7682	232-8017	
Fon Ltd., V. O., 10 Liniya 15, kv. 40	213-8030		
Fonarnye Saunas, Fonarny p. 1	312-5655		
Force Majeure, ul. Leninaa 41	230-3138	230-3138	
Formizdat, nab. kanala Griboyedova 20	312-4163	319-9673	
Fortetsiya Restaurant, Kuybysheva ul. 7	233-9468		
Fortuna International Tourism Association, Kievskaya ul. 22/24, kv. 92	298-8969		
Forum Art Gallery, V. O., 6 Liniya 17	213-6787	511-7223	
Forward Car Wash, Luzhskaya ul. 3	530-4782	531-6693	
Fregat, Torzhkovskaya ul. 15	246-1242		
Fregat Cafe, V. O., Bolshoy prosp. 39/14	213-4923		
Frunze Military Naval Academy, nab. Leytenanta Shmidta 17	213-7147		
Frunzenskaya Retail Firm, Moskovskiy prosp. 60	292-1976	292-6753	
Frunzenskiy Veterinary Center, Salova ul. 16	166-7642		
Fruzenskiy Residence Repair & Remodeling Service, ul. Budapeshtskaya 37	260-7488		
FTE, ul. Professora Popova 47,kom. 607	234-5192	234-5152	
Fuji Photo Salon, nab. reki Fontanki 23	314-4936	314-8073	
Fund for the Support of Small Enterprises, Chernomorskiy 4	210-8851	312-9090	
Fur Auction, See Pushnoy Auction			
Fural JV (Lichtenstein), Zakharyevskaya ul. 14	273-9925	279-6516	

G

	Phone	Fax	Telex
GAI, See State Automobile Inspectorate			
Galaktika, V. O., 2 Liniya 35	213-1121	218-1460	
Galereya 10-10, Pushkinskaya ul. 10, kv. 10	315-2832		
Galereya Petropol, Millionnaya ul. 27, kv. 2	315-3414		

	Phone	Fax	Telex
Galereya-102, Nevskiy prosp. 102	273-6842		
Galspe Restaurant, Leninskiy prosp. 127	254-5582		
Gamma, ul. Salova 51	166-6377		
Gangut, B. Posadskaya ul. 9/5	232-3540		
Ganzakombank, pl. Rastrelli 2	273-0521	110-7320	
Gaos Cooperative, prosp. Rimskovo-Korsakova 3	310-1449		
Garant Cooperative, ul. Pushkinskaya 68	164-4857		
Garmonia, Kamennoostrovskiy prosp. 26/28	235-0814		
Garus, Basseynaya ul. 41	298-2358		
Gavan Hotel, V. O., Sredniy prosp. 88	356-8504		
Gavana Commercial Store, Kamenoostrovskiy prosp. 2	233-5253		
Gefest, Marshala Govorova ul. 31	252-3066	252-5565	
Gelios, Bolshevikov prosp. 19	588-5707		
Gelios JV (Italia), ul. Artileriyskaya 1,Hotel Rus	273-4683	279-6144	
General Insurance Company, Novo-Litovskaya ul. 15	245-5128		
General Prosecutor's Office, ul. Yakubovicha 4	312-8469		
Geo, Ilyicha p. 10, kv. 20	164-0171		
Germes JV (Austria), Stremyannaya ul. 6	112-5516	311-7316	
Gernika, prosp. Veteranov 56	255-7610	156-6647	
Gertsen Pedagogical Institute, nab. reki Moyki 48	312-4492	312-1195	
International Dept, ul. Plekhanova 6	314-7859	314-7859	
Gifts, See Podarki			
Gigant Cinema, Kondratyevskiy prosp. 44	540-5818		
Gillette (Petersburg Product International), Sofiyskaya ul. 14	106-1061	106-3479	
Gino Ginelli Italian Icebar, Canal Griboedova 14	312-4631	311-8339	
Gippokrat, Aleksandrovskiy Park 5a	232-1853	232-5649	
Gippokrat Book Store, ul. Lenina 20	232-5469		
GlavUPDK Garage, see GlavUPDK Spetzavtotsenter			
Glinka Choir, nab. reki Moyki 20	314-1058		
Glinka Philharmonic Hall, Nevskiy prosp. 30	311-8333		
Gloria, Novosmolenskaya nab. 1	352-4438		
Godiva, Moskovskiy prosp. 179 kv. 49	294-0846	294-1388	
Gogol Library, ul. Stakhanovtsev 4-a	528-1703		
Goldstar, Lesnoy prosp. 20	542-1959	542-0989	
Golubaya Gostinaya, B. Morskaya ul. 38	315-7414		
Goluboy Delfin Restaurant, Sredneokhtinskiy prosp. 44	227-2135		
Gomeofan Homeopathic Pharmacy, P.S., Bolshoy prosp. 2	233-2381		
Goodwill Games, Inc., B. Monetnaya 19, office 321	232-7364	232-7364	
Gorodskoy Tsentr Perevodov, ul. Bronnetskaya 15	112-6515	259-6252	
Gortekhprogress Engineering Center, p. Antonenko 5	110-6600	312-9773	
Gospel House, Borovaya ul. 52b	166-2831		
Gostiny Dvor, Nevskiy prosp. 35	110-5200	110-5461	
Grace Mission Group, Kamennoostrovskiy prosp. 42	230-8017		
Granat Jewellers, Bukharestskaya ul. 72, korpus 1	268-2275		
Grand Boutique High Class Stores Ltd., Grand Hotel Europe	113-8074	315-3000	
Grand Cafe Antwerpen, Kronverkskiy prosp. 13/2	233-9446	233-9482	
Grand Hotel Europe, Mikhailovskaya ul. 1/7	119-6000	119-6001	121073
American Express	119-6009	119-6011	

	Phone	Fax	Telex
Brasserie	119-6000		
Business Center	312-0072	119-6001	121073
Car rental	113-8071		
Chop Sticks Restaurant	119-6000		
Europe Restaurant	119-6000		
Faberge by Ananov Collection,	119-6008	119-6008	
Grand Boutique High Class Stores Ltd.	113-8074	315-3000	
Mezzanine (Atrium) Cafe	119-6000		
Sadko's Restaurant	119-6000		
World Class Gym	113-8066		
Granit-91, Dibunovskaya ul. 51, kv. 61	239-3523		
Graphic Arts Center, Sverdlovskaya nab. 64	224-0622		
Grazhdanka, Prosveshcheniya prosp. 87	530-1717		
Green Party, See Public Inspectorate for Preservation of Nature			
Greta, Suvorovskiy prosp. 57	275-6246		
Greviti Ltd, Sytninskaya pl. 3	233-3744		
Griffon Int'l JV (Finland), V. O., Bolshoy prosp. 83	217-5400	356-7779	
Griffon Travel, Furshtadtskaya ul. 9	275-7215	275-8151	
Grona Ltd, ul. Blagodatnaya 40	294-0381	298-1500	
Grot, Aleksandrovskiy Park 2	238-4690		
Guazar Co. Ltd, Kamenoostrovskiy prosp. 3	233-4033		
Guild of Businessman, Vladimirskiy prosp. 2	261-6783		

H

	Phone	Fax	Telex
H. Hedman Legal Services, Nevskiy prosp. 134	274-4160	274-4355	
Haka Oy, Admiralteyskiy prosp. 6	312-3915	315-9358	
Hall of Flowers, Potemkinskaya ul. 2	272-5448		
Handicraft Union (Wholesale), See St. Petersburg Folk Art Assn.			
Hans Eike von Oppeln-Bronikowski, Zagorodny prosp. 28	112-5357	112-5357	
Harry Hedman Law Firm, Nevskiy prosp. 26	274-3968	274-4355	
Health Center Library, Italianskaya ul. 25	311-3638		
Heineken, Pobedy pl. 1	264-5816		
Helen Hotel JV (Finland), Lermontovskiy prosp. 43/1	251-6101	113-0859	121349
Helio Polis, ul. Safushkina 12	239-6719		
Hemotex, Khersonskaya ul. 3	274-5325		
Heritage Art Gallery, Nevskiy prosp. 116	279-5067		
Hermi Ltd, Pushkin,ul. Radishcheva 4	465-2820	465-3339	
Hermitage Cafe, Pushkin, ul. Kominterna 27	476-6255		
Hermitage JV (USA), Dvortsovaya nab. 30	311-3554	311-9180	
Hermitage State Museum, Dvortsovaya nab. 34	219-8625		
Hertz Interauto Firm, ul. Ispolkomovskaya 9/11	277-4032	274-2562	121488
Hi-Fi Trust, Vasi Alekseyeva ul. 14	185-0617	186-0097	
Hi-Life Electronics, ul. Karavannaya 16	314-9861	314-9861	
Hill International, ul. B. Morskaya 23	312-6701	312-5368	
Historical Museum of the Military, Aleksandrovskiy Park 7	232-0296		

	Phone	Fax	Telex
History of St. Petersburg Museum, Peter and Paul Fortress	238-4540		
Hobby, Dekabristov ul. 34	114-0639		
Holding-Kredit, nab. reki Moyki 72	314-7382		
Hollight, Baskov p. 6	279-0903	272-0369	
Home Center, prosp. Slavy 30	261-0402	260-1581	
Honda, ul. Nakhimova 5	356-7701	355-4440	
Honeywell, ul. Zakharyevskaya 31	275-3504	275-2804	
Horda, ul. Lomanaya 5	294-6462	294-6463	
Hospital No. 20, ul. Gastello 21	108-4066		
Hospital No. 9, Krestovskiy prosp. 18	235-2058		
Hotel Development Corporation, nab. kanala Griboyedova 5	314-3178	311-0471	
House of Architects, See Architects Union, RSFSR			
House of Architects Restaurant, See Dom Arkhitectora Restaurant			
House of Artists, See Artists' Union			
House of Cinema Workers, See Cinema Workers Union			
House of Friendship and Peace with Peoples of Foreign Countries, nab. reki Fontanki 21	210-4927	311-4089	
House of Music and Radio, See Dom Muzyki i Radio			
Hunter's Club Restaurant, See Okhotnichny Klub Restaurant			
Huolintakeskus Ltd SP, Lyubotinskiy p. 5	298-0083	298-6819	

I

	Phone	Fax	Telex
Ibar JV, prosp. Energetikov 24	227-4714	227-4714	
IBM, Admiralteyskiy prosp. 6	312-6017	312-3887	
Ice Rink Tavricheskovo Sada, Saltykova-Shchedrina ul. 50			
Iceberg Kafe, Shkolnaya 14	239-8356		
ICPA Corp., Konnogvardeyskiy Bulvar 4#14	311-6130	311-7822	
Idea, Kuznetskovskaya ul. 17	108-5175	108-5180	
Ideal, Laboratornaya ul. 29	540-8831		
Igma Casino, B. Porokhovskyay u. 26	224-2375	274-9376	
IGREK, Profsoyuzov bul. 19	311-9595	311-9219	
Igrushka Production Assn., Moskovskiy prosp. 25	292-3516	292-3083	
Ikar, Kubinskaya ul. 86	122-5763		
Ilim Pulp Enterprise JV(Swiss), ul. Shpalernaya 49	274-4423	274-2667	
Ilka JV (Bulgaria), V. O., Bolshoy prosp. 70	218-2968	217-2242	
Ilkopol, ul. Galernaya 25	210-9054		
IMA Press, ul. Zodchevo Rossi 1/3	110-4651	314-4823	
Imex Servis, ul. Belinskovo 13	272-4654	272-4654	
IMID	264-6614	264-6614	
Impax, nab. reki Fontanki 18	279-0259	272-1971	
Impereti Restaurant, B. Sampsoniyevskiy prosp. 104	245-5003		
Imperial, Izmaylovskiy prosp. 11	251-6128		
Imperial Restaurant, Nevskiy Palace Hotel	275-2001		
Impex, ul. B. Morskaya 35	310-9441	319-9709	121302
Import-Service, ul. Bukharestskaya 72	268-0030	109-8533	
Impuls NPO, ul. Obruchevykh 1	247-1502		

	Phone	Fax	Telex
Inavtoservice, Vitebskiy prosp. 17/2	294-0533	298-9770	
Inbankprodukt, Mokhovaya ul. 20	273-5256		
Index, ul. Shpalernaya 1	312-2025	312-2025	
Industry and Construction Bank, Nevskiy prosp. 38	110-5526	310-6173	
Inex JV (Japan), ul. Yegorova 18	292-2675	108-1030	
Inflot Maritime Agency, Gapsalskaya ul. 10	251-7326	186-1511	121505
Infokon, Isaakievskaya pl. 6	319-9543	258-6491	
Inform-Future Business Center, ul. Tombovskaya 12	312-3078	312-3078	
Informatika, nab. reki Moyki 64	314-0632		
Information and Computer Service Center, Volkovskiy prosp. 146, k. 3	269-8424	166-3624	
Information on Joint Ventures in St. Petersburg	050		
Information Plus	159-9846		
Infoservice, Universitetskaya nab. 21	213-6455	218-5065	
Infraudit, ul. Rostannaya 22	246-5090		
Inger, Professora Popova ul. 47	234-5075		
ul. B. Morskaya 53/8-12	314-8302	314-8586	121027
Ingosstrakh-St. Petersburg, ul. Zakharyevskay a 17	273-0625	275-7712	121739
Ingress Sp. Ltd, ul. Dekabristov 35	114-1135	114-3744	
Ingriya, nab. kanala Griboyedova 26	314-3159	319-9841	
Initiative, Nevskiy prosp. 104	272-0906	279-6211	
Inko 4, ul. Shkolnaya 42	239-7540	239-7510	
Inkombank, ul. Komsomola 41	248-4206	542-3807	
Inkon JV (Austria), Ligovskiy prosp. 214 ,box248	110-6592	110-6591	
Inmarkon, ul. Bekhtereva 3, korpus 2	265-1515	265-3850	
Innovation-Commercial Bank for Rail Transport, see Baltiyskiy Bank			
Inpack JV (USA), prosp. Nepokorennykh 16	535-7142	275-5554	
Inpredservice, Kutuzova nab. 34	272-1500	279-5024	
Inset Ltd, ul. Gorokhovaya 20	312-6804		121542
Instant Tour, ul. Blokhina 15	230-9840	230-4706	
Institut Aviatsionnovo Priborostroyeniya, See Aviation Instruments Institute			
Institut Fizicheskoy Kultury imeni P. F. Lesgafta, See Lesgaft Physical Culture Institute			
Institut Inzhenerov Zheleznodorozhnovo Transport, See Railway Transport Engineers Institute			
Institut Kinoinzhenerov, See Cinema Engineers Institute			
Institut Sovetskoy Torgovly imeni F. Engelsa, See Trade and Economy Institute			
Institut Teatra, Musyki i Kinematografii imeni N. K., See Cherkasov Institute of Theater, Music and Cinema			
Institut Tekstilnoy i Legkoy Promyshlennosti imeni, See Kirov Textile and Light Industry Institute			
Institut Vodnovo Transporta, See Water Transport Institute			
Institut Zhivopisi, Skulpturi i Arkhitektury imeni, See Repin Institute for Painting, Sculpture and Arch			
Instrument, Izmaylovskiy prosp. 27	311-3510		
Intaari JV, ul. Beringa 38	352-3757	352-1691	
Inteks Engineering Center, Grecheskiy 15	271-0894	271-2643	
Intep	275-5360	275-5360	

	Phone	Fax	Telex
Inter, ul. Bronnitskaya 15	259-6252	259-6252	
Inter Marco Import und Export GmbH, V. O., Bolshoy prosp. 10a	218-1625	350-5622	
Inter Ol JV, prosp. Gagarina 27	293-8359	293-8134	
Inter-Avto, prosp. Prosveshcheniya 80, kor. 2	530-8087		
Inter-Galereya, Makarova nab. 20	232-6982	312-3078	
Inter-Latis	233-1174		
Interact JV (Hungary), ul. Przhevalskovo 18/69	275-0442	275-0442	
Interbalt, Pionerskaya ul. 63	235-6046		
InterCom, Turukhtannie Ostrova 1	183-7732	232-8017	121609
Intercompeks JV (Switz.), ul. Kalinina 13	186-3439	186-3390	
Interface Cooperative, Ligovskiy prosp. 229, kv. 4	112-8760	166-3614	
Interflug Airlines, See Lufthansa			
Intergamma Cooperative, ul. Zvenigorodskaya 28/30	164-4566	164-8573	
Interhelp JV (Hungary), ul. Shvetsova 22	252-4702	252-4702	
Interier, Avtovskaya ul. 35	184-7507	184-7510	
Interior Theater-Studio, Nevskiy prosp. 114	113-0151		
Interlaks JV (FRG), ul. Chaykovskovo 43	279-0506	272-8978	
Interlenprom, Moskovskiy prosp. 119/2	298-0143		
Interlesbirzha International Timber Exchange, Mikhaylova ul. 17	541-8676	541-8750	
Intermaritime Bank/The Bank of New York	906-0673	906-0673	
Internal Affairs Department (MVD), Liteyny prosp. 4	315-0019		
International Business Services, Inc. (IBS), Rubinstein 8, Box 237	311-5838	311-3193	
International Business Machines, See IBM			
International Church, Nevskiy prosp. 39	352-7439		
International College of Art Restoration JV (Spain), nab. Kutuzova 24/1	275-8362	275-8198	
International Direct Dial Telephone Service (Int'l Codes)	274-9383		
International Document Processing Center, ul. Krasnoputilovskaya 5a	185-0336		
International Educational Centre, Universitetskaya nab. 7/9	218-1551	218-1346	
International Executive Service Corps, Belgradskaya ul. 6-4-46	109-6914	109-6914	
International Group	311-2483	311-2483	
International Management & Marketing Systems, nab. Obvodnovo kanala 30	265-1661	567-0998	
International Moscow Bank, St. Petersburg Branch, Voznesenskaya prosp. 1/12	311-9857	315-3406	
International Small Business Association, Aptekarskiy p. 3 kv. 75	310-7941		
International Transport Kompany, ul. Sofiyskaya 6	106-2841	268-5719	321682
InterOccidental, Vosstaniya ul. 49	273-4323	272-8031	
Interoptik JV (Austria), Tuchkov p. 7	218-3851	350-6475	
Interpicoat JV (FRG), nab. reki Moyki 58	314-0573	314-0573	
Interservice, Liteyny prosp. 35 kv. 4	275-3557	275-2803	
Interseverobalt Stock Exchange, V. O., Sredny prosp. 28			

	Phone	Fax	Telex
Intersotrudnichestvo Business Center,			
p. Boytsova 5	310-0169	312-7629	
Intersystem, Conrad Electronic GmbH Agency,			
Leninskiy prosp. 148	290-5565	290-5565	
Intour, Hotel Sankt Peterburg	542-8032		
Intourautoservice, ul. Sedova 5	567-8151	567-8897	122042
Intourbureau, ul. Galernaya 22	315-7876	315-7612	
Intourcreditcard, ul. Ryleyeva 5 kv. 2	119-6134		
Intourianta JV (Ireland), ul. Korablestroiteley 14	356-4185	356-0114	121276
Intourist, See St. Petersburg Travel			
Intourtrans, Hotel Pulkovskaya	299-5808		
pl. Aleksandra Nevskovo 2	274-2092	274-2121	
Invatur Cooperative, ul. Serdobolskaya 2b, kv. 33	245-6458		
Invent, Manezhny p. 19, kv. 27	275-5910	275-5320	
Invert, Chaykovskovo ul. 60	275-1567	275-7578	
Invest, ul. B. Morskaya 18	310-3954		122869
Investtrade, Fonarny p. 3	110-6267	110-6345	
Inyurkollegiya (Int'l Juridical Board),			
Pushkinskaya ul. 13	112-1679	113-3885	
Inzhener Cooperative, ul. Gorokhovaya 48	311-7094	311-7094	
IPRIS, Primorkskiy prosp. 35a	239-5796	239-6884	
IPS, Kozhevennaya liniya 34	264--0820	217-0371	
IRA, B. Morskaya ul. 45	311-5812	314-7288	
Irkutskaya Commodity & Raw Materials			
Exchange, Grivtsova p. 10	314-5221	110-6663	
Irmin, Shvernika prosp. 51	247-7894		
Iskatel, Suvorovskiy prosp. 55	275-6781		
Iskatel Book Store, nab. reki Moyki 51	312-7114		
Iskatel Cinema, Lunacharskovo prosp. 60	597-6210		
Iskorka, nab. reki Fontanki 59, kv. 444	210-8055		
Iskra, Suvorovskiy prosp. 30	271-1816		
Iskra Soft, Lesnoy prosp. 65 k 1	594-7575		
Isku Firm, prosp. Gagarina 1,office 535	294-5518		
Iskusstvo Publishers, Nevskiy prosp. 28	219-9472		
Isskustvo Bookstore, Nevskiy prosp. 16	312-8535		
Istochnik, ul. Dalya 10	234-4695	234-9026	
Istok-K, Kantemirovskaya ul. 5	245-5165	245-5165	
ITAR/TASS Press Agency, ul. Sadovaya 38	310-8840	110-6682	121832
Iter Firm, ul. Galernaya 4	315-2356		
Itmas, Bogatyrskiy prosp. 6, k. 5	395-3504		
Itochu and Co., Ltd., pl. Truda 2, kom. 41	311-8678	31107745	
Itus, Leninskiy prosp. 142a	254-7949	310-9394	
Tambasovaya ul. 21	130-2714		
Itus JV (Italy), Gorokhovaya ul. 47	310-8545	314-2273	122590
Ivan & Co. Caterers	294-0252	298-1306	
Ivan Fedorov Typography, ul. Zvenigorodskaya 11	164-4529	112-4533	
Iveria Cafe, ul. Marata 35	164-7478		
Izhora, prosp. Lenina 1	481-8150	463-9269	121435
Izhorskiy Zavod, Kolpino, prosp. Lenina 1	481-8110	463-9269	
Izmailoff Restaurant, 6 Krasnoarmeyskaya 22	292-6838		
Izmeron Factory, Novgorodskaya ul. 13	271-8560	274-0603	122215
Izobrazitelnoye Iskusstvo Publishers, Sadovaya ul. 89	114-6962		

INTERNATIONAL DOCUMENTS AND PARCELS DOOR TO DOOR

Fastest, most reliable service from and within the C.I.S.

Please call us at:
(095) 956-1000 (Moscow)
(812) 311-2649, 119-6100 (St. Petersburg)

DHL offices in Russia:
Moscow • St. Petersburg • Nizhny Novgorod • Togliatti • Novosibirsk
Khabarovsk • Vladivostok • Nakhodka • Yuzhno-Sakhalinsk

Enjoy First-Class Entertainment in an Atmosphere of Comfort & Confidence

Restaurant open from 12 noon to 2 am.
Gaming floor open from 4 pm to 6 am.
Jazz Bar open from 5 pm to 9 am.
Night Club open from 11 pm to 6 am.

Phone 945-1410

Major credit cards accepted.

	Phone	Fax	Telex
IzotermJV, Kolpino, prosp. Lenina 1	463-9270	463-9270	
Izumrud Jewellery Store, Moskovskiy prosp. 184	298-3242		
Izvestiya Editorial Office, Nevskiy prosp. 19	311-8506	311-8733	

J

JAC Travel Russia Ltd, Druzhba Hotel, suite 229-30, Chapygina ul.	234-9016	234-1797	
Jazz Club, See Kvadrat Jazz Club			
Jazz Club, Zagorodny prosp. 27	164-8565		
Jazzland JV, prosp. Obukhovskoy Oborony 86	567-8809	567-8809	
Jenart Tours, Nevskiy prosp. 40	314-2889	110-6614	
Jendrusch & Partner, ul. Belinskovo 13	272-4654	272-4654	
Jewish Cemetery, prosp. Alexandrovskoy Fermi 3a	262-0397		
John Bull Pub, Nevskiy prosp. 79	164-9877		
John the Baptist Brotherhood, 11 Krasnoarmeyskaya ul. 7, kv. 58	251-3246		
Joker Pet Shop, Sytninskaya pl. 1/47	233-7351		
Joy Boutique, Zagorodny prosp. 9	315-5315		
Joy Night Club, nab. kanala Griboyedova 28/1	311-3305		
Jubilee Palace of Sport, ul. Dobrolyubova 18	238-4114	233-4903	
Jurus JV (Yugoslavia), prosp. Gagarina 2	264-6666	264-6978	

K

K-Keskus, ul. Ordinarnaya 7	232-0723	232-0641	
Kachestvo Business Association, Rizhskiy prosp. 60	251-2739	251-4108	
Kadr, Kamennoostrovskiy prosp. 10	238-5831		
Kafe #1, prosp. Stachek 67	184-6819		
Kakadu, prosp. Chkalovskiy 58	234-6650		
Kak Dela Magazine, Nevskiy prosp. 28	219-9471		
Kalininskiy Department Store, Kondratyevskiy prosp. 40	540-5990		
Kalininskiy market, Polyustrovskiy prosp. 45	540-3039		
Kalininskiy Univermag, ul. Zamshina 29	543-3867		
Kalininskiy Veterinary Center, Vasenko ul. 3, kv. 3	540-3032		
Kalininskiy Video Center, Svetlanovskiy prosp. 62			
Kamazservis Firm, Yunnatov tupik 1	262-3034	267-6038	321448
Kammeny Ostrov, Polevaya alleya 6	234-0844	234-1266	
Kamos Cooperative, ul. Khrustalnaya 20	567-4546	272-0061	321475
Kankan Cabaret, Izmaylovskiy prosp. 7	251-7027	251-7004	
Kapella, nab. reki Moyki 20	314-7239	314-7239	
Karagach, Derptskiy p. 13	251-5945		
Karavan Restaurant, ul. Gorokhovaya 11	314-6614		
Karavan-2, ul. Shotlandskaya 1	114-9883	259-0793	
Karavella Bar, Lyoni Golikova ul. 27	152-5268		
Karavella Publishers, Solidarnosti prosp. 11, kor. 1	580-8528		
Karelia, Petrovskiy Ostrov 2-g	238-4047		
Karelia Hotel, ul. Tukhachevskovo 27/2	226-3515	226-3511	122459
Beriozka	226-3237		
Eldorado Discotec	226-3110		

	Phone	Fax	Telex
Klondyke Casino	226-3110		
Karelia Restaurant	226-3549		
Vitabank	226-3356		
Karelia Trade Oy, pl. Alexandra Nevskovo 2, Moscow Hotel	274-2037	234-2037	
Karl Fazer, Nevskiy prosp. 134	274-4160	274-4360	
Karmen, Moskovskiy prosp. 194	298-4242		
Kaskad, Ligovskiy prosp. 65	164-5333		
Kassandra, Novorossiyskaya ul. 46/3	550-0854		
Katera i Yakhty, ul. M. Morskaya 8	312-4078		
Kauko Firm, Nakhimova ul. 7, kv. 39	356-3635	356-8333	
Kaukomarkkinat Oy, See Kauko Firm			
Kazan Cathedral, Kazanskaya pl. 2	314-5838		
Kazbek, Bukharestskaya ul. 43	260-8706		
Kella, ul. Kronverkskaya 10	232-1890	2321890	
Kenguru Cooperative, P.S., Bolshoy prosp. 44	233-2563		
Kentavr Cooperative, ul. Koli Tomchaka 15	296-2701	296-2453	
Kentavr International Film and Television Center, nab. Martynova 70	230-2200	235-5318	121449
Keramika Cooperative, Yuzhnoye sh. 55	269-3676	105-7396	
Kevlar Cooperative, Fontanka 89	314-2876	310-2288	
Khachapuri Restaurant, 6 Krasnoarmeyskaya ul. 13/18	292-7377		
Kheybey Restaurant, P.S., Bolshoy prosp. 61	233-2046		
Khimchistka, Izmailovskiy prosp. 12	292-3347		
prosp. Metallistov	540-1935		
Zanevskiy prosp. 37	528-8465		
Khimiko Farmatsevticheskiy Institut, See Chemistry and Pharmaceutical Institute			
Khimiya, Nevskiy prosp. 28	219-9023		
Khimreaktivservis JV (Belgian), Khimicheskiy p. 1	252-0891	252-0981	
Khlopkotex Ltd, prosp. Obukhovskoy Oborony 86	567-7289	567-1835	
Khollait JV (Dutch), Baskov p. 6	279-0903	272-2369	
Khoros JV (Sweden), ul. Korpusnaya 28g	235-6460	230-2824	
Khudozhestvennaya Literatura Publishers, Nevskiy prosp. 28	311-3251	311-7568	
Khudozhestvennovo Stekla Factory, ul. Professora Kachalova 9	567-5267	567-6510	
Khudozhestvenny Cinema, Nevskiy prosp. 67	314-0053		
Khudozhestvennye promysli, Nevskiy prosp. 51	113-1495		
Khudozhnik Publishers, Bolsheokhtinskiy prosp. 6, korpus 2	224-0637		
Khudozhnik Training Center, Promyshlennaya 40	186-2550	314-3433	
Kievskaya Hotel, Dnepropetrovskaya ul. 49	166-0456	166-5398	
Kifa Russian Orthodox Church Center, Leninskiy prosp. 135	255-6081	470-4362	
Kinonedelya, nab. reki Fontanki 59	310-4454		
Kinoveevskoe Cemetery, Oktyabrskaya nab. 14	587-9414		
Kirov House Museum, Kamennoostrovskiy prosp. 26/28	233-3822		
Kirov Park of Culture and Leisure, Yelagin ostrov 4	239-0911		
Kirov Stadium, Krestovskiy ostrov, Morskoy prosp.	235-4877		
Kirov Textile and Light Industry Institute, ul. Gertsena 18	315-7525	315-1351	
Kirovskiy Department Store, pl. Stachek 9	186-6000		122575

	Phone	Fax	Telex
Kirovskiy Factory, prosp. Stachek 47	183-8434	183-4716	
Kirovskiy market, prosp. Stachek 54	185-0639		
Kirovskiy Residence Repair & Remodeling Service, Stachek prosp. 101	157-4444		
Kirovskiy Veterinary Center, Shvetsova ul. 47	252-7925		
Kirovspek JV (British,USA), prosp. Stachek 47	252-1730	252-1730	
Klassik Restaurant, Ligovskiy prosp. 202	166-0159		
KLM Airlines, Pulkovo II Airport	104-3440		
Klondike, Razyeszhaya u. 15	315-8217		
Klondyke Casino, Hotel Karelia	226-3110		
Klyon, Slavy prosp. 2	260-7752		
Klyonovaya Alleya, Manezhnaya pl.	219-2129		
Kniga-Pochtoy, Petrozavodskaya ul. 7	235-4064		
Knigi po Khimii, Moskovskiy prosp. 54	292-4500		
Knigolub Bookstore, Novoizmailovskiy prosp. 40, k. 1	295-9028		
Knizhnaya Lavka Pisateley, Nevskiy prosp. 66	314-4858		
KNK, Vsevoloda Vishnevdkovo ul. 20/37	230-5463	234-2501	
Know how, Divenskaya ul. 14, kv. 7	232-0045		3110965
Knyaz Konstantin, ul. Millionnaya 5/1	312-1859	312-9421	
Knyazya Vladimira Cathedral, See Cathedral of Prince Vladimir			
Kodotekinform Ltd, Apraksin p. 4	310-4364		
Kodri, Moskovskiy prosp. 5	310-3078		
Kolizey Cinema, Nevskiy prosp. 100	272-8775		
Kollektsioner, Ligovskiy prosp. 236	166-4751		
Ligovskiy prosp. 61	164-8226		
ul. Aviatsionnaya 18	291-3514		
Kolobok Restaurant, Pushkin	476-6255		
Kolomna, Rimskogo-Korsakova prosp. 24	114-3150		
Kolomyagi-RETRO Joint-Stock Association, Nevskiy prosp. 1	315-8184	312-7481	
Kombinat Tsvetnoy Pechat, prosp. Obukhovskoy Oborony 110	262-2077	267-1771	
Komeks JV(Malasiya), Beloostrovskaya ul. 13	245-3123	245-3121	
Komfort, B. Porokhovskaya ul. 24	224-2752		
Komissarzhevskoy Dramatic Theater, Italianskaya ul. 19	315-5355		
Komkon, Primakova ul. 10	184-4072	262-2151	
Kommark, ul. Sablinskaya 7	233-9965	233-3008	
Kommersant Firm, Liteyny prosp. 12 kv. 1	275-3222	275-3226	
Kommet, Moskovskiy prosp. 28, #450	259-7415	251-6553	
Komnata, Narvskiy prl 23, kor. 2	186-6358		
Kompan, ul. Dolgoozernaya 3/2	395-3623	395-3598	
Kompan Sea Structures, prosp. Marshala Govorova 52	252-0144		
Komplekt, ul. Svobody 46	132-1052	164-8573	
Komplekt Ltd., ul. Mira 6	233-4300	232-5506	
Kompressor, B. Sampsonievskiy prosp. 64	245-9418	245-6912	
Komsomolskaya Pravda, Khersonskaya ul. 12	274-0663	274-0663	
Komsomolskiy Cinema, Liony Golikova ul. 29	157-2447		
Kondiayn & Partners Architectural Bureau, ul. Plekhanova 5 flat 45	311-2878	315-2387	
Kone, Propsekt Prosveshcheniya 70, kv. 158	558-1269	112-7252	

	Phone	Fax	Telex
Konek, Marata Ul. 86	164-0722	112-4211	
Konform, B. Raznochinnaya ul. 6, kv. 28	235-4209	315-1701	
Konkurent Ltd, Ivanovskaya ul. 17	560-3645		
Konkurs Center for Science and Technology, Krasny prosp. 4a	427-9472	427-9595	
Konskor JV (Yugoslavia), Moskovskiy prosp. 119	296-3960	298-9787	
Konsofin JV (Finland), Rizhskiy prosp. 58	259-9106	251-7611	121485
Konsol, ul. Volodi Yermaka 10	219-7070		
Konstantin Cooperative, ul. Pirogova 14/7	314-1554	110-6580	
Konstruktor Stationers, Sadovaya ul.. 26	310-1815		
Konti Casino, Kondratyevskiy prosp. 44	540-5165		
Konti-Universal, Goncharnaya ul. 5	273-0949	273-0949	
Kontinent Regional Commercial Assn., ul. Sedova 37	560-9428	292-3471	
Izmaylovskiy prosp. 4	292-3471	292-3471	
Kontinental, Kronshtadt, ul. Ammermana 27	236-8311		121075
Konventsiya Research Center for the Humanities, nab. kanala Griboyedova 7	314-2252		
Konversbank (Bank of Conversion), North-West Affiliate, nab. Chyornoy Rechki 24	239-7501	239-7501	
Konwest, nab. reki Fontanki 23	311-2281		
Kopia, Izmaylovskiy prosp. 12	292-0496		
Korablestroitelny Institute, See Ship Building Institute			
Korchma, prosp. Engelsa 83	554-1449		
Koreyskiy Domik, nab. reki Fontanki 20	275-7203	591-0043	
Korona, Kamennoostrovskiy prosp. 5	232-4870		
Korona-Logovaz, Kamennoostrovskiy prosp. 5	238-1915		
Korvet, Razyezzhaya ul. 10	315-9145		
Kosmoaerogeologicheskiy Cooperative, Birzhevoy pr. 6	231-4485		
Kosmonavt Cinema, Bronnitskayay u. 24	292-2727		
Kostyor, Mytninskaya ul. 1/20	274-1572		
Kotra-Balt, Izmaylovskiy 2 kv. 34	113-0067	113-0067	
Kovcheg, ul. Chernyshevskovo 9	297-1236		
Koyolga Restaurant, Narodnaya ul. 15	263-1893		
KPMG, nab. kanala Griboyedova 7, 3rd flr.	314-5209	312-7132	
Kranex, Obvodny kanal 118	292-2856	251-0991	121313
Krasnaya Zarya Faktory, Sampsonevskiy prosp. 60	542-1222	541-8369	
Krasnaya Zarya Institute, ul. Kantemirovskaya 6	554-1613		121592
Krasnaya Zvezda, Liteyny prosp. 20	272-5825		
Krasnogvardeets, Instrumentalnaya ul. 3	234-2600		121473
Udarnikov prosp. 27, kor. 1	227-8975		
Krasnogvardeyskiy Veterinary Center, 2 Zhernovskaya ul. 46	527-0946		
Krasnoselskoye Fur Factory, Krasnoye selo, ul. Lermontova 21	132-5516	113-1799	
Krasny Khimik Factory, Khimicheskiy p. 1	252-8261	252-0809	122104
Krasny Oktyabr Cinema, Blokhina ul. 8	238-8033		
Krasny Oktyabr Machine Building Factory, ul. Politekhnicheskaya 13/15	247-9703		322194
Krasny Partizan Musical Instrument Factory, 6 Krasnoarmeyskaya ul. 7	292-2777	292-2652	
Krasota Cosmetics, Nevskiy prosp. 90	272-9325		
Kredit Petersburg, ul. Dumskaya 1	238-6058	110-4432	

	Phone	Fax	Telex
Kreyt, Pushkinskaya ul. 10, kv. 129	164-9135	312-4312	
Kris Ltd, p. Krylova 7/5	310-2796	315-2720	
Kristall, B. Konyushennaya ul. 2	113-3570	314-4267	
Krona International Timber Exchange, ul. Plekhanova 36	319-9263	319-9264	
Kross, Respublikanskaya ul. 20	528-5756		
Krug Cooperative, prosp. Bolshevikov 6, k. 2	584-5447		
Krunk Kafe, Solyanoy p. 14	273-3830	272-7286	
Krupskaya Institute of Culture, Dvortsovaya nab. 2-4	312-9521		
Krystall Jewelry Store, Nevskiy prosp. 34	311-3095		
Kulsa, ul. 3 Sovetskaya 8	275-0089		
Kultura ,Naukal Pravo Association, Moskovskiy prosp. 79a	296-1606		
Kulturnaya Initsiativa American-Russian Fund, ul. Chaykovskovo 29	272-3678	273-1128	
Kunstkamera, See Anthropology and Ethnography Museum			
Kupchinskiy Department Store, Slavy prosp. 4,12,16	261-9981		
Kurier Dansing Hall, ul. B. Morskaya 58	311-4678		
Kustanay Air	465-8810	275-5822	
Kuybyshevskiy Employment Agency, Nevskiy prosp. 78	275-1829		
Kuybyshevskiy Veterinary Center, Kolomenskaya ul. 45	164-5722		
Kuznechny market, Kuznechny p. 3	312-4161		
Kvadrat, 3 Zhernovskaya ul. 51/3			
Kvadrat Jazz Club, ul. Pravdy 10	164-8508		
Kvarta JV(USA), ul. Yakornaya 17	222-5493	227-3715	
Kvarts NPO, Piskarevskiy prosp. 63	113-2838		121654
Kvasar, Kamennoostrovskiy prosp. 5	233-4033	232-4944	

L

	Phone	Fax	Telex
L. A. -RossJV(USA), ul. Ruzovskaya 1	292-5753		
Lada, prosp. Stachek 106	158-3598		
Lada-EN 65 Car Wash, Energetikov prosp. 65	226-5678	226-5688	
Lado-Balt, Lomonosova ul. 3	310-4455	310-2231	
Ladoga Cinema, Revolyutsii sh. 31	222-5446		
Ladoga Furniture Making Factory, 12 Krasnoarmeyskaya 26	251-9792	251-0269	
Ladoga Hat Making Factory, Pevcheskiy p. 12	233-2935	233-2935	321242
Ladoga Hotel, Stakhanovtsev ul. 14	221-8014		
Ladoga Industries AG JV (Sweden), ul. Sestroretskaya 4	239-6087	239-6443	
Ladya Chess Club, Vladimirskiy prosp. 3	311-7160	113-3697	
Laktio Joint Stock Tourism Assn., ul. Italianskaya 3	110-6673		
Lampiduza, Shpalernaya ul. 18	279-5037	273-4092	
Lan International Inc., Predportovaya ul. 40-b	123-3816		
Lancome, Nevskiy prosp. 64	312-3495		
Landora, nab. reki Fontanki 136	265-0489		
Landskrona Restaurant, Nevskiy Palace Hotel	275-2001		
Lant Law Firm, Nevskiy prosp. 65	311-1927		

	Phone	Fax	Telex
Las Vegas Show Lounge, Hotel Commodore	119-6666		
LASAN, Italyanskaya ul. 23	210-4636		
Launderette, Korablestroiteley ul. 20, kor. 3	355-4025		
Ordzhonikidze ul. 31-a			
Zaytseva ul. 17	184-0503		
Lavka Khudozhnikov Art Shop, Nevskiy prosp. 31	110-5016		
Nevskiy prosp. 45	311-2196		
Nevskiy prosp. 8	312-6193		
Law Office of S. A. Stern, Nevskiy prosp. 104	275-3497	119-6186	
LDM Hotel, Professora Popova ul. 47	234-3278		
Leathertouch Fabrics U. S. A., ul. Khimikov 28	315-9382	315-7420	
Lega, 5 Krasnoarmeyskaya ul. 28, kv. 17	292-1919	312-9773	
Legal Administration, Admiralteyskaya nab. 12			
LEK Corp., Mytninskaya ul. 19	271-1420	271-4047	
Lek Estate, Nevskiy prosp. 90/92	272-1097	275-2880	
Leks JV (FRG), ul. Kalinina 13	186-8897	186-3390	
Leksa, V. O., 11 Liniya 22	213-2698		
Len-Sof, Aptekarskiy prosp. 16	234-2888	234-0117	
Lena, Myasnikova ul. 4	310-8054	310-3615	
Lenart, nab. reki Fontanki 34	275-7510	275-5096	121034
Lenaudit, Nevskiy prosp. 7/9	312-3700	312-5578	
Lenavtotrans, nab. kanala Griboyedova 5	314-6676	314-6673	
Lenbagonmash, Moskovskiy prosp. 115	298-3523		
Lenbelltelefon JV (Belgian), Malookhtinskiy prosp. 68	528-0235	528-7414	
Lenbiomed Firm, prosp. Morisa Tereza 89	553-3269		
Lenbridis JV (US), ul. Voskova 6			
Lenbytkhim Production Assn.,			
ul. Chernyakhovskovo 71	164-0429	164-6350	322118
Lencomissiontorg (Selling),			
Kamennoostrovskiy prosp. 2	233-5153		
Liteyny prosp. 34	273-6526		
Lencomissiontorg (Purchasing),			
Sadovaya ul., Apraksin dvor 35-36	310-3058		
Lencomissiontorg, ul. Plekhanova 39	312-7253		
Lenenergoremont Production Enterprise,			
Novolitovskaya ul. 16	245-4173	245-1373	
LenExpo, V. O., Bolshoy prosp. 103	355-1989	355-1985	121532
LenFilm Studio, Kamenoostrovskiy prosp. 10	232-8374	232-8881	121534
Lenfincom JV (Finland), ul. B. Morskaya 3-5	314-0060	312-3273	121979
Lenfinstroy JV(Finland), ul. 8 Krasnoarmeyskaya 23	113-0155	113-0202	
Lenfintorg, Moskovskiy prosp. 98	298-1892	296-1165	122724
Lengatur JV (FRG,Kanada), Italianskaya ul. 3	311-7960	311-7862	321893
Lengoragropromtrans 2 Transport Firm,			
prosp. Aleksandrovskoy fermi 17	262-1308	262-2589	
Lengrazhdanproekt, Fontanka 6	312-3462		
Leniko Dental and Contact Lens Center,			
V. O., 14 Liniya 97	355-8388		
Lenin Sport-Concert Complex,			
prosp. Yuri Gagarina 8	264-0472		
Leninets, Moskovskiy prosp. 212	293-7178	299-9041	
Leningrad Cinema, Potemkinskaya ul. 4	273-3116		
Leningrad Documentary Film Studio,			
Kanal Kryukova 12	114-5312	114-3304	

	Phone	Fax	Telex
Leningrad Fashion House (LDMO), Nevskiy prosp. 21	311-4448	312-2526	122892
Leningrad Regional Seed Stock Inspection, Shkapina ul. 36/40	252-6387		
Leningrad Technical Information Center Library, Sadovaya ul. 2	210-4891		
Leningrad-Goeteborg Company JV (Sweden), Leninskiy prosp. 101	153-5765	153-5748	
Leningradets Cooperative, Staro-Petergofskiy prosp. 26	252-2022		
Leningradintekh, Chkalovskiy prosp. 52	234-9223	230-1307	
Leningradskiy Alcoholic Beverages Factory, Sinopskaya nab. 56/58	271-2966	271-3138	
Leningradskiye Magistrali, Zodchevo Rossi ul. 1/3, kom. 17	311-1377		
Leninskiy Residence Repair & Remodeling Service, Moskovskiy prosp. 61	292-2102		
Lenizdat Publishers, nab. reki Fontanki 59	310-5179	315-1295	122593
Lenkhleboprodukt, 4 Predportovy pr. 5	122-0072		121499
Nevskiy prosp. 87/2	277-5030		
Lenkomissiontorg, prosp. Engelsa 66	554-0076		
Lenkontsert, nab. reki Fontanki 41	310-3766	311-2066	
LenkozhvestJV(German), Kozhevennaya Liniya 1/3	217-8206	217-2717	
Lenles, B. Konyushennaya ul. 29	312-9526	314-1976	
Lenmelioratsia, Serdobolskaya ul. 7	246-3888		
Lenmortogport Commercial Sea Port, Mezhevoy kanal 5	114-9001	251-0484	121501
Lennauchfilm Studio, ul. Melnichnaya 4	265-0151	567-7024	121063
Lenoblrestavratsiya, ul. Vosstaniya 40	273-0427	275-8812	
Lenobuv, ul. Vosstaniya 2/116	279-0530	279-1288	
Lenord Firm, Srednyaya Podyacheskaya 7 kv. 2	314-1392		
Lenpak JV (German), Sergeya Tyulenina p. 3	312-7592	312-7592	
Lenpeks JV (USA), ul. Truda 2	311-9134	311-9338	
Lenpipet JV (Finland), ul. Shvetsova 41	252-1633	186-1194	
Lenpoligrafmash, nab. reki Karpovki 5	234-2420	234-1183	
Lenpolproekt JV (Poland), ul. Kapitanskaya 3, kv. 216	352-8431	352-8431	121482
Lenprodmash Production Assn., Rizhskiy prosp. 40	251-5381	251-6920	
Lenpromstroibank, Nevskiy prosp. 38	110-4703	310-6173	
Lenptitseprom Production Assn., ul. Smolnovo 3	271-2607	274-4655	
Lenpushnina, ul. Goncharnaya 23	277-4317	277-2079	
Lenraumamebel JV (Finland), ul. Mebelnaya 5	246-7748	246-0912	121314
Lenraumamebel Shop, nab. reki Fontanki 20	272-5683	273-1322	
Lenregionbank, Kamenoovstrovskiy prosp. 10	110-4432	110-4432	
Lenremtochstanok, Lomanaya 10	298-7161	298-7161	
Lenrianta JV (Ireland), Pulkovo II Airport	104-3486	104-3468	
Lenros, nab. Obvodnovo kanala 143	113-0346	113-0346	121323
Lenryba Ltd, nab. kanala Griboyedova 56-58	310-7349		
Lenrybkholodflot, Dnepropetrovskaya 61	166-5701	166-2200	122703
Lensan JV (Brazil), prosp. Yelizarova 42	166-8622		121345
Lensey JV (FRG), ul. Sadovaya 93	114-4634	114-4634	
Lensportinvest JV (France), nab. reki Fontanki 76, korpus B	113-1419	113-1419	
Lensportkomitet, Millionnaya ul. 22	312-1541		
Lenstroyrekonstruktsia, ul. Kazanskaya 36	319-9457	312-2977	121368

	Phone	Fax	Telex
Lenstroyrekonstruktsia, V. O., 3 Liniya 6	213-2500		
Lenstroyzhilservis Association, Zakharyevskaya ul. 31	273-3139	273-0611	
Lenta JV (Finland), prosp. Chernyshevskovo 17	275-8844	275-7616	
Lentek JV (Finland), ul. B. Zelenina 43	230-3369	235-2837	121446
Lentekhgaz, B. Smolenskiy prosp. 11	265-1829	567-1244	122304
Lentekhprokat, ul. Zamshina 31	543-6939		
Lentekinvest JV (Italy), nab. Obvodnovo kanala 143	113-0824	113-0824	121511
Lentelefilm, ul. Chapygina 6	234-7775		
Lentep JV (France), Zaozernaya ul. 1	259-6717	252-6000	121478
Lentorf, P.S. Tyulenina 3	315-2485	311-6049	
Lentransagenstvo, Konyshennaya pl. 1	314-6976		
Lentruboremont Cooperative, B. Smolenskiy prosp. 4	568-0416		
Lenvars JV (Poland), Ligovskiy prosp. 56	164-5073	164-8656	
Lenvneshtrans, Mezhevoy kanal 5	259-8040	186-2883	
Lenwest Export/Import JV (FRG), Zastavskaya ul. 13	298-8647	294-0104	
Lenwest JV (FRG), ul. Tsvetochnaya 6	298-2088	294-0618	121433
Leontyevskiy Center, ul. Mayorova 16	314-4119	319-9814	
Leontyevskiy International Research Center, p. Antonenko 6	319-9624	319-9814	121465
Lesgaft Physical Culture Institute, ul. Dekabristov 35	219-5139	114-1084	
Lesotekhnik, Institutskiy p. 5 kom. 306	550-0268		
Letniy Katok LVO, nab. reki Fontanki 112	292-2128		
Leto, Pulkovskoye sh. 30	293-3495	122-6432	
Lex Telecomm, ul. Mytninskaya 19	271-1676	271-1173	
Libertas, ul. Pestelya 9	273-7127		
Library for the Blind, ul. Shamsheva 8	232-5080	232-3651	
Library of the Academy of Arts, Universitetskaya nab. 17	213-7178		
LIC, Nevskiy prosp. 28	314-5982	315-3592	
Lider, Bronnitskaya ul. 17	110-1093		
Liden & Denz, Malooktinskiy prosp. 68	528-1177	528-8977	
Lik, Telezhnaya ul. 17/19	277-2937		
LIK, Zheleznovodskaya ul. 64	350-1221		
Lilia, Sedova ul. 17	265-0489		
Limb, V. O., 5 Liniya 66	218-1424		
Lipetsk Art International, Partizana Germana ul. 3, kv. 428	164-6956	112-1213	
Lissant JV (Yugoslaviya), sh. Revolyutsii 102	527-3095	227-2312	
Litera-Nord Co Ltd, Shpalernaya ul. 18	279-5037	273-4092	
Literary Museum of the Institute of Russian Literat, nab. Makarova 4	218-0502		
Literary Plot of Volkovskoye Cemetery, Rasstannaya ul. 30	166-2383		
Literator, Shpalernaya ul. 18	279-5037	273-4092	
Literaturnaya Gazeta, ul. Shpalernaya 18	279-0873		
Literaturnoye Cafe, Nevskiy prosp. 18	312-6057		
Liteyny Food Store, Liteyny prosp. 12	272-2791		
Litsey, Kutuzova nab. 6	273-4824	273-6004	
Littlewoods, Gostiny Dvor, 2nd floor,Nevskiy 35	110-5447	110-5371	
LMZ Export-Import, Sverdlovskaya nab. 18	226-5497	542-4504	

	Phone	Fax	Telex
Logos, Pirogova p. 18	315-0810	315-0810	
Kazanskaya ul. 36, kv. 622	319-9580		121368
Logos St. Petersburg Christian College, ul. Zvezdnaya 15 bldg 2	127-5921	127-1937	
Logovaz, Oktyabrskaya nab. 6	223-5233	221-9322	
Logovaz Severo Zapad, Vitebskiy prosp. 17, kor. 2	298-4608	294-1660	
Lokomotiv Olympic Preparation Center, ul. Deputatskaya 9a	235-0412	235-3967	
Lokomotiv Swimming Pool, ul. Konstantina Zasionova 23	164-4755		
LOMO, ul. Chugunnaya 20	245-5343	542-1065	121590
Lomonosov Memorial Museum, Universitetskaya nab. 3	218-1211		
Lomonosov Porcelain Factory, prosp. Obukhovskoy Oborony 151	560-8301	560-8211	121768
London, Kamennoostrovskiy prosp. 12	232-6293		
Long Distance Telephone	07		
Los Angeles Restaurant, Hotel Commodore	119-6666		
Lost and Found, ul. Zakharevskaya 19	278-3690		
Lot Airlines, Airport Pulkovo 2	104-3437		
Pulkovo II Airport	104-3437		
ul. Karavannaya 1	273-4560	279-5352	
LST-Metall JV (FRG), Doroga na Petroslavyanku 5	267-0824	100-3263	
LT Estate, 1 Krasnoarmeyskaya ul. 11	110-1455	112-6633	
LT-Stamp JV (Finland), Lermontovskiy prosp. 24	114-2287		
ul. Rimskovo-Korsakovo 71	114-5831		
Luch, 5 Krasnoarmeyskaya ul. 22	292-3714	186-4044	
prosp. Metallistov 7	224-1775	227-3670	
Luch Cinema, Vosstaniya ul. 41	272-8630		
Lufthansa Airlines, Vosnesenskiy prosp. 7	314-4979	312-3129	
Pulkovo II Airport	104-3432		
Lukomorye Restaurant, V. O., 13 Liniya 2/19	218-5900		
Lum, Mokhovaya ul. 39			
Lumena Ltd, PO box 45	528-9605	528-9612	
Luna, B. Konyushennaya ul. 5	312-4620		
Lunacharskiy Theater Library, ul. Zodchevo Rossi 2	311-0845		
Lutheran Church, Pushkin, ul. Proletkulta 4	470-7763		
Lyogkaya Promyshlennost i Bytoviye Obsluzhivaniye, nab. reki Moyki 40, kv. 14	315-4742		
Lyubava-Lada, Canal Griboedova 126	113-7015		

M

	Phone	Fax	Telex
M. I. Kalinina Factory, Uralskaya ul. 1	352-0982	352-5735	
M. T. M. Firm, ul. B. Konyushennaya 11 kv. 37a	314-1184	314-1184	
MacTech, ul. Marata 16	314-3432	112-5359	
Madison Brands, Inc.	543-5462		
Magistral, Vosstaniya ul. 51			
Magnolia, Kamenoostrovskiy prosp. 2	233-5353		
Sadovaya ul. 46	310-0843		
Mak, ul. Sofiyskaya 6	106-2841	268-5719	
Makarov State Naval Academy, Kosaya Liniya 15-a	217-1934	217-0682	

	Phone	Fax	Telex
Maks, Nevskiy prosp. 65, Box 131	314-0121		
Malev Airlines, prosp. Voznesenskiy 7	315-5455	314-6380	
Pulkovo II Airport	104-3435		
Maltiyskiy Charitable Canteen, ul. Chaykovskovo 77	272-5294	272-3841	
Maltsevskiy market, ul. Nekrasova 52	279-2583		
Malvina, Sredny prosp. 14	213-5147		
Maly Dramatic Theater, ul. Rubinshteyna 18	113-2039	113-3366	
Maly Theater named for M. P. Musorgsky, See Musorgskiy Maly Theater			
Management Systems Corporation, Pushkin 7, Box 76	476-1550	476-0237	
Manege Central Exhibition Hall, Isaakevskaya pl. 1	314-8859		
Marble Palace, The (Russian Museum), Millionnaya ul. 5/1	312-1788		
Marcopizzi Shoes, Kamenoostrovskiy prosp. 37	233-8664	233-8554	
Mariinskiy Bank, B. Porokhovskaya ul. 52 k 2	224-0440	224-0440	
Marin-Avtoservice, Lakhtinskaya ul. 5			
Marine Computer Systems, ul. Babushkina 80	568-3947		
Marinskiy Opera & Ballet House Central Musical Note Library, ul. Zodchevo Rossi 2	312-3573		
Marinskiy Theater of Opera and Ballet, Teatralnaya pl. 1	114-1211		121460
Booking Office	114-5264		
Maritime Passenger Terminal, pl. Morskoy Slavy 1	355-1310		
Information on International Travel	355-1312		
Market Bridge Centre, Bolsheokhtinskiy prosp. 1	224-1122		
Market Bridge Firm, Nevskiy prosp. 82	275-7149	275-7150	
Mars Hotel, Narodnovo Opolcheniya prosp. 189	159-9955		
Marvel Ltd, ul. Shpalernaya 49	274-3210	274-3708	
Maservil, 5 Liniya 48, kv. 8	113-8601		
Mashinostroitel, Kolomyazhskiy prosp. 12	246-8384		
Maska Bookstore, Nevskiy prosp. 13	311-0312		
Matralen Airport Limousine Service, Lyubotinskiy pr. 5	298-3648	298-0073	121028
Matsushita Electric Industrial Co., Ltd, See Kauko Firm			
Maxim Cinema, Lanskoye sh. 35	246-4849		
Mayak Cinema, Korablestroiteley ul. 21, kor. 3	356-1212		
Mayak Sewing Production Assn., Moskovskiy prosp. 91	298-3602	296-1093	121109
Mayakovskiy Central City Library, nab. reki Fontanki 44	311-3026		
Mazda, ul. Borovaya 55a	168-5572	117-0059	
MCD Marketing, Consulting and Design, Shpalernaya ul. 52, #13	275-5623	275-5623	
McKinsey & Co., Hotelship Olympia	119-6050	119-6049	
Meandr Ltd, Sofiyskaya ul. 56	106-0904	106-0904	
Mebel, Bukharestskaya ul. 74-b	269-7603		
Mechnikov Clinical Hospital, Piskarevskiy prosp. 47	543-9329		
Medical Institute, Piskarevskiy prosp. 47	543-9609	543-1571	
Mechta Cinema, Strelbishchenskaya ul. 16	268-0097		
Meckanobr-Tekhnika, V. O., 21 Liniya 8a	213-9953		

	Phone	Fax	Telex
Medalion, ul. Sadovaya 2	210-4879		
Mediak Foreign Trade Firm, Artilleriyskiy prosp. 7	234-2144	234-2740	322168
Mediator, ul. L. Tolstova 6/8	233-7913		
Medical Export Management, ul. Voskova 27/18	233-2249	232-4220	
Medical Pediatrics Institute, Litovskaya ul. 2	245-0646	542-9695	
Medical Scientific Library, prosp. Lunacharskovo 45	592-7158		
Medikal Clinic, Moskovskiy prosp. 22	292-6272		
Medkhor, ul. Inzhenernaya 13	314-6710	311-7562	
Medpolimer, sh. Revolyutsii 69	520-6400	520-6401	
Medservice, See Vanga JV filial			
Medtekhnika, ul. Ruzovskaya 18	292-1977		
ul. Voronezhskaya 16	164-0110	164-7586	
Meduchposobiye, Kolomenskaya u. 4/6	164-4200		
MEG, Sadovaya ul. 104	113-6740	113-6672	
Mekhanicheskiy Institut imeni D. F. Ustinova, See Ustinov Mechanical Institute			
Mekhanobr Engineering, V. O., 21 Liniya 8a	213-9953		
Mekhanobr-Service, 21 Liniya 8-a			
Melodiya, Nevskiy prosp. 32/34	311-7455		
Melody JV Restaurant (Sweden), Sverdlovskaya nab. 62	227-2676	227-1596	
Mendeleev House Museum, Mendeleyevskaya liniya 2	218-2982		
Menshikov Palace Museum, Universitetskaya nab. 15	213-1112		
Meria, Cmolny	315-9883		
Meridian Cinema, Novoizmailovskiy prosp. 48	295-7670		
Meridian Restaurant, Hotel Pulkovskaya, pl. Pobedy 1	264-5177		
Merikons JV (FRG), prosp. Prosveshcheniya 46k. 1	245-3701		
Merktrans, ul. Vindavskaya 2	114-9978	251-8979	
Meta, Box 629	259-1111	312-4128	
Metallist Factory, nab. Obvodnovo kanala 150	292-9044	252-1462	
Metalloposuda, Sadovaya ul. 62	310-5806		
Metod Consulting-Expert Center of Mayor, p. Antonenko 6b	312-9312	314-7419	
Metro Oy Ab, B. Sampsionyevskiy prosp. 31	542-6842	542-6842	
Metro-Auto, Leninskiy prosp. 160	295-5449	295-8172	
Metrocom, ul. Transportnaya 1	314-5248	314-5134	
Metropol Restaurant, Sadovaya ul. 22	310-1845		
Metropoliten, Moskovskiy prosp. 28	292-9677		
Mezhsovkhozles, Muchnoy p. 2	315-7739		
MIK Publications Ltd., 10 Krasnoarmeyskaya ul. 19			
Mika, Oktyabrskiy nab. 70, kor. 1	263-9187		
Mikrofon, M. Posadskaya ul. 8	233-3274	233-3274	
Milena Art Gallery, Muchnoy p. 2	310-3482		
Milena-Inform JV (Italy), Muchnoy p. 2	110-5970	311-4633	
Military Medical Academy, Lebedeva ul. 6	542-2139		
Militia	02		
Mineral Processing Engineers, V. O., 21 Liniya 8a	213-9986	350-2024	121419
Ministry for Internal Affairs, Liteyny prosp. 4	311-1851		
Ministry for Security, Liteyny prosp. 4	278-7110		
Ministry of			
Culture and Tourism, nab. kanala Griboyedova 107	314-8234		
Foreign Economic Relations, Moskovskiy prosp. 98	298-4344	298-8514	
Foreign Affairs, nab. Kutuzova 34	272-0076	279-4847	321725

	Phone	Fax	Telex
Minolta Austrian GmbH, ul. Komissara Smirnova 15, office 285	542-0237	542-0237	
Minor-Neva Consulting Company, Serpukhovskaya ul. 4	292-4466	112-7336	
Mipros JV (FRG), Kolpino, prosp. Lenina 101	484-9104	484-1888	121253
Mir Advertising, Nevskiy prosp. 10	312-7428	110-1500	
Mir Art and Book Store, Liteyny prosp. 64	273-5012		
Nevskiy prosp. 13	311-5473		
Nevskiy prosp. 16	312-8535		
Mir Business Center, Leninskiy prosp. 161	108-4423	293-5603	
Mir Cinema, Moskovskiy prosp. 184	297-0408		
Mir Hotel, Gastello ul. 17	108-5166		
Mir Kultury, Kutuzova nab. 6	275-3864		
MIT Enterprise Forum	510-4495	122-3033	
Mits Scientific-Production Company, 1 Krasnoarmeyskaya 1	251-0894	251-2967	
Mitsar, nab. reki Pryazhki	216-0881		
MKS Sankt-Petersburg, V. O., 16 Liniya 11	217-3058	213-6447	
MMT International JV (Austria), ul. Shvetsova 22	186-8852	186-8853	
Mobil-Service, Kronshtadtskaya ul. 1	183-3868		
ul. Frunze 15	164-6066	315-8204	
Moebius Ltd., Kanal Griboedova 46	310-2467		
Molniya Cinema, P.S., Bolshoy prosp. 35	232-5600		
Molodiozhny Cinema, Sadovaya ul. 12	311-3953		
Moneta, ul. Bumazhnaya 15	186-8947	186-8215	
Moniks, Rubinshteyna ul. 22-20	310-2843		
Monna JV (Finland), Ust-Izhora, ul. Truda 2	463-9898	463-9900	
Monolitstroi, ul. Ryleyeva 29	272-1775	273-7357	
Montazh Cooperative, ul. Vereyskaya 31	292-2532		
Montazh International Ltd., Basseynaya ul. 8	296-0108	275-7150	
Moroshka Cooperative, prosp. Morisa Toreza 44	290-1786		
Morskaya Hotel, pl. Morskoy Slavy 1	355-1416		
Morskiye Computernye Systemy JV (UK), ul. Babushkina 80	262-3228	568-3993	121458
Morskiye Perevozki, Kazanskaya ul. 17-19/22	314-0659	312-3359	
Mosbiznesbank, prosp. Metallistov 115	540-3016	540-1219	
Moscow International Bank, See Moskovskiy Mezhdunarodny Bank			
Moscow Victory Park, Kuznetsovskaya ul. 25	298-3249		
Moskovskiy Cinema, Moskovskiy prosp. 129	298-7003		
Moskovskiy Department Store, Moskovskiy prosp. 205-220	293-3277	293-4871	
Moskovskiy market, ul. Reshetnikova 12	298-1189		
Moskovskiy Residence Repair & Remodeling Service, Kuznetsovskaya ul. 24, kor. 2	196-9615		
Moskovskiy Train Station, ul. Poltavskaya 9	168-0111		
Information on International Travel	168-0111		
Moskovskiy Univermag, See Moskovskiy Department Store			
Moskovskiy Veterinary Center, Ligovskiy prosp. 291	298-4694		
Moskva Cinema, Staro-Petergofskiy prosp. 6	251-2918		
Moskva Hotel, pl. Aleksandra Nevskovo 2	274-2051	274-2130	121669
Business Center	274-2051	274-2130	

	Phone	Fax	Telex
Neva Star	274-0012		
Moskva Restaurant	274-2067		
Rent-a-Car			
Vitabank	274-2127		
Mosque of the Congregation of Moslems, Kronverkskiy prosp. 7	233-9819		
Motorek Rowing Club, ul. Zhaka Dyuklo 67	533-7014		
Mramorny Dvorets Business Center, Millionaya ul. 5/1	219-3570	312-9421	
MS Audiotron, 4 Krasnoarmeyskaya ul. 4a	310-5513	310-4801	
Mukhinoy Artistic College, Solyanoy p. 13	273-3804	272-8446	121649
Muline, V. O., Sredniy prosp. 9	213-4506	230-4559	
Multipleks, Obukhovskoy Oborony prosp. 163	262-1427	262-1405	
Municipal Cultiral Centre, Belozerskiy Palace Nevskiy 41	315-4076		
Municipal Seed Stock Inspection, P.S., Maly prosp. 27	235-2641		
Municipal Veterinary Administration, 4 Sovetskaya ul. 5	277-5237	277-5237	
Murino, Tsentralnaya ul. 52	532-2252		
Museum of Anthropology and Ethnology, Universitetskaya nab. 3	218-1412		
Museum of Military Medicine, Lazaretny p. 2	113-5215		
Museum of Political History, Kuybysheva ul. 4	233-7113		
Museum of the Academy of Arts, Universitetskaya nab. 17	213-6496		
Museum of the Arctic and Antarctic, ul. Marata 24a	311-2549		
Museum of Theater and Musical Art, pl. Ostrovskovo 6a	311-2195	314-7746	
Museum of Zoology, Universitetskaya nab. 1/3	218-0112		
Music Hall – Booking office, Aleksandrovskiy Park 4	233-0243		
Music School of the Rimsky-Korsakov Conserv. See Rimsky-Korsakov Conservatory Music School			
Musical Comedy Theater, Italianskaya ul. 13	277-4760		
Musorgskiy Charitable Fand, pl. Isskustv 1	312-2040		
Musorgskiy Maly Theater (Opera and Ballet), pl. Isskusstv 1	314-3758		
Musorgskiy Music College, Mokhovaya ul. 36	273-0339		
Muza Restaurant, Rizhskiy prosp. 48	251-1724		
Muzyka Publishers, ul. Ryleyeva 17	279-0175		
Mysl Bookstore, Novocherkasskiy prosp. 41	528-8402		
Mysl Publishers, nab. kanala Griboyedova 26	314-3345		

N

	Phone	Fax	Telex
Na Fontanke Restaurant, nab. reki Fontanki 77	310-2547		
Na Sadovoy Hotel, Sadovaya ul. 53	310-6537		
Na Strazhe Rodiny, Petropavlovskaya Krepost 10/50	238-4651	238-4641	
Nadezhda, ul. Belinskovo 5	272-2952		
Nairi Restaurant, ul. Dekabristov 6	314-8093		
Nakhodka, Kustarny p. 3	310-0042	251-3900	
Narod Moy, ul. Rubinshteyna 3 kv. 50			

	Phone	Fax	Telex
Narvskiy Cinema, Bulvar Novatorov 32	254-2235		
Novatorov Bulvar 32	254-2086		
Narvskiy Department Store,			
Leninskiy prosp. 120-138	254-4359		
Nash Put, Moskovskiy prosp. 9, aud. 225	168-8497		
Natali, Labutina ul. 27	114-4487	311-7460	
Nationale, Moskovskiy prosp. 104	294-8333		
Nauchny Poisk, Voxxtaniya ul. 22/16	273-7576		
Nauka Hotel, Millionnaya ul. 27	312-3156		
Nauka Publishers, Mendeleyevskaya liniya 1	218-3912		122342
Nauka-Service Association,			
Millionnaya ul. 27, kv. 49	315-8627	311-7758	121320
Naval Museum, Birzhevaya pl. 4	218-2502		
Naval Sports Club Swimming Pool,			
Krasnogvardeyskiy prosp. 5a	528-7328		
Neapet, Nevskiy prosp. 122	277-0279		
Nechaev & Sovex, prosp. Stachek 45	252-3966	186-4044	
Nedra Coop, ul. Kuznetsovskaya 21	588-1358		
Nedra Publishers, Farforskaya ul. 18	560-9069		
Nekrasov House Museum, Liteyny prosp. 36	272-0165		
Nektar Wine Shop, Malodetskoselskiy prosp. 25	292-5244		
Neptun Hotel, nab. Obvodnovo kanala 93-a	315-4965	113-3160	
Business Center	210-1707	311-2270	
Neptun Restaurant, prosp. Stachek 25a	186-6105		
Neste Gas Stations	295-5449	295-8172	
Avangardnaya ul. 36	135-5867		
Moskovskiy prosp. 100	298-4534		
Pulkovskoye sh. 44a	123-3423		
Savushkina ul. 87	239-0415		
V.O., Maly prosp. 68	355-0879		
Neva Cables Ltd JV (Finland),			
Parnas, 9th kvartal, 8th pr.	557-9676	559-8738	
Neva Cinema, Nevskiy prosp. 108	273-7552		
Neva City Firm, Mokhovaya 12	273-3511		
Neva Construction Exchange, Liteyny prosp. 22			
Neva Hotel, Chaikovskovo ul. 17	278-0504		
Neva JV (Sweden), ul. Smolnovo 3	279-7777	279-3056	
Neva Kommerz, Isaakevskiy pl. 11	312-1620		
Neva Magazine, Nevskiy prosp. 3	315-8472	311-0817	
Neva News, ul. Pravdy 10	164-4765		
Neva Restaurant, Hotel Pribaltiyskaya	356-4409		
Neva Restaurant, Hotelship Peterhof	213-6321		
Neva Restaurant, Nevskiy prosp. 46	110-5980		
Neva Shoe Factory, Irinovskiy prosp. 2	227-3828	227-3725	
Neva Sport Club, ul. Smolenskaya 1	294-3855		
Neva Star, Hotel Moskva	274-0012		
Neva Stars Restaurant,			
See Nevskiye Zvyozdy Restaurant			
Neva Transport Trading,			
Staro-Petergofskiy prosp. 9-a	251-1215	251-0994	
Neva-Chupa-Chups, B. Sampsonievskiy prosp. 77/7	245-3613	245-3613	
Neva-Komplekt, Fontanka nab. 92, kor. 2	312-3423	113-2555	

	Phone	Fax	Telex
Neva-Kreditbank, ul. Sadovaya 21	314-7485	314-8486	
Neva-Profit, ul. Shpalernaya12	552-7690		
Neva-Sia JV (Italian), Primorskiy prosp. 52	239-3930	235-4519	
Nevis JV (Poland), ul. Voroshil 2	588-4946	588-1093	
Nevka, Moskovskiy prosp. 4/6	113-5375		
Nevmashexport Foreign Trade Firm, prosp. Obukhovskoy Oborony 51	567-6942	567-6024	121574
Nevo JV (Lichtenstein), ul. Kalinina 50-A	186-8977	186-7902	
Nevo-Tabak Ltd, Klinskiy prosp. 25	110-1062	292-3130	
Nevotal, Nevskiy prosp. 82	275-7149	275-7150	
Nevskiy, prosp. Obukhovskoy Oborony 95, korpus 9	265-3891	567-9111	
Nevskiy, ul. Perigina 22	568-0354		
Nevskiy 40, Nevskiy prosp. 40	311-9066		
Nevskiy 5, Nevskiy prosp. 5	312-6437		
Nevskiy Advertising & Publishing Co., Babushkina ul. 25	567-3007	567-3771	
Nevskiy Angel, Gorokhovaya ul. 5	315-2033	315-1463	
Nevskiy Cinema, Narodnaya ul. 4	263-3654		
Nevskiy Department Store, Inanovskaya ul. 6, 7	262-0847		
Nevskiy Employment Agency, Ivanovskaya ul. 7	560-6121		
Nevskiy market, prosp. Obukhovskoy Oborony 75a	265-3889		
Nevskiy Melody Casino, Sverdlovskaya nab. 62	227-1596		
Nevskiy Palace Hotel, Nevskiy prosp. 57	275-2001	113-1470	121279
Austrian Airlines	314-5086	164-7873	
British Airways	119-6222		
DHL Worldwide Express Center	119-6110		
Imperial Restaurant	275-2001		
Landskrona Restaurant	275-2001		
SAS	314-5086	164-7873	
Swedish Connections	113-1518		
Swissair	314-5086	164-7873	
Nevskiy Restaurant, Nevskiy prosp. 71	311-3093		
Nevskiy Vestnik, nab. reki Fontanki 59, kom. 432	315-6174	310-4073	
Nevskiy Veterinary Center, Veterenarnoe Delo, Obukhovskoy Oborony prosp. 68	567-1102		
Nevskiy Zori, Nevskiy prosp. 95	277-4252		
Nevskiye Melodii, See Melody JV Restaurant			
Nevskiye Vedomosti, Rasstannaya ul. 7	312-9554	112-9963	
Nevskiye Saunas, ul. Marata 5/7	311-1400		
Nevskiye Zori, Ligovskiy 76	164-6773		
Nevskoye Vremya, ul. B. Morskaya 47	314-2134	312-2078	
New Balance, P.S., Bolshoy prosp. 65	230-8043		
New Holland Joint Stock Company, Voznesenskiy prosp. 57	312-5740		
New Life Christian Evangelical Mission, See Novaya Zhizn Christian Evangelical Mission			
New York Restaurant, Hotel Commodore	119-6666		
Nezavisimost, Fontanka 46	311-1589		
Night Club, Hotel Pribaltiyskaya	356-0001		
Night Club Restaurant, Hotel Commodore	119-6666		
Nikolsko-Bogoyavlenskiy Cathedral, See Cathedral of Saint Nicholas and the Epiphany			
Nikolskoye Cemetery, nab. reki Monastyrki 1	274-2539		

	Phone	Fax	Telex
Nikos Translation Bureau, Moskovskiy prosp. 149b kom. 313	298-2187		
Nita, ul. Pilotov 38	104-1873	104-1813	
Niva, nab. kanala Griboyedova 15	312-3080		
Niva Weekly, nab. kanala Griboyedova 15	311-0203	110-4666	
NN Plus, ul. Karpinskovo 38			
Nochlezhka, Pushkinskaya ul. 10	164-4868	164-4868	
Nord Tourist Agency, Liteyny prosp. 64	275-5205	275-6142	121331
Nord-West, Box 11	113-2268	164-6181	
Nordiya, Zhukovskovo ul. 36	272-3472		
Nordmed, ul. Tverskaya 12/15	110-0401	552-2006	
Nordwest JV (FRG), prosp. Kima 4	350-1291	352-7529	
NormetJV (Norwegian), Len. obl. Vsevolzhskiy Rayon, Poselok Steklyanniy	164-1542		
North Hause, ul. Chekhova 5	273-4674	273-2663	
North West Union of Businessmans, nab. Obvodnovo kanala 48	166-1167	112-8758	
North-West River Shipping Company, B. Morskaya ul. 37	312-0145	312-0359	
North-West Transport Ltd, ul. B. Morskaya 37	210-8356	312-0359	121517
North-Western Copyright Agency, Nevskiy prosp. 116	279-1752	279-0774	
North-Western Regional Control of Air Transport, prosp. Rimskovo-Korsakova 39	114-1282	114-0924	
Northauto, Khimicheskiy p. 8	252-0738	252-0477	
Northern Trade Bank, ul. Nekrasova 14	275-8798	275-4559	
Notary, Nevskiy prosp. 109	277-0564		
Novaya Zhizn Christian Evangelical Mission, Saltykova-Shchedrina ul. 54	275-3662	166-3957	
Novintek Infopro, Nevskiy prosp. 104	553-9405	553-9405	
Novosty Video (Russkoye Video), Babushkina ul. 52, kv. 222	262-3028		
Novosyol, Nalichnaya ul. 40, kor. 7	350-2880		
Novy Petersburg, Nastavnikov prosp. 40	527-4821	526-6624	
NPO CKTI Power Equipment Research, ul. Krasnykh Elektrikov 3	277-9281	277-4095	
Numismatic Shop, V. O., Maly prosp. 10	213-7395		
Nurminen, John Oy, Sofiyskaya ul. 6	269-0586	268-8137	121424

O

	Phone	Fax	Telex
Oasis, Leninskiy prosp. 161	293-2247		
Ob-QuastJV (German), prosp. Morisa Toreza 40	247-8925	247-8925	
Oblik, nab. reki Fontanki 20			
Obucheniye, Zagorodny prosp. 58	292-3861	112-7254	
Ocean Restaurant, See Okean Restaurant			
Oda Firma, Tolstovo Bul. 38, #3	465-8548		
Odyssey Cooperative, ul. Zverinskaya 5	233-9546	235-3991	
Okeangeologiya Institut, ul. Maklina 1	113-8379		
Okeanpribor, Chkalovskiy prosp. 46	232-2105	235-3991	121345
Okeantekhnika Association, prosp. Stachek 88, k. 2	114-1484	114-1484	
Okhotnichny Domik Restaurant, prosp. Engelsa 28a	244-5544		

	Phone	Fax	Telex
Okhotnichny Klub Restaurant, Gorokhovaya ul. 45	310-0770		
Okhrany Prirody Cooperative, ul. Mikhailova 12, k. 2	541-8526	542-0647	
Okhta Cinema, Shaumyana prosp. 22	528-0158		
Okhtinskaya Hotel, Bolsheokhtinskiy prosp. 4	227-3767		
Okhtinskaya Restaurant	227-3767		
St. Petersburg Bank	222-8635		
Okolitsa Restaurant, Primorskiy prosp. 15	239-6984		
Oktyabr Cinema, Nevskiy prosp. 80	273-4813		
Oktyabr Pharmaceutical Factory, Aptekarskiy prosp. 5	234-2265	234-0261	121516
Oktyabrskaya Hotel, Ligovskiy prosp. 10	277-6330		
Oktyabrskaya Magistral, nab. reki Fontanki 117	315-1532	310-4209	
Oktyabrskaya Railway Freight Station, pl. Ostrovskovo 2	168-6384		
Oktyabrskiy Employment Agency, Sadovaya ul. 55/57	311-9157		
Oktyabrskiy Restaurant, Nevskiy prosp. 118	277-7042		
Oktyabrskoy Bolshoy Concert Hall, Ligovskiy prosp. 6	275-1300	275-1276	
Olgino Camping Motel, Primorskoye sh., 18 km (Olgino)	238-3009	238-3954	121758
Olgino Restaurant, Olgino Campsite, Primorskoye sh.	238-3674		
Olimpiyets, P.S., Bolshoy prosp. 76	232-8781		
Olly Ltd, V. O., 14 Liniya 39	218-0450	213-3388	
Olympia Hotel, pl. Morskoy Slavy	119-6800	119-6805	121333
White Nights Bar	119-6800	119-6805	121333
Piccolo Restaurant	119-6800	119-6805	121333
Omega, Khersonskaya ul. 12	274-0704	312-7931	
Omega Charitable Fund, ul. Khersonskaya 10, kab. 12	312-7831	274-0877	
One Hour Photo JV (Finland), Nevskiy prosp. 20	311-9974	311-9923	
Onninen-Termo St. Petersburg, Serebristy bul. 38	301-8718	301-8587	
Opposite, Izmaylovskiy prosp. 10			
Optika, Leninskiy prosp. 140	255-6595	255-6495	122205
Optima-Office, Chaykovskovo ul. 36	273-2964	273-7882	
Optos JV (German), Kondratyevskiy prosp. 2	248-3767		
Optrikto Ltd, Kubinskaya ul. 80	295-0212	122-0205	
Orange, ul. Sezzhinskaya 9/6	233-9411		
Oras Cooperative, Vladimirskiy prosp. 14	164-4422	112-2310	
Orbita-Service, prosp. Kosmonavtov 25	293-6501	293-6501	
Orgtekhnika, p. Antonenko 6	319-9259	315-7420	
Orimi Vud JV (USA), ul. Stepana Razina 8/50	113-0632	113-0960	
Orion, Piskaryovskiy prosp. 20	541-3327		
Orion JV (Austria), V. O., 1 Liniya 44	218-5169		
Orion-Service, V. O., 17 Liniya 42	350-3581		
Orkhideya Nevskiy prosp. 110	275-7124		
Ort, Krasnogvardeyskaya ul. 5-b, kv. 203-a	292-7423		
Ortex, ul. 7 Krasnoarmeyskaya 30	251-7977		
Oryol, nab. reki Fontanki 118	251-8567	251-8567	
Ostrovskiy Youth Library, Syezdovskaya liniya 21	213-5628		
Otdykh Hotel, Vasi Alekseyeva ul. 14, pod. 3	185-0690		
Otis St. Petersburg, Khimichskiy p. 12	252-3694	252-5315	
Otkrytki, Nevskiy prosp. 72	272-9031		
Otkryty Theater, Vladimirskiy prosp. 12	113-2190		

	Phone	Fax	Telex
Outpatient Medical Bureau, Nevskiy prosp. 82	272-9085		
Oven, ul. Mokhovaya 27-29 kv. 21	275-4069		
Ozerkiy Cinema, B. Ozyornaya u. 72	553-2397		
Ozon, prosp. Engelsa 42			

P

	Phone	Fax	Telex
Palace Casino, Park Lenina 4	233-9634	232-0657	
Palanga Restaurant, Leninskiy prosp. 127	254-3601		
Palitra Cooperative, Nevskiy prosp. 134, kv. 7	274-2173	274-0911	121498
Palitra Gallery, Nevskiy prosp. 166	277-1216	274-0911	121498
Palitra International, Perekupnoy p. 15/17	274-0911	274-4518	
Pallada, V. O., 13 Liniya 10	213-5640	312-4128	
Pallada Pek JV, Mikhailovskiy p. 9	542-9027	541-8810	
Palmiro Togliatti Engineering and Economics Institute, ul. Marata 27	112-0633	112-0607	
Palms & Company, Inc., ul. Dunayevskiy 51/2 (Hotel Kupchinskaya)	178-2738	176-2741	
Panda, Kanal Griboedova 26	312-8896		
Panorama Magazine, Nevskiy prosp. 53	113-1523	123-0435	
Panorama Studio, See Rus Company			
Panteleymonovskiy Antiques, ul. Pestelya 13/15	279-7235		
Papirus, B. Konyushennaya u. 2	113-3566	314-4267	
Parfum Ltd, ul. Marata 71	315-8845	315-1796	
Pargolovo Church of Our Saviour, Vyborgskoye sh. 106			
Pargolovskiy Factory, Pargolovo, ul. Zheleznodorozhnaya 11	592-3000	592-3003	321617
Paritet Ltd, ul. Lomonosova 5	310-7291	310-7291	
Pariziana, Nevskiy prosp. 80	279-5111		
Parklen Firm, Moskovskiy prosp. 212	294-8664	294-8664	
Parkovy Restaurant, Petrodvorets, Avrory ul. 14	257-9096		
Partner, Severny prosp. 23	556-3966		
Parus, Morskaya nab. 17	351-8735		
Passage Shopping Center, Nevskiy prosp. 48	315-5257	311-1426	121274
Patent Cooperative Bank, Grecheskiy prosp. 10	272-5485	272-9043	
Patriot, ul. Olgi Berggolts 40	265-1363	265-1533	
Paulig RF Ltd, ul. Generala Khruleva 7	395-2597	395-2597	
Pavlov 1st Medical Institute, ul. Lva Tolstovo 6/8	234-0821	234-0125	
Pavlov House Museum, V. O., 7 Liniya 2	213-7234		
Pearl Cafe, See Zhemchuzhina Cafe			
Pechatny Dvor, Chkalovskiy prosp. 15	235-9839		322090
Pechatny Dvor, Isakievskaya pl. 6	319-9275		
Pedagogicheskiy Institute imeni A. I. Gertsena, See Gertsen Pedagogical Institute			
Pediatricheskiy Meditsinskiy Institut, See Medical Pediatrics Institute			
Pediatrics Hospital, ul. Litovskaya 2	245-4031		
Pegas, Lotsmanskaya u. 3	114-1090		
Peggy Clothing Store, Liteyny prosp. 8/21	272-4940		
Pepper, Hamilton, & Scheetz, Shpalernaya ul. 30	273-2377	272-4317	

	Phone	Fax	Telex
See Cross Roads Business Center			
Permkombank, Moskovskiy prosp. 181	293-0620		
Personnel Corps, Nevskiy prosp. 104	275-4586	275-8323	
Pervomaiskaya Zarya Sewing Enterprise, 10 Krasnoarmeyskaya ul. 22	251-2080	251-2830	121566
Pervy Meditsinskiy Institut imeni I. P. Pavlova, See Pavlov 1st Medical Institute			
Peter Haka, Admiralteyskiy prosp. 6	312-3118	315-9358	
Peter the Great JV (Venezuela), ul. M. Konyushennaya 7	110-6497	292-4274	
Peter the Great's Domik, Petrovskaya nab. 6	232-4576		
Peter-Paul Fortress	238-4505		
Peterburgskaya Afisha, nab. reki Fontanki 32	314-3978	272-1669	
Peterburgskie Zori, Nevskiy prosp. 95, 5th floor	277-4547	277-1717	
Peterburgskiy Auktsion, p. Grivtsova 5	311-0574	311-0601	
Peterburgskiy Lesopromyshlenny Bank, Krapivny p. 5	541-8217	541-8393	
Peterhof Hotelship, Pier Makarov nab. at Tuchkov most	213-6321	213-3158	
Business Center	213-6321	213-3158	
Christina Creative Coiffure of Switzerland	213-6321	213-3158	
Neva Restaurant	213-6321		
Sky Bar	213-6321		
St. Petersburg Bank	219-9417		
Svir	213-6321		
Petersburg Commodity and Stock Exchange, B. Konyushennaya ul. 25	315-7415		
Petersburg Russian Television Company, ul. Chapygina 6	234-7753		
Petersburg Vneshtrans, Mezhevoy Kanal 5	251-0629	186-2883	121511
Petersburg-Tyumen Universal Exchange	247-2857	233-9945	
Peterstar, V. O., 16 Liniya 31	119-6060	119-9002	
Petro Service Oy, Leninskiy prosp. 160	295-3716	295-8172	121006
Petroagroprombank, nab. kanala Griboyedova 13	315-4492	314-3715	121614
Petrobalt, Zagorodny prosp. 68	292-1777	292-0636	
Petrocon, nab. reki Moyki 45	312-5514	312-5173	
Petrodvorets Watch Factory, Petrodvorets, ul. Fabrichnaya 1	420-2816	420-2804	121506
Petroff Motors (General Motors), Vyazovaya ul. 4	235-2386		
Petrograd Bookstore, Stachek prosp. 67, kor. 3	252-3316		
Petrograd-92 Firm, Hotel Astoria	210-5858	210-5859	
Servis Center, Sankt Peterburg Hotel	542-8736	542-8798	
Petrogradskaya Hotel, nab. reki Karpovki 37	234-2056	234-2056	
Petrogradskiy & Co. Innovation Commercial Firm, ul. B. Pushkarskaya 45, kv. 15	233-0275	230-4834	
Petrogradskiy Veterinary Center, nab. reki Karpovki 39	234-4055		
Petromilam, prosp. Parkhomemko 33	247-6566	247-3590	
Petropol, Nevskiy prosp. 30	311-6693		
PetroRils JV(USA), ul. Voroshilova 2	588-7453	588-6127	
Petrosnab Firm, Suvorovskiy prosp. 62	311-7371	271-9297	
Petrospek JV, Antonenko p. 5	110-6508	110-6097	

	Phone	Fax	Telex
Petrovskiy Bank, ul. Ruzovskaya 8	112-6687	292-5322	
Zakharyevskaya ul. 14, #2	275-7636	275-7635	
Petrovskiy Restaurant,			
Mytninskaya nab., across from #3	238-4793		
Petrovskiy Stadium, Petrovskiy ostrov 2g	238-4129		
Pharmacia Production Assn., ul. M. Morskaya 17	312-0214	312-4750	
Pharmacy, Nevskiy prosp. 83	277-7966		
No. 2, Kamennoostrovskiy prosp. 38/96	234-9035		
No. 5: Nevskiy prosp. 111	277-2931		
No. 7: Nevskiy prosp. 66	314-5654		
No. 48: Sadovaya ul. 36	310-8868		
No. 56: 10th Sovetskaya ul. 15	271-2577		
No. 91: Moskovskiy prosp. 167	298-0535		
P.S., Bolshoy prosp. 43	232-4679		
V. O., 17 Liniya 8	213-7140		
Philips Electronics, Suvorovskiy prosp. 2	277-4319	277-0013	
Philosophy Academy, nab. reki Fontanki 20	273-3158		
Phoenix Engineering-Productive Complex,			
ul. Mineralnaya 13	248-3678	540-8879	121428
Photo Salon, Nevskiy prosp. 54	311-0838		
Piccolo, Hotel Olympia	119-6800		
Pietari Restaurant, Moskovskiy prosp. 220	293-2397		
Pigment, nab. reki Moyki 58	314-0481	314-0535	
Pigment Scientific-Production Assn.,			
Oktyabrskaya nab. 32-38	588-3332	588-6234	321244
Pioneer Cooperative, ul. Opochinina 17, #45	217-0895	217-0895	
Pioneer Electronics, Zagorodny prosp. 11	314-2314		
Piral, Nevskiy prosp. 72	273-2314	273-2314	
Pirosmani Restaurant, P.S., Bolshoy prosp. 14	235-6456		
Piskaryovskoye Cemetery, prosp. Nepokorennykh	247-5716		
Pitanie JV (Finland), Leninskiy prosp. 160	295-3715	295-9951	
Piter-Lada, Kingisepskoye sh. 50	132-4450		
Piterskiy Department Store, Stachek pl. 9	186-6000		
Pizza Rif	290-1379		
Pizza-Express JV (Finland), Podolskaya ul. 23	292-2666	292-1039	
Planeta Bookstore, Liteyny prosp. 30	273-8815		
Planeta Cinema, Tipanova ul. 25	299-4254		
Planeta International Exchange,			
Aleksandrovskiy Park 4	232-0942	233-9945	
Planetarium, Aleksandrovskiy Park 4	233-3153		
Plastmassy, ul. Novoselov 8	263-8431	266-7453	
Plekhanov Mining Institute, V. O., 21 Liniya 2	213-6078	213-2613	
Plyke, ul. Milionnaya 4/1	315-3439	315-3439	
Pobeda Cinema, Razyeszhaya ul. 43	164-9647		
Pobeda Construction Materials Union,			
Kolpino, ul. Zagorodnaya 9	484-4212	463-9998	
Podarki, Nevskiy prosp. 54	314-1801		
Podpisniye Izdaniy Bookstore, Liteyny prosp. 57	273-5053		
Podsolnush-sunflover, Liteyny prosp. 32	273-7462		
Pogranichnik, ul. Shpalernaya 62	278-6209		
Pogrebok Restaurant, ul. M. Morskaya 7	315-5371		
Pol-Mot, ul. Nakhimova 7, #102	356-3364	356-3364	
Polar Fast Food JV (Finland), Moskovskiy prosp. 222	293-1809	293-0408	

	Phone	Fax	Telex
Polarnaya Zvezda, Nevskiy prosp. 158	277-0980		
Polesye Restaurant, Sredneokhtinskiy prosp. 4	224-2917		
Polex, Volkhovskiy p. 3	218-8344		
Poligraf, Institutskiy p. 3	550-0820		
Poligrafaktsia, Chaykovskovo ul. 30	219-9288	275-7434	
Polikomp Cooperative, nab. reki Karpovki 5	234-8564	234-1179	
Polimorf, ul. Tavricheskaya 39, kom. 231	272-9884		
Poliprofil JV (Sweden), Nevskiy prosp. 95	277-2833	114-5044	
Poliservice, Tsimlyanskaya ul. 6	224-1447		
Politechnicheskiy Institut imeni M. I. Kalinina, See Kalninin Politechnical Institute			
Politekhnika Publishers, ul. Inzhenernaya 6	312-5390	312-2136	
Poliustrovsky, Kommuny ul. 59	227-7413		
Polradis JV (Poland), prosp. Yuri Gagarina 1	294-8541	294-8783	321203
Polsib JV filial (Poland), ul. Chernyshevskovo 11	272-3036	273-8821	
Polskiy Buket Florist, Morskaya nab. 15	352-2075		
Polyarnoye Cafe, Nevskiy prosp. 79	311-8589		
Polyclinic No. 2, Moskovskiy prosp. 22	292-5904	292-5939	
Polygraph Express, Shvedskiy p. 2	311-1810		
Polymerstroimaterial Factory, Irinovskiy prosp. 53	224-9122		122407
Polyot, Vitebskiy prosp. 107	259-7648		
Polytekhnik, Politekhnicheskaya ul. 29	552-6417		
Pomoshchnik Cooperative, ul. Moyka 72	310-0052	164-3726	
Pony Express, ul. Mayakovskovo 2	279-1931	279-1931	
Popov Museum of Communications, Pochtamtskaya ul. 7	311-9255		
Porcelain, See Farfor			
Positron, ul. Kurchatova 10	552-1617	552-6081	121452
Posrednik			
Potel et Chabot, Dvortsovaya nab. 10	314-6000	315-0669	
Potential Center for Business Cooperation, Kolpino prosp. Pavlova 42	481-9524	463-9000	
Poverenny Law Firm, Moskovskiy prosp. 17	292-3127	292-3127	
Pozifort JV (Hungary), ul. Koli Tomchaka 28	294-0125	294-0411	121429
Pravda Editorial Offices, Khersonskaya ul. 12	274-0877	274-0877	
Pravovedeniye, V. O., 22 Liniya 7	355-9882		
Prazdnik, prosp. Gagapina 14	299-7079		
Preobrazhenskiy Cathedral, Liteyny ul. and ul. Pestelya	272-3662		
Press & Information Ministry, Sadovaya ul. 14, kv. 52	310-6161	310-4776	
Prestige Cooperative, pl. Truda 35	465-8102		
Prestige Ltd, Dochny prosp. 18	156-0416		
Pribaltiyskaya Hotel, ul. Korablestroiteley 14	356-0263	356-0094	121322
Baltic Star International Shopping	356-2284		
Bowling Lanes	356-1663		
Business Center	356-4563	356-0094	
Daugava Restaurant	356-4409		
Leningrad Restaurant			
Neva Restaurant	356-4409		
Night Club	356-0001		
Panorama Restaurant	356-0001		
SIT Airport Taxi Service	356-9329	356-0094	
Spielbanck Casino	356-0001		
Vitabank	356-3803		

	Phone	Fax	Telex
Pribory & Vychislitelnaya Tekhnika, Leninskiy prosp. 148	290-5530	290-5565	
Priboy Cinema, V. O., Sredny prosp. 93	217-0094		
Prime Advertising Agency, p. Pirogova 17	314-5363	312-8496	
Primorskiy Cinema, Kamennoostrovskiy prosp. 42	230-8014		
Primorskiy Department Store, Bogatyrskiy prosp. 4,5	393-2174		
Primorskiy Residence Repair & Remodeling Service, ul. Korolyova 15/30	393-6562		
Primorskiy Veterinary Center, Skholnaya ul. 32	239-1020		
Primorskiy Victory Park, Krestovskiy prosp. 21	235-2146		
Printeks Joint Stock Company, ul. Zvenigorodskaya 30	164-9822	164-9822	
Priroda Shop, Sytninskaya pl. 1/47	233-7351		
Procter & Gamble, Universitetskaya nab. 7/9	218-5173	218-5190	
Progress, Pestelya ul. 19	272-2714		
Progress Cinema, Stachek prosp. 18	252-2046		
Progress Pharmaceutical NPO, ul. Vosstaniya 4	279-1742	279-1741	
Progress-Neva, Moskovskiy prosp. 79a	275-0109	296-5965	
Prokom Computers, prosp. Stachek 47	183-6114	184-9846	121416
Proletarskoy Zavod Scientific-Production Assn., prosp. Dudko 3	567-3618	567-4466	121457
Prometey Bookstore, Narodnaya ul. 16	263-8676		
Prometey Cinema, Prosveshcheniya prosp. 80	531-2712		
Prometey Firm, ul. Rentgena 3	233-4960		
Promstroibank, ul. Mikhailovskaya 4	110-4909		
Prospekt Art Salon, Kronverskiy prosp. 9	232-3591		
Prostor Park, Krestovskiy ostrov 22	230-7972	230-7341	
Prosvescheniye, Nevskiy prosp. 28	312-1388	312-4724	
Prvni Brnenske Strojirenskiy zavod, Tverskaya ul. 27/29, kv. 8	275-5911	275-5638	
Przyv cinema, Nevskiy prosp. 176	274-2217		
Public Inspectorate for the Preservation of Nature, B. Konyushennaya ul. 8	312-4408		
Pukkila-Talot, Sverdlovskaya nab. 60, kv. 47			
Pulford Enterprises Ltd	239-6367	239-5374	
Pulkovo I Airport, ul. Pilotov 18, block 4	104-3822		
Pulkovo II Airport,			
Cargo Arrival Information	104-3494		
Cargo Dispatch Information	104-3446		
Domestic Flight Information	104-3611		
International Flight Information	104-3444		
Pulkovskaya Hotel, pl. Pobedy 1	264-5122	264-6396	121477
Business Center	264-5860	264-5860	121477
Intourtrans	299-5808		
Meridian Restaurant	264-5177		
Sberbank	299-9217		
Sezam Jewellery Store	299-9217		
Turku Restaurant	264-5716		
Puls Firm, ul. Przhevalskovo 18, korpus V	311-2234	311-2206	
Pushkin Academic Drama Theater, pl. Ostrovskovo 2	312-1545		

	Phone	Fax	Telex
Pushkin Central City Children's Library, ul. B. Morskaya 33	312-3380		
Pushkin Dacha Museum, Pushkinskaya ul. 2	476-6990		
Pushkin House Museum, nab. reki Moyki 12	311-3801		
Pushkin Museum, Catherine Palace, Komsomolskaya ul. 2	476-6411		
Pushnoy Auction, Moskovskiy prosp. 98	298-4636	298-7645	121507
Put, Krasnoputilovskaya ul. 113	291-6807		
Pyatoye Koleso, Sinopskaya nab. 30	274-0051		
Pyotr Velikiy, Sredneokhtinskiy prosp. 52	526-6631	526-6624	121637

Q

	Phone	Fax	Telex
Quality Products International	310-1850		
Quasar-Center JV, Zhdanovskaya ul. 8	235-3316	230-8358	

R

	Phone	Fax	Telex
R-Style JV (Singapur), Ligovskiy prosp. 214	167-1430	167-1429	
R. A. D. Ltd, V. O., Shiperskiy Protok 19	351-1232	352-3633	
Rabies Prevention Dept., 2 Zhernovskaya ul. 46	227-7443		
Radar, Aptekarskiy prosp. 6	234-6033	234-4365	
Kozhevennaya Liniya 38	213-4569		
Raden Firm, Leninskiy prosp. 116	158-3524		
Radio and Television Center, ul. Chapygina 6	232-0221	234-9960	
Radio-Technology Factory, Lermontovskiy prosp. 54	251-8400	251-8405	
Radius Company, Saperny p. 6 kv. 38	275-0010		
Raduga Cinema, Engelsa prosp. 133	599-3588		
Raduga Publishers, nab. reki Moyki 38	314-6960		
Raft, B. Zelinina ul. 29	235-1621	235-1621	
Railway Museum, Sadovaya ul. 50	168-8005		
Railway Transport Engineers Institute, Moskovskiy prosp. 9	310-2521	315-2621	
Rainbow, Zaitseva ul. 41	183-3096	184-1522	
Rambus, Ltd., Grazhdanskiy prosp. 14	299-4624		
Rames JV(USA), Nevskiy prosp. 140	277-7763	277-6960	
Rank Xerox, nab. Obvodnovo kanala 93a	315-7670	315-7773	
Rassvet Sewing Enterprise, Degtyarnaya ul. 5/7	271-6002	274-9139	
Ravenstvo, ul. Promyshlennaya 19	186-1860	186-4505	
Razvitiye Regional Commercial Center, prosp. Obukhovskoy Oborony 13	567-8078		
RCC (Russian Car Center), Leninskiy prosp. 160	295-5449	295-8172	
Real-Music Shop, Nevskiy prosp. 54	310-5922	310-4080	
Realis, Stremyannaya ul. 3	112-5058		
Rechnaya Hotel, prosp. Obukhovskoy Oborony 195	267-3196		
Record Cinema, Sadovaya u. 75	114-2294		
Refrigeration Industry Technological Institute, ul. Lomonosova 9	315-3617	315-0535	
Region, ul. B. Monetnaya 19, Office 311	238-8334	217-0627	
Regional Inspectorate for Freedom of the Mass Media, Sadovaya ul. 14, kv. 52	310-6161	311-2731	

	Phone	Fax	Telex
Register, Dvortsovaya nab. 8	314-0743	314-1087	
Reklama, Apraksin p. 11, #56	113-4930		
Reklama Shans, nab. reki Fontanki 59	210-8441	315-6283	
Rekord Cinema, Sadovaya ul. 75	114-2971		
Remstroyservice, Bukharestskaya ul. 22-a	268-0795		
Renaisance, M. Posadskaya ul. 17	233-8976	233-8976	
Rendezvous Casino, Moskovskiy prosp. 78	292-2996		
Renland, ul. B. Zelenina 14	230-3637		
ul. Savushkina 119	345-1697		
Rental, ul. Babushkina 3	592-9645		
Repair & Alteration Shop, Lebedeva ul. 7/9	542-0465		
Repin Institute for Painting, Sculpture and Architecture, Universitetskaya nab. 17	213-6777		
Repin Museum, Primorskoye sh. 411	231-6828		
Repinskaya Hotel, Primorskoye sh. 428, Repino	231-6637		
Repinskaya Restaurant ,Villa, Repino, Primorskoye sh. 428	231-6515		
Reskript Law Firm, ul. M. Podyazheskaya 14	113-4988		
Reson, ul. Dnepropetrovskaya 12	292-2684		
Restaurant St. Petersburg, nab. kanala Griboyedova 5	314-4947	314-3586	
Restavrator, Staro-Petergofskiy prosp. 3/5	251-6303		
ul. Marata 17	315-4807		
Restovrator Masterskaya, M. Govorova prosp. 43	252-7474		
Resurs North-Western Exchange of Production Equipment, Kamenoostrovskiy 5	233-8748	233-8045	
Retur Business Center JV (Finland), Astoria Hotel, ul. Gertsena 39	311-7362	311-7362	121304
Retur Ltd, ul. Shpalernaya 28	273-9683	273-9783	121304
Revers, Ligovskiy prosp. 56	164-8281	164-8485	
Rhapsodia Record Store, B. Konyushennaya ul. 13	314-4801		
Rikki Cooperative, Primorskiy prosp. 6, kv. 6	239-2998	239-2998	121372
Rikol JV (Latviya), Kolpino, Volodarskiy prosp. 9	481-9547	481-9547	
Rimilen Company JV (Italy), ul. Korablestroiteley 21	351-6795	352-2054	
Rimsky-Korsakov Conservatory Music School, p. Matveyeva 1a	114-1642		
Opera Studio, Teatralnaya pl. 3	311-6265		
Rimsky-Korsakov House Museum, Zagorodny prosp. 28, kv. 39	113-3208		
Ring, Apraksin dvor, kor. 1, kv. 85-95	310-1893	310-4138	
RIO, Lunacharskovo prosp. 9, kv. 113	510-8113	542-4526	
Rioni Restaurant, Shpalernaya ul. 24	273-3261		
Ritm-Tsenturion, Turbinnaya ul. 11	186-7689		
Ritos Cooperative, ul. Oraniyenbaumskaya 5	232-3847		
River Passenger Terminal, prosp. Obukhovskoy Oborony 195	262-0239		
RJR Nabisco, V. O., Sredny prosp. 36/40	213-1700	213-1835	
Romar International Inc., Yelagin Ostrov 10	239-0901	239-1261	
Romos-Video, Goncharnaya ul. 13	275-4015		
Ros Law Firm, prosp. Veteranov 78	150-1101		
Rosavtotorg, Leninskiy prosp. 146	255-9097		
RosDesign, Solyanoy p. 13	279-4196	275-3659	
Rosgalantereya Wholesale Trade Association, ul. Salova 48-50	166-2540	166-4822	121164

	Phone	Fax	Telex
Rosich i Robson JV, Galernaya ul. 27	312-0848	312-0848	
Rosinformresurs, ul. Sadovaya 2	210-4481	210-4112	
Roskhoz-Torg, Apraksin dvor, korpus 1, pom. 18-28	310-3242	310-8921	
Roskulttorga, ul. Dumskaya 9	312-2357	310-1598	
Rosmekhdesign, ul. Ivanovskaya 11	568-1798		
Rosmonumentiskusstvo, nab. Obvodnovo kanala 17	277-2797	277-2797	
Rossa JV (Austria,German), ul. Khlopina 11	534-1086		
Rossia, Sverdlovskaya nab. 44	225-9301	226-7902	
Rossia Bank, Smolny, podyezd 4, k. 422	278-1078	278-1715	
Rossia Hotel, pl. Chernyshevskovo 11	294-6322	296-3303	
Rossiya Restaurant	294-3676		
Rossiyskaya Bumaga of St. Petersburg, Sestroretskaya ul. 6	239-5628	239-5628	
Rossiyskaya Elektronnaya Kompaniya, Pobedy pl. 2	293-6757	293-5257	
Rosstrom Firm, Irinovskiy prosp. 1	224-9111	227-1925	
Rossy Agency, nab. reki Fontanki 51/53	310-1068	310-1068	
ROST, Zakharyevskyay u. 25			
Rostorgreklama, ul. Sedova 13	567-4768	567-4715	
Rostra, Shkolnaya ul. 39	239-4851	239-1898	
Rosvneshterminal, ul. Belinskovo 11	275-6161	279-7562	
Rot-Front Fur Production Assn., ul. Soyuza Pechatnikov 24	114-0973	114-7139	122426
Roza Florist, prosp. Veteranov 87	150-2362		
Roza Mira, ul. Podkovyrova 22	213-1888		
Roza Vetrov, Moskovskiy prosp. 204	293-0866		
Rozhdestvensky, Grecheskiy prosp. 15	274-9682	274-8717	
RPS JV, prosp. Stachek 18	252-1513	252-1515	
Rubezh Cinema, Veteranov prosp. 121	135-0379		
Rubicon, Lesnoy prosp. 19	542-2798	542-0989	121194
Rubin-Adgio, ul. Marata 90	210-1557	210-1442	
Ruby, See Yakhont Jewellery Store			
RUIS Industrial Building & Commodity Exchange, B. Morskaya ul. 52			
Rules and Regulations, Box 57	234-5333	234-5316	
RUMB, ul. Zaytseva 41	183-4639	185-0869	
Rumor-2, 7 Sovetskaya ul. 36	211-1814		
Runo Firm, Zhukovskovo ul. 49-3	275-3615	275-6007	
Runo Launderette, Leninskiy prosp. 155-a	164-4827		
Rus, Kvarengi p. 4	278-1694	278-1554	
Rus, V. O., 16 Liniya 85	213-0922	213-5579	121775
Rus Hotel, Artilleriyskaya ul. 1	272-0321	279-6144	
Rusar Ltd, V. O., Bolshoy prosp. 78	356-5046	355-2091	
Rusich Interior Remodeling Service, 11 Krasnoarmeyskaya ul. 7, kv. 13	251-4801		
Ruskobank, ul. B. Morskaya 15	315-7833		
Russ Service	275-8758		
Russian Academy of Sciences, St. Petersburg			
Library, Birzhevaya liniya 1	218-3592	218-7436	
Philosophy Dept., Grivtsova p. 5	315-8685		
Russian Agency for Intellectual Property, Nevskiy prosp. 116	279-1752	279-0774	
Russian American Law Firm, Lermontovskiy prosp. 7/12	114-5660	114-0740	

	Phone	Fax	Telex
Russian Antiquities, ul. Shpalernaya 11	273-0093		
Russian Arts Ltd., ul. Inzhenernaya 4	315-3183	314-4153	121364
Russian Commercial-Industrial Bank, B. Morskaya ul. 15	314-6932	311-2135	
Russian Information Services, Serpukhovskaya ul. 30	292-7420	292-7420	
Russian Institute of Prophilactic Medicine, ul. Tolstovo 10	232-3877	234-6304	
Russian Language Teaching Center, Universitetskaya nab. 7/9	218-9452		
Russian Mining Bank, ul. Shkiperskiy protok 5			
Russian Ministry of Oil and Gas Industries, See Minneftegasprom			
Russian Museum, Inzhenernaya ul. 4	219-1615	314-4153	
Russian Orthodox Theological Academy & Seminary, nab. Obvodnovo kanala 17	277-3351	277-8607	
Russian Press Service, Fontanka 46	312-3312	311-2011	
Russian Red Cross, Italianskaya ul. 25	311-3696	311-3706	
Russian Union of Theatrical Workers, Nevskiy prosp. 86	272-9482		
Russian Union of Writers, Shpalernaya ul. 18	279-0874	273-4092	
Russian Union of Composers, ul. Gertsena 45	311-3548		
Russian-Finnish Chamber of Commerce, See Finnish-Russian Chamber of Commerce			
Russkaya Literatura Magazine, nab. Makarova 4	218-1601		
Russkaya Pochta, nab. reki Fontanki 105	315-4716	315-1276	
Russkiy Chay, ul. Tombovskaya 63	168-3833		
Russkiy Diesel FTO, Vyborgskaya nab. 17	542-6851	542-3317	
Russkiy Market, 7 Krasnoarmeyskaya ul. 18-24	112-6864		
Russkiy Yazyk, Apraksin dvor, kor. 41	310-2839		
Russkiye Bliny, ul. Furmanova 13	279-0559		
Russkiye Nemtsy, Shpalernaya ul. 18	279-5037	273-4092	
Russkiye Samotsvety Production Assn., Utkin prosp. 8	528-0103	528-2378	324294
Russkiye Samovary Restaurant, ul. Sadovaya 49	314-8238		
Russkoye Iskusstvo, Millionnaya ul. 5/1	312-8115		
Russkoye Yuvelirnoye Iskusstvo Cooperative, ul. Kuybysheva 9/11	235-4251	119-6008	
Russo-Balt Exchange, pl. Morskoy Slavy 1		355-4748	
RusTex International, Belgradskaya ul. 6(4), kv. 46	109-6914	109-6914	
Ryabinushka Restaurant, ul. Oskalenko 11	239-4080		
Ryland St. Petersburg, ul. B. Morskaya 31	314-6435	314-7536	
Rzhevskiy, Ryabovskoye sh. 101	527-8007		

S

	Phone	Fax	Telex
S&A Stationers, B. Konyushennaya 27	311-8720		
S. P. I. Corp. JV (US), Konnogvardeyskiy bulvar 4/13	311-7922	311-7822	121345
S. T. B. Firm, V. O., 5 Liniya 10	312-4128	218-1181	
Saagon, ul. Shpalernaya 18	279-5933	279-5833	
Saarskaya Myza, Pushkin, ul. Kominterna 27	476-6255		
Sadko's Restaurant, Grand Hotel Europe	119-6000		
Saga, Kamennoostrovskiy prosp. 40	230-8356	230-8356	

	Phone	Fax	Telex
Saga, Kamennoostrovskiy prosp. 40	230-8356	230-8356	
Saigon-Neva JV (Vietnam), ul. Plekhanova 33	315-8772		
Saint-Peterburg Premier, ul. Professora Popva 47 kom. 705	234-5334	110-7393	
Saint-Petersburg Properties Ltd, ul. 2 Sovetskaya 14/4	277-5264	277-5264	
Sakura Restaurant, ul. Narodnaya 45	263-3594		
Salans Hertzfeld & Heilbronn, Nevskiy prosp. 70	272-4572	273-6844	
Salman Casino, B. Sampsonievskiy prosp. 29	541-8459		
Salon Sankt Peterburg, ul. Furshtadskaya 42	273-0341		
Salpi Hotel, Mozhayskaya ul. 18	292-4735		
Salpi JV (Finland), Lesnoy prosp. 65/67	534-1227	534-1227	
Saltykov-Shchedrin State Library, Sadovaya ul. 18	310-2856	310-6148	321278
Salute Pharmacy, Malookhtinskiy prosp. 92	221-1932		
Salvation Army, Kamenoostrovskiy prosp. 60, office 12	234-1062		
Salyut Sewing Production Assn., ul. Kronverkskaya 23	232-9002	238-1510	321870
Samir JV (Syria), Nevskiy prosp. 16	312-6735		
ul. Mokhovaya 32	273-6610		
Samotsvety Jewelery Store, Mikhailovskaya ul. 4	110-4915		
Samson Law Firm, Bolsheokhtinskiy prosp. 41	227-2906		
SAN, Zhernovskaya ul. 8	227-8984		
Sani JV (Poland), Tosnenskiy rayon, Fornosovo	311-2474	311-6049	
Sankt-Peterburg Restaurant, Hotel Sankt Peterburg, Pirogovskaya nab. 5/2	542-9150		
Sankt-Peterburg Art Salon, Nevskiy prosp. 54	311-4020		
Sankt-Peterburg Hotel, Vyborgskaya nab. 5/2	542-9411	248-8002	121366
Intour	542-8032		
Sankt-Peterburg Restaurant	542-9150		
Viking	542-8032		
Zerkalny (Mirrored) Restaurant	542-9155		
Sankt-Peterburgskiye Vedomosti, nab. reki Fontanki 59	314-7176	310-5141	
Sankt-Peterburgskiy Birzhevoy Bank, Ordinarnaya ul. 19	232-5980	232-5980	
Sankt-Petersburg Palace Casino, Aleksandrovskiy Park 4 (Music Hall)	233-0542	232-0657	
Santa Barbara, Ltd., ul. Goncharnaya 24-52	552-1330	312-4128	121345
Santekhkomfort JV (France), ul. Ochakovskaya 7	274-6295	529-2059	
Santekhoborydovaniye Factory, sh. Revolyutsii 88, 102	227-1296	529-2059	121492
Sapfir Jewellers, prosp. Engelsa 15	244-0723		
Sara Lee, Lermontovskiy prosp. 7/12	114-5660	114-0740	
SAS, Nevskiy Palace Hotel	314-5086	164-7873	
Sberbank, Moskovskiy prosp., 205	291-2820		
Nevskiy prosp. 82	272-9089		
Pulkovskaya Hotel	299-9217		
Vladimirskiy props. 9, Business Center	113-1671		
City Board, Voznesenskiy prosp. 16	315-5618	110-4969	121353
Regional Board, prosp. Veteranov 87	150-8143	150-8143	
Scanior Design, See Scanflot			
Schlossburg Restaurant, Bolsheokhtinskiy prosp. 41	227-2924		
Schwabskiy Domik Restaurant JV (FRG),			

	Phone	Fax	Telex
Sciences Botanikal Society of Russia, ul. Professora Popova 2	234-9602		
Scientific Technical Translation & Interpretation Assn., Galyornaya ul. 22, kv. 33	307-0913		
Scientifik Methods Inc., p. Antonenko 5	110-6508	110-6097	
Scortek JV (Italy), Tsvetochnaya ul. 6	294-1701	294-1705	
Securicor Security Services, Securicor Okrana, 22 Liniya	218-0017	218-0017	
Sedervall i Ritm JV (Sweden), Krasnogvardeyskaya pl. 2	224-0814	224-2156	121450
Seldom, nab. Kutuzova 10	275-3663	275-0973	
Selskokhoyaistvenny Institut, See Agricultural Institute			
777 Casino, ul. M. Konyushennaya 7	311-3141		
Senat-Bar, ul. Galernaya 1/3	314-9253		
Sennoy market, Moskovskiy prosp. 4	310-0217		
Serafimovskoye Cemetery, Serebryakov prosp. 1	239-3151		
Service, B. Sampsonievskiy prosp. 11/12	542-8995		
Service-Informatika Cooperative, Nevskiy prosp. 81	277-7910	277-5241	
SET-IL, Nevskiy prosp. 82	272-1007		
Seventh-Day Adventists, ul. Internatsionalnaya 7	138-9811		
Sever Bakery, Nevskiy prosp. 44	311-2589		
Kafe, Nevskiy prosp. 44/46	110-5503		
Restaurant, Nevskiy prosp. 44/46	311-3678		
Sever Textile Association, prosp. Stachek 48	184-9347	252-2976	
Severnaya Hotel, ul. Zasimova 11, Kronshtadt	236-4844	236-3372	
Severnaya Lira, Nevskiy prosp. 26	312-0796		
Severnaya Zarya NPO, ul. Kantemirovskaya 7	245-5475	542-6477	
Severnoye Siyaniye Cosmetics Salon, Nevskiy prosp. 27	315-0168		
Severnoye Siyaniye Perfume-Cosmetics Factory, ul. Marata 69	112-0050	112-0050	121471
Severny Alliance International Exchange, Sredneokhtinskiy prosp. 52	526-6630	526-6624	
Severo-Zapad Advertising, Ligovskiy prosp. 44	164-8710	164-8882	
Severo-Zapad Publishers, Admiralteyskaya ul. 4	311-1666	311-0504	
Severo-Zapadny Vodnik, B. Morskaya ul. 13	314-7034		
Severomurinskiy, Prosveshcheniya prosp. 84 ,87	531-0444		
Severtrade Ltd, ul. B. Morskaya 18	311-8166	311-8147	
Sevkabel, Kozhevennaya liniya 40	217-2323	217-2830	
Sevmorgeologiya, nab. reki Moyki 120	114-0471		121430
Sevodnya, Khersonskaya ul. 12	274-0857	274-0857	
Sevoteam JV (Norway), nab. reki Moyki 112	219-5298	219-5319	
Sezam Jewellery Store, Pobedy pl. 2 (Hotel Pulkovskaya)	299-9217		
Shalyapin House Museum, ul. Graftio 26	234-1056		
Shanghai Restaurant JV (China), Sadovaya ul. 12/23	311-2751	312-1274	
Shelkoviy Put Ltd, prosp. Prosveshcheniya 23	597-1059	597-7210	
Shepito Big Top, ul. Avtovskaya 1a	183-1501	158-5542	
Shinomontazh, Severny prosp. 23	556-3966		
Ship Building Institute, Lotsmanskaya ul. 3	114-0761	113-8109	
Shkola Sidlina, Grafskiy p. 7	311-2245		
Shoe Repair Shop, Nevskiy prosp. 153	277-3027		
Shostakovich Philharmonic, See Leningrad Philharmonic			

	Phone	Fax	Telex
Shrlotta JV (USA) Law Firm, prosp. Gagarina 1 office 617	294-5525		
Shuvalovo Church of St. Alexander Nevskiy, Vyborgskoye sh. 106a	595-0666		
Siab, bul. Serebristy 38	301-8721	301-8587	
Siar Bossard, ul. B. Morskoye 28	315-7696	315-4297	
Sibirskiy Bank, Zanevskiy prosp. 25	529-9124	528-0927	
Siemens AG, ul. Gogolya 18/20	315-3197	315-3621	121292
Sigma JV (China), Primorkskoe sh. 6	239-5536	239-5536	
Signal Production Enterprise, ul. Knipovich 4	567-2233	567-8355	121145
Sikont, Novosmolenskaya nab. 1	352-8895		
Sila, Kavalergardskaya ul. 10, kv. 19	278-5035		
Silena JV (Italy), ul. Przhevalskovo 10/12	164-4374		
Simvol Buro, ul. Yegorova 23b	292-3512	292-2074	
Sinemateka, Kamenoostrovskiy prosp. 42	230-8026	230-8028	
SIT Airport Taxi Service, Pribaltiyskaya Hotel, ul. Korablestroiteley 14	356-9329	356-0094	
Sitab Office Equipment, ul. Nekrasova 11	273-7310	273-7310	
Sitek, ul. Rentgena 3	232-1100	232-1941	
SK Johnson, Rizhskiy prosp. 26	251-7577	251-8698	251-918
Skanlen JV (Austria), ul. Plekhanova 36	312-8434	213-3446	
Skatetour, ul. Blokhina 33	233-1616	315-1701	
SKF Express, nab. reki Fontanki 116-b	251-3481	251-3390	
Skif, Vosstaniya u. 32	275-5345	275-5871	621110
Skorokhod Shoe Factory, Zastavskaya ul. 33	298-9211		122767
Sky Bar, Hotelship Peterhof	213-6321		
Sky Club Restaurant, Hotel Commodore	119-6666		
SKY Systems, ul. Egorova 18/12	292-7666	292-0094	
SL International JV (Singapoore), Konnogvardeyskiy Bulvar 4 kv. 25	311-1100	311-8139	
Slava Cinema, Bukharestskaya ul. 47	260-8726		
Slaviya-Interbuk, nab. reki Moyki 20, flat 69	315-1570	312-4128	
Smart JV (Finland), Admiralteyskiy prosp. 8/1	110-6655	314-3433	121432
Smena, nab. reki Fontanki 59	311-0219		
Smena Cinema, Sadovaya u. 42	310-2992		
Smolenskoye cemetery, V. O., Kamskaya ul. 24	355-9993		
Smolninskiy Employment Agency, Nevskiy prosp. 176	277-1859		
Smolninskiy Veterinary Center, Ligovskiy prosp. 56	164-7622		
Smolny Cathedral, pl. Rastrelli 3/1	311-3560		
Sobakovod Pet Shop, Bukharestskaya ul. 23	174-8746	166-0686	
Society of Lovers of Ex-libris & Book Illustrations, Kamennoostrovskiy prosp. 42, room 310	544-0356		
Sodruzhestvo Cooperative, See Concord Agency			
Sofi JV (Finland), Kingiseppskaya sh. 47	132-2355	135-7566	
Soft-Tronik GmbH, Fontanki nab. 88	315-9276	311-2325	
SoftUnion, ul. Schedrina 10	272-0931	272-0931	
Soinform, Kamennoostrovskiy prosp. 42	235-7146	235-7146	
Solnyshko Restaurant, prosp. Kima 3	350-2938		
Sonneks Agency, ul. Professora Popova 7/8, kv. 8	234-5800		
Sopot, Sredniy prosp. 34	213-1043		
Sopot JV (Poland), Krestovskiy prosp. 12	235-0285	315-5135	
Soppol, 2 Krasnoarmeyskaya ul. 7	110-1432	110-1209	

	Phone	Fax	Telex
Sotrudnichestvo Commercial Center, Morskaya nab. 9	355-5421	355-5422	
Sov. Can. Inc., Nevskiy prosp. 81	277-0480	277-5241	
Sovam Teleport, Nevskiy prosp. 30	311-8412	311-7129	
Sovaminco JV Filial, Millionnaya ul. 27	315-8459	542-9064	
Sovavto-St. Petersburg Shipping Company, Vitebskiy prosp. 3	298-5556	298-7760	121535
Sovetskaya Hotel, Lermontovskiy prosp. 43/1	259-3380	251-8890	
Bavaria Restaurant	259-2454		
Beriozka	251-6772		
Sovetskiy Restaurant,	259-2573		
Sovetskaya Rossia, Khersonskaya ul. 12	274-0651	274-0651	
Sovex JV (FRG), Stachek prosp. 45	252-2632	186-4044	
Sovinteravtoservice, Malodetskoselskiy prosp. 24	292-1257	292-0028	
ul. Gogolya 19	315-9758	292-0058	
Repairs, Predportovy pr. 5	290-1510		
Sovintour, Smolny, podyezd 9	271-6466	273-0871	
Sovitturs, Konnogvardeyskiy Bulvar 4	311-9715		
Sovkoopkan, nab. Makarova 30	213-7161	218-2213	
Sovmarket, 1 Sovetskaya ul. 10	277-5371	274-9460	
Sovplim JV (Sweden), sh. Revolyutsii 102	227-7853	227-2610	121284
Sovremennik Cinema, Nauki prosp. 25	535-4629		
Sovstroiservice, ul. Dostoyevskovo 30, kv. 9	164-1439	112-2366	
Sovtransavto, See Sovavto-Leningrad Shipping Company			
Sovturs Hotel, nab. Maloy Nevki 13	234-1014		
Sovyetskiy Kompozitor, ul. B. Morskaya 45	314-0921	311-5811	
Sovyetskiy Pisatel, Liteyny prosp. 36	279-0336	279-1765	
Sovyetskiy Sport, ul. Lomonosova 22	314-2417		
Soyuz, Polyustrovskiy prosp. 61	245-0046		
Soyuz Production Enterprise, ul. Kurskaya 21	166-4826	166-1582	12226
Soyuzbank, ul. Babushkina 3	567-1846		
Soyuzpechat, ul. Mirgorodskaya 1	312-8009		
Soyuzpushnina, See Fur Auction			
Soyuzteplstroi, Isaakevskaya pl. 7	312-3019		122207
Soyuzvneshtrans, Mezhevoy kanal 5	251-4197	186-2883	
Spar Market, prosp. Slavy 30	260-4121		
prosp. Stachek 9	186-9411		
Admin. Offices, B. Konyushennaya ul. 27	311-0553		
Spark Ltd, ul. Pilotov 9	122-9681	104-1602	
Spartak Cinema, Saltykova-Shchedrina ul. 8	272-2812		
Spartak Rowing Sport Center, nab. Bolshoy Nevki 24	234-3622	234-3622	
Spartak Swimming Pool, Konstantinovskiy prosp. 19	235-0583		
Spasa Preobrazhenskiy Cathedral, See Cathedral of the Transfiguration of Our Savior			
Spassis, Maly prosp. 1, kv. 3	218-6313	218-6313	
Speech Technology Center, Box 379	532-5903	532-3508	
Spektr, Degtyarny p. 1/8	274-2198		
ul. Moiseenko 15/17	271-6805	271-5672	
Spektr Center for Scientific-Technical Creativity of Youth, ul. Tsimlyanskaya 6	224-3533		
Spektr Cooperative, Khimicheskiy p. 6	252-5945		
Spektroflesh JV (German), ul. M. Zelenina 1	235-6118	235-3529	
Sphera, Box 524	126-6080	272-7669	

	Phone	Fax	Telex
Sphera, Box 524	126-6080	272-7669	
Sphinx, ul. Nekrasova 38	272-2134		
Sphinx Insurance, ul. Lomonosova 5	310-6222	310-3277	
Sphinx JV (Finland), ul. B. Morskaya 55	312-7540	312-5202	121483
Spielbanck Casino Sankt Petersburg, ul. Korablestroiteley 14 (Hotel Pribaltiyskaya)	356-0001		
SPKW, Yekaterinskiy prosp. 21	249-9088	249-7956	
Sport, Shaumyana prosp. 2	224-2874		
Sport Cinema, B. Sampsonievskiy prosp. 79	245-4522		
Sport Klass, Kamenoostrovskiy prosp. 26/28	232-7581	301-8733	
Sport Store, prosp. Shaumyana 2	224-2896		
Sport, Chelovek, Vremya, nab. reki Fontanki 59	310-4370		
Sport-Lyuks, Liteyny prosp. 57	272-6751		
Sporting Goods Shop, V. O., Nalichnaya ul. 31	356-1479		
Sportivnaya Hotel, Dekabristov ul. 34	235-1317	235-1339	
Sportivniye Tovary, Lanskoye sh. 12	246-0354		
Sports Library, Millionnaya ul. 22	311-3912		
Sportservis, Apraksin dvor, korpus 26	310-0424		
Sprint Networks	265-0571		
Sputnik, Liteyny prosp. 53	113-5021		
Sputnik Cinema, Babushkina ul. 40	560-5478		
Sputnik Hotel, prosp. Morisa Toreza 34	552-8330		
Double-K Casino	552-7991		
Sputnik International Travel Bureau, ul. Chapygina 4	234-3500	234-2304	122123
St. Catherine of Aleksandria Catholic Church, Nevskiy prosp. 32/34	311-5795		
St. Isaac's Cathedral, Isaakevskaya pl. 1	315-9732		
St. Petersburg. ., See also Sankt-Peterburg. .			
St. Petersburg Airport, Pulkovo Restaurant	104-3760		
St. Petersburg Association of Foreign Economic Cooperation, Krasnoarmeyskaya ul. 3, k. 12	292-4837	292-1453	
St. Petersburg Association of Independent Artists, Nevskiy prosp. 20	311-7777	311-2249	
St. Petersburg Association of Industries, Sovetskiy p. 5	251-4003	553-7001	
St. Petersburg Ballet on Ice, Dvortsovaya nab. 20/2	312-8637		
St. Petersburg Bank			
Head office, Vosnesenskiy prosp. 16	314-6095	110-4969	121353
Admiralteyskaya nab. 8	210-7788	315-4601	
Dom Knigi	219-9417		
Nevskiy prosp. 38	110-4945	110-4791	
Okhtinskaya Hotel	222-8635		
Peterhof Hotelship	219-9417		
Renlund Store, ul. Savushkina 119	345-1699		
Okhtinskiy Branch, Malookhtinskiy prosp. 53	528-7539	528-7539	
Gavanskiy Branch, ul. Shevchenko 1	217-1879	217-1779	
Kuibyshevskiy Branch, Nevskiy prosp. 62	319-9943	319-9943	
St. Petersburg Book Store, Nevskiy prosp. 52	311-1651		
St. Petersburg Central Customs House, V. O., 9 Liniya 10	218-6374	213-8017	
St. Petersburg Chamber of Commerce and Industry, ul. Chaykovskovo 46-48	273-4896	272-6406	122250
St. Petersburg City			

	Phone	Fax	Telex
Property Fund, p. Grivtsova 5	310-4645	319-9426	
Mayor's Office, Smolny	310-5406		
Telephone Board, ul. Gertsena 24	314-3757		
Vice-Mayor's Office, Smolny	278-1248		
St. Petersburg City Council, Isaakevskaya pl. 6	319-9485	310-4776	121575
Control Committee, Isaakevskaya pl. 6	319-9752		
Foreign Relations Dept., Isaakevskaya pl. 6	319-9381	310-4776	
Transport Depot, ul. Korolenko 5	272-5331		
St. Petersburg City Travel Bureau, B. Konyushennaya ul. 27	315-4555	314-9251	122740
St. Petersburg Clearinghouse, Ligovskiy prosp. 56g	164-6630		
St. Petersburg Council on Peace and Understanding, nab. reki Fontanki 21	210-4527	314-8321	
St. Petersburg Computer Company, ul. Mayakovskova 11	273-1112	273-0684	
St. Petersburg Commodity & Stock Exchange, V. O., 26 Liniya 15	217-8071	355-6859	
St. Petersburg Culture Fund, Nevskiy prosp. 31	311-8349	311-8349	121378
St. Petersburg Electro-Technological University, ul. Professora Popova 5	234-8925		
St. Petersburg Exchange, ul. Plekhanova 36	355-5954	355-5954	
St. Petersburg Film Actor's Guild, Fontanka 11	312-7967	312-7967	
St. Petersburg Firefighter School, Moskovskiy prosp. 149, box 227	298-1047		
St. Petersburg Folk Art Assn., ul. Chelieva 6	263-6786		
St. Petersburg Foreign Economic Association, Zagorodny prosp. 68	292-1455	113-0114	
St. Petersburg Forestry Academy, Institutskiy p. 5	550-0700		
St. Petersburg Freight Exchange, ul. Kavalergardskaya 6	275-8946	274-2966	
St. Petersburg Hunting and Fishing Union, nab. reki Pryazhki 32	219-7074	219-7074	
St. Petersburg Hermitage Orchestra Cooperative, Nevskiy prosp. 31	528-9435	311-8349	
St. Petersburg Impeks Association, ul. B. Morskaya 35	310-9441	319-9709	121575
St. Petersburg Investment & Construction Exchange, nab. reki Moyki 86	319-9575	219-1808	
St. Petersburg Information Kanal, ul. Rubinshteyna 8 kv. 3	314-4348	314-4348	
St. Petersburg Innovation Bank, ul. Chaykovskovo 24	279-0004	279-0281	
St. Petersburg Intercity Telephone Station, ul. B. Morskaya 3-5	311-4863	315-1701	
St. Petersburg International Projects Agency, ul. Klenovaya 2	210-4764	314-9272	
St. Petersburg International Solicitor's Association, ul. Furmanova 6a	275-1071	275-1135	
St. Petersburg Metro named for V. I. Lenin, Moskovskiy prosp. 28	251-6668		
St. Petersburg Mirror Factory, prosp. Yelizarova 34	560-9900	560-0219	321374
St. Petersburg Music Hall, Aleksandrovskiy Park 4	232-9466	232-5329	
St. Petersburg Musical Fund, Nevskiy prosp. 11	314-7132	314-5818	

RUSSIA'S ADDRESS FOR BUSINESS SUCCESS.

**Russia, the new frontier of business.
Expanding markets. Challenges.
Unlimited opportunity.**

**To prosper, you need an environment designed for business success.
A place to call home.**

Americom Business Centers are that place.

- ***Furnished Executive Suites.***
- ***State-of-the-art services.***
- ***Meeting and conference facilities.***
- ***Strategic downtown locations.***

Come discover why we're Russia's premier business address.

St. Petersburg:
Nevskij Palace Hotel
Tel: (7812) 275-2001
Fax: (7812) 850-1501
or 184-8923

Moscow:
Radisson Slavjanskaya Hotel
American Trade Center
Tel: (7095) 941-8815 or 8892
Int'l. fax (7502) 224-1107
Local fax: 941-8376

Visit the Stockmann shops in Moscow and St. Petersburg!

The New Fashion Store
• DOLGORUKOVSKAYA UL. 2 MOSCOW 103006

Business-to-BusinessTrading
• PROSPEKT MIRA 176 MOSCOW

Fashion and Business Store
• LENINSKY PROSPEKT 73/8 MOSCOW

Home Electronics and Car Supplies Store
• LYUSINOVSKAYA UL. 70/1 MOSCOW

Grocery Supermarket
• ZACEPSKY VAL 4/8 MOSCOW

Grocery Supermarket
• FINLYANDSKY PROSPEKT 1 ST. PETERSBURG

KALINKA · КАЛИНКА
STOCKMANN

	Phone	Fax	Telex
St. Petersburg News, See Cross Business Center			
St. Petersburg Palace for Youth, ul. Professora Popova 47	234-4215	234-9818	
St. Petersburg Philharmonic Society Music Library, Bolsheokhtinskiy prosp. 8	227-0772		
St. Petersburg Philharmonic, ul. Mikhailovskaya 2	311-7333	311-2126	
St. Petersburg Press, ul. Razyezzhaya 5	119-6080	314-2120	
St. Petersburg Radio, ul. Italianskaya 27	219-9694		
St. Petersburg Railway Agency, nab. kanala Griboyedova 24	162-3344		
St. Petersburg Record Factory, Tsvetochnaya ul. 7	298-3756	296-1254	321826
St. Petersburg Regional and City Defense Committee, nab. kanala Griboyedova 20	314-2458		
St. Petersburg Regional Committee for Television and Radio, Italianskaya ul. 27	312-4246		122116
St. Petersburg Regional Council for Tourism and Excursions, Italianskaya ul. 3	314-8786	311-9381	321893
St. Petersburg Regional Council of People's Deputies, Suvorovskiy prosp. 67	315-8665	271-5627	
St. Petersburg Regional Union of Consumer Societies, B. Konyushennaya ul. 9	314-1548	314-6287	
St. Petersburg Rock Club, ul. Rubinshteyna 13	312-3483	314-9629	
St. Petersburg Sports Committee, Karavannaya ul. 9	311-9469		
St. Petersburg State Architectural & Building Inspection, Ligovskiy prosp. 49	277-1234		
St. Petersburg State Ballet Theater Borisa Eyfmana, ul. Lizy Chaykinoy 2	232-0235	232-1862	
St. Petersburg State Music Hall, See St. Petersburg Music Hall			
St. Petersburg State Orchestra, Nevskiy prosp. 41, Belozerskiy Palace	315-3921		
St. Petersburg State University, Universitetskaya nab. 7/9	218-2000	218-1346	321074
Department of International Affairs	213-1168	218-1346	
Dormitory, ul. Shevchenko 25, korpus 1	355-0093		
St. Petersburg Stock Exchange, V. O., Bolshoy prosp. 103	355-5988	355-5988	
St. Petersburg Technical University Library, Politekhnicheskaya ul. 29	552-7559		
St. Petersburg Today, ul. Artileriyskaya 1, office 423	279-6047		
St. Petersburg Trading House, Krapivni p. 5	541-8525	541-8666	
St. Petersburg Travel Agency, Isaakevskaya pl. 11	210-0905	315-4563	121509
Pulkovo I Airport	123-8590		
Pulkovo II Airport	104-3465		
St. Petersburg Union of Journalists, Nevskiy prosp. 70	272-8513		
St. Petersburg University of Economics & Finance, Sadovaya ul. 21	310-3823		
St. Petersburg Veteran Foundation, nab. Kutuzova 22/2	279-4708	272-5294	
St. Petersburg Veterinary Center, 2 Zhernovskaya ul. 46	527-8396		

	Phone	Fax	Telex
St. Petersburg World Financial and Trade Center, Kanal Griboyedova 5	312-3557	311-0471	
St. Petersburg Youth Hostel, 3 Sovetskaya 28	277-0569	277-5102	
Stalker, Bolshoy prosp. 34	230-9966		
Stalker Center, V. O., 25 Liniya 8	217-9001	217-7229	
Stankinbank, inter-branch, Baskov p. 12	273-1671	275-5523	
Staraya Derevnya Cafe & Tours, ul. Savushkina 72	239-0000		
Stardust, Aleksandrovskiy park 4	233-2712		
Start Cooperative, Nikolskaya pl. 6	113-8186	113-7612	
Startplus, ul. Ulyany Gromovoy 8	277-0213	277-0213	
State Automobile Inspectorate (GAI), ul. Popova 42	234-2646	234-9303	
State Circus, The, nab. reki Fontanki 3	210-4411		
State Committee for Antimonopoly Policy, ul. Plekhanova 36	314-7914	319-9057	
State Committee for Conversion, Smolny	278-1248	273-5924	
State Committee for Radio Broadcasting, See St. Petersburg Radio			
State Committee for Statistics, ul. Professora Popova 39	230-7520	234-0636	
State Customs North-Western Administration, ul. Furmanova 1	275-7695	275-3154	
State Taxation Inspectorate, Liteyny prosp. 53	272-0188	272-6456	
Status, Marshala Govorova prosp. 8b	185-0860		
Stepana Razina Brewery, ul. Stepana Razina 9	251-3021	251-0825	
Stereo Cinema, Nevskiy prosp. 88	272-2729		
Stern & Co., See Law Offices of Samuel Stern			
Stiers-Sankt-Petersburg Bar, pl. Stachek 4	186-9522	186-9522	
Stilkon Ltd, ul. Gazovaya 10	235-0479	235-3407	
Stockmann Food Store (Kalinka), Finlyandskiy prosp. 1	542-2297	542-8866	
Stopolelektronika, ul. Blokhina 23	232-2800	232-2800	
Storbyork-Service, Moskovskiy prosp. 193, kv. 136	293-7175		
Stouk Ltd., nab. kanala Griboyedova 102	310-2104	310-2104	
Strela, Ligovskaya ul. 6, kv. 313	422-2098		
Strela Food Store, Izmaylovskiy prosp. 16/30	251-2709		
Stroidetal, Khimicheskiy p. 6	252-7793	252-6405	
Stroipolimer Factory, ul. Severnaya 14	484-4750	484-3388	121441
Stroitel, Lyotchika Pilyutova 34,kor. 2	144-5380		
Rubinshteyna ul. 3	312-6573		
Stroitelnaya Kniga, Bolsheokhtinskiy prosp. 3	224-0873		
Strom Cooperative, Vladimirskiy prosp. 14	164-4422	112-2310	
Stroyinvest Commercial Bank, V. O., 2 Liniya 5	218-0579	218-6946	
Stroyinvest, St. Petersburg Branch, V. O., 2 Liniya 5	218-6689	119-6190	
Stroyizdat, Birzhevoy p. 1/10	218-1896	218-1896	
Stroykeramiks Firm, Yuzhnoye sh. 49	269-3665	105-6695	
Struzh, V. O., 11 Liniya 68	213-8235		
STT Firm, ul. B. Morskaya 35	315-4696	312-1627	121422
Studiya-7, Box 264	555-9126	106-0440	
Stupeni, nab. reki Fontanki 20	275-6706		
STV, ul. Pochtamtskaya 23	315-2955		
Suburban Electric Trains-Information	168-0111		
Sudarynya Kafe, ul. Rubinshteyna 28	312-6380		

	Phone	Fax	Telex
Sudostroeniye Magazine, Promyshlennaya ul. 14a	186-1609	186-0459	
Sudostroeniye NPO, Mezhevoy kanal 4	251-2307	113-0123	121504
Sudostroeniye Publishers, ul. M. Morskaya 8	312-4479	312-0821	
Sudostroitel Bookstore, Sadovaya ul. 40	315-3117		
Sukhanov's Clinic, ul. Beloostrovskaya 26	242-2917		
Summer Gardens and Palace of Peter the Great	312-9666		
Summer Palace, Letniy sad	314-0374		
Super Siwa, ul. Savushkina 119	345-1698		
Suvorov Museum, ul. Saltykova-Shchedrina 43	279-3915		
Svarka-Welding JV(Finland), ul. Zaytseva 3	184-1456	183-1384	
Svega, Nevskiy prosp. 52/14	310-1768	314-7288	
Svellen JV, Serdobolskaya ul. 1	242-1358	242-1385	
Svet All-Union Society of the Blind, ul. Kostyushko 17a	295-1493	295-9371	321332
Svet Cinema, P.S., Bolshoy prosp. 74	232-8624		
Svetlana, prosp. Engelsa 27	554-9121	553-7001	121466
Svetlanovskiy, Engelsa prosp. 21	244-0769		
Svetoch, ul. B. Pushkarskaya 10	233-4558	233-3745	122717
Svir, Hotelship Peterhof,nab. Makarova	213-6321		
Svobodnaya Kultura, Pushkinskaya u. 10, kv. 159	164-5258	164-5207	
Svyatotroitskiy Cathedral, See Cathedral of the Holy Trinity			
Svyazmorproekt Constructive Buro, ul. M. MOrskaya 14	312-8268	315-3149	121359
Swed Car St. Petersburg, prosp. Bolshevikov 33 k 1	586-7718	586-7477	
Swed-Mobil-Service, prosp. Energetikov 59/3	225-4051	225-4051	
Swissair, Nevskiy prosp. 57, Nevskiy Palace Hotel	314-5086	164-7873	
Pulkovo II Airport	104-3443		
Synagogue, Preobrazhenskoye cemetery, prosp. Alexandrovskoy Fermi	262-0447		
Synagogue (choral), Lermontovskiy prosp. 2	114-1153	113-8975	
Sytny market, Sytninskaya ul. 3/5	233-1282		
Syuzhet, Koli Tomchaka ul. 24	307-7954		

T

	Phone	Fax	Telex
TAB International, ul. Koli Tomchaka 32, office 33	296-2527	296-2416	
Taira, V. O., Bolshoy prosp. 55a	213-5859		
Tam-Tam Club, V.O., 16 liniya at Maly prosp.			
Tambrands, Zheleznodorozhny prosp. 20	560-1319	560-9714	
Tary Coop, Liteyny prosp. 31	272-2035		
Taurus, Poliustrovskiy prosp. 32	540-9615	541-1914	
Tavricheskiy Sad, Igroteka, ul. Saltykova-Shchedrina 50	272-6044		
Taxi Reservations	312-0022		
Tbilisi Restaurant, Sytninskaya ul. 10	232-9391		
TDV-Auto, ul. Kommuny 16	521-7719	521-8547	121263
Team Deax, ul. Inzhenernaya 9	314-0215	210-4355	
Technological Institute, Zagorodny prosp. 49	292-9537	110-6285	
Tekhkompakt, Moskovskiy prosp. 181	291-0048	108-4865	
Tekhnicheskaya Kniga Bookstore, Pushkinskaya ul. 2	164-6565		
Tekhnicheskiy Tsentr, Ligovskiy prosp. 256	297-1768		
Tekhnicheskiy Universitet, ul. Politekhnicheskaya 29	247-1616	552-6086	121803

	Phone	Fax	Telex
Tekhnobalt, Shpalernaya ul. 52	275-4200	275-5308	
Tekhnoexan JV (Austria), Politekhnicheskaya ul. 26	247-9383	247-5333	121453
Tekhnoimpeks Association, V. O., 6 Liniya 27, #24	218-8091	218-4275	
Tekhnokhim Joint Stock Bank, nab. Krasnovo Flota 10	311-6994		
Tekhnokhimexport FTO, nab. Krasnovo Flota 10	314-9163	311-6847	
Tekhnologicheskiy Institut Kholodilnoy Promyshlennost, See Refrigeration Industry Tech. Inst.			
Tekhnologicheskiy Institut imeni Petrosovieta, See Technological Institute			
Teknesis, Fontanka 76	112-5832	112-5826	
Teko, Rubinshteyn ul. 13	310-0304	314-9629	
Tekobank Joint Stock Bank, Ispolkomskaya ul. 7/9	277-1875	277-4810	
Telegram Service, (dictate over the phone)	066		
Teleinform Business Association, Ligovskiy prosp. 56e, kv. 90	164-1236	164-1710	
Telemecanique, ul. Gastello 12	291-8115	291-8117	121295
Telenokia, B. Sampsonievskiy prosp. 60	542-0131	542-8860	
Teleport St. Petersburg, prosp. Gagarina 1	294-8857	294-8683	
Telets, Bryantseva ul. 7	594-5000		
Televideniye, Radio Newspaper, nab. reki Fontanki 59, #551	310-5775		
Television Exchange, Galerny p. 3	352-0669	352-0380	
Telex, Kavalergardskya ul. 10, kv. 19	278-5032		
Telinfo, nab. reki Moyki 64	315-6412	352-0380	
Tellus Ltd, Box 8	292-3564	292-5046	
Tempo Autosalon, ul. Shaumana 2	224-3609	224-2874	
Termex Cooperative, ul. Kostyushko 62	123-0002	123-2448	
Terra-Inkognita, Soyuza Pechatnikov ul. 28	219-5083	219-5847	
Testek, Shkiperskiy protok 2	356-6716	356-6716	
Tete-a-Tete Cafe, P.S., Bolshoy prosp. 65	232-7548		
Tetrapolis Bank, Zagorodny prosp. 68	292-3179	259-6069	
The Source, Hotel Moskva, room 380	274-3080	350-6475	
Theater for Musical Comedy, See Musical Comedy Theater			
3M-Lentelefonstroi, Obukhova, Garazhny prosp. 1	101-1534	172-7365	
Time	08		
Tishuten & co., Nevskiy prosp. 100	279-3311		
Tiss, Staro-Petergofskiy prosp. 52	252-4150		
Titan Cinema, Nevskiy prosp. 47	319-9726		
Titus, Serpukhovskaya ul. 1	292-3976	312-4138	
TNT Express Freight, Liteyny prosp. 50	272-5886	273-6007	121663
Tobacco Factory named for Klara Tsetkina, Klinskiy prosp. 25	110-1062	112-6466	
Tobos, ul. Karbysheva 29-a	247-5424		
Tokobank, Zagorodny prosp. 5	314-2235	113-2889	
Tolstoy Library, V. O., 6 Liniya 17	213-6787		
Tonus Medical Coop, ul. Podvoyskovo 14, k. 1	589-2647	314-9076	
Top Daily News, pl. Stachek 4,pod. 1	186-3635	186-7070	
Top-Shliop, Pushkinskaya ul. 10, kv. 123	164-5707	164-5207	
Topos, Chekhova ul. 5	273-5128		
Tor Firm, prosp. Slavy 16	119-6876	119-6876	
Uglovoy p. 6	292-7210	110-1334	121323

	Phone	Fax	Telex
Torgovy Dom Alisa Ltd, V. O., 6 Liniya 35b	218-3433	213-1777	
Tornado, Ispolkomskaya ul. 9/11	275-3065	275-3064	
V. O., Bolshoy prosp. 83	217-5306	217-5305	
Torzhkovskiy market, Torzhkovskaya ul. 20	246-8375		
Toyota, ul. M. Balkanskaya 57	101-5213	101-6426	
Trade Union Rowing Club, nab. Bolshoy Nevki 24	234-3644		
Trade Union Tennis Club, Konstantinovskiy prosp. 23	235-0407		
Trade-Economic Institute, Novorossiyskaya ul. 50	247-7806	247-4342	
Traditional Medicine Cooperative Clinic,			
ul. Serdobolskaya 57/26	245-1907		
Train Information, General	168-0111		
Domestic Tickets	162-3344		
Trans Business Line, Liteyny prosp. 50	272-9864	272-8559	
Trans-Niva, prosp. Yuriya Gagarina 32, kor. 2	299-5243		
Transelectro JV (Finland), Moskovskiy prosp. 171	294-0501	294-0443	
Transelektro OY, Box 330	294-0635	294-0443	
Transit Ltd, Nevskiy prosp. 100	259-8745	114-1698	
Translation and Interpretation Bureau,			
Isaakevskaya pl. 11	210-0933		
Transnautik, ul. Gapsalskaya 10	251-6300	251-6300	121540
Transpoint, ul. Komsomola 1/3			
Transport Publishers, ul. Goncharova 6	279-4385		
Transportnaya Kniga Bookstore, Pushkinskaya ul. 20	164-9807		
Transwell Sankt-Petersburg, Lermontovskiy prosp. 37	113-7253	114-3803	
Transworld Communications	112-4787		
Trapeza Cafe, Petrodvorets, Kalininskaya ul. 9	257-9393		
Triada, ul. Zhukovskovo 22	275-7921	272-5917	
Tribuna Sewing Production Assn., ul. Uchitelskaya 23	531-2798	594-4945	121027
Trikotazh Retail Firm, Novoizmailovskiy prosp. 10	296-6256		
Troika R. O., Zagorodny prosp. 28	112-4746		
Troika Restaurant JV (Switz.), Zagorodny prosp. 7	113-5343	113-4279	121299
Troitskiy Cathedral, See Cathedral of the Holy Trinity			
Troitskiy Trading Center Bar, Kurlyandskaya ul. 24			
Trojan Horse Kafe, V. O., 16 Liniya 20	355-9740		
Troyka Tours, Zagorodny prosp. 27	113-5376	310-4279	121299
Trubostal Factory, Zheleznodorozhny prosp. 16	560-0210	560-9874	
Trud, pl. Truda 4	314-9417	314-9417	
Trud Ltd, ul. Prazhskaya 10	268-8168		
Trud Swimming Pool, ul. Pravdy 11	210-5520		
Trudovoye Znamya, M. Monetnaya ul. 2	238-6839		
Trudovye Rezervi Swimming Pool, Gavanskaya ul. 53	352-6754		
Trutoplast JV, prosp. Obukhovskoy Oborony 53	265-1568	265-3920	
Tsarskotselskiy Bank, pl. Konstitutsii 2	123-0684		
prosp. Stachek 37	186-9796		
Tsentr Firmennoy Torgovli, nab. reki Smolenki 1	352-1134		
Novosmolenskaya nab. 1	352-0632	352-1722	
Tsentr Sudostroenie JV (Germany),			
nab. Robospyera 8/46, kv. 102	275-6072	279-3241	
Tsentralny Food Store, See Eliseevskiy Food Store			
Tsitomed Medical Center, p. Muchnoy 2	310-8011	311-5282	121484
Pharmacy	310-8011	311-5282	
Tsveti Bolgarii Florist, Kamenoostrovskiy prosp. 5	232-4685		
Tukhan, Novosyelov ul. 5-a	266-1126		

	Phone	Fax	Telex
Tukhan, Novosyelov ul. 5-a	266-1126		
Turist Hotel, Sevastyanova ul. 3	297-8183		
Turku Restaurant, Hotel Pulkovskaya, pl. Pobedy 1	264-5716		
Turner Broadcasting, See Goodwill Games, Inc.			
Turquoise, See Biryuza			
Tvel Cooperative, Yakovlevskiy p. 11	294-2355	298-5991	121253
TVID, Kamennoostrovskiy prosp. 42	230-8022		
Twentieth Trust Corporation, Nevskiy prosp. 44	311-1696	110-6448	

U

	Phone	Fax	Telex
U Petrovicha Restaurant, Sredneokhtinskiy prosp. 44	227-2135		
U Prichala Restaurant, V. O., Bolshoy prosp. 91	217-4428		
U Samovara Cafe, Piskarevskiy prosp. 52	538-3095		
U. N. O. Firm, Lesnoy prosp. 20 kor. 5	542-0402		
Nevskiy prosp. 50	310-0666		
prosp. Maklina 19	114-2925		
Umelets Cooperative, ul. Bukharestskaya 72	597-9863		
Union of German Chambers of Commerce, V. O., Bolshoy prosp. 10a	213-7991	350-5622	
Union of Industrial Associations, Smolny, 5th entrance	278-1580	278-1580	
Union of St. Petersburg Museums, Liteyny prosp. 57	279-7135	273-5792	
Union Reson, 12 Krasnoarmeyskaya ul. 7	292-3647		
Unirem JV (Switz.), pl. Dekebristov 3	311-7893	312-7958	
Uniserv Office Service Center, prosp. Prosveshcheniya 85	559-8802	559-5210	
Universal, Lebedeva ul. 31	541-8187	541-8433	
Universal Restaurant, Nevskiy prosp. 106	279-3350		
Unix Firm, ul. Italianskaya 23, floor 3	310-9745		
UPDK Service Bureau, nab. Kutuzova 34	272-1500	279-5024	
Building Oversight Committee, nab. Kutuzova 34	273-4702	279-5024	
UPS Courier Service, ul. Karavannaya 12	312-2915	314-7037	
UPS JV (Finland), ul. Saltykova-Shchedrina 31	275-8878	275-4405	121507
Ural, nab. reki Fontanki 76	112-5832	484-3231	
Uran Cinema, Yaroslavskiy prosp. 55	554-2138		
Urartu Restaurant, ul. Rudneva 25	558-6919		
Urban Sculpture Museum, Nevskiy prosp. 179/2	274-2635		
Uritskiy Tobacco Factory, Sredny prosp. 36/40	213-8509	213-1955	321845
USIS JV (Bulgarian), ul. Rosenshteyna 34	252-2521	186-8494	
Uspekh Shop, Kamenoostrovskiy 16b	534-8315		
Ustinov Mechanical Institute, 1 Krasnoarmeyskaya ul. 1	292-2341	292-2409	
UVIR, ul. Saltykova-Shchedrina 4	278-2418		

V

	Phone	Fax	Telex
V. A. Instruments JV (UK), Rizhskiy prosp. 26	252-6759	252-1003	
Vacuum Analytical Instruments JV (UK), prosp. Marshala Govorova 52	251-8889	252-1003	121549
Valeodent Ltd, ul. Artileriyskaya 1, Hotel Rus, 1st fl., office 5	279-6920		

	Phone	Fax	Telex
VAMI Research and Design Institute,			
V. O., Sredny prosp. 86	213-5458	217-5242	
Vana Information, ul. Millionnaya 11	311-1717	311-3391	
Vanda, Gatchinskaya ul. 5			
Vanda Cosmetics, Nevskiy prosp. 11	279-4341		
Vanga Medservice, 3 Sovetskaya ul. 6	271-0900		
Variant, Vosstaniya u. 40	273-6536		
Variant Bookstore, Komsomola ul. 16	542-4971		
Varlen JV (Poland), Obvodnovo Kanala nab. 154a	186-0267	186-0267	
Varshavskiy Train Station,			
nab. Obvodnovo kanala 118	168-2972		
Varvara Firm, ul. Lermontova 46	132-6816		
Vas-Fed Agrofirm, V. O., 25 Liniya 8	217-4503	355-1448	
Vasileostrovskiy Home Repair & Renovation			
Service, V. O., 11 Liniya 40	213-1378		
Vasileostrovskiy Veterinary Center,			
V. O., 17 Liniya 56	355-9912		
Vasileostrovskiy market, V. O., Bolshoy prosp. 18	213-6687		
Vasilievskiy Ostrov, Uralskaya ul. 33	351-5885		
Vecher Restaurant, ul. Tallinskaya 20	221-1676		
Vecherny Peterburg, nab. reki Fontanki 59	311-8875	314-3105	
Veda, p. Pirogova 18	315-2665	312-8396	
Vega Cooperative, V. O., 17 Liniya 62	355-7324	271-9211	122621
Vekom Bookstore, Slavy prosp. 15	261-8682		
Vektor, Kolomenskaya ul. 4/6	164-4200		
ul. Akademika Pavlova 14a	234-7511		
Vena Ltd, Farforovskaya 1	560-0628	560-0601	
Venice Restaurant, ul. Korablestroiteley 21	352-1432		
Venita, Vernosti ul. 10, kor. 3	535-4620		
Vereteno Knitwear Factory,			
nab. Obvodnovo kanala 223/225	251-4993		
Veronika Cooperative, Vyborgskaya nab. 65	246-5754		
Veronika Hotel, Generala Khrulyova ul. 6	395-1373		
Very Well, nab. reki Fontanki 118-4	251-3461		
Ves Peterburg, See All Petersburg			
Vesko, Kupchinskaya ul. 16/1-52	176-1045		
Vesna Cinema, Avtovskaya u. 15	183-0517		
Vesnushka Cinema, Marshala Kazakova ul. 1	157-9355		
Vesti Newspaper, ul. Millionaya 3, 4th flr.	314-1985	314-1986	
Vestnik Lensoveta, Isaakiyevskaya pl. 6	319-9031		
Vestnik Merii, Gertsena ul. 47, kor. 2	312-0200	311-0493	
Vet Cooperative, nab. reki Fontanki 90, kv. 17	314-4226	314-4226	
Veteran, Varshavskaya ul. 110	233-1320		
Vial Stationers, ul. Belinskovo 11	278-8680		
Vibrator Production Assn., Petrogradskaya nab. 18	233-4212		
Victoria, Vyazovaya ul. 10	235-6519	235-5003	
Victoria Hotel JV (USA), Millionnaya ul. 22	315-1279		
Victoria Restaurant, Kamennoostrovskiy prosp. 24	232-5130		
Video Center, V. O., 7 Liniya 36	213-4357		
Vika, nab. Obvodnovo kanala 215, kv. 12	251-4333	251-4333	
Vikart, Professora Popova ul. 41/5, kv. 11	234-9676	312-9385	
Viking, Sankt Peterburg Hotel	542-8032		
Viking JV (German), Grecheskiy p. 10	272-5485	314-6131	

	Phone	Fax	Telex
Viking JV (Sweden), nab. reki Moyki 72	315-0772		
Viktoria, Industrialny prosp. 9	524-1966		
Vilena, Nauki prosp. 44	538-2533		
Viliya, Leninskiy prosp. 118 pod. 7	153-5900	153-5900	
Virilis, Bronnitskaya ul. 17	110-1093		
VIS JV(USA), p. Pirogova 8	311-4789	311-4789	
Visa and Registration office, See UVIR			
Visavi, ul. Italyanskaya 28	588-5010		
Visla Restaurant, Gorokhovaya ul. 17	210-6807		
Vista, Grecheskiy prosp. 15 kv. 27	271-2916	271-2758	
Vista Communications, Shpalernaya ul. 53, kv. 113	278-1928	271-3227	
Vista Cooperative, Primorskiy prosp. 32	239-2584	294-0411	121449
Vistar-SP, Kolomenskaya ul. 5	112-0768		
Vita, Box 86	226-2617	226-2617	
Vitabank, Karelia Hotel	226-3356		
Moskva Hotel	274-2127		
Pribaltiyskaya Hotel	356-3803		
ul. B. Morskaya 59	311-5193	311-8161	
Vitalis, Lagody ul. 3	227-1962		
Vitebskiy Train Station, Zagorodny prosp. 52	168-5390		
Vitebskiy Universam, ul. Dmitrova 5	172-4622		
Vityaz Restaurant, Pushkin, Moskovskaya ul. 20	476-6255		
Vizion Express, ul. Lomonosova 5	310-1595		
Vizit Cooperative, nab. reki Fontanki 26 kv. 43	273-4289	273-7984	
Vladen, ul. Gorokhovaya 7	307-7954		
VMB, Pisareva ul. 6, kv. 8	114-7589	114-7589	
Vnesheconombank (Foreign Economic Bank), ul. B. Morskaya 29	314-6059	312-7818	121515
Vneshposyltorg, prosp. Stachek 14/2	252-5223		
Vneshstroiservis JV (Norway), ul. Galernaya 6,office 64	315-2610		
Vneshtorgizdat, ul. Kuybysheva 34	233-5263	232-0160	
VNIITVCh NPO, ul. Tolstovo 7	234-9585	234-4652	321493
Vody Lagidze Restaurant, ul. Belinskovo 3	279-1104		
Volkhov Restaurant ,Casino, Liteyny prosp. 28	273-4736		
Volkovskoye Cemetery (Orthodox), Rasstanny pr. 7a	166-0400		
Volkswagen Sales and Service, See Fisherman's Harbor			
Volna, Galernaya ul. 55	311-0000		
Volna Cinema, Korablestroiteley ul. 33	352-3454		
Volna Sewing Production Assn., Leninskiy prosp. 140	255-9747	255-9247	
Volshebny Krai Bakery, P.S., Bolshoy prosp. 15/3	233-3253		
Volt Cooperative, ul. Mineralnaya 13	248-3031	540-0319	
Voprosy Kinologii, Klub Kinologov, V. O., 17 Liniya 38	213-7560		
Voskhod, ul. Sedova 12			
Voskhod Cinema, Pogranichnika Garkavovo ul. 22	144-6100		
Voskhod Scientific Cooperative Center, prosp. Yuri Gagarina 35, box 505	113-0298		
Vostochnye Sladosti Candy Shop, Moskovskiy prosp. 27	292-7556		
Vostochnye Sladosti Candy Shop, Nevskiy prosp. 104	273-7436		

	Phone	Fax	Telex
Nevskiy prosp. 104	273-7436		
Vostok-Orient JV Restaurant (India), Primorskiy Park Pobedy	235-5984		
Voyage Association, Rizhskiy prosp. 34 kv. 26	251-0121	101-5939	
Voyazh Firm, Ligovskiy prosp. 36	164-1262		
Voznesenskiy Financial and Economic Institute, ul. Sadovaya 21	310-3823	110-5674	
Vozrozhdeniye, ul. Plekhanova 50	311-9160		
Vozrozhdeniye Cotton Mill, Piskarevskiy prosp. 3	227-4874	227-3704	
Vperyod Machine Building Factory, nab. reki Smolenki 19/21	218-0139	218-2885	
Vseleniye Cooperative, prosp. Sizova 24, korpus 1	395-3623	395-3598	
Vsyo Dlya Vsekh, Kondryatevskiy 24	542-3055	542-8774	
Art Shop, ul. Pochtamtskaya 5	311-2643		
VTM & K-90, Leninskiy prosp. 101	153-5797		
Vtorchermet Production Assn., Khimicheskiy p. 4	252-1074	252-6544	121313
Vulkan Machine-Building Factory Ltd, Pionerskaya ul. 50	235-6431	235-6445	
Vyborgskaya Hotel, ul. Torzhkovskaya 3	246-2319		321064
Vyborgskaya Storona, B. Sampsonievskiy prosp. 88	245-1045		
Vyborgskiy, Lesnoy prosp. 37	245-0131		
Vyborgskiy Employment Agency, B. Sampsonievskiy prosp. 75			
Vyborgskiy Veterinary Center, Zelenogorskaya ul. 16	244-1548		

W

	Phone	Fax	Telex
Wal-Rus Ltd, ul. Nekrasova 40/1	273-6746	273-5192	
Warsteiner Forum, Nevskiy prosp. 120	277-2914		
Water Transport Institute, Dvinskaya ul. 5/7	259-0325	251-7620	
Wax Figures Museum, ul. Kuybysheva 2/4	233-7189		
Wella Salon Debut JV (FRG), Nevskiy prosp. 54	312-3026	312-3026	
West-Ingriya, Nevskiy prosp. 86			
White Horse Restaurant, See Belaya Loshchad Restaurant			
White Nights Bar, Hotel Olympia	119-6880	119-6805	121333
White Nights Restaurant, See Belye Nochi Restaurant			
Wind Instrument Factory, ul. Bely Kuna 28	269-6214		122864
World Class Gym, Grand Hotel Europe	113-8066		
Hotel Astoria, 4th floor	210-5869		
Kamennoostrovskiy prosp. 26	232-7581		
Worldwide Laboratory (Vsemirnaya Laboratoriya), Zhdanovskaya ul. 8	235-4342		121391
Writer's Bookshop, The, See Knizhnaya Lavka Pisateley			
Writers' Union, See Union of Writers			

	Phone	Fax	Telex
Xerox-Rotator, Sennaya pl. 3	310-9975		

Y

Name	Phone	Fax	Telex
Yakhont Jewellery Store, ul. B. Morskaya 24	314-6447		
Yakutskaya Commodity Stock Exchange, Moskovskiy prosp. 216	108-5920	108-5920	
Yana-Print, Konnogvardeyskiy Bulvar 4, kv. 33	311-2413	110-6496	
Yanus Juridical Agency, Universitetskaya nab. 7/9/11	218-7621	218-0402	
Yaroslav, ul. Millionnaya 5,rm. 2	312-9076	110-6450	
Yedinstvo, Bronnitskaya ul. 17	110-1448	112-6030	
Yenisey, Artilleriyskaya ul. 1	279-3469		
Yevropeyskaya Hotel, See Grand Hotel Europe			
Yevrosib International Exchange, Tavricheskaya ul. 39	271-3649	271-7650	
Yit-Yhtyma, Voronezhskaya ul. 33	167-0356	167-0357	
Yubiley Department Store, Sverdlovskaya nab. 60	224-2598	224-3451	
Yubileyny Bakery, Nevskiy prosp. 10	312-6086		
pl. Chernyshevskovo 3	298-1547		
V. O., 7 Liniya 40	213-1162		
Yubileyny Sports Palace, prosp. Dobrolyubova 18	238-4122		
Yugo-Zapad Avto, Petergofskoye sh. 3, kor. 2	155-6311	155-6311	
Yulena, Lanskoye sh. 14, k. 3	246-6897	242-2091	121345
Yuma Electronics, Malookhtinskiy prosp. 68	528-9566	528-8400	
Yuniks Inc., Italyanskaya ul. 23	142-1386	315-1701	
Yunost, nab. reki Moyki 48	312-4222		
Novo-Izmaylovskiy prosp. 4	296-6264		
Yunost Cinema, Savushkina ul. 21	239-2881		
Yupiter Kholding Firm, ul. Tsiolkovskovo 9	251-3900	251-3900	
Yuridicheskaya Literatura, Nevskiy prosp. 28	219-9465	311-9895	
Yuriskonsult, Millionnaya ul. 17	312-1852		
Yusta, Fontanka 39	552-5506	552-5506	
Yustas Agency, ul. Sergievskaya 17	278-0583		
YuVM, Bronnitskaya ul. 26	292-3503	292-0672	
Yuzhnaya, Rasstannaya ul. 2-b	166-1088		
Yuzhno-Primorskiy Park, Petergofskoye sh. 27	151-5287		
Yuzhny Univermag (Groceries) No. 2, ul. Yaroslava Gasheka 6	176-1829		
Yves Rocher, Nevskiy prosp. 61	113-1506	113-1496	

Z

Name	Phone	Fax	Telex
Zagreb Hotel, Ispytateley prosp. 31	395-3629		
Zanevkaprokat JV (Finland), Poselok Zanevka 48/1	521-8558	521-8558	121057
Zanevskiy Cinema, Krasnogvardeyskiy prosp. 47, kor. 1	221-3785		
Zapstroitrans Transport Association, Ligovskiy prosp. 56	164-6794		121204
Zarya, ul. Plekhanova 7	312-9643		
Zashchita, ul. Dobrolyubova prosp. 13	233-8262		
Zavod Bolshevik, prosp. Obukhovskoy Oborony 120	267-9860		
Zelyony Popugay Kafe, Sredneokhtinskiy prosp. 48	227-3912		

	Phone	Fax	Telex
Zelyonaya Pharmacy, Nevskiy prosp. 41	312-3773		
Zenit, Nevskiy prosp. 100	272-2831		
Zenit Cinema, ul. Gastello 7	293-1320		
Zenit Sports Palace, ul. Butlerova 9	535-0171		
Zerkalo Amateur Photographers' Organization, nab. Obvodnovo kanala 114, Marx Palace of Culture	168-2948		
Zhemchug, Slavy prosp. 5	261-3720		
Zhemchuzhina Cafe, ul. Shkiperskiy protok 2	355-2063		
Zhenskoye Schastye, Akademika Konstantinova ul. 8/2	550-8910	550-8689	
Zhilservice, Yefimova ul. 1/4	310-4789		
Zhurnal Tekhnicheskoy Fiziki, Politekhnicheskaya ul. 26	247-9906	218-3712	
Zimny Sad Restaurant, Hotel Astoria	210-5838		
Zimny Sports Center, Manezhnaya pl. 2	311-0771		
Znamya Oktyabrya, ul. Trefoleva 2	252-0111	252-3400	
Znaniye, ul. Kavalergardskaya 10	275-6108		
Znaniye Cinema, Nevskiy prosp. 72	273-5183		
Zodiak Bookstore, Gorokhovaya ul. 50	310-7965		
Zolotoy Klyuchik, Marshala Govorova ul. 10	184-8318		
Zolotoy Uley Candy Shop, Nevskiy prosp. 22	312-2394		
Zoo, Park Lenina 1	232-2839		
Zvezda, Kubinskaya ul. 1	296-6250		
Zvezda Magazine, ul. Mokhovaya 20	272-8948		

Not listed?

This is a very qualitative directory and no attempt is made to be comprehensive, to cover all St. Petersburg enterprises or businesses. Instead, the intent is to focus on those businesses, institutions and enterprises of immediate importance to the Western business person and traveler. If your company provides goods or services for this community, you should be listed here. Please send us information (to either of the addresses printed on the reverse of the title page) about the services or goods you provide, so that we can determine how best to place you.

Error?

If you find that information about your company or another company or entity listed in this directory is given incorrectly, please do not hesitate to contact us. While we re-verify all the information in *Where in St. Petersburg* prior to publication, companies are constantly moving, changing phone numbers and status. The task of providing up-to-date directory information is much as what one astute observer said about tracking Russian law, it is "like changing a tire on a moving car." We appreciate your input and assistance in making this guide more useful to its thousands of users.

124 items.
52 publishers.
One catalogue.

Access Russia

Access Russia is a 24-page catalogue presenting the finest and most useful publications on Russia and the CIS, of both Western and Russian manufacture. Many of the items in this catalogue are hard-to-find. All are for Russophiles and frequent travelers to Russia and the CIS.

Fonts. **Language tapes**. History books. **Periodicals**. Cookbooks. **Directories**. Travel gadgets. **Maps**. Software. Travel essays. Atlases. **Dictionaries**. Business guides. **Magazines**. Reference books.

To receive your FREE copy of ***Access Russia*** by mail,

call:
1-800-639-4301

or:
1-802-223-4955

or fax:
1-802-223-6105

or write to:
Access Russia
89 Main St., Suite 2
Montpelier, VT 05602

A grand welcome

"A distinguished envoy steps down from the carriage to be cordially ushered by the doorman into a peaceful chamber. After long hours the representatives of worldwide importance affix their seals to the deed. With a handshake they depart to be escorted to their rooms. The day has been a success."

Times change but not that special something at the Grand Hotel Europe: Today, too, we bid you, the traveller in modern business, a grand welcome, giving you all our attention to make your stay a success.

GRAND HOTEL EUROPE

★★★★★

ST. PETERSBURG

RUSSIA

Nevsky Prospekt/Mikhailovskaya Ulitsa 1/7, 191073 St. Petersburg, Russia
MAILING ADDRESS: P.O. Box 53 FIN-53501 Lappeenranta, Finland

RESO HOTELS

NATIONAL: TEL. (812) 1196000 FAX (812) 119 6001 TELEX 64121073
INTERNATIONAL: TEL. +7 (812) 3296000 FAX +7 (812) 329 6001 TELEX +64121073

Reservations worldwide via SUPRANATIONAL.

YOUR BUSINESS PARTNER IN ST. PETERSBURG.

It's something new.
Dramatically different.
A business partnership unlike any other.

Introducing Americom Business Centers - St. Petersburg, the first facility created to help you meet the demands and seize the opportunities of today's Russia.

- ***State-of-The-Art Services.***

- ***Open 24-Hours.***

- ***Knowledgeable Support Staff.***

- ***Convenient Downtown Location.***

Americom Business Centers, we're your partner in business success.

Nevskij Palace Hotel
Tel: (7812) 275-2001
Fax: (7812) 850-1501 or 184-8923.

St. Petersburg Business Yellow Pages

International Country and City Codes

To dial an international call from Russia, first dial 8, wait for a dial tone, then 10, then the country code and city code as listed below, then the local number.

Algeria	**213**
Argentina	**54**
Buenos Aires	1
Armenia	**7**
Australia	**61**
Melbourne	3
Sydney	2
Austria	**43**
Vienna	1
Azerbaidzhan	**7**
Bahrain	**973**
Belarus	**7**
Belgium	**32**
Brussels	2
Bolivia	**591**
Santa Cruz	33
Canada	**1**
Montreal	514
Ottawa	613
Toronto	416
Vancouver	604
Cameroon	**237**
Chile	**56**
Santiago	2
China	**86**
Beijing	1
Columbia	**57**
Bogota	1
Costa Rica	**506**
Croatia	**385**
Cyprus	**357**
Czech Republic	**42**
Prague	2
Denmark	**45**
Copenhagen	1 or 2
Ecuador	**593**
Egypt	**20**
El Salvador	**503**
Estonia	**372**
Tallinn	2
Ethiopia	**251**
Finland	**358**
Helsinki	0
France	**33**
Paris	1
Georgia	**7**
Germany	**49**
Berlin	30
Bonn	228
Dusseldorf	211
Frankfurt	69
Munich	89
Greece	**30**
Athens	1
Guatemala	**502**
Haiti	**509**
Honduras	**504**
Hong Kong	**852**
Hong Kong	5
Hungary	**36**
Budapest	1
Iceland	**354**
India	**91**
Bombay	22
New Delhi	11
Indonesia	**62**
Jakarta	21
Iran	**98**
Teheran	21
Iraq	**964**
Baghdad	1
Ireland	**353**
Dublin	1
Israel	**972**
Jerusalem	2
Tel Aviv	3
Italy	**39**
Florence	55
Milan	2
Rome	6
Venice	41
Ivory Coast	**225**
Japan	**81**
Tokyo	3
Yokohama	45
Jordan	**962**
Amman	6
Kazakhstan	**7**
Kenya	**254**
Kirgizistan	**7**
Korea, South	**82**
Seoul	2
Kuwait	**965**
Latvia	**371**
Riga	2
Liberia	**231**
Libya	**218**
Liechtenstein	**4175**
Lithuania	**370**
Vilnius	2
Luxembourg	**352**
Malawi	**265**
Malaysia	**60**
Mexico	**52**
Mexico City	5
Moldova	**373**
Chisinau	2
Monaco	**3393**
Morocco	**212**
Namibia	**264**
Nepal	**977**
Netherlands	**31**
Amsterdam	20
The Hague	70
New Zealand	**64**
Nicaragua	**505**
Nigeria	**234**
Norway	**47**
Oslo	2
Oman	**968**
Pakistan	**92**
Islamabad	51
Panama	**507**
Peru	**51**
Phillipines	**63**
Manila	2
Poland	**48**
Warsaw	22
Portugal	**351**
Lisbon	1
Qatar	**974**
Romania	**40**
Bucharest	0
Russia	**7**
Moscow	095
St. Petersburg	812
Saudi Arabia	**966**
Senegal	**221**
Singapore	**65**
Slovakia	**42**
South Africa	**27**
Spain	**34**
Madrid	1
Sri Lanka	**94**
Suriname	**597**
Sweden	**46**
Stockholm	8
Switzerland	**41**
Geneva	22
Zurich	1
Tadzhikistan	**7**
Taiwan	**886**
Thailand	**66**
Bangkok	2
Tunisia	**216**
Turkey	**90**
Istanbul	1
Turkmenistan	**7**
Ukraine	**7**
United Arab Emirates	**971**
UK	**44**
Belfast	232
Glasgow	41
London	71 (inner) 81 (outer)
United States	**1**
Boston	617
Chicago	312
Dallas	214
Houston	713
Los Angeles	213
Montpelier	802
New York	212
San Francisco	415
Seattle	206
Washington	202
Uruguay	**598**
Uzbekistan	**7**
Vatican City	**396**
Venezuela	**58**
Yemen Arab Republic	**967**
Yugoslavia	**381**
Belgrade	11

☑ **See page 6 for Russian and CIS city codes.**

Cross-reference Guide

The following is a list of cross-reference topics for use with the St. Petersburg Business Yellow Pages. Bolded subheadings appear in the Yellow Pages.

Accounting
Advertising
Aerobics, see Gym
Airlines, Charter
Airlines, Commercial
Airports
Ambulance
Antiques
Apartment cleaning
Apartments
Art galleries
Art museums
 see Museums
Associations
ATMs, see Cash advance
Autos, see Cars
Bakeries
Banks, Domestic
Banks, Foreign
Ballet
 see Theater/Ballet
Bars
Beauty salon
 see Hair cutting
Beepers, see Telecom
Bodyguards, see Security
Boat Rides
Books
Bowling
Bridges
Brunch
Bus
Business cards, see Printing
Business Centers
Business publications
 see News
Cable Television
Calling home
 see International phone
Car phone
Car washes
Cars, parts & supplies
Cars, rental
Cars, sales
Cars, service
Cash advances
Casinos
Catering
Cellular phones
Changing money
 see Money changing
Chambers of Commerce
Charitable organizations,
 see Non-profits
Charters, see Airlines, Charters
Churches
 see Religious services
Children, see Recreation, Schools, Clothing, Children's, Toys
Circus
Clothing
Clothing, Children's
Clubs
Coffee shops
Communication
 see International phone, Telegram/Telex, Telecom
Computers, Sales
Computers, Service
Computers, Software
Conference rooms, see Business Centers
Construction
Consulates
Consulting firms
Contact lenses, see Optical
Copiers, Repair
Copiers, Sales
Copying
Cosmetics
Courier, City/Domestic
Courier, International
Credit card loss
Customs
Decor
Dentists
Department stores
Desktop publishing
 see Printing
Dinner
 see Restaurants
Doctors
 see Medical care
Drug stores
Dry cleaning
Electronic mail
Electronics
Electronics, Service
Electronic mail
Embassies, see Consulates
Eye care, see Optical
Exercise
 see Swimming, Gym, Horseback Riding, Golf
Exchanges
Exhibitions
Express mail
Farmer's markets
 see Markets
Fax, see Business Centers
Film

IMPORTANT NUMBERS

01	**FIRE**
02	**Militia**
03	**Ambulance**
07	**Long Distance Telephone**
08	**Time**
09	**Directory Assistance**
006	**Aeroflot Schedules**
061	**Address Information**
066	**Telegram Service**

ACCOUNTING

Current Russian law requires regular auditing for all firms with foreign ownership. This has strained the already busy Western and joint venture accounting firms. Listed below are the major Western firms and joint ventures that can provide a full range of services.

Arthur Andersen, V. O., Bolshoy prosp. 10 ph. 350-4984

Audit Firm, ul. Gorokhovaya 30, ph. 310-4805

Auditor, ul. Dumskaya 1/3, 3rd flr., ph. 110-5999

Bosy, 1 Krasnoarmeyskaya ul. 11, ph. 292-1595

Coopers & Lybrand, Astoria Hotel, room 528, ph. 210-5528

Key to Abbreviations

Abbrev.	Full word	English
bul./bulv.	bulvar	boulevard
	kanal	canal
kor./k.	korpus	building
kv.	kvartira	apartment
	most	bridge
nab.	naberezhnaya	embankment
	ostrov	island
P.S.	Petrogradskaya Storona	Petrograd Side
p.	pereulok	lane
pl.	ploshchad	square
pod.	podyezd	entrance
prosp.	prospekt	avenue
pro.	protok	canal
pr.	proyezd	passage
	reka/reki	river
sh.	shosse	highway
str.	stroyenie	building
	tupik	dead-end
ul.	ulitsa	street
V.O.	Vasiliyevskiy Ostrov	Vasiliyev Island
	val	rampart

Deloitte & Touche, Petropavlovskiy krepost 11, ph. 238-4408

Ernst and Young, ul. M. Morskaya 11, ph. 312-9911

ICPA Corp., Konnogvardeyskiy bul. 4#14, ph. 311-6130

Infraudit, ul. Rostannaya 22, ph. 246-5090

KPMG, nab. kanala Griboyedova 7, 3rd flr., ph. 314-5209

Lenaudit, Nevskiy prosp. 7/9, ph. 312-3700

Leningradintekh, Chkalovskiy prosp. 52, ph. 234-9223

Storbyork-Service, Moskovskiy prosp. 193, kv. 136, ph. 293-7175

Yustas Agency, ul. Sergievskaya 17, ph. 278-0583

ADVERTISING

See also Radio, News

The amazing increase in available media outlets in Russia has likewise increased options for advertising. Listed below are both Western and Russian firms that provide advertising services. To advertise in a specific newspaper, see the White Pages under the paper's name.

Advertising Agency, Yurii Gagarin prosp. 28, k. 1, ph. 299-3982

Blaze Productions, Inc., nab. kanala Griboyedova 97, ph. 311-0459

BMP Reklama A/O, Mezhevoy kan. 5, ph. 114-9541

East Media Advertising GmbH, Chapygina ul. 6, ph. 234-8358

Express Media, Manezhny p. 19, kv. 39, ph. 273-1748

IGREK, Profsoyuzov bul. 19, ph. 311-9595

IMA Press, ul. Zodchevo Rossi 1/3, ph. 110-4651

Imex Servis, ul. Belinskovo 13, ph. 272-4654

Impex, ul. B. Morskaya 35, ph. 310-9441

Instrument, Izmaylovskiy prosp. 27, ph. 311-3510

International Business Services, Inc. (IBS), Rubinstein 8, Box 237, ph. 311-5838

Kommet, Moskovskiy prosp. 28, #450, ph. 259-7415

Len-Sof, Aptekarskiy prosp. 16, ph. 234-2888

Lentelefilm, ul. Chapygina 6, ph. 234-7775

LIC, Nevskiy prosp. 28, ph. 314-5982
Mikrofon, M. Posadskaya ul. 8, ph. 233-3274
Mir Advertising, Nevskiy prosp. 10, ph. 312-7428
Mir Business Center, Leninskiy prosp. 161, ph. 108-4423
Multipleks, Obukhovskoy Oborony prosp. 163, ph. 262-1427
Neva News, ul. Pravdy 10, ph. 164-4765
Nevskiy Advertising & Publishing Co., Babushkina ul. 25, ph. 567-3007
Novy Petersburg, Nastavnikov prosp. 40, ph. 527-4821
Oda Firma, Tolstovo Bul. 38, #3, ph. 465-8548
Reklama, Apraksin p. 11, #56, ph. 113-4930
Rossy Agency, nab. reki Fontanki 51/53, ph. 310-1068
Rostorgreklama, ul. Sedova 13, ph. 567-4768
RUMB, ul. Zaytseva 41, ph. 183-4639
⇨ **Russian Information Services**, Serpukhovskaya ul. 30, ph. 292-7420 {*Where in St. Petersburg, Where in Moscow, Russia Survival Guide, Russian Travel Monthly*}
Severo-Zapad Advertising, Ligovskiy prosp. 44, ph. 164-8710
Smart JV (Finland), Admiralteyskiy prosp. 8/1, ph. 110-6655
Sonneks Agency, ul. Professora Popova 7/8, kv. 8, ph. 234-5800
Sovmarket, 1 Sovetskaya ul. 10, ph. 277-5371
Startplus, ul. Ulyany Gromovoy 8, ph. 277-0213
Svega, Nevskiy prosp. 52/14, ph. 310-1768
Teko, Rubinshteyn ul. 13, ph. 310-0304
TVID, Kamennoostrovskiy prosp. 42, ph. 230-8022
Vika, nab. Obvodnovo kanala 215, kv. 12, ph. 251-4333
VTM & K-90, Leninskiy prosp. 101, ph. 153-5797

AIRLINES, CHARTER

Aero-Balt Service, Pilotov ul. 38, ph. 104-1875
Alak, ul. Pilotov 8, ph. 178-2725
Alfa-700, Gorokhovaya ul. 25
Arctic Road, Boytsova p. 4, ph. 314-1992
ARK Co., Razyeschaya ul. 5, ph. 113-3329
DisCo Plus, Bukharestskaya ul. 6, kor. 3, ph. 269-9324
Europa-Asia Airlines, Rizhskiy prosp. 3, ph. 251-4341
Euro-Flite Oy, Box 187, Vantaa, Finland, ph 358-0-870-2544, fax 358-0-870-2507 {flights to points throughout Russia, originating in Helsinki}
Kustanay Air, ph. 465-8810 {helicopter charters to/from Vyborg and surr. areas}

AIRLINES, COMMERCIAL

Most airlines have offices in Pulkovo II airport and, if not listed here, can be contacted with the help of a hotel service bureau or, in any case, by calling one of these numbers. For addresses, fax or telex numbers, see the Telephone Directory ***(numbers in bold are the airline's office phone number at Pulkovo Airport):***

Aeroflot Airlines, ph. 310-4581, **104-3444**
Air France Airlines, Pulkovo II Airport, ph. **104-3433** or 122-6485
Austrian Airlines, Nevskiy prosp. 57, Nevskiy Palace Hotel, ph. 314-5086
Balkan Airlines, ul. B. Morskaya 36, ph. 315-5030, **104-3436**
British Airways, Nevskiy Palace Hotel, ph. 119-6222, **104-3438**
Czechoslovak Airlines, ul. B. Morskaya 36, ph. 315-5259; **104-3430**
Delta Airlines, ul. B. Morskaya 36, ph. 311-5819; **104-3438**
Finnair Airlines, ul. M. Morskaya 19, ph. 314-3646, 315-9736, **104-3439**
KLM Airlines, Pulkovo II Airport, ph. 104-3440, **104-3440**
Lot Airlines, ul. Karavannaya 1, ph. 273-4560; **104-3437**
Lufthansa Airlines, Vosnesenskiy prosp. 7, ph. 314-4979; **104-3432**
Malev Airlines, prosp. Voznesenskiy 7, ph. 315-5455; **104-3435**
SAS, Nevskiy prosp. 57, Nevskiy Palace Hotel, ph. 314-5086
Swissair, Nevskiy prosp. 57, Nevskiy Palace Hotel, ph. 314-5086; **104-3443**

AIRPORTS

See also Taxis, Car Rental

Pulkovo I Airport, ul. Pilotov 18, block 4, ph. 104-3822
Pulkovo II Airport
Cargo Arrival Information, ph. 104-3494
Cargo Dispatch Information, ph. 104-3446
Domestic Flight Information, ph. 104-3611
International Flight Info., ph. 104-3444

AMBULANCE DIAL 03

⇨**American Medical Center**, nab. reki Fontanki 77, ph. 310-9611
Gastello Hospital, ul. Gastello 21, ph. 108-4066, 108-4808

ANTIQUES

Antiques, Nalichnaya ul. 21, ph. 217-1010
Heritage Art Gallery, Nevskiy prosp. 116, ph. 279-5067
Kollektsioner, Ligovskiy prosp. 61, ph. 164-8226; Ligovskiy prosp. 236, ph. 166-4751; ul. Aviatsionnaya 18, ph. 291-3514
Restovrator Masterskaya, M. Govorova prosp. 43, ph. 252-7474
Salon Sankt Peterburg, ul. Furshtadskaya 42, ph. 273-0341

APARTMENT CLEANING

Agency for Apartment Cleaning, Zakharevskaya ul. 14, ph. 273-3851 {hours 10-17:30}
Cleaning Services Losk, Shpalernaya ul. 30, ph. 272-9141 {offices only, hours 9-17:30}
Gefest, Marshala Govorova ul. 31, ph. 252-3066 {M-Sat. hours 10-17}
Peterburgskie Zori, Nevskiy prosp. 95, 5th floor, ph. 277-4547 {hours 9-18}

INCREASED SALES

No other directory of St. Petersburg touches as wide a Western audience and offers such exclusive advertising. To find out more about advertising in ***Where in St. Petersburg****, phone RIS in the US at 802-223-4955, fax 802-223-6105.*

APARTMENTS

More and more Russians are renting their apartments to cover the rising cost of living. There are hundreds of firms, varying in reputability, that will help you find such an apartment. Below is a list of reliable Western and Russian agencies. The best of these provide both rental and renovation services.

Astoria-Service, Borovaya ul. 11/13, ph. 112-1583
Deon, Suvorovskiy prosp. 62, ph. 271-2868
Dom Plus, nab. kanala Griboyedova 3, ph. 312-8873; ul. Karavannaya 4, ph. 117-2181
Ecopolis, Zanevskiy prosp. 32, k. 2, kv. 3, ph. 528-2666
Finservis, ul. Engelsa 51, ph. 554-3755
Inform-Future Business Center, ul. Tambovskaya 12, ph. 312-3078
Inpredservice, Kutuzova nab. 34, ph. 272-1500 {Dachas, hours 9-13, 14-18}
K-Keskus, ul. Ordinarnaya 7, ph. 232-0723
LT Estate, 1 Krasnoarmeyskaya ul. 11, ph. 110-1455
Luch, 5 Krasnoarmeyskaya ui. 22, ph. 292-3714
Nevskiy Zori, Nevskiy prosp. 95, ph. 277-4252
North Hause, ul. Chekhova 5, ph. 273-4674
Oven, ul. Mokhovaya 27-29 kv. 21, ph. 275-4069
Restavrator, ul. Marata 17, ph. 315-4807

ART GALLERIES

Andreyevskiy Dom, V. O., 8 Liniya 43, ph. 218-0614
Antiques, Nalichnaya ul. 21, ph. 217-1010
Ariadna, Profsoyuzov bul. 11, #17, ph. 311-6997
Art Boutique, Nevskiy prosp. 51, ph. 113-1495
Art Shop Varyag, V. O., Sredny prosp. 88, ph. 356-6139
Aster, Kuybysheva ul. 4, ph. 233-7300
Autograph, ul. Lomonosova 5, ph. 310-2602 {9-18}
Blok Central Library Art Gallery, Nevskiy prosp. 20, ph. 311-7777
Borey Art Gallery, The, Liteyny prosp. 58, ph. 273-3693

Decorative Design Center, prosp. Rimskovo-Korsakova 24/135, ph. 114-3766

Elena, Morskaya nab. 15, ph. 356-0313

Exhibition Center of the Association of Artists, ul. B. Morskaya 38, ph. 314-6432 {13-19, closed Mondays}

Forum Art Gallery, V. O., 6 Liniya 17, ph. 213-6787

Galereya 10-10, Pushkinskaya ul. 10, kv. 10, ph. 315-2832

Galereya Petropol, Millionnaya ul. 27, kv. 2, ph. 315-3414

Galereya-102, Nevskiy prosp. 102, ph. 273-6842

Garmonia, Kamennoostrovskiy prosp. 26/28, ph. 235-0814

Golubaya Gostinaya, B. Morskaya ul. 38, ph. 315-7414

Graphic Arts Center, Sverdlovskaya nab. 64, ph. 224-0622

Heritage Art Gallery, Nevskiy prosp. 116, ph. 279-5067

Inter-Galereya, Makarova nab. 20, ph. 232-6982

Klyonovaya Alleya, Manezhnaya pl., ph. 219-2129

Kolomna, Rimskogo-Korsakova prosp. 24, ph. 114-3150

Lavka Khudozhnikov Art Shop, Nevskiy prosp. 31, ph. 110-5016; Nevskiy prosp. 45, ph. 311-2196; Nevskiy prosp. 8, ph. 312-6193

Lipetsk Art International, Partizana Germana ul. 3, kv. 428, ph. 164-6956

Manege Central Exhibition Hall, Isaakevskaya pl. 1, ph. 314-8859

Milena Art Gallery, Muchnoy p. 2, ph. 310-3482

Mir Art and Book Store, Liteyny prosp. 64, ph. 273-5012; Nevskiy prosp. 13, ph. 311-5473; Nevskiy prosp. 16, ph. 312-8535

Palitra Gallery, Nevskiy prosp. 166, ph. 277-1216

Prospekt Art Salon, Kronverskiy prosp. 9, ph. 232-3591

Ritm-Tsenturion, Turbinnaya ul. 11, ph. 186-7689

RosDesign, Solyanoy p. 13, ph. 279-4196

Rosmonumentiskusstvo, nab. Obvodnovo kanala 17, ph. 277-2797

Russian Arts Ltd., ul. Inzhenernaya 4, ph. 315-3183 {closed Mon.}

Salon Sankt Peterburg, ul. Furshtadskaya 42, ph. 273-0341

Sankt-Peterburg Art Salon, Nevskiy prosp. 54, ph. 311-4020

Shkola Sidlina, Grafskiy P. 7, ph. 311-2245

ASSOCIATIONS

Academy of Sciences Geographical Society, p. Grivtsova 10, ph. 315-8535

All-Russian Society of Handicapped Persons, Krasnogvardeyskiy p. 8, ph. 245-2779

All-Union Society of the Deaf, Pavlovsk, ul. Kommunarov 16, ph. 470-6244

ArgosYoung Business Persons Assn., Gatchinskaya ul. 11/56, ph. 232-7123

Association for Eastern and Central European Businesspeople, ul. M. Morskaya 14, ph. 312-8097

Association of Commercial Banks, ul. Plekhanova 36, ph. 319-9249

Association of Joint Ventures, ul. Plekhanova 36, ph. 312-7954

AVEKS Association, 3 Krasnoarmeyskaya 12, ph. 292-4837

Baltika-1 Association, Konnogvardeyskiy bulvar 4, pod. 6, ph. 314-1287

Baltrans Transport Enterprises Assn., ul. Dvinskaya 3, ph. 315-8986

Biokompleks Ltd, ul. Pochtamtskaya 14, ph. 312-7840

Center for Humanitarian and Business Cooperation, nab. reki Moyki 59, ph. 315-6028

Etude Fraternity of Artists, Zagorodny prosp. 14, pom. 77, ph. 315-4318

Fortuna International Tourism Association, Kievskaya ul. 22/24, kv. 92, ph. 298-8969

Fund for the Support of Small Enterprises, Chernomorskiy 4, ph. 210-8851

Kachestvo Business Association, Rizhskiy prosp. 60, ph. 251-2739

Kontinent Regional Commercial Assn., Izmaylovskiy prosp. 4, ph. 292-3471; ul. Sedova 37, ph. 560-9428

North-West Union of Businessmen, nab. Obvodnovo kanala 48, ph. 166-1167

Potential Center for Business Cooperation, Kolpino prosp. Pavlova 42, ph. 481-9524

Russian Union of Theatrical Workers, Nevskiy prosp. 86, ph. 272-9482
Russian Union of Writers, Shpalernaya ul. 18, ph. 279-0874
Sciences Botanical Society of Russia, ul. Professora Popova 2, ph. 234-9602
St. Petersburg Assn. of Independent Artists, Nevskiy prosp. 20, ph. 311-7777
St. Petersburg Culture Fund, Nevskiy prosp. 31, ph. 311-8349
St. Petersburg Folk Art Assn., ul. Chelieva 6, ph. 263-6786
St. Petersburg Foreign Economic Assn., Zagorodny prosp. 68, ph. 292-1455
Svet All-Union Society of the Blind, ul. Kostyushko 17a, ph. 295-1493
Teleinform Business Association, Ligovskiy prosp. 56e, kv. 90, ph. 164-1236
Union of Industrial Associations, Smolny, 5th ent., ph. 278-1580
Voyage Association, Rizhskiy prosp. 34 kv. 26, ph. 251-0121
Vtorchermet Production Assn., Khimicheskiy p. 4, ph. 252-1074

B

BAKERIES

Neva-Chupa-Chups, B. Sampsonievskiy prosp. 77/7, ph. 245-3613
Sever Bakery, Nevskiy prosp. 44, ph. 311-2589
Volshebny Kray Bakery, P.S., Bolshoy prosp. 15/3, ph. 233-3253

BANK, DOMESTIC

Russian banks have been springing up faster than mushrooms after rain. Here is a list of the larger Russian banks.

ABINSET Bank, Zakharyevskaya ul. 35, ph. 275-6636
Association of Commercial Banks, ul. Plekhanova 36, ph. 319-9249
Astrobank, Nevskiy prosp. 58, ph. 311-3600; ***Kuibyshevskiy Branch***, ul. Dostoyevskovo 5, ph. 164-0278
AvtoVAZbank, 2 Sovetskaya ul. 3/7, ph. 274-4948
Baltiyskiy Bank, ul. Sadovaya 34, ph. 310-0580
Bamkredit, prosp. Yuriya Gagarina 1, ph. 294-8536
Central Bank of Russia, St. Petersburg Branch, nab. reki Fontanki 70/72, ph. 312-3940
Credobank, ul. Mokhovaya 26, ph. 275-0333
Ekonombank, Nevskiy prosp. 78-19, ph. 275-5845
Energomash Joint Stock Bank, ul. Karavannaya 1, ph. 314-9954
Ganzakombank, Pl. Rastrelli 2, ph. 273-0521
Inbankprodukt, Mokhovaya ul. 20, ph. 273-5256
Industry and Construction Bank, Nevskiy prosp. 38, ph. 110-5526; ul. Mikhailovskaya 4, ph. 110-4909
Konversbank (Bank of Conversion), North-West Affiliate, nab. Chyornoy Rechki 24, ph. 239-7501
Kredit Petersburg, ul. Dumskaya 1, ph. 238-6058
Mariynskiy Bank, B. Porokhovskaya ul. 52 k 2, ph. 224-0440
Neva-Komplekt, Fontanka nab. 92, kor. 2, ph. 312-3423
Neva-Kreditbank, ul. Sadovaya 21, ph. 314-7485
Northern Trade Bank, ul. Nekrasova 14, ph. 275-8798
Patent Co-operative Bank, Grecheskiy prosp. 10, ph. 272-5485
Peterburgskiy Lesopromyshlenny Bank, Krapivniy P. 5, ph. 541-8217
Petroagroprombank, nab. kanala Griboyedova 13, ph. 315-4492
Petrovskiy Bank, ul. Ruzovskaya 8, ph. 112-6687; Zakharyevskaya ul. 14, #2, ph. 275-7636
Rossia Bank, Smolny, podyezd 4, k. 422, ph. 278-1078
Rozhdestvenskiy, Grecheskiy prosp. 15, ph. 274-9682
Ruskobank, ul. B. Morskaya 15, ph. 315-7833
Russian Commercial-Industrial Bank, B. Morskaya ul. 15, ph. 314-6932
Russian Mining Bank, ul. Shkiperskiy pro. 5
Sankt-Peterburgskiy Birzhevoy Bank, Ordinarnaya ul. 19, ph. 232-5980

Sberbank, a centrally-located Sberbank (Savings Bank) is at: Nevskiy prosp. 82, ph. 272-9089 {For a list of several other branches of Sberbank, which (since it used to be the only bank for consumers) are all over St. Petersburg and thus too numerous to list here, see the White Pages, under Sberbank.}

St. Petersburg Bank, Head office, Vosnesenskiy prosp. 16, ph. 314-6095 {open 9-18}; Admiralteyskaya nab. 8, ph. 210-7788; Dom Knigi, ph. 219-9417 {open 9-21}; Nevskiy prosp. 38, ph. 110-4945 {open 9-21}; **Gavanskiy Branch**, ul. Shevchenko 1, ph. 217-1879; **Kuybyshevskiy Branch**, Nevskiy prosp. 62, ph. 319-9943; **Okhtinskiy Branch**, Malookhtinskiy prosp. 53, ph. 528-7539

St. Petersburg Clearinghouse, Ligovskiy prosp. 56g, ph. 164-6630

St. Petersburg Innovation Bank, ul. Chaykovskovo 24, ph. 279-0004

Stankinbank, inter-branch, Baskov P. 12, ph. 273-1671

Stroyinvest, V.O., 2 Liniya 5, ph. 218-6689

Tekhnokhim Joint Stock Bank, nab. Krasnovo Flota 10, ph. 311-6994

Tekobank Joint Stock Bank, Ispolkomskaya ul. 7/9, ph. 277-1875; Zagorodny prosp. 5, ph. 314-2235

Tsarskotselskiy Bank, pl. Konstitutsiy 2, ph. 123-0684

Veda, p. Pirogova 18, ph. 315-2665

Vitabank, ul. B. Morskaya 59, ph. 311-5193

Vnesheconombank (Foreign Economic Bank), ul. B. Morskaya 29, ph. 314-6059

BANKS, FOREIGN

A recent law allows foreign banks to open full-service banks in Russia. A few have chosen to open such branches in St. Petersburg. A few simply maintain representations.

Credit Lyonnais Russie, Nevskiy prosp. 12, box 139, ph. 210-3100

Deutsche Bank, nab. kanala Griboyedova 101, ph. 315-0216

Dresdner Bank, Isakievskaya pl. 11, ph. 312-2100

Intermaritime Bank/The Bank of New York, ph. 906-0673

International Moscow Bank, Voznesenskaya prosp. 1/12, ph. 311-9857

BARS

Almost all major tourist hotels have bars. Many new bars have also opened up outside hotels to meet the needs of the growing foreign community. Some of the better choices in both categories are:

Angleterre Bar, Hotel Astoria, ph. 210-5838

Baku Restaurant, Sadovaya ul. 12, ph. 315-0752

⇨**Basil Piano Bar**, Hotel Olympia, ph. 119-6800

Bavaria Restaurant, Lermontovskiy prosp. 43/1 (Hotel Sovetskaya), ph. 259-2454

Beer Garden, Nevskiy prosp. 86, ph. 275-7620

Beer Stube, Nevskiy Palace Hotel, ph. 311-6366

Cafe-Bar, Nevskiy Palace Hotel, ph. 311-6366

Chaika, nab. kanala Griboyedova 14, ph. 312-4631

Desertholl, ul. Belinskovo 5, ph. 273-2952

Diana, Sadovaya ul. 56, ph. 310-3332

Eldorado Discotec, Hotel Karelia, ul. Tukhachevskovo 27, k. 2, ph. 226-3110 {cc, open 22-5}

Elefant, prosp. Kosygina 7, kor. 1

Galspe Restaurant, Leninskiy prosp. 127, ph. 254-5582 {open 12-6}

Garus, Basseynaya ul. 41, ph. 298-2358

Greta, Suvorovskiy prosp. 57, ph. 275-6246

Grot, Aleksandrovskiy Park 2, ph. 238-4690

Heineken, Hotel Pribaltiyskaya, ph. 264-5816

John Bull Pub, Nevskiy prosp. 79, ph. 164-9877 {cc, closed 18-19}

Kakadu, prosp. Chkalovskiy 58, ph. 234-6650

Karavella Bar, Lyoni Golikova ul. 27, ph. 152-5268

Kazbek, Bukharestskaya ul. 43, ph. 260-8706

Kodri, Moskovskiy prosp. 5, ph. 310-3078

Korchma, prosp. Engelsa 83, ph. 554-1449

Korvet, Razyezzhaya ul. 10, ph. 315-9145

Kvadrat Jazz Club, ul. Pravdy 10, ph. 164-8508 {open 19-23}

Las Vegas Show Lounge, Hotel Commodore, ph. 119-6666
Lum, Mokhovaya ul. 39
Luna, B. Konyushennaya ul. 5, ph. 312-4620
Malvina, Sredny prosp. 14, ph. 213-5147
Melody JV Restaurant (Sweden), Sverdlovskaya nab. 62, ph. 227-2676 {cc, open 12-18, 19-1}
Nadezhda, ul. Belinskovo 5, ph. 272-2952
New Orleans Night Club, Hotel Commodore, ph. 119-6666
Night Bar, Hotel Astoria, ph. 311-4206
⇨ **Night Club**, Grand Hotel Europe, ph. 119-6000
Nevskiy 40, Nevskiy prosp. 40, ph. 311-9066 {cc, open 12-24}
Palm Beach Pool Bar, Hotel Commodore, ph. 119-6666
⇨ **Panorama Bar**, Peterhof Hotelship, ph. 213-6321 {cc}
Pietari Restaurant, Moskovskiy prosp. 220, ph. 293-2397 {cc, open 12-3}
Roza Vetrov, Moskovskiy prosp. 204, ph. 293-0866
Rumor-2, 7 Sovetskaya ul. 36, ph. 211-1814
⇨ **Sadko's**, Grand Hotel Europe, ph. 119-6000
Sakura Restaurant, ul. Narodnaya 45, ph. 263-3594
Sky bar, Hotel Commodore, ph. 119-6666
Troitskiy Trading Center Bar, Kurlyandskaya ul. 24
Viktoria, Industrialny prosp. 9, ph. 524-1966
⇨ **White Nights Bar**, Hotel Olympia, ph. 119-6800
Warsteiner Forum, Nevskiy prosp. 120, ph. 277-2914 {cc, open 12-2}

BOAT RIDES

One of the most pleasant activities for a sunny, summer day is a cruise along the rivers and canals of St. Petersburg. It offers great scenery for newcomers, and plenty of sunshine and water for experienced residents. There is, perhaps, no better way to see the "Venice of the North."

Aqua Excurs, nab. reki Moyki 8, ph. 314-5645
Central Yacht Club, Petrovskaya Kosa 7, ph. 235-7217
Maritime Passenger Terminal, Pl. Morskoy Slavy 1, ph. 355-1310 {to Helsinki/Stockholm}; Information on International Travel, ph. 355-1312
River Passenger Terminal, prosp. Obukhovskoy Oborony 195, ph. 262-0239
Rivers of St. Petersburg: Departures every 15 minutes from landings by Anichkov bridge (where Nevskiy prosp. meets nab. reki Fontanka, **J16**, or oppposite the main entrance of the Hermitage museum, **H15**. There are also night tours of the rivers during White Nights.
Suburbs & Kronshtadt: In summer (May to October), boats leave for Petrodvorets every 30 minutes from the landing in front of the Hermitage. Boats leave every 30 minutes or so for Kronshtadt from Tuchkov bridge, **G14**.

BOOKS

Book vendors are on every street corner and in every downtown underpass. They carry a range of 10-cent romances, dictionaries, and an occasional classic. Quality art books, classics, and dictionaries are now available in many Russian book stores, but the best selection is still found in front of the major tourist sites, and especially along Nevskiy prospekt. Western literature is not widely available in St. Petersburg, although there are a few well-hidden caches, in particular the Bukinist in the courtyard of Liteyny pr. 59.

Die-hard book lovers will want to visit the weekend book fair near Yelizarovskaya metro station.

Antikvarno-Bukinisticheskaya Kniga, Nevskiy prosp. 18, ph. 315-5078
Bukinist, Liteyny prosp. 59, ph. 273-2504 {used and new Western fiction}
Burevestnik Book Store, Nevskiy prosp. 141, ph. 277-1522
Dom Knigi, Nevskiy prosp. 28, ph. 219-9422 {St. Petersburg's largest}
Dom Stroitelnoy Knigi, Bolsheokhtinskiy prosp. 1, ph. 224-1575 {construction/engineering books}
Dom Voyennoy Knigi, Nevskiy prosp. 20, ph. 311-5792 {military literature}
Economic Literature & Business Press, ul. Razyezhaya 16/18, ph. 312-9500

Energia, Moskovskiy prosp. 189, ph. 293-0147

Gelios, Bolshevikov prosp. 19, ph. 588-5707

Gippokrat Book Store, ul. Lenina 20, ph. 232-5469 {medical books}

Hobby, Dekabristov ul. 34, ph. 114-0639

Iskatel Book Store, nab. reki Moyki 51, ph. 312-7114

Isskustvo Bookstore, Nevskiy prosp. 16, ph. 312-8535 {art books; 11-20, closed Sun.}

Knigolub Bookstore, Novoizmailovskiy prosp. 40, k. 1, ph. 295-9028

Knizhnaya Lavka Pisateley, Nevskiy prosp. 66, ph. 314-4858

Maska Bookstore, Nevskiy prosp. 13, ph. 311-0312

Mir Art and Book Store, Liteyny prosp. 64, ph. 273-5012; Nevskiy prosp. 13, ph. 311-5473; Nevskiy prosp. 16, ph. 312-8535

Mysl Bookstore, Novocherkasskiy prosp. 41, ph. 528-8402

Petrograd Bookstore, Stachek prosp. 67, kor. 3, ph. 252-3316

Planeta Bookstore, Liteyny prosp. 30, ph. 273-8815

Podpisniye Izdaniy Bookstore, Liteyny prosp. 57, ph. 273-5053

Prometey Bookstore, Narodnaya ul. 16, ph. 263-8676

Russkoye Iskusstvo, Millionnaya ul. 5/1, ph. 312-8115 {art books}

St. Petersburg Book Store, Nevskiy prosp. 52, ph. 311-1651

Sudostroitel Bookstore, Sadovaya ul. 40, ph. 315-3117 {maritime books}

Tekhnicheskaya Kniga Bookstore, Pushkinskaya ul. 2, ph. 164-6565

Transportnaya Kniga Bookstore, Pushkinskaya ul. 20, ph. 164-9807

Variant Bookstore, Komsomola ul. 16, ph. 542-4971

Vekom Bookstore, Slavy prosp. 15, ph. 261-8682

Zodiak Bookstore, Gorokhovaya ul. 50, ph. 310-7965

Petersburg Under Glass

Full-sheet laminated versions of the map in the back of this book are available from the publisher.

BOWLING

Kirov Stadium, Krestovskiy ostrov, Morskoy prosp., ph. 235-4877 {open 9-22}

Pribaltiyskaya Hotel Bowling Lanes, Hotel Pribaltiyskaya, ph. 356-1663 {$25/hr., 12-22; reservations recommended}

BRIDGES

St. Petersburg is unique for its bridges. If you are out carousing early in the morning, when the bridges are raised for river traffic, you may find yourself stranded if you don't plan ahead.

Bridge-raising schedule (Apr-Oct)

Aleksandra Nevskovo: 2:35-4:50
Birzhevoy: 2:25-3:20 and 3:40-4:40
Bolshoy Okhtinskiy: 2:45-4:45
Bolshoy Krestovskiy: 2:05-2:35 and 4:45-5:20
Bolshoy Petrovskiy: 1:25-2:00 and 5:00-5:45
Dvortsovy: 1:55-3:05 and 3:15-4:45
Grenedirskiy: 2:45-3:45 and 4:20-4:50
Kamenoostrovskiy: 2:15-3:00 and 4:05-4:50
Kantemirovskiy: 2:45-3:45 and 4:20-4:50
Leytenant Shmidta: 1:55-2:55 and 3:15-4:50
Liteyny: 2:10-4:40
Sampsioniyevskiy: 2:10-2:25 and 3:20-4:25
Stroitely: 2:25-3:20
Troitskiy: 2:00-4:40
Tuchkov: 2:00-3:10 and 3:40-4:40
Ushakovskiy: 2:15-2:55 and 3:55-4:30
Volodarskiy: 2:05-3:55 and 4:30-5:50

BRUNCH

Astoria Hotel, ul. B. Morskaya 39, ph. 210-5838, offers a top-rate brunch.

⇨ **Grand Hotel Europe**, Mikhailovskaya ul. 1/7, ph. 113-8066, Jazz Brunch for $30 per person, from 12-15 each Sunday.

Nevskiy 27 (located at Nevsky prosp. 27) offers good pastries and coffee.

⇨ Ship hotels **Olympia** and **Peterhof**. On a warm Sunday, try brunching on the top deck restaurants of these exclusive hotels.

Schwabskiy Domik, Krasnogvardeyskiy prosp. 28/19, ph. 528-2211, serves a very good selection of pastries and coffees, open 8-20, Sunday 12-19, closed 11:30-12 and 15-16.

BUS

Finnord, Italianskaya ul. 37, ph. 314-8951, daily bus service to and from Finland (the city of Lahti), open 9:30-18, Saturday and Sunday 12-17. Cost is $52.

Hotel Moskva, pod. 5, room 114, ph. 274-2095, twice weekly bus to Helsinki, cost is $37 or $30 for students.

Sovtransavto, Hotel Pulkovskaya, ph. 264-5125, daily bus from this hotel, the Grand Hotel Europe and the Hotel Helen to Helsinki. Cost is $60.

BUSINESS CENTERS

Most of the centers listed below can help if you need to send a fax, make an international call, make copies or use a conference room.

Agfa Salon, Nevskiy prosp. 20, ph. 311-9974 {open 9-21, color copies}

Alliance Ltd., Lermontovskiy prosp. 43/1, ph. 259-3442

⇨**Americom Business Center**, Nevskiy Palace Hotel, ph. 275-2001

Business Center, Nevskiy prosp. 87/2, ph. 279-4376; Suvorovskiy prosp. 47, ph. 275-6436

Business Center T. A. M., Nevskiy prosp. 16, ph. 312-7214

Cross Roads Business Center, Poltavskaya ul. 10, ph. 277-4197

⇨**Europe Business Center, Grand Hotel Europe**, Mikhaylovskaya ul. 1/7, ph. 312-0072

Expo-Center, nab. Obvodnovo kanala 93a, ph. 210-1820

Fax Service, ul. B. Morskaya 3/5, ph. 314-0140

International Business Services, Inc. (IBS), Rubinstein 8, Box 237, ph. 311-5838

Intersotrudnichestvo Business Center, p. Boytsova 5, ph. 310-0169

Mir Business Center, Leninskiy prosp. 161, ph. 108-4423

Mramorny Dvorets Business Center, Millionaya ul. 5/1, ph. 219-3570

Neptun Business Center, nab. Obvodnovo kanala 93-a, ph. 210-1707

Orgtekhnika, p. Antonenko 6, ph. 319-9259

Pribaltiyskaya Business Center, Hotel Pribaltiyskaya, ph. 356-4563

Razvitiye Regional Commercial Center, prosp. Obukhovskoy Oborony 13, ph. 567-8078

Retur Business Center JV (Finland), Astoria Hotel, ul. Gertsena 39, ph. 311-7362

C

CABLE TELEVISION

Most St. Petersburg apartment buildings are wired for cable. These companies can tap in to that cable to provide access to international TV channels.

Baltic Sputnik, Litovskaya ul. 10, ph. 245-2160

Pyotr Velikiy, Sredneokhtinskiy prosp. 52, ph. 526-6631

CAR PHONE

Delta Telecom, ul. Chekhova 18, ph. 275-4149; **Showroom**, ul. B. Morskaya 22, ph. 314-6126

CAR WASHES

Autobaltservice, Nakhimova ul. 5, kor. 1, ph. 356-7701 {hours 8-12, 13-20, HC & Rbls}

Avto-Motors (Opel), Novoizmailovski 4, ph. 296-5587

Forward Car Wash, Luzhskaya ul. 3, ph. 530-4782 {hours 8-20}

Lada-EN 65 Car Wash, Energetikov prosp. 65, ph. 226-5678 {hours 8-21}

Logovaz Severo Zapad, Vitebskiy prosp. 17, kor. 2, ph. 298-4608 {hours 9-22}

CARS, PARTS & SUPPLIES

See also Hardware, Security and Cars, Service

4 Kolesa, Irinovskiy prosp. 2, ph. 222-4216

Agro, Utkin prosp. 13/6, ph. 528-6959

Autokhim, prosp. Stachek 106, ph. 158-3598

Avtosalon, ul. Marshala Zakharova 21, ph. 142-5527

Cars Auto Parts Store, prosp. Energetikov 65, ph. 226-1922

Elena, Kolomenskaya ul. 29, ph. 312-7072

Faeton, prosp. Stachek 55, ph. 184-5108

Favorit, Saperny p. 15

Feya-2, Moskovskiy prosp. 124

Karavan-2, ul. Shotlandskaya 1, ph. 114-9883

Konsol, ul. V. Yermaka 10, ph. 219-7070

Kvadrat, 3 Zhernovskaya ul. 51/3

Lada, prosp. Stachek 106, ph. 158-3598

Lenkomissiontorg, prosp. Engelsa 66, ph. 554-0076

Libertas, ul. Pestelya 9, ph. 273-7127

Lik, Telezhnaya ul. 17/19, ph. 277-2937

Mika, Oktyabrskiy nab. 70, kor. 1, ph. 263-9187

Neste, Pulkovskoye sh. 44a, ph. 123-3423

Nezavisimost, Fontanka 46, ph. 311-1589

Orion-Service, V. O., 17 Liniya 42, ph. 350-3581

Ow-QuastJV (German), prosp. Morisa Toreza 40, ph. 247-8925 {Audi, VW}

Partner, Severny prosp. 23, ph. 556-3966

Poliustrovsky, Kommuny ul. 59, ph. 227-7413

Pyatoye Koleso, Sinopskaya nab. 30, ph. 274-0051

Rosavtotorg, Leninskiy prosp. 146, ph. 255-9097

Shinomontazh, Severny prosp. 23, ph. 556-3966

Sovinteravtoservice, ul. Gogolya 19, ph. 315-9758

Telets, Bryantseva ul. 7, ph. 594-5000

Tempo Autosalon, ul. Shaumana 2, ph. 224-3609 {American cars}

Universal, Lebedeva ul. 31, ph. 541-8187

Yugo-Zapad Avto, Petergofskoye sh. 3, kor. 2, ph. 155-6311

CARS, RENTAL

See also Limos

A number of car rental opportunities are available. As in the West, your best bet is to call around and compare prices and models, and bargain.

Astoria Rent-A-Car, Vyborgskaya nab. 5/2, ph. 210-5858

Astoria-Servis, Borovaya ul. 11/13, ph. 112-1583

Auto-Vo Firm, prosp. Stachek 106, ph. 158-5777

Autohouse, nab. reki Moyki 56, ph. 312-9045

Avis Rent-a-Car, Konnogvardeyskiy bul. 4, ph. 312-6318

⇨**Grand Hotel Europe Car Rental**, Grand Hotel Europe, ph. 113-8071

Hertz Interauto Firm, ul. Ispolkomovskaya 9/11, ph. 277-4032

Itmas, Bogatyrskiy prosp. 6, k. 5, ph. 395-3504

Matralen Airport Limousine Service, Lyubotinskiy pr. 5, ph. 298-3648

Mobil-Service, ul. Frunze 15, ph. 164-6066

Petrograd-92 Firm, Hotel Astoria, ph. 210-5858

Sovinteravtoservice, Malodetskoselskiy prosp. 24, ph. 292-1257

Tekhnicheskiy Tsentr, Ligovskiy prosp. 256, ph. 297-1768

Transwell Sankt-Petersburg, Lermontovskiy prosp. 37, ph. 113-7253

CARS, SALES

Car sales is one of the fastest growing businesses in Russia. This is directed not so much at the Western community, as it is at the nouveau-riche *Russian business class. You can now purchase virtually any make or model of car in Russia. Call around to get complete information and verify taxation expenses.*

Accis, ul. Shota Rustavelli 31a, ph. 538-6781

Americar (Chrysler), Piskarevskiy prosp. 39, ph. 544-0590

Ancher-Auto, prosp. Prosvoshcheniya 80, ph. 540-8746

ARS, Leninskiy prosp. 121, ph. 254-7611

Art-Motors, Kubinskaya ul. 81, ph. 122-5418 {Opel}

Avto-Motors, Novoizmailovskiy 4, ph. 296-5587 {Opel, GM}

Auto Star, prosp. Energetikov 65, ph. 226-9980

Autohaus St. Petersburg, ul. Rubinshteyna 6-8, ph. 113-1895

Avtomobili, prosp. Stachek 106, ph. 157-0459

Avtozapchasti, Kubinskaya ul. 76, ph. 290-4833
Bast, prosp. Rayevskovo 16, ph. 247-7412
Deymos, Smolny prosp. 11, ph. 110-0267
EFO, Omskaya ul. 21, ph. 246-9242
Faeton, Poklonnogorskaya ul. 14, ph. 292-3038
Honda, ul. Nakhimova 5, ph. 356-7701
Inter-Avto, prosp. Prosveshcheniya 80, kor. 2, ph. 530-8087
Korona-Logovaz, Kamennoostrovskiy prosp. 5, ph. 238-1915 {Mercedes}
Lan International Inc., Predportovaya ul. 40-b, ph. 123-3816
Lider, Bronnitskaya ul. 17, ph. 110-1093
Metro-Auto, Leninskiy prosp. 160, ph. 295-5449
Neste, Pulkovskoye sh. 44a, ph. 123-3423
Oblik, nab. reki Fontanki 20
Ow-QuastJV (German), prosp. Morisa Toreza 40, ph. 247-8925 {Audi, VW}
Petroff Motors (General Motors), Vyazovaya ul. 4, ph. 235-2386
Peter-Lada, Kingisepskoye sh. 50, ph. 132-4450
RCC (Russian Car Center), Leninskiy prosp. 160, ph. 295-5449
Sitek, ul. Rentgena 3, ph. 232-1100
SPKW, Yekaterinskiy prosp. 21, ph. 249-9088 {BMW}
Swed Car St. Petersburg, prosp. Bolshevikov 33 k 1, ph. 586-7718 {Volvo}
TDV-Auto, ul. Kommuny 16, ph. 521-7719 {Ford}
Titus, Serpukhovskaya ul. 1, ph. 292-3976
Tornado, Ispolkomskaya ul. 9/11, ph. 275-3065
Triada, ul. Zhukovskovo 22, ph. 275-7921
Ural, nab. reki Fontanki 76, ph. 112-5832
West-Ingriya, Nevskiy prosp. 86

CARS, SERVICE

ACD AutoJV (USA), ul. Kalinina 59a, ph. 186-0000
Aksel V, ul. Savushkina 15, ph. 538-6781
Art-Motors, Kubinskaya ul. 81, ph. 122-5418 {Opel}
ArtAG, Kubinskaya ul. 86, ph. 122-2072
Autoservice, Oktyabrskaya nab. 40-42, ph. 587-7249
Avto, ul. Kalinina 59-a, ph. 186-0000
Avto-Motors, Novoizmailovskiy 4, ph. 296-5587 {Opel, GM}
Avtobaltservice JV (Sweden), ul. Nakhimova 5, k. 1, ph. 356-4525
Avtodvor, ul. Rustaveli 7, ph. 249-1370
Avtomobilist Coop, Lodeynopolskaya ul. 7, ph. 235-2817
Avtoremont, Moskovskiy prosp. 181, ph. 293-3373; Telezhnaya ul. 7/9
Avtotekhobsluzhivanie, Bogatyrskiy prosp. 12, ph. 395-3095
AvtoVAZtekhobsluzhivaniye, Kingisepskoye sh. 50, ph. 132-4789
Ayaks, Krasnoputilovskaya ul. 69, ph. 184-6073
Baltiya Firm, ul. Shkapina 10, ph. 252-1062
Barvas, 8 Sovetskaya ul. 4, ph. 271-2069
Bikar, Cheliyeva p. 16, ph. 586-9528
Car-Service, Bukharetskaya ul. 1, ph. 166-9267
Doroga, prosp. Narodnovo Opolcheniya 201-a, ph. 155-9150
Driver, Leninskiy prosp. 146, ph. 255-9097
Elkom, Sotsialisticheskaya ul. 16, ph. 112-5906
Fakt, Khimicheskiy p. 6, ph. 252-0738
Gamma, ul. Salova 51, ph. 166-6377
Ideal, Laboratornaya ul. 29, ph. 540-8831
Ikar, Kubinskaya ul. 86, ph. 122-5763
Inavtoservice, Vitebskiy prosp. 17/2, ph. 294-0533
Itus, Leninskiy prosp. 142a, ph. 254-7949
Karelia, Petrovskiy Ostrov 2-g, ph. 238-4047
Kassandra, Novorossiyskaya ul. 46/3, ph. 550-0854
Kross, Respublikanskaya ul. 20, ph. 528-5756
Kvarta JV(USA), ul. Yakornaya 17, ph. 222-5493
Marin-Avtoservice, Lakhtinskaya ul. 5
Mekhanobr-Service, 21 Liniya 8-a
Mobil-Service, Kronshtadtskaya ul. 1, ph. 183-3868
Neste, Pulkovskoye sh. 44a, ph. 123-3423
Nevskiy, ul. Perigina 22, ph. 568-0354
NN Plus, ul. Karpinskovo 38
Northauto, Khimicheskiy p. 8, ph. 252-0738
Opposite, Izmaylovskiy prosp. 10
Ort, Krasnogvardeyskaya ul. 5-b, kv. 203-a, ph. 292-7423

Ow-Quast JV (German), prosp. Morisa Toreza 40, ph. 247-8925 {Audi, VW}
Ozon, prosp. Engelsa 42
Petro Service Oy, Leninskiy prosp. 160, ph. 295-3716
Petrograd-92, Servis Center, Sankt Peterburg Hotel, Vyborgskaya nab. 5/2, ph. 542-8736
Petromilam, prosp. Parkhomemko 33, ph. 247-6566
Polyot, Vitebskiy prosp. 107, ph. 259-7648
Raft, B. Zelinina ul. 29, ph. 235-1621
Remstroyservice, Bukharestskaya ul. 22-a, ph. 268-0795
Rostra, Shkolnaya ul. 39, ph. 239-4851
SAN, Zhernovskaya ul. 8, ph. 227-8984
Service, B. Sampsonievskiy prosp. 11/12, ph. 542-8995
Sovinteravtoservice, Malodetskoselskiy prosp. 24, ph. 292-1257; Predportovy pr. 5, ph. 290-1510
Soyuz, Polyustrovskiy prosp. 61, ph. 245-0046
Sputnik, Liteyny prosp. 53, ph. 113-5021
STV, ul. Pochtamtskaya 23, ph. 315-2955
Swed-Mobil-Service, prosp. Energetikov 59/3, ph. 225-4051
Tobos, ul. Karbysheva 29-a, ph. 247-5424
Trans-Niva, prosp. Yuriya Gagarina 32, kor. 2, ph. 299-5243
Varvara Firm, ul. Lermontova 46, ph. 132-6816
Vasiliyevskiy Ostrov, Uralskaya ul. 33, ph. 351-5885
Victoria, Vyazovaya ul. 10, ph. 235-6519
Vista, Grecheskiy prosp. 15 kv. 27, ph. 271-2916
Voskhod, ul. Sedova 12

CASH ADVANCE

The locations below provide cash advance services off AMEX, MC, VISA or Eurocard cards. You can also have money wired to you instantly via Western Union. To find out where in St. Petersburg you can receive cash via Western Union, you can call WU in Moscow at 095-119-8250.

AMEX

American Express, Grand Hotel Europe, ph. 315-7487

VISA/MC/Eurocard

Astrobank, Nevskiy prosp. 58, ph. 311-3600
Baltiyskiy Bank, ul. Sadovaya 34, ph. 310-0580
Credobank, ul. Mokhovaya 26, ph. 275-0333
Industry and Construction Bank, Nevskiy prosp. 38, ph. 110-5526; ul. Mikhailovskaya 4, ph. 110-4909
Sberbank, Moskovskiy prosp., 205, ph. 291-2820; Nevskiy prosp. 82, ph. 272-9089; Pulkovskaya Hotel, ph. 299-9217; Vladimirskiy prosp. 9, Business Center, ph. 113-1671
St. Petersburg Bank, Vosnesenskiy prosp. 16, ph. 314-6095 {open 9-18}; Dom Knigi, ph. 219-9417 {open 9-21}; Nevskiy prosp. 38, ph. 110-4945 {open 9-21}; Okhtinskaya Hotel, ph. 222-8635; Peterhof Hotelship, ph. 219-9417; Renlund Store, ul. Savushkina 119, ph. 345-1699
Tsarskotselskiy Bank, pl. Konstitutsiy 2, ph. 123-0684; prosp. Stachek 37, ph. 186-9796
Vitabank, Karelia Hotel, ph. 226-3356; Moskva Hotel, ph. 274-2127; Pribaltiyskaya Hotel, ph. 356-3803; ul. B. Morskaya 59, ph. 311-5193

WESTERN UNION

Call the Moscow head office, 095-119-8250 for a full list of all locations where a Western Union wire can be sent from or received. Here are a few:

Inkombank, ul. Komsomola 41, ph. 542-9713
Industry and Construction Bank, ul. Galernaya 24, ph. 312-4342
St. Petersburg Bank, pl. Ostrovskovo 7, ph. 310-3383

Western Union in the US: 1-800-325-6000

CASINOS

Admiral, Hotel Astoria {open 18-6}
Casino na Sadovoy, Sadovaya ul. 25, ph. 310-0404
Conti Casino, Kondratyevskiy prosp. 44, ph. 540-0122

Double-K Casino, prosp. Morisa Tereza 34, Hotel Sputnik, ph. 552-7991

Galspe Restaurant, Leninskiy prosp. 127, ph. 254-5582 {open 12-6}

Igma Casino, B. Porokhovskyay u. 26, ph. 224-2375

Konti Casino, Kondratyevskiy prosp. 44, ph. 540-5165

Klondike, Razyeszhaya u. 15, ph. 315-8217

Nevskiy Melody Casino, Sverdlovskaya nab. 62, ph. 227-1596 {cc, open 12-18, 19-1}

Palace Casino, Park Lenina 4, ph. 233-9634

SET-IL, Nevskiy prosp. 82, ph. 272-1007

Spielbanck Casino Sankt Petersburg, ul. Korablestroiteley 14 (Hotel Pribaltiyskaya), ph. 356-0001

Volkhov Restaurant, Casino, Liteyny prosp. 28, ph. 273-4736

CATERING

See also Restaurants

Ivan & Company, ph. 294-0252

Potel et Chabot, Dvortsovaya nab. 10, ph. 314-6000

CELLULAR PHONES

Delta Telecom, ul. Chekhova 18, ph. 275-4149; **Showroom**, ul. B. Morskaya 22, ph. 314-6126

CEMETERIES

Bogoslovskovo Cemetery, Laboratornaya ul. 4, ph. 544-7524

Bolsheokhtinskovo Cemetery, prosp. Metallistov 5, ph. 224-2729

Jewish Cemetery, prosp. Alexandrovskoy Fermi 3a, ph. 262-0397

Kinoveevskoe Cemetery, Oktyabrskaya nab. 14, ph. 587-9414

Nikolskoye Cemetery, nab. reki Monastyrki 1, ph. 274-2539 {largest of three major cemeteries on grounds of Alexander Nevskiy Lavra – many famous political and literary persons}

Piskaryovskoye Memorial Cemetery, prosp. Nepokorennykh 74, ph. 247-5716 {victims of the seige of Leningrad}

Serafimovskoye Cemetery, Serebryakov prosp. 1, ph. 239-3151

Smolenskoye cemetery, V. O., Kamskaya ul. 24, ph. 355-9993

Volkovskoye Cemetery (Orthodox), Rasstanny pr. 7a, ph. 166-0400 {plots of famous literary and artistic personages}

CHAMBERS OF COMMERCE

Finnish-Russian Chamber of Commerce, 4 Krasnoarmeyskaya ul. 4a, ph. 292-1641

St. Petersburg Chamber of Commerce and Industry, ul. Chaikovskovo 46/48, ph. 273-4896

Union of German Chambers of Commerce, V.O., Bolshoy prosp. 10a, ph. 213-7991

CIRCUS

Shepito Big Top, ul. Avtovskaya 1a, ph. 183-1501

State Circus, The, nab. reki Fontanki 3, ph. 210-4411

CLOTHING

There are hundreds of shops that sell imported clothing. Check out the following locations if you're looking for better-quality work or casual wear.

Algo, V. O., 18 Liniya 7 flat 11, ph. 217-4246

Babylon, Liteyniy prosp. 61, ph. 273-4212; Nevskiy prosp. 69, ph. 314-6237; Nevskiy prosp. 130, ph. 277-0730; P.S., Bolshoy prosp. 94, ph. 234-9068; Bolshoy prosp. 38, ph. 232-5243; Sadovaya ul. 26, ph. 310-1815

Benetton, Nevskiy prosp. 147, ph. 277-1732

Bolshevichka Clothing, Ligovskiy prosp. 107, ph. 164-9310

Godiva, Moskovskiy prosp. 179 kv. 49, ph. 294-0846

Heinemann, Grand Hotel Europe, ph. 312-0072

Joy Boutique, Zagorodny prosp. 9, ph. 315-5315

Littlewood's, Gostiny dvor, ph. 110-5967

Neva Star, Hotel Moskva, ph. 274-0012

Real-Music Shop, Nevskiy prosp. 54, ph. 310-5922

Renland, ul. B. Zelenina 14, ph. 230-3637; ul. Savushkina 119, ph. 345-1697

CLOTHING, CHILDREN'S

DLT, B. Konyushennaya 21/23, ph 312-2627

Peggy, Liteyny prosp. 8/21, ph. 272-4940

CLUBS

See also Bars

For the more-adventurous, Russian clubs are frequently a special cross-breed of disco, bar, and floor show. Security is not tight at most of them, so be careful with your belongings.

Eldorado Night Club, ul. Tukhachevskovo 27/2, ph. 226-3110

Evropa Plus Dance Hall, Kamennoostrovskiy prosp. 68 {weekends 23-6}

Galspe, Leninskiy prosp. 127, ph. 254-4482

Stardust, Aleksandrovskiy park 4, ph. 233-2712 {Tu-Su 22-6:30}

Tam-Tam Club, V.O., 16 liniya at Maly prosp.

COFFEE SHOPS

Most of the newer, Western-run hotels have nice coffee shops where you can take a break during the day or have a short business meeting:

Astoria Hotel Restaurant, ul. B. Morskaya 39 {excellent coffee and fine service}

Chaika Restaurant, Nab. Kanala Griboyedova 14, {expensive, but a very nice atmosphere and close to the center}

⇨**Grand Hotel Europe**, Mikhailovskaya ul. 1/7{nice Piano bar on the second floor}

Nevskiy 27, Nevskiy prosp. 27,{good pastries and coffee}

Nevskiy 44, Nevskiy prosp. 44 {a bier-stube atmosphere}

⇨**Olympia Hotel**, pl. Morskoy Slavy {nice open-air coffee shop/bar, as well as indoor shop}

⇨**Peterhof Hotel**, nab. Makarova near Tuchkov bridge {tasty Swiss pastries in the Panorama bar}

THE ORIGINAL

Where in St. Petersburg contains, in one handy book, the city's first yellow pages, only business white pages and best, most-accurate city street map (in handy book format). Accept no substitutes, copy-cats or derivations. Nothing else comes close.

COMPUTERS, SALES

See also Electronics

Computers are widely available for sale in St Petersburg, as are peripherals and supplies. Be sure you are getting what you expect – watch out for shoddy, over-priced Asian imports. Few firms offer full system installation and maintenance programs with guarantees.

Azimut International Ltd, ul. M. Pasadskaya 30, ph. 238-7802

Baltex Assn., ul. Blagodatnaya 55, ph. 294-1023

Catalog Express, Sadovaya ul. 34

Computerland, Sverdlovskaya nab. 64, ph. 224-0243

Connolly International, Ltd., ph. 122-3033

Cooperative Computer, Perekupnoy p. 12, ph. 274-7160

Creat, Kazanskaya ul. 49, ph. 311-1301

Digital Equipment Corporation, Moskovskiy prosp. 108, ph. 298-2370

Elegant Logic, Inc., nab. reki Fontanki 46, ph. 311-1064

IBM, Admiralteyskiy prosp. 6, ph. 312-6017

Inform-Future Business Center, ul. Tambovskaya 12, ph. 312-3078

MacTech, Povarskoy p. 8, ph. 112-3844 {Apple}

Marvel Ltd, ul. Shpalernaya 49, ph. 274-3210

Ortex, ul. 7 Krasnoarmeyskaya 30, ph. 251-7977

Polradis JV (Poland), prosp. Yuri Gagarina 1, ph. 294-8541

Prokom Computers, prosp. Stachek 47, ph. 183-6114

Ramec, ul. Obruchovikh 1, ph. 277-6960

Rames, Nevskiy prosp. 140, ph. 277-7763

Rubicon, Lesnoy prosp. 19, ph. 542-2798

SKY Systems, ul. Egorova 18/12, ph. 292-7666

Soft-Tronik GmbH, Fontanki nab. 88, ph. 315-9276

Sphinx JV (Finland), ul. Gertsena 55, ph. 312-7540

Yuma, Malookhtinskiy prosp. 68, ph. 528-9566

UniRem, Dobrolyubova prosp. 6/2, ph. 232-6155

COMPUTERS, SERVICE

All of the companies in the previous listing can arrange computer repairs, as can:

Bikar, 3 Sovetskaya ul. 19, ph. 274-4291

Information and Computer Service Center, Volkovskiy prosp. 146, k. 3, ph. 269-8424

Tor Firm, Uglovoy p. 6, ph. 292-7210

COMPUTERS, SOFTWARE

Most firms listed under the Computers, Sales heading above stock and support software, from fonts to LANs to Word Processing, as do:

Arnica Prima, Aptekarskiy prosp. 10, ph. 234-2018

ELCO, ul. Goncharnaya 26, ph. 277-7175

Soft-Tronik, nab. reki Fontanki 88, ph. 315-9276

SoftUnion, ul. Schedrina 10, ph. 272-0931

CONCERTS

See also Theaters/Ballet

Dom Muzyki i Radio, Grazhdanskiy prosp. 15, block 1, ph. 534-4218

Glinka Choir, nab. reki Moyki 20, ph. 314-1058

Glinka Philharmonic Hall, Nevskiy prosp. 30, ph. 311-8333

Lenkontsert, nab. reki Fontanki 41, ph. 310-3766

Music Hall Booking office, Aleksandrovskiy Park 4, ph. 233-0243

Oktyabrskoy Bolshoy Concert Hall, Ligovskiy prosp. 6, ph. 275-1300

Rimsky-Korsakov Conservatory (Opera Studio), Teatralnaya pl. 3, ph. 311-6265; **Music School**, p. Matveyeva 1a, ph. 114-1642

Russian Union of Composers, ul. Gertsena 45, ph. 311-3548

Severnaya Lira, Nevskiy prosp. 26, ph. 312-0796

St. Petersburg Hermitage Orchestra Cooperative, Nevskiy prosp. 31, ph. 528-9435

St. Petersburg Music Hall, Aleksandrovskiy Park 4, ph. 232-9466

St. Petersburg Musical Fund, Nevskiy prosp. 11, ph. 314-7132

St. Petersburg Philharmonic, ul. Mikhailovskaya 2, ph. 311-7333

St. Petersburg Rock Club, ul. Rubinshteyna 13, ph. 312-3483

CONSTRUCTION

Domostroy Cooperative, ul. Rubinshteyna 3, ph. 311-2060

Energomashzhilstroy Architectural-Construction Assn, prosp. Suslova 21, #4, ph. 156-0866

Finnrefit Ltd, nab. reki Moyki 3A, ph. 312-9998

Haka Oy, Admiralteyskiy prosp. 6, ph. 312-3915

International Group, ph. 311-2483

Lek Estate, Nevskiy prosp. 90/92, ph. 272-1097

Lenstroyrekonstruktsia, ul. Kazanskaya 36, ph. 319-9457; V. O., 3 Liniya 6, ph. 213-2500

Management Systems Corporation, Pushkin 7, Box 76, ph. 476-1550

Monolitstroi, ul. Ryleyeva 29, ph. 272-1775

Pobeda Construction Materials Union, Kolpino, ul. Zagorodnaya 9, ph. 484-4212

Polymerstroymaterial Factory, Irinovskiy prosp. 53, ph. 224-9122

Ryland St. Petersburg, ul. B. Morskaya 31, ph. 314-6435

Santekhoborydovaniye Factory, Sh. Revolyutsii 88, 102, ph. 227-1296

Siab, bul. Serebristy 38, ph. 301-8721

Sovstroyservice, ul. Dostoyevskovo 30, kv. 9, ph. 164-1439

Soyuzteplstroi, Isaakevskaya pl. 7, ph. 312-3019

St. Petersburg World Financial and Trade Center, Kanal Griboyedova 5, ph. 312-3557
Stroidetal, Khimicheskiy p. 6, ph. 252-7793
Stroipolimer Factory, ul. Severnaya 14, ph. 484-4750
Svyazmorproekt Construction Buro, ul. M. Morskaya 14, ph. 312-8268
Twentieth Trust Corporation, Nevskiy prosp. 44, ph. 311-1696
VMB, Pisareva ul. 6, kv. 8, ph. 114-7589
Yit-Yhtyma, Voronezhskaya ul. 33, ph. 167-0356

CONSULATES

Several foreign governments maintain consulates in St. Petersburg. A few alaso have commercial offices or attaches attached to the consulate. Check the White Pages listings under Consulate of...

CONSULTING FIRMS

See also Accounting, Advertising, Information, Legal Advice

Listed below are only better-known firms:

Arctis, Ltd., ul. Promyshlennaya 7, ph. 252-9587
Arthur Andersen, V. O., Bolshoy prosp. 10, ph. 350-4984
Azbuka JV (Finland), ul. Gangutskaya 4, ph. 272-5860
Baker & McKenzie, nab. kanala Griboyedova 36, ph. 310-5446
Connolly International, Ltd., ph. 122-3033
Coopers & Lybrand, Astoria Hotel, room 528, ph. 210-5528
Costa Inc. JV (USA), Tavricheskaya ul. 39, kv. 353, ph. 271-4110
Deloitte & Touche, Petropavlovskiy krepost 11, ph. 238-4408
Dialog Invest Group, Inc., ul. Dostoyevskovo 19/21, ph. 164-8747
Ernst and Young, ul. M. Morskaya 11, ph. 312-9911
Ekon Firm, ul. Myasnaya 19, ph. 184-6861
Euroconsel, p. Bankovskiy 3, ph. 310-6543
Florman Information Systems, Kamenoostrovskiy prosp. 14b, ph. 233-7682
Hans Eike von Oppeln-Bronikowski, Zagorodny prosp. 28, ph. 112-5357
Hermi Ltd, Pushkin,ul. Radishcheva 4, ph. 465-2820
Infokon, Isaakievskaya pl. 6, ph. 319-9543
International Business Services, Inc. (IBS), Rubinstein 8, Box 237, ph. 311-5838
KPMG, nab. kanala Griboyedova 7, 3rd flr., ph. 314-5209
Law Office of S. A. Stern, Nevskiy prosp. 104, ph. 275-3497
MCD Marketing, Consulting and Design, Shpalernaya ul. 52, #13, ph. 275-5623
McKinsey & Co., Hotelship Olympia, ph. 119-6050
Metod Consulting-Expert Center of Mayor, p. Antonenko 6b, ph. 312-9312
Minor-Neva Consulting Company, Serpukhovskaya ul. 4, ph. 292-4466
Palms & Company, Inc., ul. Dunayevskiy 51/2 (Hotel Kupchinskaya), ph. 178-2738
Petrocon, nab. reki Moyki 45, ph. 312-5514
Russkiy Market, 7 Krasnoarmeyskaya ul. 18-24, ph. 112-6864
RusTex International, Belgradskaya ul. 6(4), kv. 46, ph. 109-6914
Scientifik Methods Inc., p. Antonenko 5, ph. 110-6508
Siar Bossard, ul. B. Morskeye 28, ph. 315-7696
St. Petersburg International Projects Agency, ul. Klenovaya 2, ph. 210-4764
Transelectro JV (Finland), Moskovskiy prosp. 171, ph. 294-0501
Vana Information, ul. Millionnaya 11, ph. 311-1717

COPIERS, REPAIR

See also Repair Services

Fotrelle Copier Service Center, Volkovskiy prosp. 146, ph. 268-6125
Rank Xerox, nab. Obvodnovo kanala 93a, ph. 315-7670

COPIERS, SALES

See also ***Electronics***

Buying a copier, as with all office equipment, has become much easier. Be sure to check out the service and guarantee policy. For sure-fire copier purchases try:

EastMarket, B. Konyushennaya 27, ph. 312-8889 {Canon}
Hitachi, Sinopskaya nab. 76, ph. 271-5051
Ipris, Primorskiy prosp. 35a, ph. 239-6884
Rank Xerox, nab. Obvodnovo kanala 93a, ph. 315-7670

COPYING

See also ***Business Centers***

Copy centers have sprung up all over St. Petersburg and, odds are, you will be able to find one in your neighborhood (or hotel, see Business Centers). It's a good idea to carry a few sheets of stationary or letterhead with you, if you need a quick, but quality copy.

Apogey, Gospitalny p. 3, ph. 274-0310
Delta, Plovdivskaya ul. 9, ph. 108-1917
Informatika, nab. reki Moyki 64, ph. 314-0632
Kopia, Izmaylovskiy prosp. 12, ph. 292-0496
Xerox-Rotator, Sennaya pl. 3, ph. 310-9975

COSMETICS

See also ***Shops***

Babylon-7, Bolshoy prosp. 65, ph. 232-0466
Krasota Cosmetics, Nevskiy prosp. 90, ph. 272-9325
Lancome, Nevskiy prosp. 64, ph. 312-3495
Magnolia, Kamenoostrovskiy prosp. 2, ph. 233-5353
Parfum Ltd, ul. Marata 71, ph. 315-8845
Severnoye Siyaniye Cosmetics Salon, Nevskiy prosp. 27, ph. 315-0168
Vanda Cosmetics, Nevskiy prosp. 11, ph. 279-4341
Yves Rocher, Nevskiy prosp. 61, ph. 113-1506

COURIER, CITY/DOMESTIC

Aerocourier JV (Germany), ul. Vzletnaya 7/1, Pulkovo Airport, ph. 104-3496 {deliveries, express services}
⇨ **DHL**, nab. kanala Griboyedova 5, office 325, ph. 311-2649; **Express Center**, Nevskiy Palace Hotel, ph. 119-6110
Express Mail, Konnogvardeyskiy bul. 4, ph. 311-9671
Itec, Manezhnaya p. 19, ph. 275-8811

COURIER, INTERNATIONAL

See also ***Express Mail***

⇨ **DHL**, nab kanala Griboyedova 5, office 325, ph. 311-2649; **Express Center**, Nevskiy Palace Hotel, ph. 119-6110
Federal Express, ul. Mayakovskaya 2, ph. 279-1287
TNT Express Freight, Liteyny prosp. 50, ph. 272-5886
UPS Courier Service, ul. Karavannaya 12, ph. 312-2915

CREDIT CARD LOSS

American Express: contact the AMEX office in the Grand Hotel Europe, ph. 315-7487
VISA/MC/ Eurocard: contact Intourcreditcard at ul. Gorokhovaya 1, ph. 312-6015

CUSTOMS

See also ***Shipping, Warehouses***

There are a large number of customs clearing agents operating in Russia. Unfortunately, most operate out of Moscow, since most trade transits there (see our ***Where in Moscow*** *for a full listing). Still, some good agents are operating in St. Petersburg.*

Customs clearing agents:

Petersburg Vneshtrans, Mezhevoy kanal 5, ph. 251-1877
Rosvneshterminal, ul. Belinskovo 11, ph. 279-7586
Sovtransavto, Vitebskiy prosp. 3, ph. 298-4650

Customs points:

Baltic Customs, Mezhevoy kanal ul. 5, ph. 113-9945

Customs Administration, Pulkovo II Airport, ph. 104-3401

St. Petersburg Central Customs House, V. O., 9 Liniya 10, ph. 218-6374

State Customs North-Western Administration, ul. Furmanova 1, ph. 275-7695

D

DECOR

See also Renovation, Furniture

There are several stores with everything you need to decorate your apartment or office.

Babylon-8, P.S., Bolshoy prosp. 38, ph. 232-5243

Fairn & Swanson, Nevskiy prosp. 96, ph. 275-5385

Home Center, prosp. Slavy 30, ph. 261-0402

Renlund, B. Zelenina 14, ph. 232-3607

DENTISTS

Medi, 10 Sovetskaya ul. 13, ph. 274-6480

Nordmed, ul. Tverskaya 12, ph. 110-0654

Raden Firm, Leninskiy prosp. 116, ph. 158-3524

DEPARTMENT STORES

Dom Leningradskoy Torgovli (DLT), B. Konyushennaya ul. 21/23, ph. 312-2627

Passage Shopping Center, Nevskiy prosp. 48, ph. 315-5257

DRUG STORES

See also Medical Care

Adonis Pharmacy, Svechnoy p. 7, ph. 315-8487

⇨ **This symbol points you to one of our valued advertisors. Look for their advertisement in this book.**

Aguaservice, ul. Kolomenskaya 10 kv. 65, ph. 164-5806

Damian Pharmacy, Moskovskiy prosp. 22, ph. 110-1744

Farmadom Pharmacy, Zagorodny prosp. 21, ph. 113-3340

Farmaservice Pharmacy, nab. Kutuzova 14, ph. 279-0660

Feniks, Yaroslava Gasheka ul. 9, ph. 176-9602

Gomeofan Homeopathic Pharmacy, P.S., Bolshoy prosp. 2, ph. 233-2381

Pharmacy, Nevskiy prosp. 83, ph. 277-7966; No. 48: Sadovaya ul. 36, ph. 310-8868; No. 56: 10th Sovetskaya ul. 15, ph. 271-2577; No. 5: Nevskiy prosp. 111, ph. 277-2931; No. 7: Nevskiy prosp. 66, ph. 314-5654; No. 91: Moskovskiy prosp. 167, ph. 298-0535; P.S., Bolshoy prosp. 43, ph. 232-4679; V. O., 17 Liniya 8, ph. 213-7140

Pharmacy No. 2, Kamennoostrovskiy prosp. 38/96, ph. 234-9035

Salute Pharmacy, Malookhtinskiy prosp. 92, ph. 221-1932

Stouk Ltd., nab. kanala Griboyedova 102, ph. 310-2104

Tsitomed-Peptos Pharmacy, p. Muchnoy 2, ph. 310-8011

Zelyonaya Pharmacy, Nevskiy prosp. 41, ph. 312-3773 {medicinal herbs}

DRY CLEANING

See also Hotels

All major hotels offer dry cleaning services, as do the following independent firms:

Khimchistkas (Dry Cleaners), Izmailovskiy prosp. 12, ph. 292-3347; prosp. Metallistov, ph. 540-1935; Zanevskiy prosp. 37, ph. 528-8465 {open 8-21}

Polar Cleaners, ul. Pestelya 8, ph. 272-9655

ELECTRONIC MAIL

Prices are fast becoming competitve in this, the easiest, cheapest, and most reliable way to communicate with Russia. See the chapter on

Telecommunicationsin our Russia Survival Guide for Western addresses of Email providers.

Glasnet, (Moscow office), Denezhny p. 9/5, ph. 241-8243
Infocom (Moscow office), Kuznetskiy most 4, ph. 925-1235
Istok-K, Kantemirovskaya ul. 5, ph. 245-5165
⇨**Sovam Teleport**, Nevskiy prosp. 30, ph. 311-8412 {best overall value}
Sprint Networks, Sinopskaya nab. 14, ph. 265-0571

ELECTRONICS

Baltic Star, Hotel Pribaltiyskaya, ph. 356-2284
Baltica, prosp. M. Toreza 2/40, ph. 247-8203
Electrolux, Robespera nab. 16, ph. 275-5512; ul. Zakharievskaya 31, ph. 275-3685
Elektronika Gallery and Shop, prosp. Yuri Gagarina 12, korp. 1, ph. 299-3849
Electronics Store, Pulkovo 1 Airport, ph. 123-8778
Fairn & Swanson, Nevskiy prosp. 96, ph. 275-5385
High Life, Karavannaya ul. 16, ph. 314-9861
Intep, ul. Ryleyeva 10, ph. 275-5360
Kauko Firm, Nakhimova ul. 7, kv. 39, ph. 356-3635
Neva Star, Hotel Moskva, ph. 274-0012
Philips Electronics, Suvorovskiy prosp. 2, ph. 277-4319 {hours 10-14, 15-20}
Pioneer Electronics, Zagorodny prosp. 11, ph. 314-2314 {hours Mon-Sat, 11-19}
Rubikon, Lesnoy prosp. 19, ph. 542-0065
Siemens AG, ul. Gogolya 18/20, ph. 315-3197
Yuma Electronics, Malookhtinskiy prosp. 68, ph. 528-9566

ELECTRONICS, SERVICE

Arnika Prima, Aptekarskiy prosp. 10, ph. 234-2018
Askod, ul. Sovetskaya 3, ph. 110-7401
Commark Ltd., ul. Sablinskaya 7, ph. 233-3008
Creat, ul. Plekhanova 49, ph. 314-3081
Elektronika Bekas, Mytninskaya ul. 1, ph. 274-4291
Orbita-Service, prosp. Kosmonavtov 25, ph. 293-6501
Sikont, Novosmolenskaya nab. 1, ph. 352-8895

EXCHANGES

Interlesbirzha International Timber Exchange, Mikhaylova ul. 17, ph. 541-8676
Interseverobalt Stock Exchange, V. O., Sredny prosp. 28
Irkutsk Commodity & Raw Materials Exchange, Grivtsova p. 10, ph. 314-5221
Krona International Timber Exchange, ul. Plekhanova 36, ph. 319-9263
LEK Corp., Mytninskaya ul. 19, ph. 271-1420
Neva Construction Exchange, Liteyny prosp. 22
Petersburg Commodity and Stock Exchange, B. Konyushennaya ul. 25, ph. 315-7415
Petersburg-Tyumen Universal Exchange, ph. 247-2857
Petrosnab Firm, Suvorovskiy prosp. 62, ph. 311-7371
Planeta International Exchange, Aleksandrovskiy Park 4, ph. 232-0942
Resurs North-Western Exchange of Production Equipment, Kamenoostrovskiy 5, ph. 233-8748
Rossiyskaya Bumaga of St. Petersburg, Sestroretskaya ul. 6, ph. 239-5628
Rossiyskaya Elektronnaya Kompaniya, Pobedy pl. 2, ph. 293-6757
RUIS Industrial Building & Commodity Exchange, B. Morskaya ul. 52
Russo-Balt Exchange, pl. Morskoy Slavy 1
Severny Alliance Int'l Exchange, Sredneokhtinskiy prosp. 52, ph. 526-6630
St. Petersburg Commodity & Stock Exchange, V.O., 26 Liniya 15, ph. 217-8071
St. Petersburg Exchange, ul. Plekhanova 36, ph. 355-5954
St. Petersburg Investment & Construction Exchange, nab. reki Moyki 86, ph. 319-9575
St. Petersburg Stock Exchange, V.O., Bolshoy prosp. 103, ph. 355-5988
Television Exchange, Galerniy P. 3, ph. 352-0669

Yakutsk Commodity Stock Exchange, Moskovskiy prosp. 216, ph. 108-5920

Yevrosib International Exchange, Tavricheskaya ul. 39, ph. 271-3649

EXHIBITIONS

Expoconsta JV (Finland), V. O., Bolshoy prosp. 103, ph. 355-1991

Lenart, nab. reki Fontanki 34, ph. 275-7510

LenExpo, V.O., Bolshoy prosp. 103, ph. 355-1989

Neva Kommerz, Isaakevskiy pl. 11, ph. 312-1620

EXPRESS MAIL

⇨**DHL**, nab. kanala Griboyedova 5, office 325, ph. 311-2649; **Express Center**, Nevskiy Palace Hotel, ph. 119-6110

EMS Garantpost, Konnogvardeyskiy bul. 4, ph. 311-1120 {also has a collection or sending point at the Main Post Office, desk #25, ul. Pochtamtskaya 9}

Federal Express, ul. Mayakovskaya 2, ph. 279-1287

Huolintakeskus, Lyubotinskiy p. 5, ph. 298-0083

Sovinteravtoservice, Malodetskoselskiy prosp. 24, ph. 292-1257

TNT Express Freight, Liteyny prosp. 50, ph. 272-5886

UPS Courier Service, ul. Karavannaya 12, ph. 312-2915

Vneshtransavto, Sofiyskaya ul. 6, ph. 166-0891 {weekly Helsinki truck}

F

FILM

See also Photo Developing

Western Kodak and Fuji film can be purchased in hotel shops and most stores listed under the heading Food, as well as at Photo Developing shops. When buying film, always check the expiration date. Also, avoid purchasing ORWO NC-21 or DC-4 film, which can only be developed in Russia.

FIRE DIAL 01

FLOWERS

Alenkiy Tsvetochek, Prosveshcheniya prosp. 46, ph. 597-2694

Alinda, Mayakovskovo ul. 19, ph. 272-8358

Azalia, B. Sampsonievskiy prosp. 70, ph. 245-4619

Baccara, P.S., Bolshoy prosp. 86, ph. 232-8407

Ekzot, Professora Popova ul. 2, ph. 234-8448

Ekzotika, Leninskiy prosp. 119, ph. 254-7591

Fialka, Stachek prosp. 96, ph. 183-2287

Flora, ul. Shpalernaya 44b, ph. 271-1161 {delivery service}

Gloria, Novosmolenskaya nab. 1, ph. 352-4438

Hall of Flowers, Potemkinskaya ul. 2, ph. 272-5448

Karmen, Moskovskiy prosp. 194, ph. 298-4242

Korona, Kamennoostrovskiy prosp. 5, ph. 232-4870

Landora, nab. reki Fontanki 136, ph. 265-0489

Lilia, Sedova ul. 17, ph. 265-0489

Magnolia, Sadovaya ul. 46, ph. 310-0843

Nevskiy 5, Nevskiy prosp. 5, ph. 312-6437

Nordiya, Zhukovskovo ul. 36, ph. 272-3472

Orange, ul. Sezzhinskaya 9/6, ph. 233-9411

Polskiy Buket Florist, Morskaya nab. 15, ph. 352-2075

Roza Florist, prosp. Veteranov 87, ph. 150-2362

Tsveti Bolgarii Florist, Kamenoostrovskiy prosp. 5, ph. 232-4685

FOOD

Alfa Express, ph. 234-3968

Almaz, Sredneokhtinskiy 5, ph. 224-2048

Antanta, Novoizmailovskiy prosp. 46, ph. 295-0165; Moskovskiy prosp. 161, ph. 298-7496

Babylon-2, Nevskiy prosp. 69, ph. 314-6237

Baltic Star, Hotel Pribaltiyskaya, ph. 356-2284

Belochka Candy Shop, V. O., Sredniy prosp. 28, ph. 213-1763

Eliseyevskiy Food Store, Nevskiy prosp. 56, ph. 311-9323

Express Market, Moskovskiy prosp. 73, ph. 252-4144; Stary Nevskiy prosp. 113, ph. 277-7771

Inter-Latis, ph. 233-1174 {24 hour}

Liteyny Food Store, Liteyny prosp. 12, ph. 272-2791

Neva Star, Hotel Moskva, ph. 274-0012

Paulig RF Ltd, ul. Generala Khruleva 7, ph. 395-2597 {coffee, tea, spices}

Pizza Rif, ph. 290-1379 {24 hour}

Russ Service, ph. 275-8758 {24 hour}

⇨**Stockmann Food Store (Kalinka)**, Finlyandskiy prosp. 1, ph. 542-2297

Strela Food Store, Izmaylovskiy prosp. 16/30, ph. 251-2709

Troika R. O., Zagorodniy prosp. 28, ph. 112-4746

Viking, Sankt Peterburg Hotel, ph. 542-8032

Vostochnye Sladosti Candy Shop, Moskovskiy prosp. 27, ph. 292-7556; Nevskiy prosp. 104, ph. 273-7436

Yubileyny Bakery, Nevskiy prosp. 10, ph. 312-6086; Pl. Chernyshevskovo 3, ph. 298-1547; V. O., 7 Liniya 40, ph. 213-1162

Zolotoy Uley Candy Shop, Nevskiy prosp. 22, ph. 312-2394

FOOD, WHOLESALE

Karl Fazer, Nevskiy prosp. 134, ph. 274-4160 {candy, cookies}

Paulig RF Ltd, ul. Generala Khruleva 7, ph. 395-2597 {coffee, tea, spices}

Pitanie JV (Finland), Leninskiy prosp. 160, ph. 295-3715

Quality Products International, ph. 310-1850

FURNITURE

Aldi Firm, Malookhtinskiy prosp. 68, ph. 528-9566

Apit, prosp. Kima 28, ph. 119-6130

Babylon-8, Bolshoy prosp. 25, ph. 235-6400

Bon-Servis, V.O., Bolshoy prosp. 63, ph. 217-3137

Capricorn, Lesnoy prosp. 19a, ph. 542-5588

Cartas, Dibunovskaya ul. 37, ph. 239-4728

Dresden, prosp. Morisa Toreza 40, ph. 552-2808

Ekoparts JV (Finland), Bolsheokhtinskiy prosp. 19, ph. 239-3930

Elegant, P.S., Bolshoy prosp. 55, ph. 232-8601

Interbalt, Pionerskaya ul. 63, ph. 235-6046

Karagach, Derptskiy p. 13, ph. 251-5945

Klyon, Slavy prosp. 2, ph. 260-7752

Ladoga Furniture Making Factory, 12 Krasnoarmeyskaya 26, ph. 251-9792

Leathertouch Fabrics U. S. A., ul. Khimikov 28, ph. 315-9382

Lenraumamebel Shop, nab. reki Fontanki 20, ph. 272-5683

Mebel, Bukharestskaya ul. 74-b, ph. 269-7603

Nakhodka, Kustarny p. 3, ph. 310-0042

Neva-Sia JV (Italian), Primorskiy prosp. 52, ph. 239-3930

Nevka, Moskovskiy prosp. 4/6, ph. 113-5375

Novosyol, Nalichnaya ul. 40, kor. 7, ph. 350-2880

Orion, Piskaryovskiy prosp. 20, ph. 541-3327

Plyke, ul. Milionnaya 4/1, ph. 315-3439

Teknesis, Fontanka 76, ph. 112-5832

Yaroslav, ul. Millionnaya 5, rm. 2, ph. 312-9076

Yupiter Kholding Firm, ul. Tsiolkovskovo 9, ph. 251-3900

FURS

Krasnoselskoye Fur Factory, Krasnoye selo, ul. Lermontova 21, ph. 132-5516

Lena, Myasnikova ul. 4, ph. 310-8054

Pushnoy (Fur) Auction, Moskovskiy prosp. 98, ph. 298-4636

Rot-Front Fur Production Assn., ul. Soyuza Pechatnikov 24, ph. 114-0973

WHAT'S MISSING?

Since we don't let our Yellow Pages get cluttered-up with lots of little ads, you get more listings in less space. You get a user-driven (vs. advertiser-driven) guide with more in it (like a white pages and full-color city street map). While other guides force you to lug around hundreds of pages of advertisements, ***WIS*** *gives you more information for your money.*

G

GAS STATIONS

Below is a list of St. Petersburg city gas stations, by geographical location. All are indicated on the map in the back of the book.

Center: Moskvoskiy prosp. 100 • Teatralnaya pl. 8 • Park Lenina 1 • Nab. Reki Fontanki 156 • Tavricheskiy per. 18

South: Vitebskiy prosp. 9 • Prosp. Yuriya Gagarina 18 • Prosp. Yuriya Gagarina 32 • Pulkovskoye shosse 13th km • Kubinskaya ul. 90 • ul. Pilotov 6a • Prosp. Stachek 108a • Prosp. Narodnovo Opolcheniya 16 • Moskovskoye shosse 35 • Krasnoye Selo, posyolok Gorelovo

Southeast: ul. Matyushenko 3 • Sovyetskiy prosp. 37

North: Vyborgskoye shosse 4 • Primorskiy prosp. 56 • Prosp. Nepokorennikh 47 • Polyustrovsky prosp. 73 • Suzdalskiy prosp. 12 • ul. Rustaveli 25

Northwest: Primorskoye shosse 18th km • ul. Savushkina 87

Northeast: Obyezdnoe shosse 15 • Ekaterininsky prosp. 11

Vasilevsky ostrov: Detskaya ul. 50

There are also some newer, Western-style stations:

Neste Gas Stations
Avangardnaya ul. 36, ph. 135-5867
Moskovskiy prosp. 100, ph. 298-4534
Pulkovskoye sh. 44a, ph. 123-3423
Savushkina ul. 87, ph. 239-0415
V.O., Maly prosp. 68, ph. 355-0879

Petro Service Oy, Leninskiy prosp. 160, ph. 295-3716

RUSSIA GUIDE

Our flagship publication, ***Russia Survival Guide: Business & Travel,*** *the definitive guide to Russia, is now totally updated for 1994. For more info, contact RIS at the addresses given in the front or back of the book.*

GOVERNMENT

For most government bodies, see the White pages under Russia, Government of..., or State Committee for... The organs listed below may not be as easy to find in the White pages under their common name.

Russia

General Prosecutor's Office, ul. Yakubovicha 4, ph. 312-8469

Internal Affairs Department (MVD), Liteyny prosp. 4, ph. 315-0019

Legal Administration, Admiralteyskaya nab. 12

Press & Information Ministry, Sadovaya ul. 14, kv. 52, ph. 310-6161

Russian Agency for Intellectual Property, Nevskiy prosp. 116, ph. 279-1752

State Automobile Inspectorate (GAI), ul. Popova 42, ph. 234-2646

State Taxation Inspectorate, Liteyny prosp. 53, ph. 272-0188

UVIR (Visa office), ul. Saltykova-Shchedrina 4, ph. 278-2418

St. Petersburg

St. Petersburg City Council, Isaakevskaya pl. 6, ph. 319-9485

- **Architectural and Building Committee**, Lomonosova pl. 2, ph. 315-5216
- **Committee on the Administration of City Property (KUGI)**, Smolny, 6th ent., ph. 278-1557
- **Control Committee**, Isaakevskaya pl. 6, ph. 319-9752
- **Dept. of Foreign Relations**, Isaakevskaya pl. 6, ph. 319-9381
- **Property Fund**, p. Grivtsova 5, ph. 310-4645
- **Transport Depot**, ul. Korolenko 5, ph. 272-5331

St. Petersburg City Mayor's Office, Smolny, ph. 310-5406

St. Petersburg City Vice-Mayor's Office, Smolny, ph. 278-1248

St. Petersburg Regional Council of People's Deputies, Suvorovskiy prosp. 67, ph. 315-8665

GYMS

See also Recreation, Sports

There are a plethora of Russian gyms with adequate facilities for lifting weightsand getting in your daily exercise. For a fairly comprehensive list, look under the Recreation, Sports heading. There are also several World Class gym locations, with everything from Nautilus to solaria.

World Class Gym, Grand Hotel Europe, ph. 113-8066; Hotel Astoria, 4th floor, ph. 210-5869; Kamennoostrovskiy prosp. 26, ph. 232-7581

HAIR CUTTING

See also Hotels

Most major hotels have hairdressers and you don't necessarily have to be a guest there to use the service.

⇨**Christina Creative Coiffure of Switzerland**, Hotel Peterhof, ph. 213-6321

Dom Modeley Prichosok 'Studia M', prosp. Morisa Toreza 30, ph. 552-6981

Wella Salon Debut JV (FRG), Nevskiy prosp. 54, ph. 312-3026

World Class Gym, Grand Hotel Europe, ph. 113-8066

HARDWARE STORES

Babylon Shop, Liteyny prosp. 63, ph. 273-5254

East Way/Lappeenrannan Rautakauppa Oy JV, ul. Sofiyskaya 6, ph. 268-5719

Home Store, Slavy prosp. 30, ph. 261-0402

Littlewoods, Gostiny Dvor, 2nd fl.,Nevskiy 35, ph. 110-5447

Renlund, B. Zelenina ul., ph. 232-3607

HORSEBACK RIDING

Horse can be hired out at:

Olgino Motel and Campsite, ph. 238-3132, open 10-12 and 15-18. Closed Mondays. Take the train from Finlyandskiy station to Olgino.

Kirov Stadium, Krestovskiy ostrov, Morskoy prosp. 4, open 9-12, 16-21, closed Tuesdays, ph. 235-5448.

Prostor Park, Krestovskiy ostrov 20, ph. 230-7873, open 16-20, 10-15 on Su.

HOTELS

See also Youth Hostels

Bolded information (i.e. **D17(9)**) *is the map coordinates and page on the map where you will find the hotel.For a listing of major hotels' relative standards and prices, see our* ***Russia Survival Guide.***

Antraks Hotel, Vyazemskiy P. 5, ph. 234-0700 **H11(6)**

Astoria Hotel, ul. B. Morskaya 39, ph. 210-5020 **H16(21)**

Avangard Hotel, Zavoda Komponent, Metallistov prosp. 115, ph. 540-4815 **N14(11)**

Avtotur Hotel, Klyuchevaya ul. 32, ph. 544-7728 **N11(7)**

Beliye Nochi Hotel, Narodnaya ul. 93, kor. 1, ph. 263-2104 **Q22(16)**

Chaika Hotel, Serebristy bulvar 38, ph. 301-7969 **G7(6)**

Commodore Hotel, prosp. Morskoy Slavy 1, ph. 119-6666 **D17(9)**

Deson Hotel, Shaumyana prosp. 26, ph. 528-5628 **N16(11)**

Druzhba Hotel, ul. Chapygina 4, ph. 234-1844 **H11(6)**

Fiodorovskiy Gorodok Hotel, Akademicheskiy prosp. 14, Pushkin, ph. 476-3600

Gavan Hotel, V. O., Sredniy prosp. 88, ph. 356-8504 **E16(9)**

⇨**Grand Hotel Europe**, Mikhailovskaya ul. 1/7, ph. 119-6000 **I15(22)**

Helen Hotel JV (Finland), Lermontovskiy prosp. 43/1, ph. 251-6101 **G18(25)**

Karelia Hotel, ul. Tukhachevskovo 27/2, ph. 226-3515 **O12(8)**

Kiev Hotel, Dnepropetrovskaya ul. 49, ph. 166-0456 **K18(27)**

Ladoga Hotel, Stakhanovtsev ul. 14, ph. 221-8014 **N16(11)**

LDM Hotel, Professora Popova ul. 47, ph. 234-3278 **G12(17)**

Mars Hotel, Narodnovo Opolcheniya prosp. 189, ph. 159-9955 **G25(14)**

Mir Hotel, Gastello ul. 17, ph. 108-5166 I24(14)

Morskaya Hotel, pl. Morskoy Slavy 1, ph. 355-1416 D16(9)

Moskva Hotel, Pl. Aleksandra Nevskovo 2, ph. 274-2051 M17(28)

Na Sadovoy Hotel, Sadovaya ul. 53, ph. 310-6537 H17(25)

Nauka Hotel, Millionnaya ul. 27, ph. 312-3156 I15(22)

Neptun Hotel, nab. Obvodnovo kanala 93-a, ph. 315-4965 H18(25)

Neva Hotel, Chaikovskovo ul. 17, ph. 278-0504 J14(22)

Nevskiy Palace Hotel, Nevskiy Prosp. 57, ph. 275-2001 J16(22)

Okhtinskaya Hotel, Bolsheokhtinskiy Prosp. 4, ph. 227-3767 N14(11)

Oktyabrskaya Hotel, Ligovskiy prosp. 10, ph. 277-6330 K16(23)

Olgino Camping Motel, Primorskoye Sh., 18 km (Olgino), ph. 238-3009

⇨ **Olympia Hotel**, pl. Morskoy Slavy, ph. 119-6800 D16(9)

Otdykh Hotel, Vasi Alekseyeva ul. 14, pod. 3, ph. 185-0690 F22(14)

⇨ **Peterhof Hotelship**, Pier Makarov nab. at Tuchkov most, ph. 213-6321 {cc} G14(21)

Petrogradskaya Hotel, nab. reki Karpovki 37, ph. 234-2056 H12(17)

Pribaltiyskaya Hotel, ul. Korablestroiteley 14, ph. 356-0263 C15(9)

Pulkovskaya Hotel, Pl. Pobedy 1, ph. 264-5122 I26(14)

Rechnaya Hotel, prosp. Obukhovskoy Oborony 195, ph. 267-3196 Q23(16)

Repinskaya Hotel, Primorskoye Sh. 428, Repino, ph. 231-6637

Rossia Hotel, Pl. Chernyshevskovo 11, ph. 294-6322 H23(14)

Rus Hotel, Artilleriyskaya ul. 1, ph. 272-0321 K15(23)

Salpi Hotel, Mozhayskaya ul. 18, ph. 292-4735 I18(26)

Sankt-Peterburg Hotel, Vyborgskaya nab. 5/2, ph. 542-9411 J13(18)

⇨ This symbol points you to one of our valued advertisors. Look for their advertisement in this book. Tell them you saw their ad here.

Severnaya Hotel, ul. Zasimova 11, Kronshtadt, ph. 236-4844

Sovetskaya Hotel, Lermontovskiy prosp. 43/1, ph. 259-3380 G18(25)

Sovturs Hotel, nab. Maloy Nevki 13, ph. 234-1014 G11(6)

Sportivnaya Hotel, Dekabristov ul. 34, ph. 235-1317 F11(6)

Sputnik Hotel, prosp. Morisa Toreza 34, ph. 552-8330 K8(7)

St. Petersburg Youth Hostel, 3 Sovetskaya 28, ph. 277-0569 {$5-10/night, issues visas, train tickets, tours} L16(24)

Turist Hotel, Sevastyanova ul. 3, ph. 297-8183 I22(14)

Veronika Hotel, Generala Khrulyova ul. 6, ph. 395-1373 G9(6)

Vyborgskaya Hotel, ul. Torzhkovskaya 3, ph. 246-2319 H10(6)

Yenisey, Artilleriyskaya ul. 1, ph. 279-3469 K15(23)

Yuzhnaya, Rasstannaya ul. 2-b, ph. 166-1088 J18(26)

Zagreb Hotel, Ispytateley prosp. 31, ph. 395-3629 F8(6)

I

ICE CREAM

Baskin-Robbins Ice Cream, Nevskiy prosp. 79, ph. 164-6456

Diana, Gavanskaya u. 19, ph. 217-0222

Fiesta, Zverinskaya ul. 42, ph. 232-7813

Spektr, Degtyarny p. 1/8, ph. 274-2198

Tishuten & co., Nevskiy prosp. 100, ph. 279-3311

Vilena, Nauki prosp. 44, ph. 538-2533

INFORMATION

Address Bureau, Liteyny prosp. 6, ph. 278-3119

Addresses of St. Petersburg Residents, (during working hours), ph. 009

Aircraft Arrivals and Departures, Information, ph. 297-2509

Directory Assistance, ph. 09

Emergency Medical Assistance, ph. 278-0025

Hotelship  Peterhof
★ ★ ★ ★

Swiss Quality & Russian Hospitality

Enjoy an exquisite dining experience
in the romantic atmosphere
with a breathtaking view of the Neva River.

Delicious international specialities prepared with
imported high-quality products under
the supervision of a Swiss Chef de Cuisine.

Live music and entertainment nightly.

"Svir" à la carte restaurant
Famous ethnic Food Festivals every month.
Russian and International cuisine.
12–2 p.m., 6–11 p.m.

"Neva" restaurant
Table d'hôte menu. Business lunch.
7–10 a.m., 12–14 p.m., 6–10 p.m.

"Sky Bar" night club
The best music band in town.
Dancing. Hot meals until 2 a.m.

"Panorama Bar"
A quiet place for drinks, coffee and
mouthwatering Swiss pastry.

Sun Deck Café
Cooling drinks under palm-trees
on a hot summer day.

The Hotelship Peterhof**** is located at the Makarov Embankment,
near the Tuchkov bridge, a 5 minute drive from the Hermitage museum.

For reservations please call 213 63 21

Information on Joint Ventures in St. Petersburg, ph. 050
International Direct Dial Telephone Service (Int'l Codes), ph. 274-9383
Long Distance Telephone, ph. 07
Lost and Found, ul. Zakharevskaya 19, ph. 278-3690
Militia, ph. 02
⇨**Russian Information Services**, Serpukhovskaya ul. 30, ph. 292-7420 {publishers of this guide}
State Committee for Statistics, ul. Professora Popova 39, ph. 230-7520
Telegram Service, (dictate over the phone), ph. 066
Time, ph. 08

INSURANCE

ASKO-Petersburg, Yuriya Gagarina prosp. 1, ph. 297-8500
Baltiyskoye Strakhovoye Obshchestvo, Ligovskiy prosp. 44, kv. 571, ph. 164-0635
Delta Consulting, KIMa prosp. 22, kv. 501-511, ph. 350-7961
Deposit, Ligovskiy prosp. 230, ph. 166-5583
General Insurance Company, Novo-Litovskaya ul. 15, ph. 245-5128
Geo, Ilyicha p. 10, kv. 20, ph. 164-0171
Hi-Fi Trust, Vasi Alekseyeva ul. 14, ph. 185-0617
Ingosstrakh-St. Petersburg, Zakharyevskaya ul. 17, ph. 273-0625
Lado-Balt, Lomonosova ul. 3, ph. 310-4455
Maks, Nevskiy prosp. 65, Box 131, ph. 314-0121
Progress-Neva, Moskovskiy prosp. 79a, ph. 275-0109
Rus, Kvarengi p. 4, ph. 278-1694
SKF Express, nab. reki Fontanki 116-b, ph. 251-3481
Sphinx Insurance, ul. Lomonosova 5, ph. 310-6222
Virilis, Bronnitskaya ul. 17, ph. 110-1093

INTERNATIONAL PHONE

See Business Centers, Telecom
See Car phone

International phones (in booths) payable by credit card or debit card are available in most major tourist hotels and at selected tourist sites. Always be sure of the costs before you dial; these booths are very expensive!

International calls can now be dialed directly from apartments, depending on overall line traffic. See the instructions and dialing codes for direct international dialing at the beginning of the Yellow Pages. Call 315-0012 for current rates.

If you can't get through by dialing direct from your hotel or apartment, you can book a call or use the services of business centers and telecom companies providing satellite switching to the international phone network, bypassing the local network, i.e. Delta Telecom, Lenfincom and BCL (see listings under Telecom).

Also try calling from the long distance phone center at ul. B. Morskaya 3/5 between 9 and 17 daily. Expect to stand in line.

AT&T and US Sprint have put their direct dialing systems in place in Moscow, and you can access them from St. Petersburg by prefacing their numbers with 8-095.

AT&T USA Direct, ph. 155-5042
Long distance call booking: 315-0012
Sprint Express , ph. 155-6133

JAZZ

Dixie Swing Club, Zagorodny prosp. 27, ph. 164-8565, open Sun, Tu-Th 19-23:30, Fr-Sa 19-00:30, closed Mo. Call for schedule and locations of performances.
Jazz Brunch, Grand Hotel Europe, Sundays 12-15. Cost is $30 per person, ph. 113-8066.
Jazz Philharmonic Hall (a.k.a. Jazz Club), Zagorodniy prosp. 27, ph. 164-8565
Kvadrat Jazz Club, ul. Pravdy 10, ph. 164-8508 {open 19-23}

JEWELRY

Almaz Jewelery, prosp. Veteranov 87, ph. 150-4401
Amethyst Jewelery Store, Petrogradskaya Storona, Bolshoy prosp. 64, ph. 232-0102
Aquamarine Jewelery, Novosmolenskaya nab. 1, ph. 352-0766

Biryuza Jewelery Store, Nevskiy prosp. 69, ph. 312-2176
Granat Jewelers, Bukharestskaya ul. 72, k. 1, ph. 268-2275
Izumrud Jewelery Store, Moskovskiy prosp. 184, ph. 298-3242
Krystall Jewelery Store, Nevskiy prosp. 34, ph. 311-3095
Russkiye Samotsvety Production Assn., Utkin prosp. 8, ph. 528-0103
Samotsvety Jewelery Store, Mikhailovskaya ul. 4, ph. 110-4915
Sapfir Jewelers, prosp. Engelsa 15, ph. 244-0723
Yakhont Jewelery Store, ul. B. Morskaya 24, ph. 314-6447
Zhemchug, Slavy prosp. 5, ph. 261-3720

L

LANGUAGE COURSES

See also Translation

The opportunities are virtually endless; call around, bargain for the best rate. Listed below are just a few of the more widely-advertised and well-established programs.

Many institutes and technical colleges also have programs which are very good. Consult our ***Russia Survival Guide*** *for universities offering language study programs in St. Petersburg.*

International Business Services (IBS), Rubinstein 8, Box 237, ph. 311-5838
Liden & Denz, Malookhtinskiy prosp. 68, ph. 528-1177
Obucheniye, Zagorodny prosp. 58, ph. 292-3861
Russian Language Teaching Center, Universitetskaya nab. 7/9, ph. 218-9452

LAUNDRIES, SELF SERVE

Launderette, Korablestroiteley ul. 20, kor. 3, ph. 355-4025; Ordzhonikidze ul. 31-a; Zaytseva ul. 17, ph. 184-0503
Runo Launderette, Leninskiy prosp. 155-a, ph. 164-4827

LEGAL ADVICE

Western law firms have finally started entering St. Petersburg. These are listed below, along with better-established Russian firms.

AZ Law Firm, ul. Mayakovskovo 50, ph. 272-4132
Baker & McKenzie, nab. kanala Griboyedova 36, ph. 310-5446
Booz-Allen & Hamilton, Nevskiy prosp. 77, kv. 3, ph. 164-5289
H. Hedman Legal Services, Nevskiy prosp. 134, ph. 274-4160
Inyurkollegiya (Int'l Juridical Board), Pushkinskaya ul. 13, ph. 112-1679
Law Office of S. A. Stern, Nevskiy prosp. 104, ph. 275-3497
Pepper, Hamilton, & Scheetz, Shpalernaya ul. 30, ph. 273-2377
Poverenny Law Firm, Moskovskiy prosp. 17, ph. 292-3127
Russian American Law Firm, Lermontovskiy prosp. 7/12, ph. 114-5660
Salans Hertzfeld & Heilbronn, Nevskiy prosp. 70, ph. 272-4572
St. Petersburg Bar Assn., Sadovaya ul. 32/1, ph. 315-8510
Stouk Ltd., nab. kanala Griboyedova 102, ph. 310-2104
Yuriskonsult, Millionnaya ul. 17, ph. 312-1852

LIBRARIES

Russian libraries often have strict admission and usually non-existent borrowing policies. But if you can read Russian and are interested in visiting a library, take your passport along (call ahead for hours) and give it a go. Don't take a bag or briefcase with you, you will likely not be able to take it in with you. The major libraries are listed below.

Agricultural Library, ul. B. Morskaya 42, ph. 314-4914
All-Union Geological Library, V.O., Sredniy prosp. 74, ph. 218-9228
Asian and African Literature Book Repository, Liteyny prosp. 49, ph. 272-5776
Baltiyskiy Zavod Shipyard Library, V.O., Bolshoy prosp. 78, ph. 217-9406

Belinskiy Central District Library, Grazhdanskiy prosp. 83, kor. 1, ph. 217-2923
Blok Central Library, Nevskiy prosp. 20, ph. 311-0106
Central Archives of the Navy, ul. Millionnaya 36, ph. 315-9054
Central Naval Library, Sadovaya ul. 2, ph. 210-4365
Chernyshevskiy Library, prosp. Kima 4, ph. 350-1200
Filosofskaya Akademiya Library, nab. reki Fontanki 20, ph. 273-9484
Gogol Library, ul. Stakhanovtsev 4-a, ph. 528-1703
Health Center Library, Italianskaya ul. 25, ph. 311-3638
Leningrad Technical Information Center Library, Sadovaya ul. 2, ph. 210-4891
Library for the Blind, ul. Shamsheva 8, ph. 232-5080
Library of the Academy of Arts, Universitetskaya nab. 17, ph. 213-7178
Lunacharskiy Theater Library, ul. Zodchevo Rossi 2, ph. 311-0845
Marinskiy Opera & Ballet House Central Musical Note Library, ul. Zodchevo Rossi 2, ph. 312-3573
Mayakovskiy Central City Library, nab. reki Fontanki 44, ph. 311-3026
Medical Scientific Library, prosp. Lunacharskovo 45, ph. 592-7158
Ostrovskiy Youth Library, Syezdovskaya liniya 21, ph. 213-5628
Pushkin Central City Children's Library, ul. B. Morskaya 33, ph. 312-3380
Russian Academy of Sciences Library, Birzhevaya liniya 1, ph. 218-3592
Saltykov-Shchedrin State Library, Sadovaya ul. 18, ph. 310-2856
Sports Library, Millionnaya ul. 22, ph. 311-3912
St. Petersburg Philharmonic Society Music Library, Bolsheokhtinskiy prosp. 8, ph. 227-0772
St. Petersburg Technical University Library, Politekhnicheskaya ul. 29, ph. 552-7559
Tolstoy Library, V. O., 6 Liniya 17, ph. 213-6787

LIQUOR

Most all the shops listed under Food and under Shops offer a variety of wine, spirits and beer. Kiosks also sell liquor, but this should be a last resort – there has been a rash of liquor poisoning cases from liquor bought through kiosks, which are poorly regulated.

Also try:

Nektar Wine Shop, Malodetskoselskiy prosp. 25, ph. 292-5244

M

MAIL

See also Courier

American Express offers a service worldwide that allows cardholders to receive mail sent to their name at the Amex office. Mail should be sent to the cardholder, *c/o American Express, P.O. Box 87, SF-53501, Lapeenranta, Finland.* The St. Petersburg office is located in the Grand Hotel Europe.
Central Post Office, ul. Pochtamtskaya 9, ph. 312-8302
International Post Offfice, Nevskiy prosp. 6, open 10-20, handles foreign mail, telegrams and phone calls.

MAPS

Maps in Russian of the city can be bought at just about any kiosk that sells newspapers. The two best stores for consistent stocks of Russian-produced maps are:

Dom Knigi, Nevskiy prosp. 28
Plakat, Lermontovskiy prosp. 38 (across from the Sovetskaya Hotel.

*The best, most-current English-language map of St. Petersburg is the one printed in the back of this book. The map is available in full-sheet, fold-out form (**The New St. Petersburg: City Map and Guide**) from the publisher (see office addresses at front or back of this guide) or at fine stores in St. Petersburg, Moscow and worldwide.*

Quality Western Health Care for the St. Petersburg Community

Highly qualified Western doctors and Registered Nurses

•

Family medicine, including pediatric and prenatal care

•

24-hour emergency service for AMC members

•

State-of-the-art diagnostic and lab facilities

•

Comprehensive Western pharmacy

•

Coordination of medical evacuations

AMC also offers the following customized membership plans:

• Corporate • Family • Individual
• Tourist • Student

The American Medical Center

For appointments, or to discuss membership, call:
(812) 119-61-01, fax (812) 119-61-20

Hours: M-F 8:30 am – 6 pm

HOTEL OLYMPIA

★★★

ST. PETERSBURG

Welcome to the *new* Hotel Olympia!

Hotel Olympia offers you generous value for money in totally remodelled, more spacious and comfortable rooms.

RESTAURANT

Exciting kitchen in a friendly atmosphere.

BAR

Summertime rendezvous under the midnight sun.

Hotel Olympia, Sea Glory Square, 199106 St.Petersburg, Russia.
Phone: +7-812-119 68 00. Telex: +64-121 333. Fax: +7-812-119 68 05.

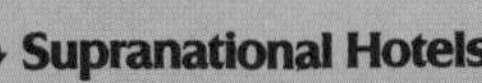

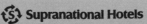

MARKETS

You will find the best domestic produce at farmers' markets. Bargaining with vendors is expected. Kuznechny and Nekrasovskiy markets enjoy the best reputations.

Kalininskiy, Polyustrovskiy prosp. 45, ph. 540-3039

Kirovskiy, prosp. Stachek 54, ph. 185-0639

Kuznechny, Kuznechny p. 3, ph. 312-4161

Maltsevskiy, ul. Nekrasova 52, ph. 279-2583

Moskovskiy, ul. Reshetnikova 12, ph. 298-1189

Nevskiy, prosp. Obukhovskoy Oborony 75a, ph. 265-3889

Sennoy, Moskovskiy prosp. 4, ph. 310-0217

Sytny, Sytninskaya ul. 3/5, ph. 233-1282

Torzhkovskiy, Torzhkovskaya ul. 20, ph. 246-8375

Vasileostrovskiy, V. O., Bolshoy prosp. 18, ph. 213-6687

MASSAGE

Major hotels and gyms (see Gyms above) have masseuses on staff. Also try:

Nevskiye Saunas, ul. Marata 5/7, ph. 311-1400

World Class Gym, Grand Hotel Europe, ph. 113-8066; Hotel Astoria, 4th floor, ph. 210-5869; Kamennoostrovskiy prosp. 26, ph. 232-7581

MEDICAL CARE

See also Ambulance, Dentists, Drug Stores

⇨ **American Medical Center**, nab. reki Fontanki 77, ph. 310-9611 {staffed with Western-trained doctors and best equipment; offers traveler's medical plan and membership rates on all services}

Avalanche Ltd, Vladimirskiy prosp. 2, ph. 113-1384; Izmailovskiy prosp. 14, ph. 112-6510

Avicenna JV (Syria), ul. Professora Popova 15/17, ph. 234-5028

Center for Lazer Technology JV (FRG), ul. Politekhnicheskaya 29, ph. 535-5247

Clinical Center of New Medical Technology, prosp. Severny 1, ph. 511-0961

Euro-Flite Oy, Box 187, 01531, Vantaa, Finland, ph. 358-0-870-2544, fax 870-2507 {emergency medical evacuations}

Hospital No. 20, ul. Gastello 21, ph. 108-4066 {foreigners' hospital}

Hospital No. 9, Krestovskiy prosp. 18, ph. 235-2058

Medkhor, ul. Inzhenernaya 13, ph. 314-6710

Medtekhnika, ul. Ruzovskaya 18, ph. 292-1977; ul. Voronezhskaya 16, ph. 164-0110

Nordmed, ul. Tverskaya 12/15, ph. 110-0401

Outpatient Medical Bureau, Nevskiy prosp. 82, ph. 272-9085

Polyclinic No. 2, Moskovskiy prosp. 22, ph. 292-5904

Russian Institute of Prophilactic Medicine, ul. Tolstovo 10, ph. 232-3877

Sukhanov's Clinic, ul. Beloostrovskaya 26, ph. 242-2917

Tonus Medical Cooperative, ul. Podvoyskovo 14, k. 1, paradnaya 9, ph. 589-2647

Traditional Medicine Cooperative Clinic, ul. Serdobolskaya 57/26, ph. 245-1907

Tsitomed Medical Center, p. Muchnoy 2, ph. 310-8011

MONEY CHANGING

See Banks, Domestic
See American Express, Cash Advances

More liberal Russian hard-currency regulations, combined with mass-printing of large denomination bills has eased many of the former difficulties of changing money. At the same time, the steady decline in the ruble's value means that it does not make sense to change more money for rubles than you will need for the near term (i.e. 1-2 weeks).

Money exchange points have popped up on practically every street corner, and almost every bank has an Обмен валюты–'Obmen valyuty' (Bureau de change). Bank rates are usually pegged to the MICE (Moscow Interbank Currency Exchange) rate, which is based on twice-weekly currency auctions.

MOVIES

See also Video Rental

There is no lack of movie theaters in St. Petersburg. However, movies from the 70's-early 80's, and dubbed grade-B American action films are the usual features. There are billboards at strategic points throughout the city with current theater listings. You can also call theaters directly to find out their programs — you will find the address and phone of most St. Petersburg theaters in the White Pages Telephone Directory.

MOVING

See also Shipping Agents

Avtokolonna 1106, nab. reki Volkovki 13, ph. 166-6216

EuroDonat JV (Belgian), ul. Yakornaya 17, ph. 224-1144 {leader in St. Petersburg-based removal services}

Galaktika, V. O., 2 Liniya 35, ph. 213-1121

Hertz Interauto Firm, ul. Ispolkomovskaya 9/11, ph. 277-4032

Intourautoservice, ul. Sedova 5, ph. 567-8151

Kamazservis Firm, Yunnatov tupik 1, ph. 262-3034

Lenavtotrans, nab. kanala Griboyedova 5, ph. 314-6676

Lengoragropromtrans 2 Transport Firm, prosp. Aleksandrovskoy fermi 17, ph. 262-1308

Mak, ul. Sofiyskaya 6, ph. 106-2841

North-West Transport Ltd, ul. B. Morskaya 37, ph. 210-8356

Petersburg Vneshtrans, Mezhevoy Kanal 5, ph. 251-0629

Transpoint, ul. Komsomola 1/3

Zapstroitrans Transport Association, Ligovskiy prosp. 56, ph. 164-6794

MUSEUMS

Aleksandr Nevskiy Abbey, Pl. Aleksandra Nevskovo, ph. 274-0409

Anna Akhmatova Museum, Liteyniy prosp. 53,or nab. Fontanki 34, ph. 272-1811

Aurora Cruiser Ship, Petrovskaya nab. 4, ph. 230-5202

Blok House Museum, ul. Dekabristov 57, ph. 113-8633

Botanical Gardens Museum, ul. Professora Popova 2, ph. 234-0673

Botanical Gardens of St. Petersburg State University, Universitetskaya nab. 7/9, ph. 218-9721

Brodskiy House Museum, ul. Mkhailovskaya 3, ph. 314-3658

Dokuchayev Museum of Soil Science, Birzhevoy pr. 6, ph. 218-5501

Dostoevskiy House Museum, Kuznechny p. 5/2, ph. 164-6950

Emperor Paul I Residence, Pavlovsk Park, Pavlovsk, ul. Revolyutsii 20, ph. 470-2156

Ethnographic Museum of the Peoples of Russia, Inzhenernaya ul. 4/1, ph. 219-1174

Exhibition Hall of the Artists' Union, Sverdlovskaya nab. 64, ph. 224-0633; ul. B. Morskaya 38, ph. 314-4734 {open 13-18, closed Sun., Mon.}

Hermitage State Museum, Dvortsovaya nab. 34, ph. 219-8625

Historical Museum of the Military, Aleksandrovskiy Park 7, ph. 232-0296

History of St. Petersburg Museum, Peter and Paul Fortress, ph. 238-4540 {open 11-17}

Kirov House Museum, Kamennoostrovskiy prosp. 26/28, ph. 233-3822

Literary Museum of the Institute of Russian Literature, nab. Makarova 4, ph. 218-0502

Literary Plot of Volkovskoye Cemetery, Rasstannaya ul. 30, ph. 166-2383

Lomonosov Memorial Museum, Universitetskaya nab. 3, ph. 218-1211

Marble Palace, The (Russian Museum), Millionnaya ul. 5/1, ph. 312-1788

Mendeleev House Museum, Mendeleyevskaya liniya 2, ph. 218-2982

Menshikov Palace Museum, Universitetskaya nab. 15, ph. 213-1112

Museum of Anthropology and Ethnology, Universitetskaya nab. 3, ph. 218-1412

Museum of Military Medicine, Lazaretniy p. 2, ph. 113-5215

Museum of Political History, Kuybysheva ul. 4, ph. 233-7113

Museum of the Academy of Arts, Universitetskaya nab. 17, ph. 213-6496

Museum of the Arctic and Antarctic, ul. Marata 24a, ph. 311-2549

Museum of Theater and Musical Art, pl. Ostrovskovo 6a, ph. 311-2195

Museum of Zoology, Universitetskaya nab. 1/3, ph. 218-0112

Naval Museum, Birzhevaya pl. 4, ph. 218-2502

Nekrasov House Museum, Liteyny prosp. 36, ph. 272-0165

Pavlov House Museum, V. O., 7 Liniya 2, ph. 213-7234

Peter the Great's Domik, Petrovskaya nab. 6, ph. 232-4576

Peter-Paul Fortress, ph. 238-4505

Piskaryovskoye Cemetery, prosp. Nepokorennykh, ph. 247-5716

Planetarium, Aleksandrovskiy Park 4, ph. 233-3153

Popov Museum of Communications, Pochtamtskaya ul. 7, ph. 311-9255

Pushkin Dacha Museum, Pushkinskaya ul. 2, ph. 476-6990

Pushkin House Museum, nab. reki Moyki 12, ph. 311-3801

Pushkin Museum, Catherine Palace, Komsomolskaya ul. 2, ph. 476-6411

Railway Museum, Sadovaya ul. 50, ph. 168-8005

Repin Museum, Primorskoye sh. 411, ph. 231-6828

Rimsky-Korsakov House Museum, Zagorodny prosp. 28, kv. 39, ph. 113-3208

Russian Museum, Inzhenernaya ul. 4, ph. 219-1615

Shalyapin House Museum, ul. Graftio 26, ph. 234-1056

St. Issac's Cathedral, Isaakevskaya pl. 1, ph. 315-9732

St. Petersburg State Orchestra, Nevskiy prosp. 41, Belozerskiy Palase, ph. 315-3921

Summer Palace, Letniy sad, ph. 314-0374

Suvorov Museum, ul. Saltykova-Shchedrina 43, ph. 279-3915

Union of St. Petersburg Museums, Liteyny prosp. 57, ph. 279-7135

Urban Sculpture Museum, Nevskiy prosp. 179/2, ph. 274-2635

MUSIC STORES

Baltic Star and **Neva Star** stores (see addresses in White Pages), sell CDs and tapes of Western music.

Dom Muzyki i Radio, Grazhdanskiy prosp. 15, ph. 535-0314

Globus Photoshop, Nevskiy prosp. 72, ph. 272-9031

Melodiya, Nevskiy prosp. 32/34, ph. 311-7455 {open 11-20, lunch 14-15}

Real-Music Shop, Nevskiy prosp. 54, ph. 310-5922

Rhapsodiya Record Store, B. Konyushennaya ul. 13, ph. 314-4801

N

NEWS

Major hotels (i.e. the Grand Hotel Europe and Nevskiy Palace) now have live satellite feed of CNN and European news channels. These hotels/shops will also have fairly current editions of national news magazines like TIME or Stern, as well as the IHT and other foreign language papers, including the Moscow Times and the St Petersburg Press, both English language papers aimed at the cities' expatriate communities.

For local businessand other news, the major newspapers and journals are:

Chas Pik Newspaper, Nevskiy prosp. 81, ph. 279-2270

Chasa Newspaper, 24, ul. Rimskovo-Korsakovo 9, ph. 310-6375

Delovie Lyudi, (Business in the Ex-USSR) also published in English, available at most kiosks and hotel shops.

Ekonomika i Zhizn, ul. Lomonosova 22, ph. 315-3148

ITAR/TASS Press Agency, ul. Sadovaya 38, ph. 310-8840

Izvestiya Editorial Office, Nevskiy prosp. 19, ph. 311-8506

Kak Dela, Nevskiy prosp. 28, ph. 219-9471 {monthly English/Russian business journal}

Komsomolskaya Pravda, Khersonskaya ul. 12, ph. 274-0663

Literaturnaya Gazeta, ul. Shpalernaya 18, ph. 279-0873
Neva News, ul. Pravdy 10, ph. 164-4765 {English language}
Nevskiye Vedomosti, Rasstannaya ul. 7, ph. 312-9554
Sankt-Peterburgskiye Vedomosti, nab. reki Fontanki 59, ph. 314-7176
Smena, nab. reki Fontanki 59, ph. 311-0219
St. Petersburg Press, ul. Razyezzhay 5, ph. 119-6080 {English language weekly for the foreign community – should be required reading for any long- or short-term visitor}
St. Petersburg Today, ul. Artileriyskaya 1, office 423, ph. 279-6047

NON-PROFITS

There are numerous charitable, non-profit and non-governmental organizations now operating in Russia and providing various types of aid or technical assistance. Some of the major ones are listed below. See the White Pages for other listings.

Aist, Raznochinnaya B. ul. 6, kv. 28
Center for Citizen Initiatives, V. O., 4th Galernaya Liniya, room 418, ph. 271-0467
Citizens' Democracy Corps, Inc., ul. Sadovaya 38, ph. 315-7393
Cultural Initiative, ul. Chaykovskovo 29, ph. 273-5538
Deti Blokady-900, ul. Saltykova-Shchedrina 32/34, ph. 273-1109
Dolg Soldiers & Reserve Corps Club, V. O., 1 Liniya 20, ph. 213-8037
House of Friendship and Peace with Peoples ofForeign Countries, nab. reki Fontanki 21, ph. 210-4927
International Executive Service Corps, Belgradskaya ul. 6-4-46, ph. 109-6914
Iskatel, Suvorovskiy prosp. 55, ph. 275-6781
Kapella, nab. reki Moyki 20, ph. 314-7239
Maltiyskiy Charitable Canteen, ul. Chaykovskovo 77, ph. 272-5294
Nevskiy Angel, Gorokhovaya ul. 5, ph. 315-2033
Nochlezhka, Pushkinskaya ul. 10, ph. 164-4868
Oasis, Leninskiy prosp. 161, ph. 293-2247
Russian Red Cross, Italianskaya ul. 25, ph. 311-3696
St. Petersburg Veteran Foundation, nab. Kutuzova 22/2, ph. 279-4708
Veteran, Varshavskaya ul. 110, ph. 233-1320

OFFICE EQUIPMENT

Absolut St. Petersburg, Kosmonavtov prosp. 54, ph. 264-6527
Alcatel Business Systems, ul. B. Morskaya 16, ph. 315-8938
Amela, Vladimirskiy prosp. 3, ph. 113-2284
Bive, Konnogvardeyskiy bul. 4, kv. 20, ph. 312-7835
Commark, ul. Sablinskaya 7, ph. 233-3008
Etal, B. Morskaya ul. 53, ph. 312-3382
Hi-Life Electronics, ul. Karavannaya 16, ph. 314-9861
Invent, Manezhny p. 19, kv. 27, ph. 275-5910
Invert, Chaykovskovo ul. 60, ph. 275-1567
IPRIS, Primorkskiy prosp. 35a, ph. 239-5796
Kvasar, Kamennoostrovskiy prosp. 5, ph. 233-4033
Leksa, V. O., 11 Liniya 22, ph. 213-2698
London, Kamennoostrovskiy prosp. 12, ph. 232-6293
MKS Sankt-Petersburg, V. O., 16 Liniya 11, ph. 217-3058
Nevotal, Nevskiy prosp. 82, ph. 275-7149
Pribory & Vychislitelnaya Tekhnika, Leninskiy prosp. 148, ph. 290-5530
Rainbow, Zaitseva ul. 41, ph. 183-3096
Rank Xerox, nab. Obvodnovo kanala 93a, ph. 315-7670
Renaisance, M. Posadskaya ul. 17, ph. 233-8976
Rossa JV (Austria,German), ul. Khlopina 11, ph. 534-1086
Skif, Vosstaniya ul. 32, ph. 275-5345
Stalker, Bolshoy prosp. 34, ph. 230-9966
Strela, Ligovskaya ul. 6, kv. 313, ph. 422-2098
Testek, Shkiperskiy protok 2, ph. 356-6716
Vikart, Professora Popova ul. 41/5, kv. 11, ph. 234-9676

OFFICE SPACE

See also Real Estate

Inform-Future Business Center, ul. Tambovskaya 12, ph. 312-3078

Market Bridge Centre, Bolsheokhtinskiy prosp. 1, ph. 224-1122

Market Bridge Firm, Nevskiy prosp. 82, ph. 275-7149

OFFICE SUPPLIES

Babylon Shop, Sadovaya ul. 26, ph. 310-1815

Imperial, Izmaylovskiy prosp. 11, ph. 251-6128

Konstruktor Stationers, Sadovaya ul.. 26, ph. 310-1815

S&A Stationers, B. Konyushennaya 27, ph. 311-8720

Sphinx JV (Finland), ul. Gertsena 55, ph. 312-7540

Vial Stationers, ul. Belinskovo 11, ph. 278-8680

OPTICAL

Leniko Dental and Contact Lens Center, V. O., 14 Liniya 97, ph. 355-8388

Vizion Express, ul. Lomonosova 5, ph. 310-1595

P

PARKS

See also Recreation, Boat Rides

On a free afternoon, try walking through Kirov Park on Yelagin island. It has walking paths, boating, a bathing beach as well as an exhibition hall and theaters. Boating is also possible at Park Pobedy (Victory Park). Lenin Park and the Botanical Gardens, on opposite sides of Petrogradskiy island, are also nice.

If you have a day free, the former Imperial Palaces in Petrodvorets, Pushkin and Pavlovsk, all just outside the city, are quite beautiful in the late spring and summer.

Botanical Garden of the Academy of Sciences, ul. Professora Popova 2, ph. 234-1764

Botanical Gardens of St. Petersburg State University, Universitetskaya nab. 7/9, ph. 218-9721

Dvorets Tvorchestva Yunikh, Nevskiy prosp. 39, ph. 314-7281

Kirov Park of Culture and Leisure, Yelagin ostrov 4, ph. 239-0911

Moscow Victory Park, Kuznetsovskaya ul. 25, ph. 298-3249

Primorskiy Victory Park, Krestovskiy prosp. 21, ph. 235-2146

Summer Gardens and Palace of Peter the Great, ph. 312-9666

Tavricheskiy Garden, Igroteka, ul. Saltykova-Shchedrina 50, ph. 272-6044

Yuzhno-Primorskiy Park, Petergofskoye sh. 27, ph. 151-5287

PASSPORT PHOTOS

Agfa Salon, Nevskiy prosp. 20, ph. 311-9923. {while-you-wait service}

Obyektiv Fotographia, Nevskiy prosp. 24, ph. 312-0122 {makes pictures for passports, visas and other documents. 4 hour turn-around time}

Srochnaya Foto, (Quick Photo) stores can be found on nearly ever main street in St. Petersburg and canmake photosfor documents at any time.

PERSONNEL

Artar-Innery, Belgradskaya ul. 40, ph. 260-1888

Baltink Ltd., nab. reki Fontanki 40, ph. 279-7463

Hill International, ul. B. Morskaya 23, ph. 312-6701

Konform, B. Raznochinnaya ul. 6, kv. 28, ph. 235-4209

Kuybyshevskiy Employment Agency, Nevskiy prosp. 78, ph. 275-1829

Nevskiy Employment Agency, Ivanovskaya ul. 7, ph. 560-6121

Oktyabrskiy Employment Agency, Sadovaya ul. 55/57, ph. 311-9157

Personnel Corps, Nevskiy prosp. 104, ph. 275-4586

Smolninskiy Employment Agency, Nevskiy prosp. 176, ph. 277-1859
Soinform, Kamennoostrovskiy prosp. 42, ph. 235-7146
Viliya, Leninskiy prosp. 118 pod. 7, ph. 153-5900
Vyborgskiy Employment Agency, B. Sampsonievskiy prosp. 75

PETS

Elita Pet Shop, Stachek prosp. 67, kor. 1, ph. 184-5698
Joker Pet Shop, Sytninskaya pl. 1/47, ph. 233-7351
Priroda Shop, Sytninskaya pl. 1/47, ph. 233-7351
Sobakovod Pet Shop, Bukharestskaya ul. 23, ph. 174-8746
Vitalis, Lagody ul. 3, ph. 227-1962

PHOTO DEVELOPING

Agfa Salon, Nevskiy prosp. 20, ph. 311-9974 {open 9-21, color copies}
Fuji Photo Salon, nab. reki Fontanki 23, ph. 314-4936
Peter the Great JV (Venezuela), ul. M. Konyushennaya 7, ph. 110-6497
Photo Salon, Nevskiy prosp. 54, ph. 311-0838

POLICE — DIAL 02

PRINTING

See also Copying

Aiyu, Voronezhskaya ul. 33, ph. 166-0320
Aleksander Print, nab. reki Fontanki 18, ph. 279-0259
Ales, Basseynaya ul. 20, Box 261, ph. 294-0455
Ankor, 6 Krasnoarmeyskaya ul. 17, ph. 292-0475
Baltika-St. Petersburg, Box 48, ph. 543-6211
Baltinvest, Goncharnaya ul. 25, ph. 271-8153
Begemot, Shpalernaya ul. 60/1, ph. 278-5968
Biont, Furmanova ul. 25, kv. 8, ph. 275-8757
Dilar-6, ul. Komsomola 33, ph. 541-8372
Ekobalt, Voznesenskiy prosp. 36 kv. 11, ph. 310-2731
Express Printing, Konnogvardeyskiy bulv. 4, ph. 311-2346
Express-Print, Pushkinskaya ul. 20, ph. 113-1808
Hemotex, Khersonskaya ul. 3, ph. 274-5325
Hollight, Baskov p. 6, ph. 279-0903
Impax, nab. reki Fontanki 18, ph. 279-0259
Inger, Professora Popova ul. 47, ph. 234-5075
Kaskad, Ligovskiy prosp. 65, ph. 164-5333
Kella, ul. Kronverkskaya 10, ph. 232-1890
Konti-Universal, Goncharnaya ul. 5, ph. 273-0949
Lega, 5 Krasnoarmeyskaya ul. 28, kv. 17, ph. 292-1919
Lenart, nab. reki Fontanki 34, ph. 275-7510
Lenta JV (Finland), prosp. Chernyshevskovo 17, ph. 275-8844
Maservil, 5 Liniya 48, kv. 8, ph. 113-8601
Mitsar, nab. reki Pryazhki, ph. 216-0881
Pallada, V. O., 13 Liniya 10, ph. 213-5640
Petropol, Nevskiy prosp. 30, ph. 311-6693
Petrospek JV, Antonenko p. 5, ph. 110-6508
Polex, Volkhovskiy p. 3, ph. 218-8344
Poligraf, Institutskiy p. 3, ph. 550-0820
Poligrafaktsia, Chaykovskovo ul. 30, ph. 219-9288
Polimorf, ul. Tavricheskaya 39, kom. 231, ph. 272-9884
Polygraph Express, Shvedskiy p. 2, ph. 311-1810
Realis, Stremyannaya ul. 3, ph. 112-5058
Restavrator, Staro-Petergofskiy prosp. 3/5, ph. 251-6303
Revers, Ligovskiy prosp. 56, ph. 164-8281
Smart JV (Finland), Admiralteyskiy prosp. 8/1, ph. 110-6655

Where in Moscow, this book's parallel guide to the Russian capital, is the only guide you'll need to the "Third Rome." Call Russian Information Services at: (in the US) 802-223-4955, (in Moscow) 095-254-9275, (in St. Petersburg) 812-292-7420.

Sovmarket, 1 Sovetskaya ul. 10, ph. 277-5371
Status, Marshala Govorova prosp. 8b, ph. 185-0860
Struzh, V. O., 11 Liniya 68, ph. 213-8235
Syuzhet, Koli Tomchaka ul. 24, ph. 307-7954
Tekhnobalt, Shpalernaya ul. 52, ph. 275-4200
Telex, Kavalergardskya ul. 10, kv. 19, ph. 278-5032
Terra-Inkognita, Soyuza Pechatnikov ul. 28, ph. 219-5083
Topos, Chekhova ul. 5, ph. 273-5128
Very Well, nab. reki Fontanki 118-4, ph. 251-3461
Vika, nab. Obvodnovo kanala 215, kv. 12, ph. 251-4333
Vista Communications, Shpalernaya ul. 53, kv. 113, ph. 278-1928
Vistar-SP, Kolomenskaya ul. 5, ph. 112-0768
Vladen, ul. Gorokhovaya 7, ph. 307-7954

R

RADIO

Here is where to tune for news, sports and music:

BBC {1260 AM}
Deutsche Welle {1200 AM}
Evropa Plus, ul. Prof. Popova 47, ph. 234-4080 {72.6 & 100.5 FM}
Magic Radio, nab reki Karpovki 43, ph. 234-9085 {68.2 FM}
Radio Baltika, Kamennoostrvskiy prosp. 67, ph. 235-5850 {71.2 FM}
Radio Rocks {102 FM; wide selection of both new and old rock music}
Radio Rossii, Italyanskaya ul. 27, ph. 219-9608 {66.3 FM}

REAL ESTATE

See also Apartments, Office Space

20 Vek Agency, Vladimirskiy prosp. 9, ph. 113-1676
ACCEPT, ul. Borovaya 19, ph. 164-7683
Alivekt, nab. reki Moyki 40, ph. 315-7302
Atlantic Investment, Ryleyeva ul. 18, ph. 275-8590
BusinessLink, V. O., 13 Liniya 14, ph. 218-6900
Dinas, Ligovskiy prosp. 249, ph. 166-1155
DINAT'F, prosp. Entuziastov 18/3, ph. 315-6794
Ferguson Hollis, Nevskiy prosp. 30, ph. 312-1490
Haka Oy, Admiralteyskiy prosp. 6, ph. 312-3915
Hotel Development Corporation, nab. kanala Griboyedova 5, ph. 314-3178
Inform-Future Business Center, ul. Tambovskaya 12, ph. 312-3078
International Group, ph. 311-2483
InterOccidental, Vosstaniya ul. 49, ph. 273-4323
Investtrade, Fonarniy P. 3, ph. 110-6267
Jendrusch & Partner, ul. Belinskovo 13, ph. 272-4654
Kulsa, ul. 3 Sovetskaya 8, ph. 275-0089
Lek Estate, Nevskiy prosp. 90/92, ph. 272-1097
Management Systems Corporation, Pushkin 7, Box 76, ph. 476-1550
Muline, V. O., Sredniy prosp. 9, ph. 213-4506
Peter Haka, Admiralteyskiy prosp. 6, ph. 312-3118
Pukkila-Talot, Sverdlovskaya nab. 60, kv. 47
Ryland St. Petersburg, ul. B. Morskaya 31, ph. 314-6435
St. Petersburg World Financial and Trade Center, Kanal Griboyedova 5, ph. 312-3557
Twentieth Trust Corporation, Nevskiy prosp. 44, ph. 311-1696
VMB, Pisareva ul. 6, kv. 8, ph. 114-7589
Wal-Rus Ltd, ul. Nekrasova 40/1, ph. 273-6746

RECREATION, CHILDREN

See also Parks, Horseback Riding, Museums, Skating, Zoo

Bolshoy Puppet Theater, ul. Nekrasova 10, ph. 273-6672
Museum of Zoology, Universitetskaya nab. 1/3, ph. 218-0112

Railway Museum, Sadovaya ul. 50, ph. 168-8005

Tavricheskiy Sad, Shchedrina ul. 50

RECREATION, SPORTS

See also Gyms, Saunas, Swimming

Here are the major sports facilities in St. Petersburg. Membership rules and fees differ widely from place to place. Call ahead to see if you will be welcomed.

Army Sports Club, Inzhenernaya ul. 13, ph. 219-2967

Baltika Sports Center, Petrovskiy prosp. 16, ph. 235-5164

Dinamo Sports Center, prosp. Dinamo 44, ph. 235-0170

Elektrosila Sports Club, Moskovskiy prosp. 139, ph. 298-2075

Jubilee Palace of Sport, ul. Dobrolyubova 18, ph. 238-4114

Lenin Sport-Concert Complex, prosp. Yuri Gagarina 8, ph. 264-0472

Lokomotiv Olympic Preparation Center, ul. Deputatskaya 9a, ph. 235-0412

Motorek Rowing Club, ul. Zhaka Dyuklo 67, ph. 533-7014

Petrovskiy Stadium, Petrovskiy ostrov 2g, ph. 238-4129

Spartak Rowing Sport Center, nab. Bolshoy Nevki 24, ph. 234-3622

Sport Klass, Kamenoostrovskiy prosp. 26/28, ph. 232-7581

Trade Union Rowing Club, nab. Bolshoy Nevki 24, ph. 234-3644

Trade Union Tennis Club, Konstantinovskiy prosp. 23, ph. 235-0407

Trud Swimming Pool, ul. Pravdy 11, ph. 210-5520

Yubileyny Sports Palace, prosp. Dobrolyubova 18, ph. 238-4122

Zenit Sports Palace, ul. Butlerova 9, ph. 535-0171

Zimny Sports Center, Manezhnaya pl. 2, ph. 311-0771

RELIGIOUS SERVICES

Amal Charitable Islamic Fund, Dvortsovaya nab. 18, ph. 311-5101

Baptist Church, B. Ozernoy ul. 29a, ph. 553-4578

Buddhist Temple, Primorskiy prosp. 91, ph. 239-0341

Christ Church, ul. Prof. Popova 47, ph. 110-1870

Christian Lutheran Evangelical Society, Sredny prosp. 18, ph. 184-9111

Evangelical Christian Church, Slavyanskaya ul. 13, ph. 100-4092

Grace Mission Group, Kamennoostrovskiy prosp. 42, ph. 230-8017

Gospel House, Borovaya ul. 52b, ph. 166-2831

International Church, Nevskiy prosp. 39, ph. 352-7439 {services Sunday mornings}

John the Baptist Brotherhood, 11 Krasnoarmeyskaya ul. 7, kv. 58, ph. 251-3246

Kifa Russian Orthodox Church Center, Leninskiy prosp. 135, ph. 255-6081

Lutheran Church, Ligovskiy prosp. 65, ph. 164-3091

Mosque of the Congregation of Moslems, Kronverkskiy prosp. 7, ph. 233-9819

Novaya Zhisn Christian Evangelical Mission, Saltykova-Shchedrina ul. 54, ph. 275-3662

St. Catherine of Aleksandria Catholic Church, Nevskiy prosp. 32/34, ph. 311-5795

Seventh-Day Adventists, ul. Internatsionalnaya 7, ph. 138-9811

Synagogue, Preobrazhenskoye cemetery, prosp. Alexandrovskoy Fermi, ph. 262-0447

Synagogue (choral), Lermontovskiy prosp. 2, ph. 114-1153

Some working Orthodox Churches:

Cathedral of Prince Vladimir, ul. Blokhina 26, ph. 232-7625

Cathedral of St. Nicholas & the Epiphany, Nikolskaya pl. 1/3, ph. 114-0862

Cathedral of the Holy Trinity, Alexander Nevskiy Monastery, nab. Reki Monastyrki 1, ph. 274-0409

Cathedral of the Transfiguration of Our Saviour, Pl. Radishcheva 1, ph. 272-3662

Church of Our Lady of Lourdes, Kovenskiy p. 7, ph. 272-5002

Church of Saint Seraphim of Sarovo, Serafimovskoye Cemetery, Serebryakov p. 1, ph. 239-1432

Church of St. Nicholas, prosp. Metallistov 5, ph. 224-2708
Church of the Apostle & Evangelist St. John the Divi, nab. Obvodnovo kanala 17, ph. 277-3350
Church of the Holy Prophet Job, Volkovo Cemetery, Kamchatskaya ul. 6, ph. 166-2544
Church of the Smolensk Cemetery, Kamskaya ul. 24, ph. 213-5414
Church of the Trinity (Kulich v Paskhe), prosp. Obukhovskoy Oborony 235, ph. 262-1387
Kazan Cathedral, Kazanskaya pl. 2, ph. 314-5838
Pargolovo Church of Our Saviour, Vyborgskoye sh. 106
Preobrazhenskiy Cathedral, Liteyny ul. and ul. Pestelya, ph. 272-3662
Shuvalovo Church of St. Alexander Nevskiy, Vyborgskoye sh. 106a, ph. 595-0666
Smolny Cathedral, Pl. Rastrelli 3/1, ph. 311-3560

RENOVATION (REMONT)

Agra, Engelsa prosp. 111, kor. 1, kv. 46
Anata, Izmaylovskiy prosp. 14, ph. 112-6678
Atlant, Yuriya Gagarina prosp. 1, ph. 297-8194
Beta, Marinesko ul. 1, ph. 184-1383
Brok, Dnepropetrovskaya ul. 31, ph. 164-0133
Chernavin, Basseynaya ul. 33/1, ph. 122-4789
Dekon, Tovarishcheskiy prosp. 3, kor. 1, ph. 527-3442
Elen, Moskovskiy prosp. 7, ph. 310-9537
Fregat, Torzhkovskaya ul. 15, ph. 246-1242
Granit-91, Dibunovskaya ul. 51, kv. 61, ph. 239-3523
Grazhdanka, Prosveshcheniya prosp. 87, ph. 530-1717
Interier, Avtovskaya ul. 35, ph. 184-7507
Komfort, B. Porokhovskaya ul. 24, ph. 224-2752
Komnata, Narvskiy prosp. 23, kor. 2, ph. 186-6358
Krasnogvardeets, Udarnikov prosp. 27, kor. 1, ph. 227-8975
Kreyt, Pushkinskaya ul. 10, kv. 129, ph. 164-9135
Moniks, Rubinshteyna ul. 22-20, ph. 310-2843
Nevskiye Zori, Ligovskiy 76, ph. 164-6773
Primorskiy Residence Repair & Remodeling Service, ul. Korolyova 15/30, ph. 393-6562
Reson, ul. Dnepropetrovskaya 12, ph. 292-2684
Restavrator, ul. Marata 17, ph. 315-4807
Rusich Interior Remodeling Service, 11 Krasnoarmeyskaya ul. 7, kv. 13, ph. 251-4801
Stroitel, Lyotchika Pilyutova 34,kor. 2, ph. 144-5380
Stroitel, Rubinshteyna ul. 3, ph. 312-6573
Union Reson, 12 Krasnoarmeyskaya ul. 7, ph. 292-3647
Venita, Vernosti ul. 10, kor. 3, ph. 535-4620
Vozrozhdeniye, ul. Plekhanova 50, ph. 311-9160
Zvezda, Kubinskaya ul. 1, ph. 296-6250

RESTAURANTS

The assertion of the ruble as the singular cash currency in Russia means that all restaurants must (if they deal in cash payments) accept payment in rubles. The reality is that nicer restaurants accept credit cards, print prices on their menus in dollars, and offer clients the opportunity to pay in rubles, based on a "house rate" of exchange. In such instances, it is usually best to pay with credit card, as house rates tend to be inflated.

If a restaurant is known to accept credit cards (most all do, certainly all those in the city center and all those catering to foreign clientele), then a "cc" follows the listing. ***Information in bold is map coordinates of the restaurant*** *(i.e.* F14(17) *= section F14, page 17)*

ARMENIAN

Nairi Restaurant, ul. Dekabristov 6, ph. 314-8093 **H16(21)**

AZERI

Zhemchuzhina Cafe, ul. Shkiperskiy protok 2, ph. 355-2063 **D16(9)**

BULGARIAN

Balkany Restaurant, Nevskiy prosp. 27, ph. 315-4748 **I15(22)**

BYELORUSSIAN

Polesye Restaurant, Sredneokhtinskiy prosp. 4, ph. 224-2917 **N14(11)**

CAUCASIAN

Iveria Cafe, ul. Marata 35, ph. 164-7478 **K17(27)**

Urartu Restaurant, ul. Rudneva 25, ph. 558-6919 **L3(3)**

CHINESE

⇨**Chop Sticks**, Grand Hotel Europe, ph. 119-6000 {cc, open 11-23} **I15(22)**

Kheybey, P.S., Bolshoy prosp. 61, ph. 233-2046 {open 1-22} **H12(17)**

Shanghai Restaurant JV (China), Sadovaya ul. 12/23, ph. 311-2751 {cc} **J15(22)**

DESSERT

Bristol Restaurant, Nevskiy prosp. 22/24, ph. 311-7490 **I15(22)**

Briz Kafe, Kolokolnaya ul. 8, ph. 110-6225 **J16(22)**

Bushe Restaurant, ul. Ryleyeva 23, ph. 272-0168 **K15(23)**

Ryabinushka Restaurant, ul. Oskalenko 11, ph. 239-4080 **F10(6)**

Solnyshko Restaurant, prosp. Kima 3, ph. 350-2938 **E13(9)**

EUROPEAN

Admiralteystvo Restaurant, Yekaterinskiy park, ul. Komsomolskaya 7, Pushkin, ph. 465-3549

Assambleya Restaurant, ul. B. Konyushennaya 13, ph. 314-1537 **I15(22)**

Bella Liona Restaurant, Vladimirskiy prosp. 9, ph. 113-1670 {open 12-2} **J16(22)**

Belye Nochi Restaurant, Voznesenskiy prosp. 41, ph. 319-9660 **H17(25)**

Brigantina Restaurant, Dvinskaya ul. 3, ph. 259-0815 **E18(9)**

Chaika Restaurant, nab. kanala Griboyedova 14, ph. 312-4631 {cc} **I15(22)**

Daddy's Steak Room and Pizza, Moskovskiy prosp. 73, ph. 252-7744 {cc, open 12-23} **I19(10)**

Daugava Restaurant, Hotel Pribaltiyskaya, ul. Korablestroiteley 14, ph. 356-4409 **C15(9)**

Grand Cafe Antwerpen, Kronverkskiy prosp. 13/2, ph. 233-9446 **I13(18)**

Koyolga Restaurant, Narodnaya ul. 15, ph. 263-1893 **Q22(16)**

Melody JV Restaurant (Sweden), Sverdlovskaya nab. 62, ph. 227-2676 {cc, open 12-18, 19-1} **N14(11)**

Meridian Restaurant, Hotel Pulkovskaya, Pl. Pobedy 1, ph. 264-5177 **I26(14)**

Metropol Restaurant, Sadovaya ul. 22, ph. 310-1845 **I15(22)**

Muza Restaurant, Rizhskiy prosp. 48, ph. 251-1724 **G18(25)**

Na Fontanke Restaurant, nab. reki Fontanki 77, ph. 310-2547 **I16(22)**

⇨**Neva Restaurant**, Hotelship Peterhof, ph. 213-6321

Neva Restaurant, Nevskiy prosp. 46, ph. 110-5980 **J16(22)**

Nevskiy 40, Nevskiy prosp. 40, ph. 311-9066 {cc, open 12-24} **I15(22)**

Night Club, Hotel Pribaltiyskaya, ul. Korablestroiteley 14, ph. 356-0001 {cc} **C15(9)**

Oktyabrskiy Restaurant, Nevskiy prosp. 118, ph. 277-7042 **K16(23)**

Olgino Restaurant, Olgino Campsite, Primorskoye sh., ph. 238-3674

Palanga Restaurant, Leninskiy prosp. 127, ph. 254-3601 **F25(14)**

⇨**Piccolo**, Hotel Olympia, ph. 119-6800 **D16(9)**

Pietari Restaurant, Moskovskiy prosp. 220, ph. 293-2397 {cc, open 12-3} **I25(14)**

Polyarnoye Cafe, Nevskiy prosp. 79, ph. 311-8589 **K16(23)**

Repinskaya Restaurant, Villa, Repino, Primorskoye sh. 428, ph. 231-6515

Russkiy Chay, ul. Tambovskaya 63, ph. 168-3833 **J18(26)**

Sankt-Peterburg Restaurant, Hotel Sankt Peterburg, Pirogovskaya nab. 5/2, ph. 542-9150 {cc} **J13(18)**

Schlossburg Restaurant, Bolsheokhtinskiy prosp. 41, ph. 227-2924 {cc} **N13(11)**

Sovetskiy Restaurant, Lermontovskiy prosp. 43/1, ph. 259-2573 **G18(25)**

St. Petersburg-Airport Pulkovo Restaurant, ph. 104-3760

Staraya Derevnya Cafe, ul. Savushkina 72, ph. 239-0000 **F10(6)**

⇨ **Svir**, Hotelship Peterhof, nab. Makarova, ph. 213-6321 {cc} G14(21)

Tete-a-Tete Cafe, P.S., Bolshoy prosp. 65, ph. 232-7548 H12(17)

Turku Restaurant, Hotel Pulkovskaya, Pl. Pobedy 1, ph. 264-5716 I26(14)

Victoria Restaurant, Kamennoostrovskiy prosp. 24, ph. 232-5130 H13(17)

Vityaz Restaurant, Pushkin, Moskovskaya ul. 20, ph. 476-6255

Warsteiner Forum, Nevskiy prosp. 120, ph. 277-2914 {cc, open 12-2} K16(23)

Zimny Sad Restaurant, Hotel Astoria, ph. 210-5838 {cc} H16(21)

FINNISH

Aphrodite Restaurant, Nevskiy prosp. 86, ph. 275-7620 {cc, open 12-24} K16(23)

Klondyke Casino, Hotel Karelia, ph. 226-3110 {cc} O12(8)

FISH

Aphrodite Restaurant, Nevskiy prosp. 86, ph. 275-7620 {cc, open 12-24} K16(23)

Demyanova Ukha Restaurant, Kronverkskiy prosp. 53, ph. 232-8090 {cc} H13(17)

Goluboy Delfin Restaurant, Sredne-okhtinskiy prosp. 44, ph. 227-2135 N13(11)

GEORGIAN

Aragvi Restaurant, ul. Tukhachevskovo 41, ph. 225-0082 N11(7)

Impereti Restaurant, B. Sampsoniyevskiy prosp. 104, ph. 245-5003 I9(6)

Khachapuri Restaurant, 6 Krasno-armeyskaya ul. 13/18, ph. 292-7377 H18(25)

Rioni Restaurant, Shpalernaya ul. 24, ph. 273-3261 J14(22)

Tbilisi Restaurant, Sytninskaya ul. 10, ph. 232-9391 H13(17)

GERMAN

Bavaria Restaurant, Lermontovskiy prosp. 43/1 (Hotel Sovetskaya), ph. 259-2454 G18(25)

Restaurant St. Petersburg, nab. kanala Griboyedova 5, ph. 314-4947 {cc, open 12-17, 19-2} I15(22)

Schwabskiy Domik Restaurant JV (FRG), Novocherkaskiy prosp. 28/19, ph. 528-2211 {cc} N16(11)

INDIAN

Vostok-Orient JV Restaurant (India), Primorskiy Park Pobedy, ph. 235-5984 {cc, open 12-04:30} E12(5)

ITALIAN

Venice Restaurant, ul. Korablestroiteley 21, ph. 352-1432 {cc} C14(9)

JAPANESE

Sakura Restaurant, ul. Narodnaya 45, ph. 263-3594 R21(16)

KOREAN

Koreyskiy Domik (Korean House), nab. reki Fontanki 20, ph. 275-7203 {cc} J15(22)

PIZZA

Daddy's Steak Room and Pizza, Moskovskiy prosp. 73, ph. 252-7744 {cc, open 12-23, home delivery} I19(10)

Pizza House (Finland), Podolskaya ul. 23, ph. 292-2666 {cc, open 11-24} I18(26)

⇨ **Sky Bar**, Hotelship Peterhof, ph. 213-6321 {cc} E16(9)

Venice Restaurant, ul. Korablestroiteley 21, ph. 352-1432 {cc, take-out} C14(9)

POLISH

Visla Restaurant, Gorokhovaya ul. 17, ph. 210-6807 I16(22)

RUSSIAN

Admiralteyskiy Restaurant, ul. B. Morskaya 27, ph. 314-4514 H16(21)

Astoria Restaurant, Astoria Hotel, ul. Gertsena 39, ph. 210-5906 {cc} H16(21)

Austeria Restaurant, Peter and Paul Fortress, Ioannovskiy Ravelin, ph. 238-4262 I14(22)

Belaya Loshad Cafe, Chkalovskiy prosp. 16, ph. 235-1113 G13(17)

Dom Architectora Restaurant, ul. B. Morskaya 52, ph. 311-0531 H16(21)

Druzhba Restaurant, Hotel Druzhba, ul. Chapygina 4, ph. 234-4556 H11(6)

Eldorado Discotec, Hotel Karelia, ul. Tukhachevskovo 27, k. 2, ph. 226-3110 {cc, open 22-5} O12(8)

Elf Cafe, Stremyannaya ul. 11, ph. 311-2217 K16(23)

Fortetsiya Restaurant, Kuybysheva ul. 7, ph. 233-9468 {cc} I13(18)

Fregat Cafe, V.O., Bolshoy prosp. 39/14, ph. 213-4923 F15(10)

Hermitage Cafe, Pushkin, ul. Kominterna 27, ph. 476-6255

John Bull Pub, Nevskiy prosp. 79, ph. 164-9877 {cc, closed 18-19} K16(23)

Kafe #1, prosp. Stachek 67, ph. 184-6819 E23(13)

Klassik Restaurant, Ligovskiy prosp. 202, ph. 166-0159 J18(26)

Knyaz Konstantin, ul. Millionnaya 5/1, ph. 312-1859 I15(22)

Kolobok Restaurant, Pushkin, ph. 476-6255

Literaturnoye Cafe, Nevskiy prosp. 18, ph. 312-6057 {cc, open 12-17, 19-23} I15(22)

Lukomorye Restaurant, V. O., 13 Liniya 2/19, ph. 218-5900 F16(10)

Moskva Restaurant, Hotel Moskva, Pl. Alexandra Nevskovo 2, ph. 274-2067 {cc} M17(28)

Neptun Restaurant, prosp. Stachek 25a, ph. 186-6105 F20(14)

Neva Restaurant, Hotel Pribaltiyskaya, ul. Korablestroiteley 14, ph. 356-4409 C15(9)

Nevskiy Restaurant, Nevskiy prosp. 71, ph. 311-3093 K16(23)

Okhotnichny Domik Restaurant, prosp. Engelsa 28a, ph. 244-5544 I8(6)

Okhotnichny Klub Restaurant, Gorokhovaya ul. 45, ph. 310-0770 I16(22)

Okolitsa Restaurant, Primorskiy prosp. 15, ph. 239-6984 G10(6)

Parkovy Restaurant, Petrodvorets, Avrory ul. 14, ph. 257-9096

Petrovskiy Restaurant, Mytninskaya nab., across from #3, ph. 238-4793 H14(21)

Pogrebok Restaurant, ul. M. Morskaya 7, ph. 315-5371 H15(21)

Rossiya Restaurant, Hotel Rossiya, Pl. Chernyshevskovo 11, ph. 294-3676 H23(14)

Russkiye Bliny, ul. Furmanova 13, ph. 279-0559 J14(22)

Russkiye Samovary Restaurant, ul. Sadovaya 49, ph. 314-8238 H17(25)

Saarskaya Myza, Pushkin, ul. Kominterna 27, ph. 476-6255

⇨**Sadko's Restaurant**, Grand Hotel Europe, ph. 119-6000 {cc, open 12-24} I15(22)

Sever Restaurant, Nevskiy prosp. 44/46, ph. 311-3678 J15(22)

Trapeza Cafe, Petrodvorets, Kalininskaya ul. 9, ph. 257-9393

Troika Restaurant JV (Switz.), Zagorodny prosp. 7, ph. 113-5343 {cc, open 19:30-00:30} J17(26)

Trojan Horse Kafe, V. O., 16 Liniya 20, ph. 355-9740 F15(10)

U Petrovicha Restaurant, Sredneokhtinskiy prosp. 44, ph. 227-2135 N13(11)

U Prichala Restaurant, V.O., Bolshoy prosp. 91, ph. 217-4428 E16(9)

U Samovara Cafe, Piskarevskiy prosp. 52, ph. 538-3095 O9(8)

Universal Restaurant, Nevskiy prosp. 106, ph. 279-3350 K15(23)

Vecher Restaurant, ul. Tallinskaya 20, ph. 221-1676 N17(11)

Vody Lagidze Restaurant, ul. Belinskovo 3, ph. 279-1104 J15(22)

Volkhov Restaurant, Casino, Liteyny prosp. 28, ph. 273-4736 J15(22)

SCANDINAVIAN

Karelia Restaurant, Hotel Karelia, ul. Marshala Tukhachevskovo 27/2, ph. 226-3549 {cc} O12(8)

SPANISH

Galspe Restaurant, Leninskiy prosp. 127, ph. 254-5582 {open 12-6} K16(23)

RUBBER STAMPS

There are stamp-making operations all around the city and service is getting better and faster. If you can't find a shop nearby, try:

LT Stamp, prosp. Rimskovo-Korsokova 71, ph. 114-5831

U. N. O. Firm, Lesnoy prosp. 20 kor. 5, ph. 542-0402; Nevskiy prosp. 50, ph. 310-0666; prosp. Maklina 19, ph. 114-2925

S

SAUNAS

See also Gyms, Swimming

Most major hotelsalso have sauna facilities.

Fonarnye Saunas, Fonarniy P. 1, ph. 312-5655

Nevskiye Sauna, ul. Marata 5/7, ph. 311-1400

World Class Gym, Grand Hotel Europe, ph. 113-8066; Hotel Astoria, 4th floor, ph. 210-5869; Kamennoostrovskiy prosp. 26, ph. 232-7581

SEAMSTRESS/TAILOR

Progress, Pestelya ul. 19, ph. 272-2714

Repair & Alteration Shop, Lebedeva ul. 7/9, ph. 542-0465

SECURITY

See also Hardware Stores

Alex Detective Services, ul. Kapitanskaya 3, ph. 352-5754 {from electronic devices to bodyguards and transport security}

Elektronika Bekas, Mytninskaya ul. 1, ph. 274-4291 {electronic security devices}

Honeywell, ul. Zakharyevskaya 31, ph. 275-3504

Konek, Marata Ul. 86, ph. 164-0722

Securicor Security Services, Securicor Okrana, 22 Liniya, ph. 218-0017

Soppol, 2 Krasnoarmeyskaya ul. 7, ph. 110-1432 {open 24 hrs.}

Valeri, ul. Pochtamtskaya 5, #1, ph. 312-8654

YuVM, Bronnitskaya ul. 26, ph. 292-3503

Zashchita, ul. Dobrolyubova prosp. 13, ph. 233-8262 {bodyguards}

SHIPPING AGENTS

Aeroflot, Aviagorodok Warehouse ul. Pilotov, ph. 104-3411

Ahlers Lines, Suvorovskiy prosp. 2, ph. 277-2006

Anna Laine Ltd, ul. Lenina 1a, ph. 291-2546

Arctic & Antarctic Marine Shipping Company, nab. reki Fontanki 34, ph. 273-3725

Baltic Sea Shipping, Mezhevoy kanal 5, ph. 114-9001

Ennek, Malookhtinskiy prosp. 68, ph. 528-0225

EuroDonat JV (Belgian), ul. Yakornaya 17, ph. 224-1144

Fedorov Trans Express, ul. Shturmanskaya 32, ph. 104-3449

Huolintakeskus Ltd SP, Lyubotinski p. 5, ph. 298-0083

Inflot Maritime Agency, Gapsalskaya ul. 10, ph. 251-7326

Infoservice, Universitetskaya nab. 21, ph. 213-6455

Kevlar Cooperative, Fontanka 89, ph. 314-2876

Lenvneshtrans, Mezhevoy kanal 5, ph. 259-8040

Morskiye Perevozki, Kazanskaya ul. 17-19/22, ph. 314-0659

Neva Transport Trading, Staro-Petergofskiy prosp. 9-a, ph. 251-1215

North-West River Shipping Company, B. Morskaya ul. 37, ph. 312-0145

Nurminen, John Oy, Sofiyskaya ul. 6, ph. 269-0586

Oktyabrskaya Railway Freight Station, Pl. Ostrovskovo 2, ph. 168-6384

Petersburg Vneshtrans, Mezhevoy Kanal 5, ph. 251-0629

Petrobalt, Zagorodny prosp. 68, ph. 292-1777

Romar International Inc., Yelagin Ostrov 10, ph. 239-0901

Rosvneshterminal, ul. Belinskovo 11, ph. 275-6161

Sofi JV (Finland), Kingiseppskaya sh. 47, ph. 132-2355

Sovavto-St. Petersburg Shipping Company, Vitebskiy prosp. 3, ph. 298-5556

Transit Ltd, Nevskiy prosp. 100, ph. 259-8745

USIS JV (Bulgarian), ul. Rosenshteyna 34, ph. 252-2521

SHOES

Adidas, P.S., Bolshoy prosp. 51, ph. 232-2092
Lenwest JV (FRG), ul. Tsvetochnaya 6, ph. 298-2088
Marcopizzi Shoes, Kamenoostrovskiy prosp. 37, ph. 233-8664
Monna JV (Finland), Ust-Izhora, ul. Truda 2, ph. 463-9898
New Balance, P.S., Bolshoy prosp. 65, ph. 230-8043

SHOPPING

See Food, Souvenirs, Electronics, Books

Shopping hours throughout St. Petersburg can vary greatly. Beware the afternoon break, which usually falls between 13-14:00 for food stores, and 14-15:00 for all others. The major department stores like DLT and Gostiny Dvor work without a lunch break, as do the many Western-run stores (indeed, there are even 24 hour convenience stores popping up around the city). Most all shops are open six days a week and some stores, particularly food stores and bread stores, are open on Sundays.

Typical hours for food stores are 9-20:00, while for central department stores it is 8-21:00. Expect to encounter the infamous "sanitary day", "closed for technical reasons" or "closed for inventory". These days occur at random and mean the store is closed for the entire day. They are more likely to happen at the start of the month.

Buying goods in most larger stores still requires a fairly round-a-bout procedure. You first choose your product and tell the attendant to wrap it. Then you go to the cashier and tell her the price and department number to ring in on her register. Finally, you return to the attendant and exchange your sales slip for the goods.

SHOPS

In this "transitional" period, there are many retail shops that defy easy classification. Either they sell everything from clothing to perfume to books and liquor, or they are chameleon shops, whose inventory varies from week to week. In any case, all those cited below are worth becoming familiar with, as they may lead to some interesting "finds."

Alivekt, Lanskoe Sh. 27, ph. 246-1515; Liteyniy prosp. 59, ph. 272-3301; Nevskiy prosp. 112, ph. 275-0107; Nevskiy prosp. 2/24, ph. 315-5978; Nevskiy prosp. 23, ph. 311-4645; P.S., Bolshoy prosp. 82, ph. 232-0283; ul. B. Pushkarskaya 34, ph. 230-4740
Apraksin Dvor Second Hand Shop, Sadovaya ul. 32, ph. 310-7350
Gavana Commercial Store, Kamenoostrovskiy prosp. 2, ph. 233-5253
Intour, Hotel Sankt Peterburg, ph. 542-8032
Kovcheg, ul. Chernyshevskovo 9, ph. 297-1236
Sopot, Sredniy prosp. 34, ph. 213-1043
Super Siwa, ul. Savushkina 119, ph. 345-1698

SIGHTSEEING

See also Museums, Parks, Boat Rides

If you have some time for independent sightseeing and want to go on a tour, contact a tour agency listed under Travel Agencies below. Individuals can sign up for excursions at the Hotel Astoria travel bureau desk 24 hours in advance.

SKATING

Ice Rink Tavricheskovo Sada, Saltykova-Shchedrina ul. 50, ph. {hours 9-20}
Letniy Katok LVO, nab. reki Fontanki 112, ph. 292-2128 {Year-round. Hours 7-23}
Yubileyny Palace of Sports, Dobrolyubova ul. 18, ph. 238-4061 {Year-round. Hours 11-18}

SOUVENIRS

Khudozhestvennye promysli, Nevskiy prosp. 51, ph. 113-1495
Otkrytki, Nevskiy prosp. 72, ph. 272-9031
Podarki, Nevskiy prosp. 54, ph. 314-1801
Polarnaya Zvezda, Nevskiy prosp. 158, ph. 277-0980

SPORTING GOODS

Evrika, Piskaryovskiy prosp. 52, ph. 249-0950

Irmin, Shvernika prosp. 51, ph. 247-7894
Neapet, Nevskiy prosp. 122, ph. 277-0279
Olimpiyets, P.S., Bolshoy prosp. 76, ph. 232-8781
Parus, Morskaya nab. 17, ph. 351-8735
Ring, Apraksin dvor, kor. 1, kv. 85-95, ph. 310-1893
Sport Store, prosp. Shaumyana 2, ph. 224-2896
Sport-Lyuks, Liteyny prosp. 57, ph. 272-6751
Sporting Goods Shop, V. O., Nalichnaya ul. 31, ph. 356-1479
Sportivniye Tovary, Lanskoye sh. 12, ph. 246-0354
World Class Gym, Hotel Astoria, 4th floor, ph. 210-5869; Kamennoostrovskiy prosp. 26, ph. 232-7581
Zenit, Nevskiy prosp. 100, ph. 272-2831

SWIMMING

The Pribaltiyskaya, Sankt-Peterburg and Pulkovskaya Hotels all have swimming pools as does the Grand Hotel Europe and the Hotel Astoria. See the White Pages for contact numbers and addresses. Below are some more public alternatives. In all cases bathing cap and goggles are recommended. Some pools willrequire a 'spravka' from a doctor attesting to your good health.

Army Sports Club Swimming Pool, Litovskaya ul. 3, ph. 542-0162
Dinamo Swimming Pool, prosp. Dinamo 44, ph. 235-6606
Lokomotiv Swimming Pool, ul. Konstantina Zasionova 23, ph. 164-4755
Naval Sports Club Swimming Pool, Krasnogvardeyskiy prosp. 5a, ph. 528-7328
Spartak Swimming Pool, Konstantinovskiy prosp. 19, ph. 235-0583
Trudovye Rezervi Swimming Pool, Gavanskaya ul. 53, ph. 352-6754

T

TAXIS

See Car Rental

Price hikes due to the increase in gas prices have, in general, made taxis more available. Prices are usually agreed upon with the driver beforehand. There are very few taxis that work by the meter anymore. Many drivers also try to make some money on the side by giving rides ('gypsy cabs').

With recent increases in crime, it is best to avoid gypsy cabs if you are not a Russian speaker or do not know your way around the city fairly well. NEVER GET INTO A CAR WHICH ALREADY HAS A RIDER IN IT.

Taxi prices are climbing too fast to be worth quoting. Given the stable value of the dollar, however, you can figure on paying $2-4 in rubles for a 10 minute ride. To hire a taxi out by the hour will run you $5-10 in equivalent rubles.

Matralen Airport Limousine Service, Lyubotinskiy pr. 5, ph. 298-3648
SIT Airport Taxi Service, Pribaltiyskaya Hotel, ul. Korablestroiteley 14, ph. 356-9329
Taxi Reservations, ph. 312-0022
Transwell Sankt-Petersburg, Lermontovskiy prosp. 37, ph. 113-7253

Unequaled Access

Where in St. Petersburg reaches over ten thousand active users inside Russia and out. It is the only guide of its type with national bookstore distribution in North America and Europe. It has earned a reputation as an objective, detailed, qualitative and easy-to-use guide. And it is used year-round as a reference tool and guide. A very limited number of advertising spaces are available in this guide (limited so as to maximize each ad's value). To find out how your company can become a part of ***Where in St. Petersburg***, contact Russian Information Services at 89 Main St., Suite 2, Montpelier, VT 05602, ph. 802-223-4955, fax 802-223-6105. In Moscow, call our office at 095-254-9275.

TELECOM

See also Electronic Mail, International Phone

3M-Lentelefonstroi, Obukhova, Garazhny prosp. 1, ph. 101-1534
Alcatel Business Systems, ul. B. Morskaya 16, ph. 315-8938; Varshavskaya ul. 11, ph. 296-3978
AT&T, Liflyandskaya ul. 4, ph. 186-7537
Baltic Communications Ltd. (BCL), ul. Marata 6, ph. 314-5548
Catalog Express, Sadovaya ul. 34
Dalnyaya Svyaz NPO, Petrogradskaya nab. 34, ph. 233-5502
Delta Telecom, ul. Chekhova 18, ph. 275-4149; **Showroom**, ul. B. Morskaya 22, ph. 314-6126
Lenfincom JV (Finland), ul. B. Morskaya 3-5, ph. 314-0060
Lex Telecomm, ul. Mytninskaya 19, ph. 271-1676
Metrocom, ul. Transportnaya 1, ph. 314-5248
Siemens AG, ul. Gogolya 18/20, ph. 315-3197
⇨ **Sovam Teleport**, Nevskiy prosp. 30, ph. 311-8412
Spassis, Maly prosp. 1, kv. 3, ph. 218-6313
Sprint Networks, Sinopskaya nab. 14, ph. 265-0571
St. Petersburg City Telephone Board, ul. Gertsena 24, ph. 314-3757
St. Petersburg Intercity Telephone Station, ul. B. Morskaya 3-5, ph. 311-4863
Teleport St. Petersburg, prosp. Gagarina 1, ph. 294-8857
Transworld Communications, ph. 112-4787

TELEGRAM/TELEX

To send a telegram, go to the Central Telegraph Office at Soyuza Svyazi 14 (hotels also have telegram and telex capabilities). You can also dictate a telegram over the phone by calling 066. In the center, go to Central Telegraph at B. Morskaya 3/5.

THEATER/BALLET

Hotel service desks (often a separate theater desk exists) are the best place to turn to for tickets. For places like the Kirov, you can often hang around outside the theater the day of the performance and buy tickets from scalpers, for varying prices and seat locations. Russian speakers should also try the Teatralniye kassi (on the streets or at a specific theater) since the dramatic increase in ruble ticket prices for Russians has also made tickets more widely available.

Akimova Comedy Theater, Nevskiy prosp. 56, ph. 312-4555
Bolshoy Dramatic Theater (Gorkiy Theater), nab. reki Fontanki 65, ph. 310-0401
Bolshoy Puppet Theater, ul. Nekrasova 10, ph. 273-6672
Buff Plus Cabaret and Bar, ul. Narodnaya 1, ph. 266-4356 {bar}
Choreographic Miniatures State Ballet, ul. Mayakovskovo 15, ph. 273-1997
Estrada Theater, ul. Zhelyabova 27, ph. 314-6661
Interior Theater-Studio, Nevskiy prosp. 114, ph. 113-0151
Komissarzhevskoy Dramatic Theater, Italianskaya ul. 19, ph. 315-5355
Maly Dramatic Theater, ul. Rubinshteyna 18, ph. 113-2039
Marinskiy Theater of Opera and Ballet (Kirov), Teatralnaya pl. 1, ph. 114-1211; Booking Office, ph. 114-5264
Musical Comedy Theater, Italianskaya ul. 13, ph. 277-4760
Musorgskiy Maly Theater, pl. Isskusstv 1, ph. 314-3758
Otkryty Theater, Vladimirskiy prosp. 12, ph. 113-2190
Pushkin Academic Drama Theater, pl. Ostrovskovo 2, ph. 312-1545
Russian Union of Theatrical Workers, Nevskiy prosp. 86, ph. 272-9482
St. Petersburg Ballet on Ice, Dvortsovaya nab. 20/2, ph. 312-8637
St. Petersburg State Ballet Theater Borisa Eyfmana, ul. Lizy Chaykinoy 2, ph. 232-0235

TIME — DIAL 08

Seasonal time changes are as follows: clocks are set one hour ahead the last weekend of March and back one hour the last weekend in September. Check time differences across Rus-

September. Check time differences across Russia on the map on pages 2 and 3 of our ***Russia Survival Guide.***

TOYS

Babylon-9, Bolshoy prosp. 38, ph. 232-5243

Elma, Lesnoy prosp. 73, ph. 245-4588

Zolotoy Klyuchik, Marshala Govorova ul. 10, ph. 184-8318

TRAINS, INFORMATION

Domestic Tickets, ph. 162-3344

General, ph. 168-0111

Order tickets by phone: 162-3344

Suburban Trains, ph. 168-0111

TRAINS, STATIONS

Baltiyskiy, nab. Obvodnovo kanala 120, ph. 168-2972 {serves southern city outskirts and Petrodvorets}

Finlyandskiy, pl. Lenina 6, ph. 168-7685 {serves Vyborg, Repino, Razliv and Finland}

Moskovskiy, ul. Poltavskaya 9, ph. 168-0111; Information on International Travel, ph. 168-0111 {Serves Moscow, the Northeast and South of Russia}

Varshavskiy, nab. Obvodnovo kanala 118, ph. 168-2972 {serves the Baltics and Western destinations}

Vitebskiy, Zagorodny prosp. 52, ph. 168-5390 {serves Pushkin, Pavlovsk, Belarus and Ukraine}

TRANSLATION

Services of this nature are widely available and have a very wide quality range. For best results, make sure the service can draw on native speakers of the language you are having something translated into.

AT&T offers a unique over-the-phone translation service. You call them up, any time day or night in the US at (800) 628-8486, and for $3.50 per minute, plus long distance charges, you can have a translated telephone conversation. Internationally, call (800) 843-8420.

AsLANTIS, Box 398, ph. 298-9007

Asta-Information, P.S., Bolshoy prosp. 82, kv. 17, ph. 230-7898

Gorodskoy Tsentr Perevodov, ul. Bronnetskaya 15, ph. 112-6515

Inter, ul. Bronnitskaya 15, ph. 259-6252

IPS, Kozhevennaya liniya 34, ph. 264-0820

Konwest, nab. reki Fontanki 23, ph. 311-2281

Nauchny Poisk, Voxxtaniya ul. 22/16, ph. 273-7576

Nikos Translation Bureau, Moskovskiy prosp. 149b kom. 313, ph. 298-2187

Optima-Office, Chaykovskovo ul. 36, ph. 273-2964

Rambus, Ltd., Grazhdanskiy prosp. 14, ph. 299-4624

Scientific Technical Translation & Interpretation Assn., Galyornaya ul. 22, kv. 33, ph. 307-0913

Sila, Kavalergardskaya ul. 10, kv. 19, ph. 278-5035

Sphinx JV (Finland), ul. Gertsena 55, ph. 312-7540

Transelectro JV (Finland), Moskovskiy prosp. 171, ph. 294-0501

Translation and Interpretation Bureau, Isaakevskaya pl. 11, ph. 210-0933

Unix Firm, ul. Italianskaya 23,fioor 3, ph. 310-9745

Yuniks Inc., Italyanskaya ul. 23, ph. 142-1386

Znaniye, ul. Kavalergardskaya 10, ph. 275-6108

TRAVEL AGENCIES

American Express, in Grand Hotel Europe, Mikhailovskaya ul. 1/7, ph. 119-6009

Atlas Firm, ul. B. Morskaya 35, ph. 110-6550

Balkantourist, ul. B. Morskaya 36, ph. 315-5030

Cairos Travel Agency, Teatralnaya pl. 4, ph. 312-2517

Duncan Travel Firm, Millionaya ul. 23, ph. 275-1337

Finnord JV, Italianskaya ul. 37, ph. 314-8951 {bus service to Lahti, Finland, $50}

Fortuna International Tourism Assn., Kievskaya ul. 22/24, kv. 92, ph. 298-8969

Galaktika, V. O., 2 Liniya 35, ph. 213-1121

Griffon, Furshtadtskaya ul. 9, ph. 275-7215

Instant Tour, ul. Blokhina 15, ph. 230-9840

International Business Services, Rubinstein 8, Box 237, ph. 311-5838

Intourbureau, ul. Galernaya 22, ph. 315-7876

Intourtrans, Hotel Pulkovskaya, ph. 299-5808; Pl. Aleksandra Nevskovo 2, ph. 274-2092

JAC Travel Russia Ltd, Druzhba Hotel, suite 229-30, Chapygina ul., ph. 234-9016

Nord Tourist Agency, Liteyniy prosp. 64, ph. 275-5205

Pol-Mot, ul. Nakhimova 7, #102, ph. 356-3364

Sovintour, Smolny, podyezd 9, ph. 271-6466

Sputnik International Travel Bureau, ul. Chapygina 4, ph. 234-3500

Staraya Derevnya, ul. Savushkina 72, ph. 239-0000 {customized city tours}

St. Petersburg City Travel Bureau, B. Konyushennaya ul. 27, ph. 315-4555

St. Petersburg Reg. Council for Tourism and Excursions, Italianskaya ul. 3, ph. 314-8786

St. Petersburg Travel Agency, Isaakevskaya pl. 11, ph. 210-0905; Pulkovo I Airport, ph. 123-8590; Pulkovo II Airport, ph. 104-3465

Troyka Tours, Zagorodny prosp. 27, ph. 113-5376 {nights of St. Petersburg tours}

Vet Cooperative, nab. reki Fontanki 90, ph. 314-4226 {historic/literary city tours}

V

VETERINARIANS

Aibolit, Kolomenskaya ul. 45, ph. 164-6211

Evradonat, Olgi Forsh ul. 5, ph. 558-9820

Municipal Veterinary Administration, 4 Sovetskaya ul. 5, ph. 277-5237

Rabies Prevention Department, 2 Zhernovskaya ul. 46, ph. 227-7443

VIDEO RENTAL

Kalininskiy Video Center, Svetlanovskiy prosp. 62

Romos-Video, Goncharnaya ul. 13, ph. 275-4015

Video Center, V. O., 7 Liniya 36, ph. 213-4357

VISA OFFICE

UVIR, ul. Saltykova-Schedrina 4, ph. 278-2481, open 10-18 weekdays.

WAREHOUSES

AB, Kamenoostrovskiy 26/28, ph. 560-6187

EuroDonat JV (Belgian), ul. Yakornaya 17, ph. 224-1144

Huolintakeskus Ltd SP, Lyubotinskiy p. 5, ph. 298-0083

Interservice, Liteyny prosp. 35 kv. 4, ph. 275-3557

Petersburg Vneshtrans, Mezhevoy Kanal 5, ph. 251-0629

Poliservice, Tsimlyanskaya ul. 6, ph. 224-1447

Rosvneshterminal, ul. Belinskovo 11, ph. 275-6161

Sofi JV (Finland), Kingiseppskaya sh. 47, ph. 132-2355

WATER, BOTTLED

ClearWater, V. O., 6 Liniya 37, ph. 213-5733

YOUTH HOSTEL

St. Petersburg Youth Hostel, 3 Sovetskaya 28, ph. 277-0569 {$14/night, issues visas, train tickets, tours}

Z

ZOO

Zoo, P.S., Park Lenina 1, ph. 232-2839 {open May-August 10-22, Sep-Nov 10-18, Dec-Feb 10-16, Mar-Apr 10-19}

Now getting through to Russia is no problem at all.

SOVAM TELEPORT

the world's premier communication service to the former Soviet Union is your solution.

- Fast reliable electronic mail
- Global fax and telex access
- Regional offices throughout the CIS*
- Daily CIS newswire
- Russian business weeklies
- Personalized service
- Installation and training on site
- Rouble accounts available

SOVAM TELEPORT *USA*
3220 Sacramento Street
San Francisco, CA 94115
Tel: (800) 257-5107
(415) 931-8500
Fax: (415) 931-2885

* Commonwealth of Independent States

SOVAM TELEPORT CIS locations

Moscow (095)229-3466 • St. Petersburg (812)311-8412
Baku (8922)66-3995 • Kazan (8432)76-2366 • Kiev (044)296-4238
Kurgan (35222)7-1637 • Mariupol (0629)33-1391 • Minsk (0172)26-4560
Perm (3422)39-1500 • Petrozavodsk (81400)5-1189 • Riga (0132)55-1133
Tashkent (3712)44-6360 • Ufa (3472)22-4827 • Vladivostok (4232)25-2598
Yekaterinburg (3432)60-5175 • Yerevan (8852)28-2951

Corporate Forwarding
Your partner in the former USSR

Shipping to and from all points and ports in the republics of the former USSR:

- Armenia
- Azerbaidzhan
- Belarus
- Estonia
- Georgia
- Kazakhstan
- Kirgizistan
- Latvia
- Lithuania
- Moldova
- Russia
- Russian Far East
- Tadzhikistan
- Turkmenistan
- Ukraine
- Uzbekistan

Air Shipments
Daily Air consolidation to all major cities. From small parcels to Truckloads and full charter shipments.

Ocean Shipments
Our specialty is auto shipments.
Ocean containers, break bulk & LTL.
Weekly Express Service to all major points and ports.

Door to Door Service
Including pick-up throughout the CIS, Baltics, USA, Europe, Hong Kong, Brazil, Mexico and other regions.

Storage
Bonded, high-security storage in Moscow, St. Petersburg, Tallinn, Riga, Odessa and other cities. Packing, sorting, distribution and on site-inspection.

Documentation
All air and ocean shipping documents, customs clearance. We submit letter of credit documentation to your bank.

Corporate Forwarding, Inc.

102 Southfield Ave.
Stamford Landing
Stamford, CT 06902 USA
ph. (203) 353-1441
fax (203) 353-1497
tlx 4961 4503 CORPFWDG

St. Petersburg City Street Map

ST. PETERSBURG
Scale 1:35,000
N
Restaurant
Metro Stations
Park or Cemetery
Railroad & Station
Boat Stop
Cinema
Consulate
Gas Station
Market
Theater
Christian Church
Russian Orthodox
Synagogue
Mosque
Buddhist Temple
Kilometers
Miles
A
B
C
D
E
F
G
H
I
J
K
L
M
N
O
P
Q
R
1
2
3
4
5
6
7
8
9
10
11
12
1
2
3
4
5
6
7
8
17
18
19
20
Parnas
Devyatkino
Murino
Shuvalovo
Ozerki
Derevnya
Udelnayas
Kolomyagi
Sosnovka
Udelnoe
Grazhdanka
Rybatskaya
Novaya Derevnya
Staraya Derevnya
Stoyka
Polyustrovo
See Central St. Petersburg Map for Detail

9
10
11
12
13
14
15
16
21
22
23
24
25
26
27
28
Gulf of Finland
Yablonovka
Malaya Okhta
Vesyoly Poselok
Volkovo
Smolenskoye
Farforovaya
Alekseyevka
Avtovo
Troitskoye Pole
Aleksandrovskoye
Kupchino
Dachnoye
Ligovo

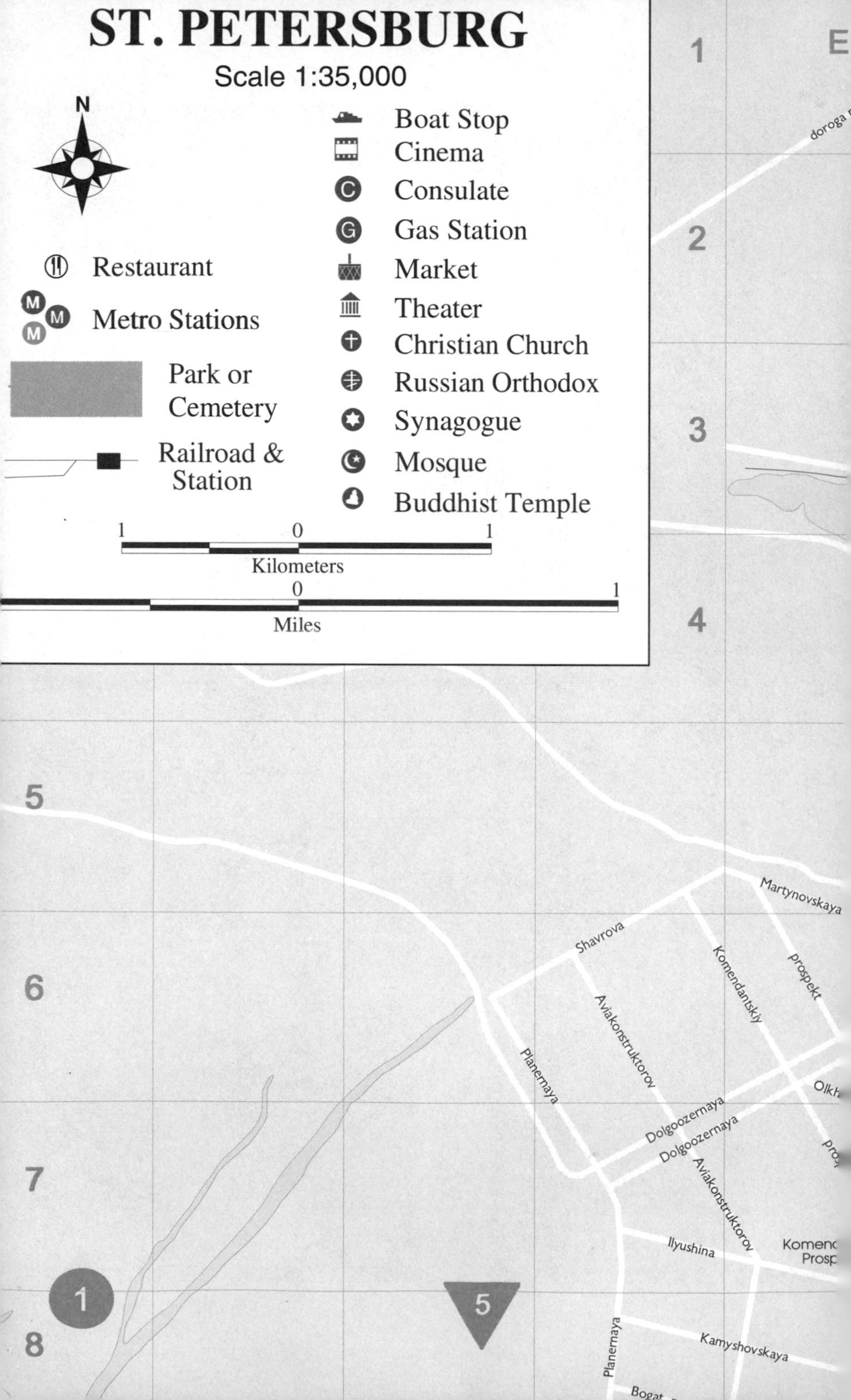
ST. PETERSBURG
Scale 1:35,000
N
Boat Stop
Cinema
Consulate
Gas Station
Market
Theater
Christian Church
Russian Orthodox
Synagogue
Mosque
Buddhist Temple
Restaurant
Metro Stations
Park or Cemetery
Railroad & Station
Kilometers
Miles
1
2
3
4
5
6
7
8
E
doroga
Martynovskaya
Shavrova
Komendantskiy
prospekt
Aviakonstruktorov
Planernaya
Olkh
Dolgoozernaya
Dolgoozernaya
Aviakonstruktorov
Ilyushina
Komend
Prosp
Kamyshovskaya
Planernaya
1
5

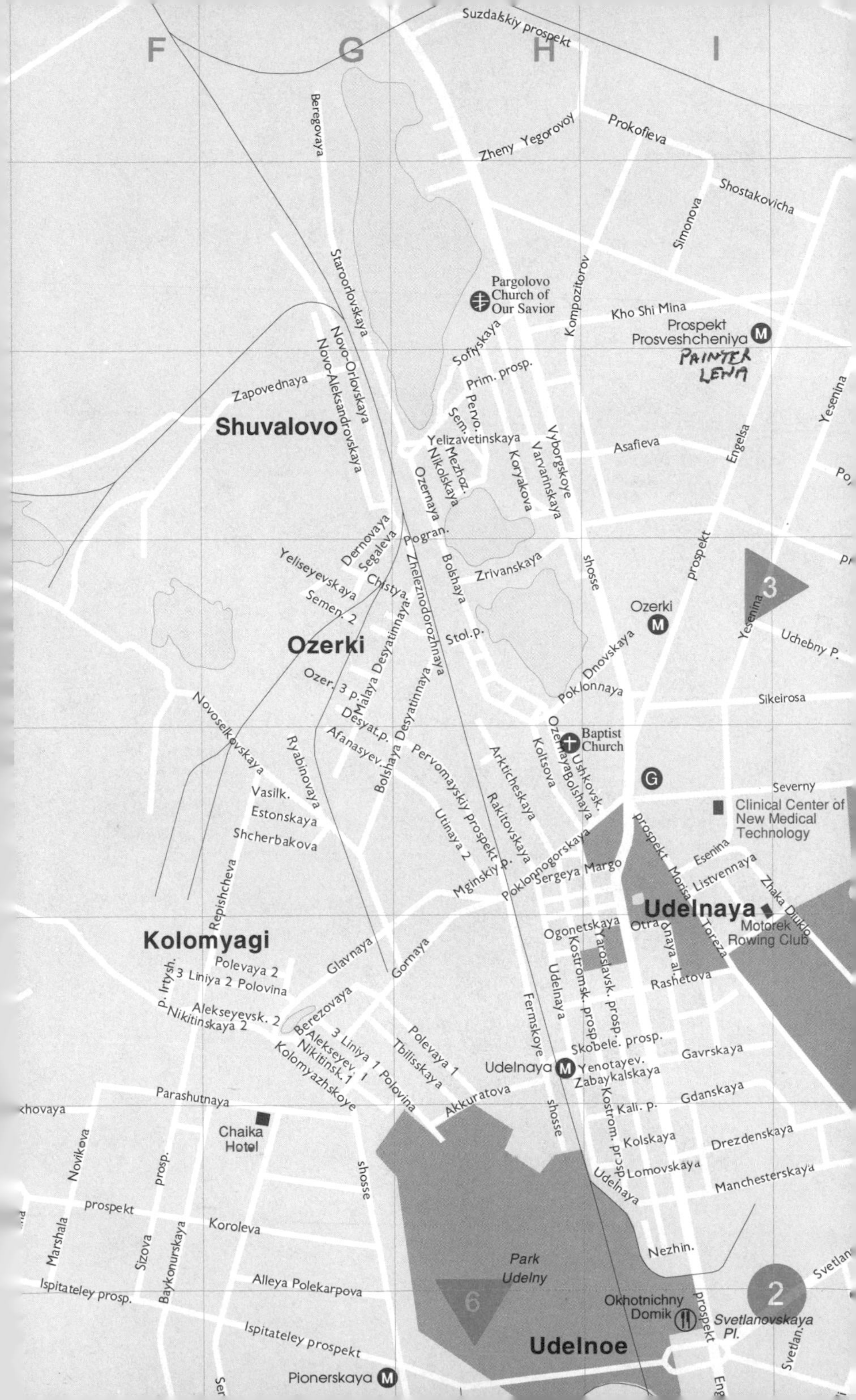
F
G
H
I
Suzdalskiy prospekt
Beregovaya
Zheny Yegorovoy
Prokofieva
Shostakovicha
Simonova
Staroorlovskaya
Pargolovo Church of Our Savior
Kompozitorov
Kho Shi Mina
Prospekt Prosveshcheniya
PAINTER LENA
Novo-Orlovskaya
Novo-Aleksandrovskaya
Zapovednaya
Sofiyskaya
Prim. prosp.
Pervo.
Sem.
Shuvalovo
Yelizavetinskaya
Mezhoz.
Nikolskaya
Koryakova
Vyborgskoye
Varvarinskaya
Asafieva
Engelsa
Yesenina
Ozernaya
Dernovaya
Segaleva
Pogran.
Yeliseyevskaya
Chistya.
Zheleznodorozhnaya
Bolshaya
Zrivanskaya
shosse
prospekt
3
Semen. 2
Ozerki
Malaya Desyatinnaya
Stol.p.
Ozerki
Yesenina
Uchebny P.
Dnovskaya
Poklonnaya
Sikeirosa
Ozer. 3 p.
Desyat.p.
Bolshaya Desyatinnaya
Novoselkovskaya
Ryabinovaya
Afanasyev.
Pervomayskiy prospekt
Arkticheskaya
Koltsova
Baptist Church
Ozernaya
Bolshaya
Ushkovsk.
Severny
Clinical Center of New Medical Technology
Vasilk.
Estonskaya
Shcherbakova
Utinaya 2
Rakitovskaya
Poklonnogorskaya
prospekt Morisa
Esenina
Listvennaya
Repishcheva
Mginskiy p.
Sergeya Margo
Zhaka Diuklo
Udelnaya
Motorek Rowing Club
Kolomyagi
Ogonetskaya
Otra
dnaya al.
Toreza
Glavnaya
Gornaya
Kostromsk. prosp.
Yaroslavsk. prosp.
Polevaya 2
p. Irtysh.
3 Liniya 2 Polovina
Udelnaya
Rashetova
Berezovaya
Alekseyevsk. 2
Nikitinskaya 2
Fermskoye
Skobele. prosp.
3 Liniya 1 Polovina
Alekseyev. 1
Nikitinsk. 1
Polevaya 1
Tbilisskaya
Udelnaya
Yenotayev.
Gavrskaya
Zabaykalskaya
Kolomyazhskoye
Kostrom. prosp
Parashutnaya
Akkuratova
Kali. P.
Gdanskaya
Chaika Hotel
shosse
Kolskaya
Drezdenskaya
Novikova
prosp.
shosse
Lomovskaya
Manchesterskaya
Udelnaya
prospekt
Koroleva
Marshala
Sizova
Baykonurskaya
Nezhin.
Park Udelny
Alleya Polekarpova
Ispitateley prosp.
6
Okhotnichny Domik
2
Svetlanovskaya Pl.
prospekt
Svetlan.
Ispitateley prospekt
Udelnoe
Pionerskaya

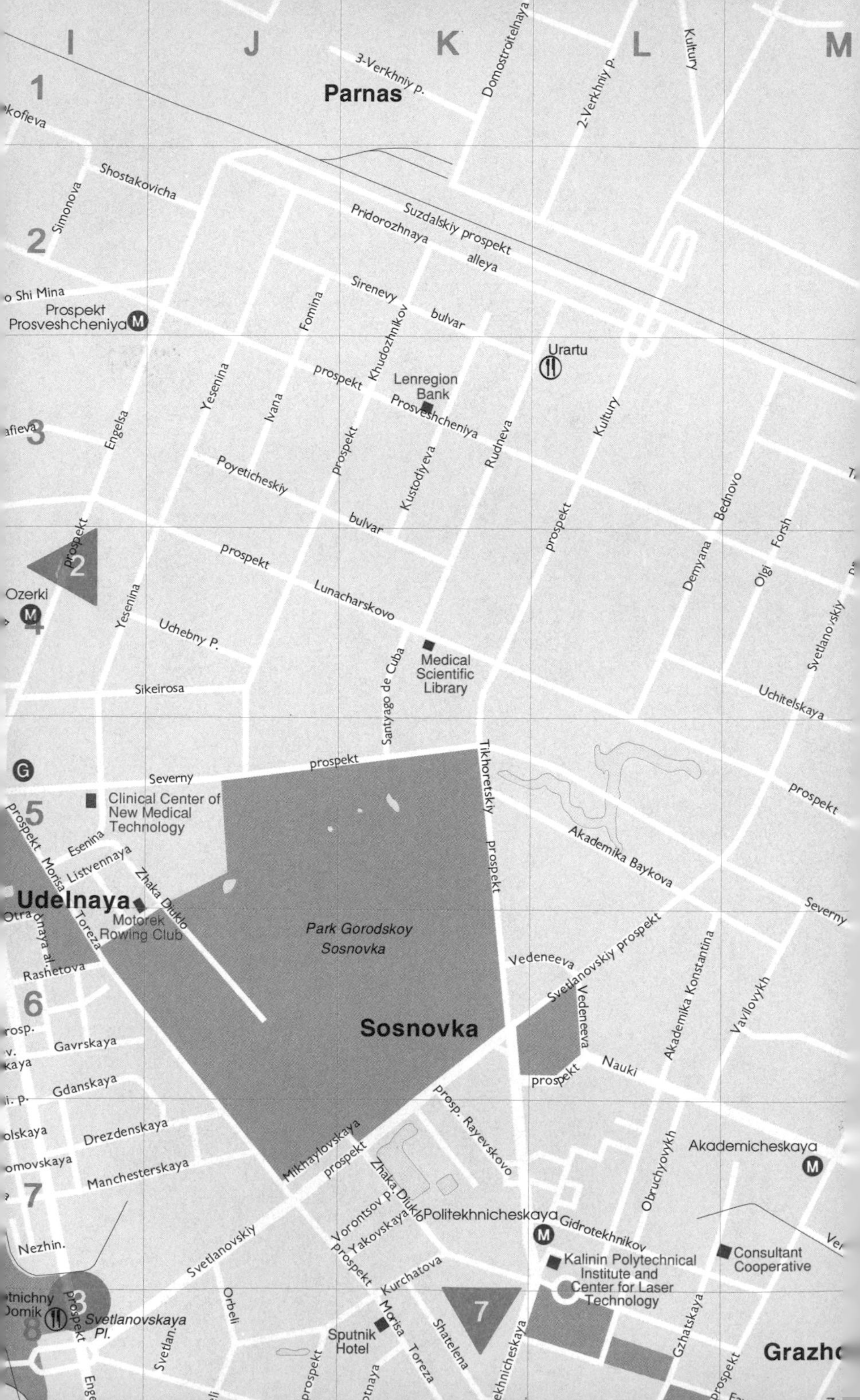
I
J
K
L
M
1
2
3
4
5
6
7
8
Parnas
3-Verkhniy p.
Domostroitelnaya
2-Verkhniy p.
Kultury
Shostakovicha
Simonova
Suzdalskiy prospekt
Pridorozhnaya
alleya
Sirenevy
bulvar
o Shi Mina
Prospekt
Prosveshcheniya
Fomina
Khudozhnikov
prospekt
Prosveshcheniya
Lenregion
Bank
Urartu
Yesenina
Ivana
Engelsa
Rudneva
Kultury
prospekt
Poyeticheskiy
bulvar
Kustodiyeva
prospekt
prospekt
2
Ozerki
Lunacharskovo
Bednovo
Forsh
Demyana
Olgi
Svetlanovskiy
Yesenina
Uchebny P.
Medical
Scientific
Library
Santyago de Cuba
Sikeirosa
Uchitelskaya
G
Severny
prospekt
Tikhoretskiy
prospekt
prospekt
Clinical Center of
New Medical
Technology
Esenina
Listvennaya
Morisa
Toreza
Zhaka Duklo
Akademika Baykova
Udelnaya
Motorek
Rowing Club
Park Gorodskoy
Sosnovka
Severny
Vedeneeva
Svetlanovskiy prospekt
Akademika Konstantina
Vavilovykh
Rashetova
Vedeneeva
Sosnovka
Gavrskaya
Nauki
prospekt
Gdanskaya
prosp. Rayevskovo
Drezdenskaya
Obruchyovykh
Akademicheskaya
Mikhaylovskaya
prospekt
Manchesterskaya
Zhaka Duklo
Voronts ov p.
Yakovskaya
Politekhnicheskaya
Gidrotekhnikov
Nezhin.
Svetlanovskiy
prospekt
Kurchatova
Kalinin Polytechnical
Institute and
Center for Laser
Technology
Consultant
Cooperative
Orbeli
7
3
Svetlanovskaya
Pl.
prospekt
Sputnik
Hotel
Morisa
Toreza
Shatelena
Gzhatskaya
Svetlan.
prospekt
prospekt

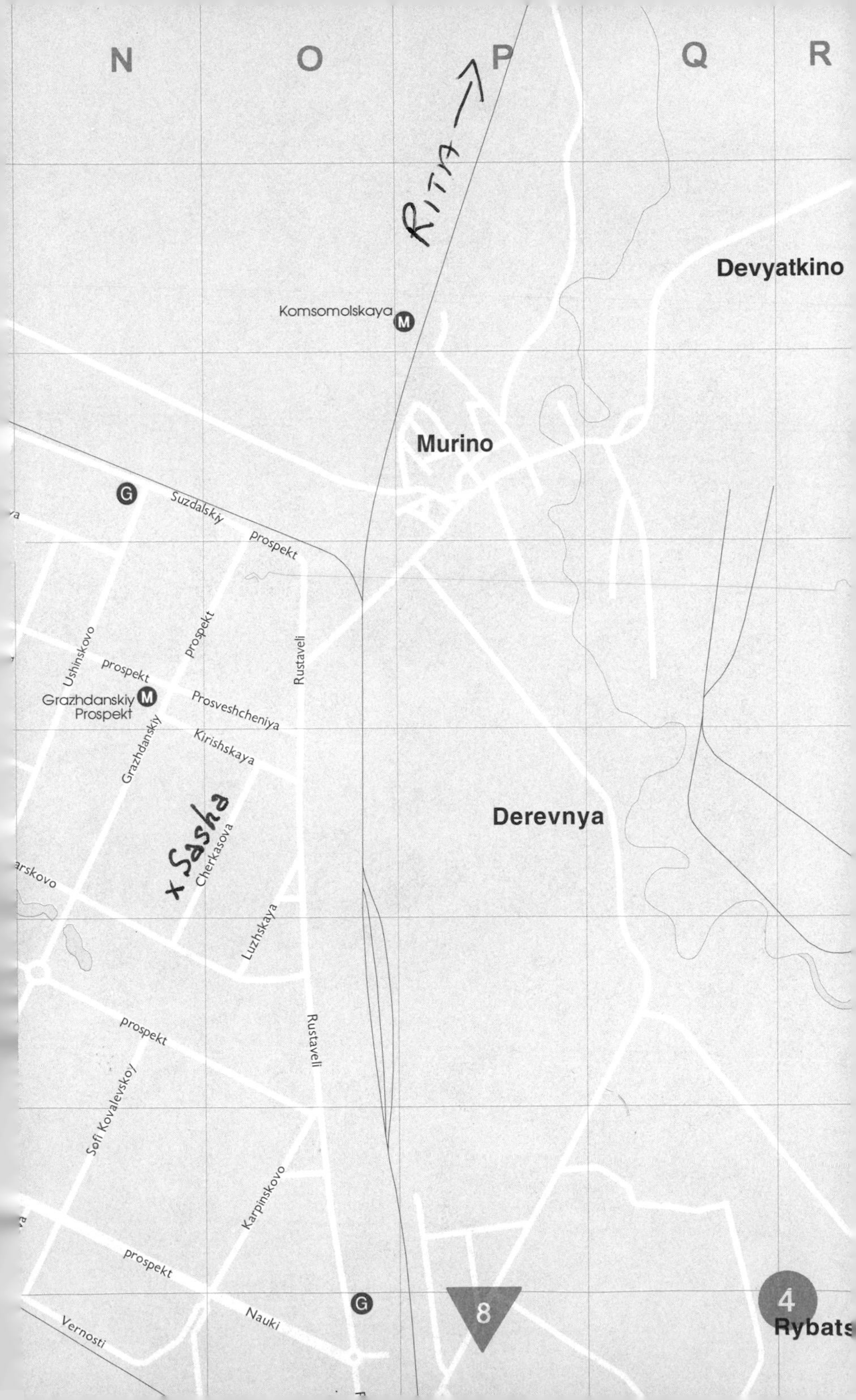
N
O
P
Q
R
Rita →
Devyatkino
Komsomolskaya
Murino
Suzdalskiy
prospekt
prospekt
Ushinskovo
prospekt
Rustaveli
Grazhdanskiy
Prospekt
Prosveshcheniya
Grazhdanskiy
Kirishskaya
Derevnya
x Sasha
Cherkasova
arskovo
Luzhskaya
prospekt
Rustaveli
Sofi Kovalevskoy
Karpinskovo
prospekt
Nauki
Vernosti
8
4
Rybats

A
B
C
D
E
7
8
9
10
11
12
13
1
5
9
Dolgoozern
Aviakonstruktorov
Ilyushina
Komendo
Prospe
Planernaya
Kamyshovskaya
Bogat. prosp.
Sitstevaya
Optikov
Tortyanaya doroga
Primorskoye shosse
Shkolnaya
Begovaya
Savushkina
Yakhtennaya
Primorsk. prosp.
Staraya
Derevnya
Polevaya doroga
Starod.3
Starod.2
Starod.1
Staraya
Derevnya
Buddhist Temple
Primorskiy
Tsentralny Pa
Otdykha im
YELAGIN
Srednyaya
Martynov
Kirov
Stadium
KRESTOVSKIY OSTROV
(Island)
Kemskaya
Primorskiy Park Pobedy
Morskoy
prospe
Yuzhnaya alleya
Vostok
Orient
Yacht Club
Petrovsk. Kosa
Plo
Petr
Morskaya nab.
Kapitansk.
Korablestroiteley
Nalichnaya
(Island)
OSTROV
DEKABRISTOV
Solnyshko
Dekabristov p.
Zhelezno
Kakhavskovo p.
prospekt Kima
Zheleznovodskaya
Leningrads
Novosmolenskaya nab.
nab. Reki Smol
Primorskaya
Odoyevskovo
Armenian Apostolic

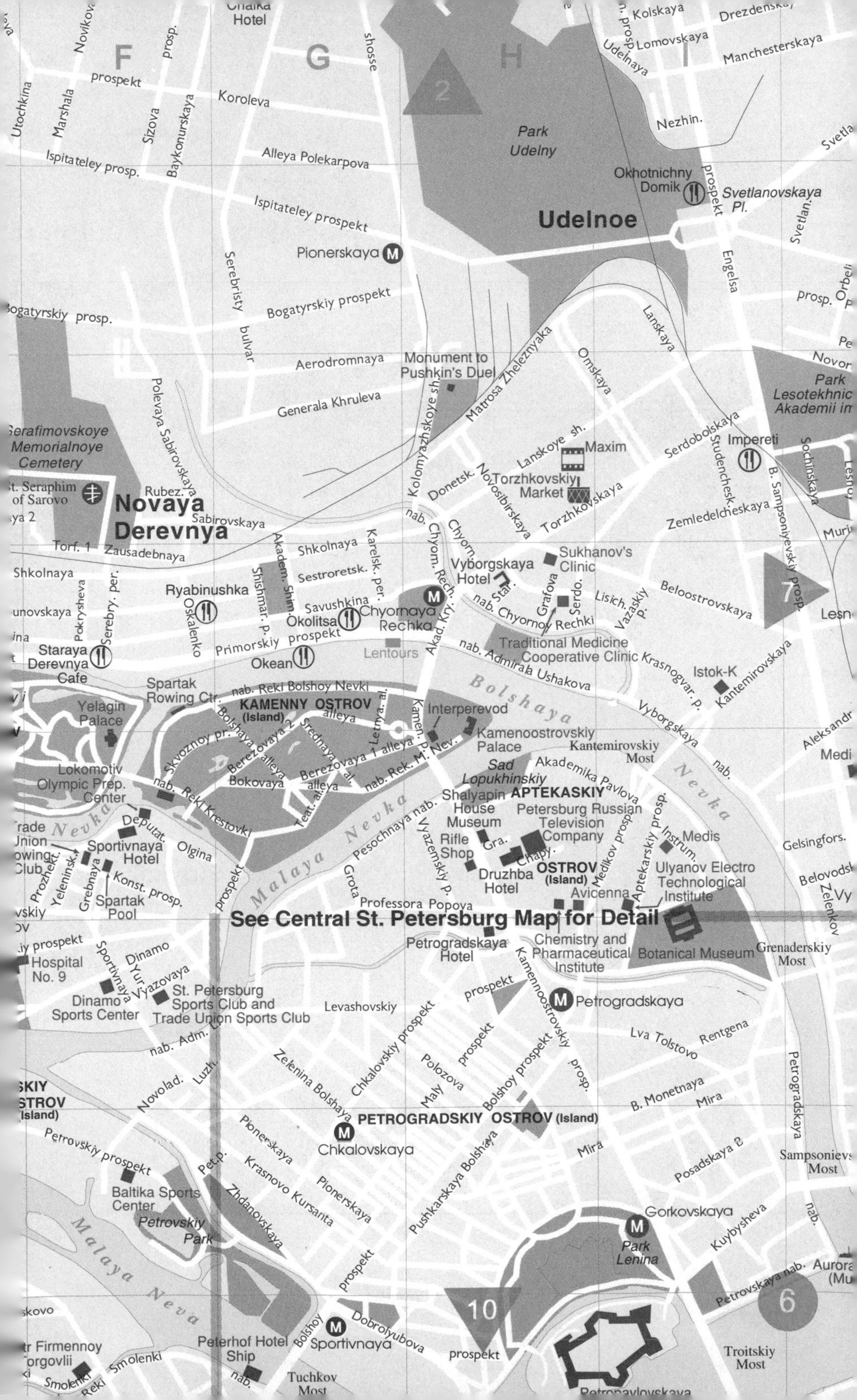
F
G
H
2
7
10
6
Chaika Hotel
Novikova
prosp.
prospekt
Utochkina
Marshala
Sizova
Baykonurskaya
Koroleva
shosse
Ispitateley prosp.
Alleya Polekarpova
Ispitateley prospekt
Kolskaya
Drezdenskaya
Lomovskaya
Udelnaya
Manchesterskaya
Nezhin.
Park Udelny
Okhotnichny Domik
Svetlanovskaya Pl.
Svetlan.
Udelnoe
Pionerskaya
Engelsa
prospekt
Serebristy bulvar
Bogatyrskiy prosp.
Bogatyrskiy prospekt
Lanskaya
prosp.
Orbeli
Aerodromnaya
Monument to Pushkin's Duel
Matrosa Zheleznyaka
Omskaya
Novor
Park Lesotekhnic Akademii im
Generala Khruleva
Polevaya Sabirovskaya
Kolomyazhskoye sh.
Serafimovskoye Memorialnoye Cemetery
St. Seraphim of Sarovo
Lanskoye sh.
Maxim
Serdobolskaya
Impereti
Studenchesk.
B. Sampsoniyevskiy prosp.
Sochinskaya
Donetsk.
Novosibirskaya
Torzhkovskiy Market
Torzhkovskaya
Zemledelcheskaya
Rubez.
Novaya Derevnya
Sabirovskaya
Torf. 1
Zausadebnaya
Shkolnaya
Akadem. Shim.
Karelsk. per.
nab. Chyom. Rech.
Chyom.
Vyborgskaya Hotel
Sukhanov's Clinic
Sestroretsk.
Shishmar. p.
Beloostrovskaya
Ryabinushka
Oskalenko
Savushkina
Okolitsa
Chyornaya Rechka
Star.
nab. Chyornoy Rechki
Grafova
Serdo.
Lisich.
Vazaskiy p.
Pokrysheva
Serebry. per.
Primorskiy prospekt
Staraya Derevnya Cafe
Okean
Lentours
Akad. Kry.
Traditional Medicine Cooperative Clinic
nab. Admirala Ushakova
Krasnogvar. p.
Istok-K
Kantemirovskaya
Spartak Rowing Ctr.
nab. Reki Bolshoy Nevki
KAMENNY OSTROV (Island)
alleya
Letnya. al.
Interperevod
Bolshaya
Yelagin Palace
Kamenoostrovskiy Palace
Kantemirovskiy Most
Vyborgskaya
Skvoznoy pr.
Bolshaya
Berezovaya 2
Srednaya al.
Kamen. p.
Berezovaya 1 alleya
nab. Rek. M. Nev.
Sad Lopukhinskiy
Akademika Pavlova
Nevka
nab.
Aleksandr
Medi
Lokomotiv Olympic Prep. Center
nab. Reki Krestovki
Bokovaya
Teat. al.
Shalyapin House Museum
APTEKASKIY
Petersburg Russian Television Company
Medikov prosp.
Aptekarskiy prosp.
Instrum.
Medis
Trade Union Rowing Club
Nevka
Deputat.
Sportivnaya Hotel
Olgina
Malaya Nevka
Pesochnaya nab.
Vyazemskiy p.
Rifle Shop
Gra.
Chapy.
Gelsingfors.
Prozhekt.
Yeleninsk.
Grebnaya
Konst. prosp.
Spartak Pool
prospekt
Grota
Druzhba Hotel
OSTROV (Island)
Ulyanov Electro Technological Institute
Belovodsk
Professora Popova
Avicenna
Zelenkov
See Central St. Petersburg Map for Detail
prospekt
Hospital No. 9
Sportivnaya
Dinamo
Yur
Vyazovaya
Petrogradskaya Hotel
Kamennoostrovskiy prosp.
Chemistry and Pharmaceutical Institute
Botanical Museum
Grenaderskiy Most
Dinamo Sports Center
St. Petersburg Sports Club and Trade Union Sports Club
Levashovskiy
Chkalovskiy prospekt
Petrogradskaya
nab. Adm. L.
Luzh.
Zelenina Bolshaya
Polozova
Maly prospekt
Bolshoy prospekt
Lva Tolstovo
Rentgena
Novolad.
B. Monetnaya
Mira
Petrogradskaya
SKIY OSTROV (Island)
PETROGRADSKIY OSTROV (Island)
Chkalovskaya
Pionerskaya
Petrovskiy prospekt
Pet.p.
Krasnovo Kursanta
Pionerskaya
Pushkarskaya Bolshaya
Mira
Posadskaya 2
Sampsonievs Most
Baltika Sports Center
Petrovskiy Park
Zhdanovskaya
Gorkovskaya
Kuybysheva
nab.
Malaya Neva
Park Lenina
prospekt
Aurora (Mu
Petrovskaya nab.
skovo
Bolshoy
Sportivnaya
Dobrolyubova
prospekt
Troitskiy Most
Firmennoy Torgovlii
Smolenki
Smolenki
Reki
Peterhof Hotel Ship
nab.
Tuchkov Most
Petropavlovskaya

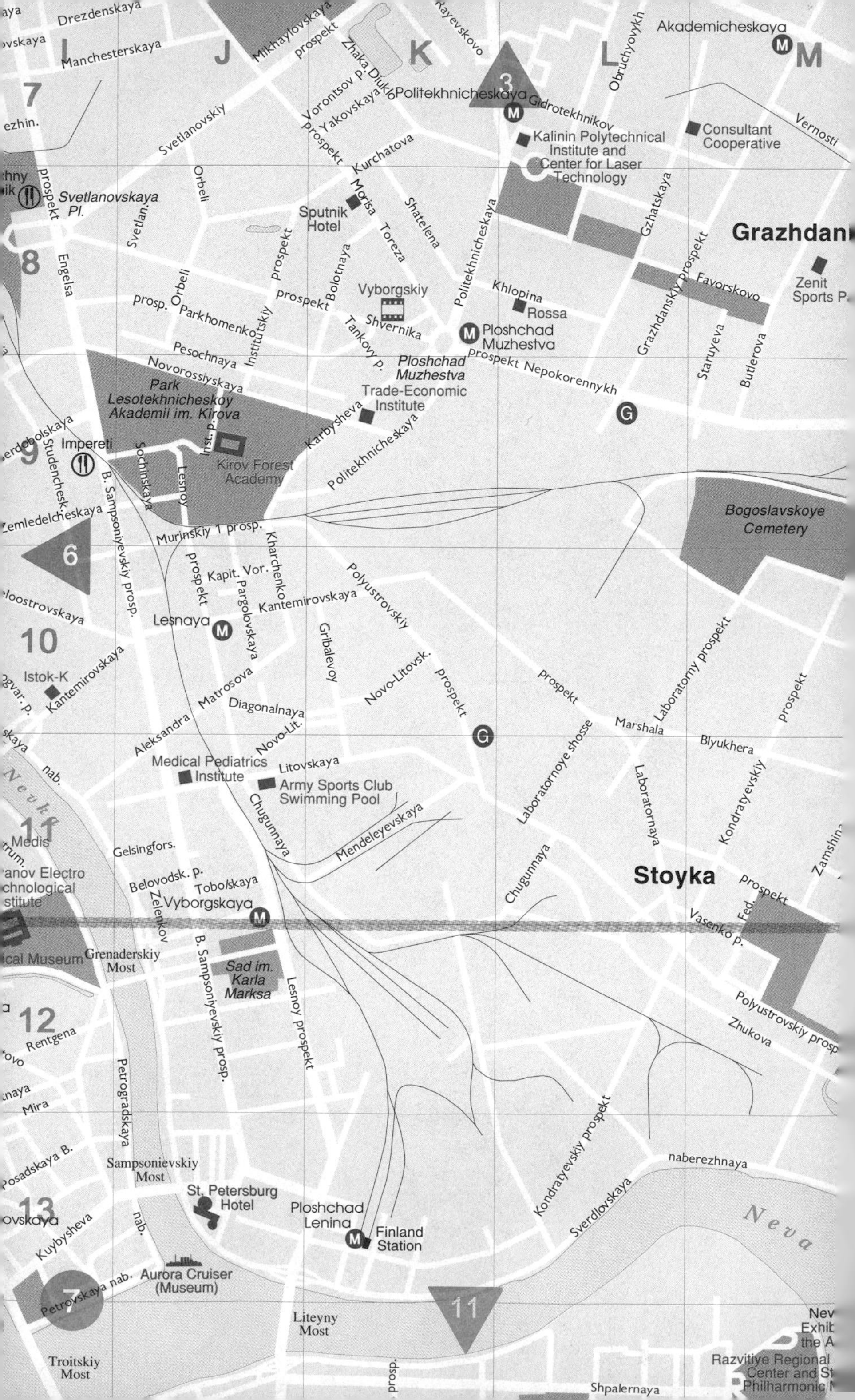

I
J
K
L
M
7
8
9
10
11
12
13
3
6
11
Drezdenskaya
Manchesterskaya
Mikhaylovskaya
prospekt
Zhaka Duklo
Rayevskovo
Obruchyovykh
Akademicheskaya
Politekhnicheskaya
Gidrotekhnikov
Vorontsov p.
Yakovskaya
Kurchatova
Svetlanovskiy
Kalinin Polytechnical Institute and Center for Laser Technology
Consultant Cooperative
Vernosti
Svetlanovskaya Pl.
Orbeli
Engelsa
Svetlan.
Sputnik Hotel
Morisa
Toreza
Shatelena
Gzhatskaya
Grazhdanskiy prospekt
Favorskovo
Zenit Sports P
Politekhnicheskaya
Institutskiy
Bolotnaya
Vyborgskiy
Khlopina
Rossa
Parkhomenko
Shvernika
Ploshchad Muzhestva
Pesochnaya
Novorossiyskaya
Tankovy p.
prospekt Nepokorennykh
Staruyeva
Butlerova
Park Lesotekhnicheskoy Akademii im. Kirova
Trade-Economic Institute
Karbysheva
Impereti
Studenchesk.
Sochinskaya
Lesnoy
Inst. p.
Kirov Forest Academy
Politekhnicheskaya
Zemledelcheskaya
B. Sampsoniyevskiy prosp.
Muriniskiy 1 prosp.
Kharchenko
Bogoslavskoye Cemetery
Kapit. Vor.
Pargolovskaya
Kantemirovskaya
Polyustrovskiy
Lesnaya
Gribalevoy
Istok-K
Kantemirovskaya
Matrosova
Diagonalnaya
Novo-Litovsk.
prospekt
Marshala
Blyukhera
Laboratorny prospekt
Aleksandra
Novo-Lit.
Medical Pediatrics Institute
Litovskaya
Army Sports Club Swimming Pool
Laboratornoye shosse
Laboratornaya
Kondratyevskiy
Neva
nab.
Chugunnaya
Mendeleyevskaya
Gelsingfors.
Belovodsk. p.
Tobolskaya
Zelenkov
Vyborgskaya
Chugunnaya
Stoyka
Fed.
Vasenko p.
Zamshina
Grenaderskiy Most
Sad im. Karla Marksa
B. Sampsoniyevskiy prosp.
Lesnoy prospekt
Polyustrovskiy prosp.
Zhukova
Rentgena
Petrogradskaya
Mira
Kondratyevskiy prospekt
Posadskaya B.
Sampsonievskiy Most
naberezhnaya
St. Petersburg Hotel
Ploshchad Lenina
Sverdlovskaya
Neva
Kubysheva
nab.
Finland Station
Aurora Cruiser (Museum)
Petrovskaya nab.
Liteyny Most
Troitskiy Most
prosp.
Shpalernaya
Razvitiye Regional Center and St Philharmonic

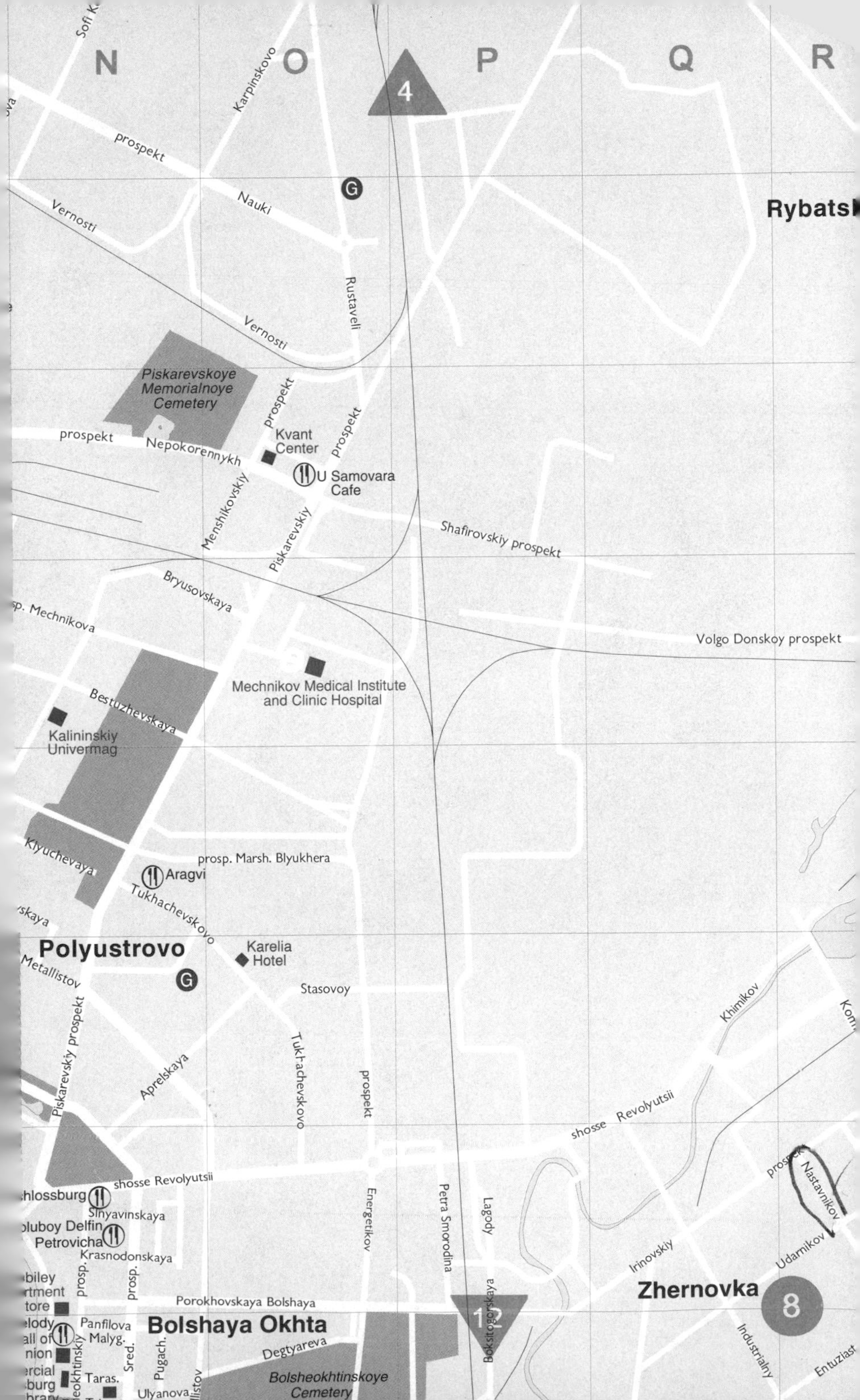

N
O
P
Q
R
4
Karpinskovo
prospekt
Nauki
Vernosti
Rustaveli
Vernosti
Rybatsk
Piskarevskoye Memorialnoye Cemetery
prospekt
prospekt
Nepokorennykh
prospekt
Kvant Center
U Samovara Cafe
Menshikovskiy
Piskarevskiy
Shafirovskiy prospekt
Bryusovskaya
Mechnikova
Volgo Donskoy prospekt
Mechnikov Medical Institute and Clinic Hospital
Bestuzhevskaya
Kalininskiy Univermag
Klyuchevaya
prosp. Marsh. Blyukhera
Aragvi
Tukhachevskovo
Polyustrovo
Metallistov
Karelia Hotel
Stasovoy
Piskarevskiy prospekt
Aprelskaya
Tukhachevskovo
prospekt
Khimikov
shosse Revolyutsii
shosse Revolyutsii
Energetikov
Petra Smorodina
Lagody
Nastavnikov
Slnyavinskaya
Petrovicha
Krasnodonskaya
Irinovskiy
Udarnikov
Zhernovka
8
Porokhovskaya Bolshaya
12
Panfilova
Malyg.
Bolshaya Okhta
Degtyareva
Bokshitogorskaya
Industrialny
Entuziast
Taras.
Sred.
Pugach.
Bolsheokhtinskoye Cemetery
Ulyanova

A
B
C
D
E
13
14
15
16
17
18
19
9
13
Gulf of Finland
Morskaya nab.
Kapitansk.
Korablestroiteley
Nalichnaya
(Island)
OSTROV
DEKABRISTOV
Solnyshko
Dekabristov p.
Zheleznovo
Kakhavskovo p.
prospekt
Kima
Zheleznovodskaya
Novosmolenskaya nab.
Primorskaya
Odoyevskovo
Leningradskay
Armenian Apostolic
nab. Reki Smolenki
Venice
Michmansk.
Church of the
Smolensk Cemetery
Smolenskoye
Cemetery
Beringa
Beriozka
Pol-Mot
Nakhimova
Pribaltiyskaya
Hotel
Television
Exchange
Trudovye
Reservi
Swimming Pool
Maly prospekt
St. Petersburg
Uni-Hostel
Ost.
Intourbureau
Sredniy
Gavan
Hotel
Kirov Pala
of Cultur
Shkiperskiy protok
Kartashikhina
Gavanskaya
Opochinina
Shevchenko
Detskaya
Srednegavanskiy pr.
Bolshoy prospekt
Vesel.
Lenexpo
U Prichala
Morskaya
Hotel
Ploshchad
Morskoy Slavy
Intourtrans
(Maritime Passenger
Terminal)
Admiral Mak
Sea Engineers'
Kozhevennaya liniya
Customs
Administratio
Mezhevoy kana
Dvinskaya
Water
Transport Institu
GUTUYEVSKIY OSTROV
(Island)
KANONERSKIY OSTROV (Island)
Kanala
Nevelskaya
nab. Reki Yekate
REZVY BOLSHOY
OSTROV (Island)
Morskovo
nab.
Pekezskiy per.
Kalinina
Kem.
Khudozh
RSFS
Train

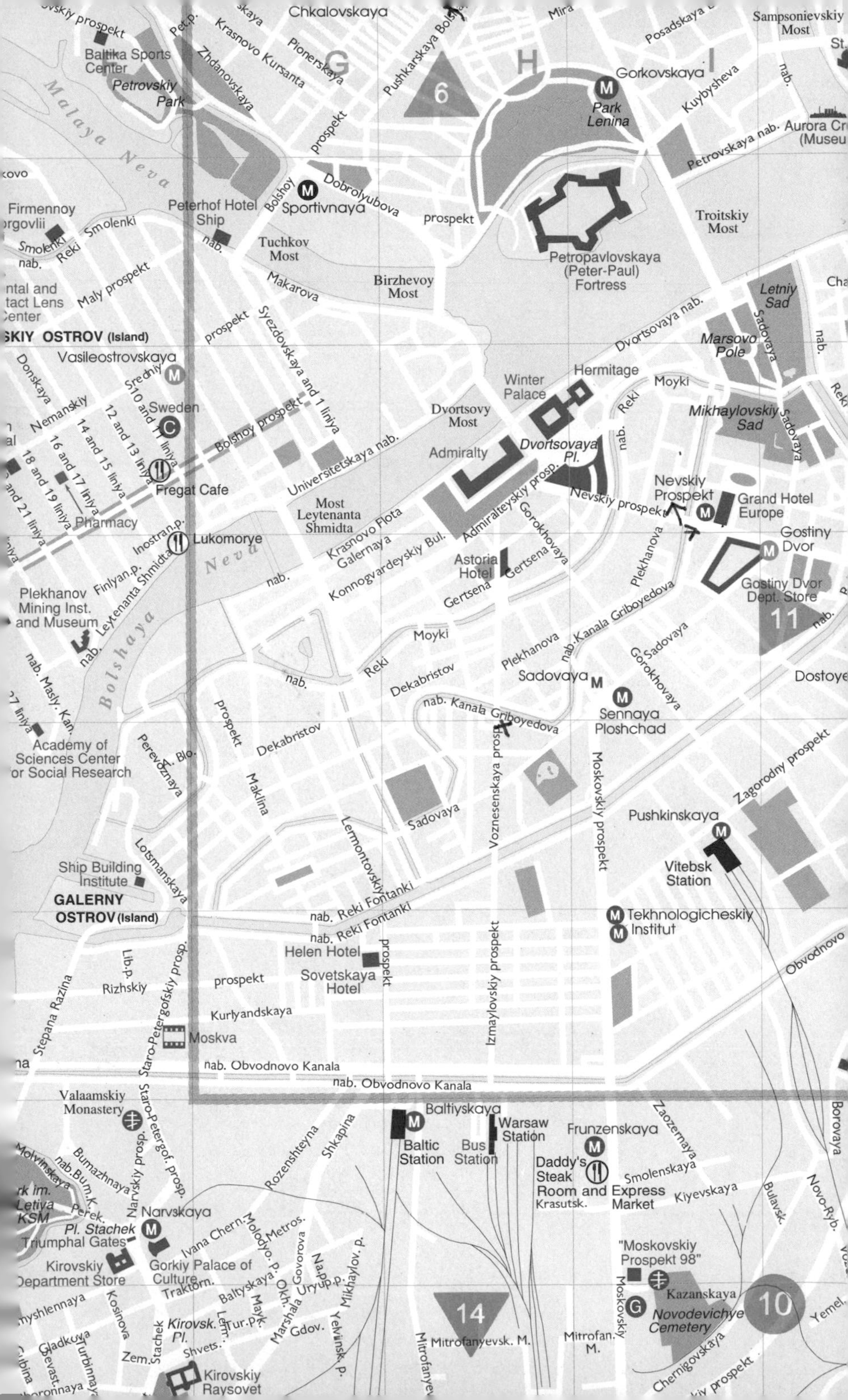

Chkalovskaya
Sampsonievskiy Most
Baltika Sports Center
Petrovskiy Park
Malaya Neva
Krasnovo Kursanta
Zhdanovskaya
Pionerskaya
Pushkarskaya
Posadskaya
Gorkovskaya
Park Lenina
Kuybysheva
Aurora Cr (Museu
Petrovskaya nab.
Firmennoy
Smolenki
Reki
Peterhof Hotel Ship
Bolshoy
Sportivnaya
Dobrolyubova
prospekt
Tuchkov Most
Troitskiy Most
Petropavlovskaya (Peter-Paul) Fortress
Makarova
Birzhevoy Most
Maly prospekt
Syezdovskaya and 1 linija
SKIY OSTROV (Island)
Letniy Sad
Dvortsovaya nab.
Marsovo Pole
Sadovaya
Vasileostrovskaya
Sredniy
Hermitage
Winter Palace
Moyki
Donskaya
10 and 11 linija
Sweden
Nemanskiy
12 and 13 linija
Bolshoy prospekt
Dvortsovy Most
Mikhaylovskiy Sad
14 and 15 linija
16 and 17 linija
18 and 19 linija
Fregat Cafe
Admiralty
Dvortsovaya Pl.
Universitetskaya nab.
Pharmacy
Most Leytenanta Shmidta
Krasnovo Flota
Admiralteyskiy prosp.
Gorokhovaya
Nevskiy Prospekt
Nevskiy prospekt
Grand Hotel Europe
Inostran.p.
Lukomorye
Neva
Galernaya
Konnogvardeyskiy Bul.
Astoria Hotel
Gertsena
Plekhanova
Gostiny Dvor
Gostiny Dvor Dept. Store
Finlyan.p.
Leytenanta Shmidta
Plekhanov Mining Inst. and Museum
Kanala Griboyedova
Bolshaya
Moyki
Reki
Dekabristov
Sadovaya
Sennaya Ploshchad
Dostoye
Masly. Kan.
Academy of Sciences Center for Social Research
Perevoznaya
A. Blo.
Dekabristov
Maklina
Voznesenskaya prosp.
Moskovskiy prospekt
Zagorodny prospekt
Pushkinskaya
Lermontovskiy
Sadovaya
Vitebsk Station
Ship Building Institute
Lotsmanskaya
GALERNY OSTROV (Island)
nab. Reki Fontanki
Tekhnologicheskiy Institut
Helen Hotel
Sovetskaya Hotel
Izmaylovskiy prospekt
Obvodnovo
Lib.p.
Rizhskiy
Kurlyandskaya
Stepana Razina
Staro-Petergofskiy prosp.
Moskva
nab. Obvodnovo Kanala
Valaamskiy Monastery
Baltiyskaya
Baltic Station
Bus Station
Warsaw Station
Frunzenskaya
Zaozernaya
Borovaya
Rozenshteyna
Shkapina
Daddy's Steak Room and Express Market
Krasutsk.
Smolenskaya
Kiyevskaya
Bulavsk.
Novo-Ryb.
Narvskiy prosp.
Bumazhnaya
Narvskaya
Pl. Stachek
Triumphal Gates
Kirovskiy Department Store
Gorkiy Palace of Culture
Ivana Chern.
Metros.
Traktorn.
Baltyskaya
Govorova
Mikhaylov. p.
"Moskovskiy Prospekt 98"
Kazanskaya
Novodevichye Cemetery
Kirovsk. Pl.
Gdov.
Mitrofanyevsk. M.
Mitrofan. M.
Chernigovskaya
Yemel.
Kosinova
Gladkova
Turbinnaya
Shvets.
Zem.
Stachek
Kirovskiy Raysovet

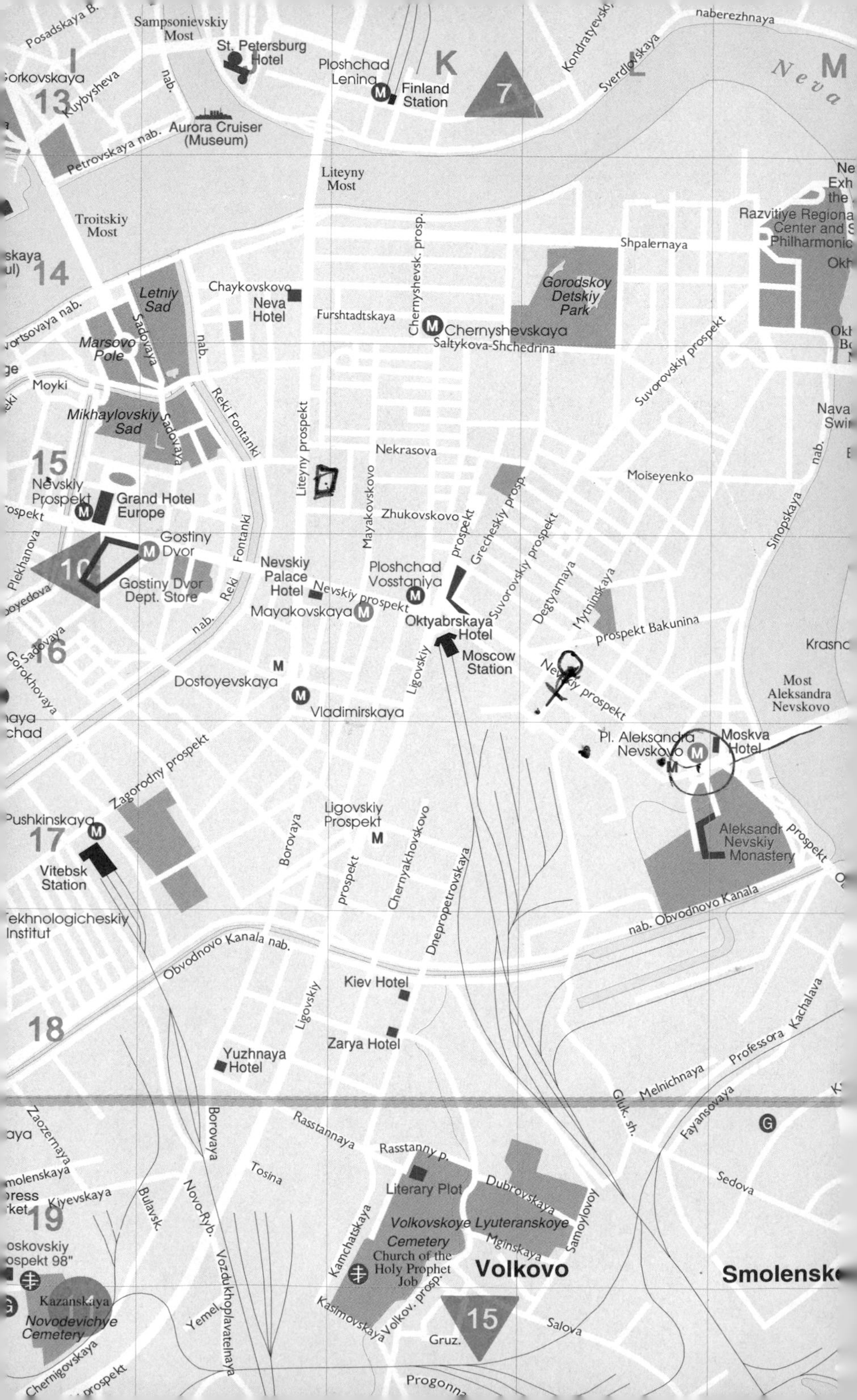

Sampsonievskiy Most
St. Petersburg Hotel
Ploshchad Lenina
Finland Station
Aurora Cruiser (Museum)
Petrovskaya nab.
Kuybysheva
Gorkovskaya
Posadskaya B.
Kondratyevskiy
Sverdlovskaya
naberezhnaya
Neva
I
K
L
M
7
13
14
15
16
17
18
19
Liteyny Most
Troitskiy Most
Razvitiye Regional Center and Philharmonic
Shpalernaya
Gorodskoy Detskiy Park
Chaykovskovo
Neva Hotel
Furshtadtskaya
Chernyshevsk. prosp.
Chernyshevskaya
Saltykova-Shchedrina
Letniy Sad
Marsovo Pole
Sadovaya
Moyki
Mikhaylovskiy Sad
Reki Fontanki
Liteyny prospekt
Nekrasova
Mayakovskovo
Zhukovskovo
Suvorovskiy prospekt
Moiseyenko
Sinopskaya
Nevskiy Prospekt
Grand Hotel Europe
Gostiny Dvor
Gostiny Dvor Dept. Store
Plekhanova
Nevskiy Palace Hotel
Nevskiy prospekt
Ploshchad Vosstaniya
Mayakovskaya
Oktyabrskaya Hotel
Moscow Station
Grecheskiy prosp.
Degtyarnaya
Mytninskaya
prospekt Bakunina
Most Aleksandra Nevskovo
Gorokhovaya
Dostoyevskaya
Vladimirskaya
Ligovskiy
Pl. Aleksandra Nevskovo
Moskva Hotel
Aleksandr Nevskiy Monastery
Zagorodny prospekt
Pushkinskaya
Vitebsk Station
Tekhnologicheskiy Institut
Borovaya
Ligovskiy Prospekt
Chernyakhovskovo
Dnepropetrovskaya
nab. Obvodnovo Kanala
Obvodnovo Kanala nab.
Kiev Hotel
Zarya Hotel
Yuzhnaya Hotel
Professora Kachalava
Melnichnaya
Gluk. sh.
Fayansovaya
Zaozernaya
Rasstannaya
Rasstanny p.
Tosina
Literary Plot
Dubrovskaya
Volkovskoye Lyuteranskoye Cemetery
Church of the Holy Prophet Job
Mginskaya
Samoylovoy
Sedova
Kamchatskaya
Volkovo
Smolensk
Kiyevskaya
Bulavsk.
Novo-Ryb.
Vozdukhoplavatelnaya
Kazanskaya
Novodevichye Cemetery
Yemel.
Kasimovskaya
Volkov. prosp.
15
Gruz.
Salova
Chernigovskaya
Progonna

N
O
P
Q
R
shosse Revolyutsii
Sinyavinskaya
Krasnodonskaya
Porokhovskaya Bolshaya
Bolshaya Okhta
Panfilova
Malyg.
Degtyareva
Bolsheokhtinskoye Cemetery
Nikolskaya Bolsheokhtinskaya
Spektr Center
Polesye
Kontorsk.
Shepetov.
Partizanskaya
prospekt Metallistov
Krasnogvardeyskaya Pl.
Yakornaya
Energetikov
Petra Smorodina
Lagody
Boksitogorskaya
Irinovskiy
Udarnikov
Zhernovka
Industrialny
Entuziastov
Peredovikov
Kosygina
Magnitogorskaya
prospekt
Lenskaya
Khasanskaya
Sport Store
Utkin
Ladozhskaya
Yablonovka
Respublikanskaya
Sergiyev.
Krzhizhanovskovo
Deson-Ladoga Hotel
Zanevskiy
Schwabskiy Domik
Shaumyana
Latyshskikh Strelkov
Vaneeva
Malaya Okhta
Tallinskaya
Gromova
Rizhskaya
Krasnogvardeyskiy prospekt
Granitnaya
Rossiyskiy
Kollontai
Prospekt Bolshevikov
Tovarishcheskiy
Dalnevostochny prospekt
Belysheva
Tonus Medical Cooperative
Podvoyskovo
prospekt Bolshevikov
Kinoveyevskoye Cemetery
Oktyabrskaya nab.
Antonovo-Ovseyenko
Ulitsa Dybenko
Neva
Iskrovskiy prospekt
Vesyoly Poselok
Dybenko
Shotmana
Progonny p.
Nevskiy Market
Yelizarovskaya
A.O. Nevskiy Center
Smolenskiy
Babushkina
Olminskovo
Yelizarova
Olgi Bergolts
Yevdokima Ogneva
Krylenko
Dalnevos
16
12

A
B
C
D
E
19
20
21
22
23
24
25
26
9
13
KANONERSKIY OSTROV (Isla
nab.
Morskovo
Kanala
Nevelskaya
REZVY BOLSHOY
OSTROV (Island)
nab. Reki Ye
Pekezskiy per.
Kalinina
Kem.
Khudozh
RSFS
Train
Cen
Korabelnaya
Gaza
Kir
Komsomolsk
Korabelnaya
doroga na Turukhtannye Ostrova
Portovaya
Morskoy Pekhoty
Zhukova
Marshala
Kozakova
Leninskiy
prospekt
Kotina
Marshala
Marshala
Zakharova
Kuznetsova
Brestskiy bul.
Desantnikov
prospekt
Stachek
Tretyevo Internatsionala
Rikharda Zorge
Rikharda Zorge
no-Primorskiy
im. Lenina
Petergofskoye
shosse
prospekt
Zhukova
Marshala
Soldata
Veteranov
Tankista
Tretyev
Prospekt
Veteranov

Baltic Station
Bus Station
Daddy's Steak Room and Express Market
Narvskaya
Pl. Stachek
Triumphal Gates
Kirovskiy Department Store
Gorkiy Palace of Culture
Kirovsk. Pl.
Kirovskiy Raysovet
Detskiy Park im. 9 Yanvarya
Neptun
Khimicheskiy pereulok
Mitrofanyevskoye shosse
Mitrofanyevskoye Cemetery
"Moskovskiy Prospekt 98"
Kazanskaya
Novodevichye Cemetery
Chernigovskaya
Ligovskiy prospekt
Moscow Triumphal Gates
Pl. Moskovskiye Vorota
Moskovskiye Vorota
Lenwest
Zastavskaya
Roshchinskaya
Elektrosila Sports Club
Elektrosila
Mariinskaya
Reshetnikova
Moskovskiy Market
Alekseyevka
Avtovo
Korpusnoy proyezd
Blagodatnaya
Kuznetsovskaya
Park Kosmonavtov
Yubileyny Bakery
Rossia Hotel
Pl. Chernyshevskovo
Moskovskiy Park Pobedy
Pharmacy No. 91
Park Pobedy
Basseynaya
Shepito Big Top
Chervonnovo Kazachestva
Krasnenkoye Cemetery
Frunze
Rossa
Central Naval Museum
Zenit
Gastello
Hospital No. 20
Mir Hotel
Knigolub Bookstore
Aviatsionnaya
Moskovskaya
Meridian
Moskovskaya Ploshchad
Leninskiy prospekt
Leninskiy Prospekt
Altayskaya
Pietari
Moskovskiy Department Store
Pulkovskaya Hotel
Ploshchad Pobedy
Business Center T.A.M.
Galstyana
Ordzhonikidze
Kostyushko
Krasnoputilovskaya
Novo-Izmaylovskiy prospekt
Varshavskaya
Moskovskiy prospekt
prospekt Narodnovo Opolchenya
bulvar Novatorov
Schastlivaya
Avtovskaya
Kubinskaya
Syzranskaya
Yuriya Gagarina
10
15
14

Volkovo
Smolenskoy
Kupchino
Volkovskoye Lyuteranskoye Cemetery
Church of the Holy Prophet Job
Literary Plot
Novodevichye Cemetery
Moscow Triumphal Gates
Moskovskiye Vorota
Lenwest
Elektrosila Sports Club
Reshetnikova
Moskovskiy Market
Novo-Volkovskoye Cemetery
Rosgalantereya Wholesale Trade Association
Moskovskiy Park Pobedy
Park Pobedy
Sport-Concert Complex
Central Naval Museum
Mir Hotel
Gastello
Moskovskaya Ploshchad
Moskovskaya
Pietari
Ploshchad Pobedy
Slava
Sparmarket
Kupichinskiy Department Store
Vitebskiy Department Store
Tosina
Dubrovskaya
Sedova
Kiyevskaya
Bulavsk.
Novo-Ryb.
Kamchatskaya
Mginskaya
Samoylovoy
Kazanskaya
Kasimovskaya
Volkov. prosp.
Salova
Gruz.
Yemel.
Vozdukhoplavatelnaya
Chernigovskaya
Ligovskiy prospekt
Progonnaya
Loman.
Parkovaya
Bukharestskaya
Tsvetochnaya
Koli Tomchaka
Zastavskaya
Kondraten.
Lyubotinskiy prospekt
Vitebskiy prospekt
Volkovskiy prospekt
Strelbishchenskaya
Koz.p.
Pulkovsk.
Irkutskaya
Roshchinskaya
Fuchika
Sofiyskaya
Blagodatnaya
Belgradskaya
Sevastyanova
Sveaborgskaya
prospekt
Budapeshtskaya
Kuznetsovskaya
Kosmonavtov
Bela Kuna
Turku
Prazhskaya
Yuriya Gagarina
Vitebskiy prospekt
Basseynaya
prospekt Kosmonavtov
Frunze
Lensoveta
Aviatsionnaya
prospekt Slavy
Tipanova
Alpiyskiy p.
Altayskaya
Zagrebskiy bul.
Dimitrova
Ordzhonikidze
Malaya Balkanskaya
Plovdivskaya

N
O
P
Q
12
Vesyoly Poselok
Proyezdnaya
Pere. nab.
Obsh.p.
Progonny p.
Nevskiy Market
Bolshoy prosp.
Smolenskiy
Pineg.
Olminskovo
Babushkina
Yelizarovskaya
A.O. Nevskiy Center
Sedova
prosp. Yelizarova
Olgi Bergolts
Tkachey
Zub.
Krupskoy
Uyezdny prosp.
Kanat.
Dudko
prospekt
Dybenko
Shotmana
Yevdokima Ogneva
Krylenko
Dalnevostochny
Telmana
prosp.
Novoselov
Sakura
Narodnaya
Koyolga
Tsimbalina
P. Kir.
Zheleznodorozhny prosp.
Park im. Babushkina
Obukhovskoy
Farforovaya
Varfolomeyevskaya
Farforovskaya
Babushkina
Sedova
Polyarnikov
Matyush.p.
Nevskiy Raysovet
Pryamoy prosp.
Chesn.
Lomonosovskaya
Ivanovskaya
Oborony
Dalnevostochny
Oktyabrskaya
nab.
bulvar Krasnykh Zor
Nevskiye Zvyozdy
Rechnaya Hotel
(River Passenger Terminal)
Lesnozavodskaya
Neva
Slavy
prospekt
Kibalchicha
Sedova
Shelgunova
Novo-Aleksandrovskaya
Proletarskaya
Holy Trinity
Chernova
Sofiyskaya
Yuszhnoye shosse
Shelgunova
Fermy prosp.
Babushkina
prospekt
Synagogue
Tikhaya
Yevreyskoye (Jewish) Cemetery
Aleksandrovskoy
Troitskoye Pole
Obkhovskoy
Gribakinykh
Troitskoye pole
Oborony
Aleksandrovskoye
Devyatoyo Yanvarya
Cemetery im. Zhertv 9 Yanvarya
Malaya
Bukharestskaya
Devyatovo Yanvarya
Obukhovo
Zaporozhskaya
Progonny p.
Sofiyskaya
Maly p.
Foreign Trade Industrial-Commercial Center
Ivanovskiy p.
Skladskoy proyezd
Gruzovoy proyezd
16

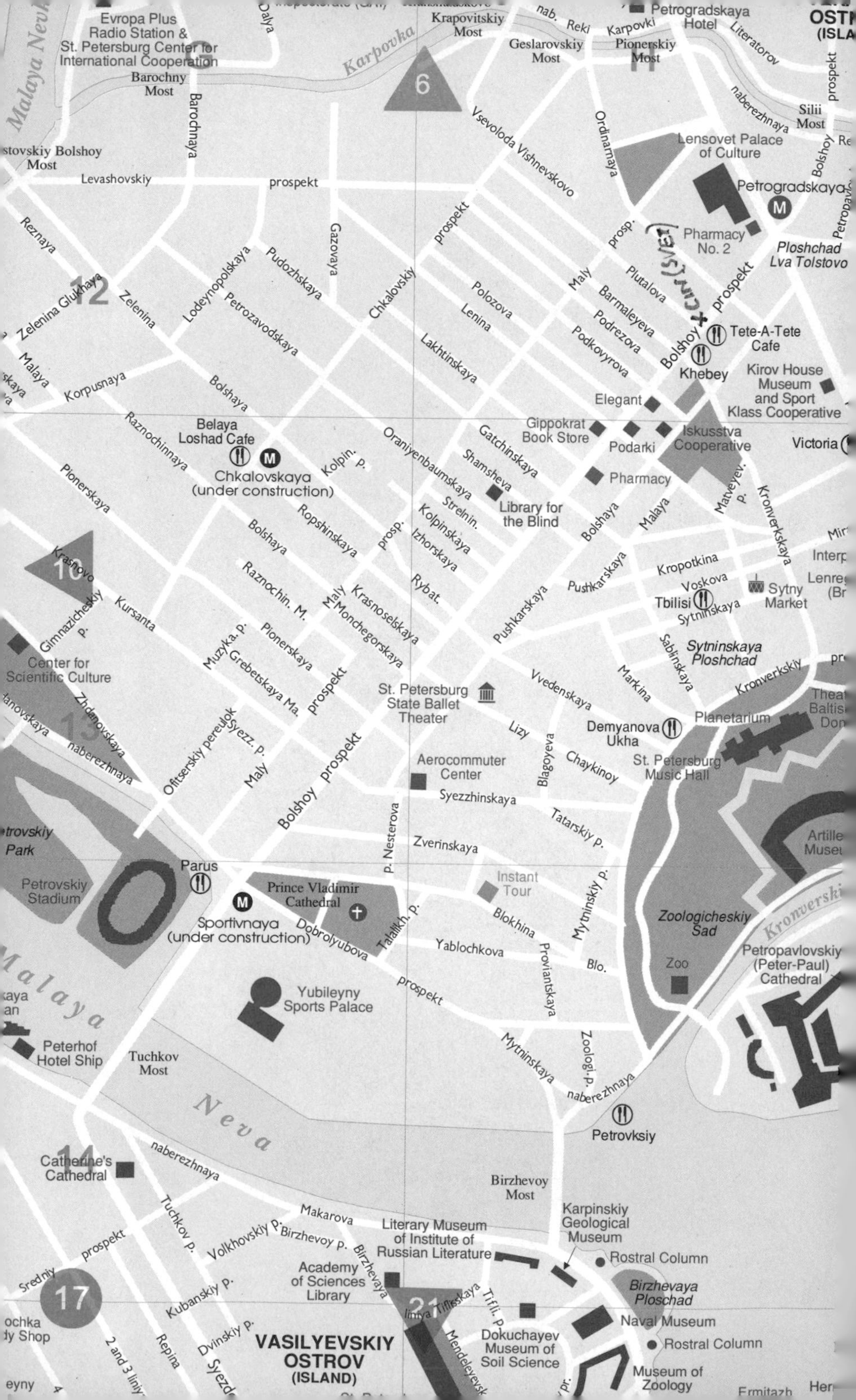

Malaya Neva
Evropa Plus Radio Station & St. Petersburg Center for International Cooperation
Barochny Most
Dalya
Krapovitskiy Most
Karpovka
nab. Reki Karpovki
Geslarovskiy Most
Pionerskiy Most
Petrogradskaya Hotel
Literatorov
OSTR (ISLA
6
Barochnaya
Vsevoloda Vishnevskovo
Ordinarnaya
naberezhnaya
Silii Most
prospekt
Lensovet Palace of Culture
stovskiy Bolshoy Most
Levashovskiy
prospekt
Petrogradskaya
Bolshoy
Petropavl
Pharmacy No. 2
Ploshchad Lva Tolstovo
Reznaya
Gazovaya
prospekt
prosp.
Maly
Plutalova
Barmaleyeva
Podrezova
Podkovyrova
Bolshoy prospekt
12
Zelenina Glukhaya
Zelenina
Lodeynopolskaya
Pudozhskaya
Petrozavodskaya
Chkalovskiy
Polozova
Lenina
Tete-A-Tete Cafe
Khebey
Kirov House Museum and Sport Klass Cooperative
Malaya
Korpusnaya
Bolshaya
Lakhtinskaya
Elegant
Belaya Loshad Cafe
Raznochinnaya
Chkalovskaya (under construction)
Kolpin. p.
Oraniyenbaumskaya
Gatchinskaya
Shamsheva
Gippokrat Book Store
Podarki
Iskusstva Cooperative
Victoria
Pharmacy
Pionerskaya
Library for the Blind
Strelnin.
Kolpinskaya
Izhorskaya
Ropshinskaya
prosp.
Bolshaya
Malaya
Matveyev. p.
Kronverkskaya
10
Krasnovo
Bolshaya
Raznochin. M.
Maly
Krasnoselskaya
Rybat.
Pushkarskaya
Pushkarskaya
Kropotkina
Voskova
Tbilisi
Sytninskaya
Sytny Market
Interp
Lenreg (Br
Gimnazicheskiy p.
Kursanta
Monchegorskaya
Pionerskaya
Muzyka. p.
Grebetskaya Ma.
prospekt
Sablinskaya
Markina
Sytninskaya Ploshchad
Center for Scientific Culture
St. Petersburg State Ballet Theater
Vvedenskaya
Kronverkskiy
Planetarium
Theat Baltis Dom
13
Zhdanovskaya
naberezhnaya
Syezz. p.
Oftserskiy pereulok
Maly
Bolshoy prospekt
Lizy
Demyanova Ukha
Aerocommuter Center
Chaykinoy
Blagoyeva
St. Petersburg Music Hall
Syezzhinskaya
Tatarskiy p.
Petrovskiy Park
Zverinskaya
p. Nesterova
Artille Museu
Parus
Petrovskiy Stadium
Prince Vladimir Cathedral
Instant Tour
Mytninskiy p.
Sportivnaya (under construction)
Dobrolyubova
Talalikh. p.
Blokhina
Zoologicheskiy Sad
Kronverski
Yablochkova
Proviantskaya
Blo.
Zoo
Petropavlovskiy (Peter-Paul) Cathedral
Malaya
prospekt
Yubileyny Sports Palace
Peterhof Hotel Ship
Tuchkov Most
Mytninskaya
Zoologi. p.
naberezhnaya
Neva
Petrovksiy
14
Catherine's Cathedral
naberezhnaya
Birzhevoy Most
Tuchkov p.
Makarova
Literary Museum of Institute of Russian Literature
Karpinskiy Geological Museum
prospekt
Volkhovskiy p.
Birzhevoy p.
Rostral Column
Sredniy
Academy of Sciences Library
Birzhevaya
Birzhevaya Ploschad
17
Kubanskiy p.
Tiflisskaya
Tifli. p.
21
liniya
Naval Museum
ochka dy Shop
Dvinskiy p.
Dokuchayev Museum of Soil Science
Rostral Column
Repina
Mendeleyevsk
2 and 3 liniy
Syezd
VASILYEVSKIY OSTROV (ISLAND)
Museum of Zoology
eyny
pr.
Ermitazh
Her

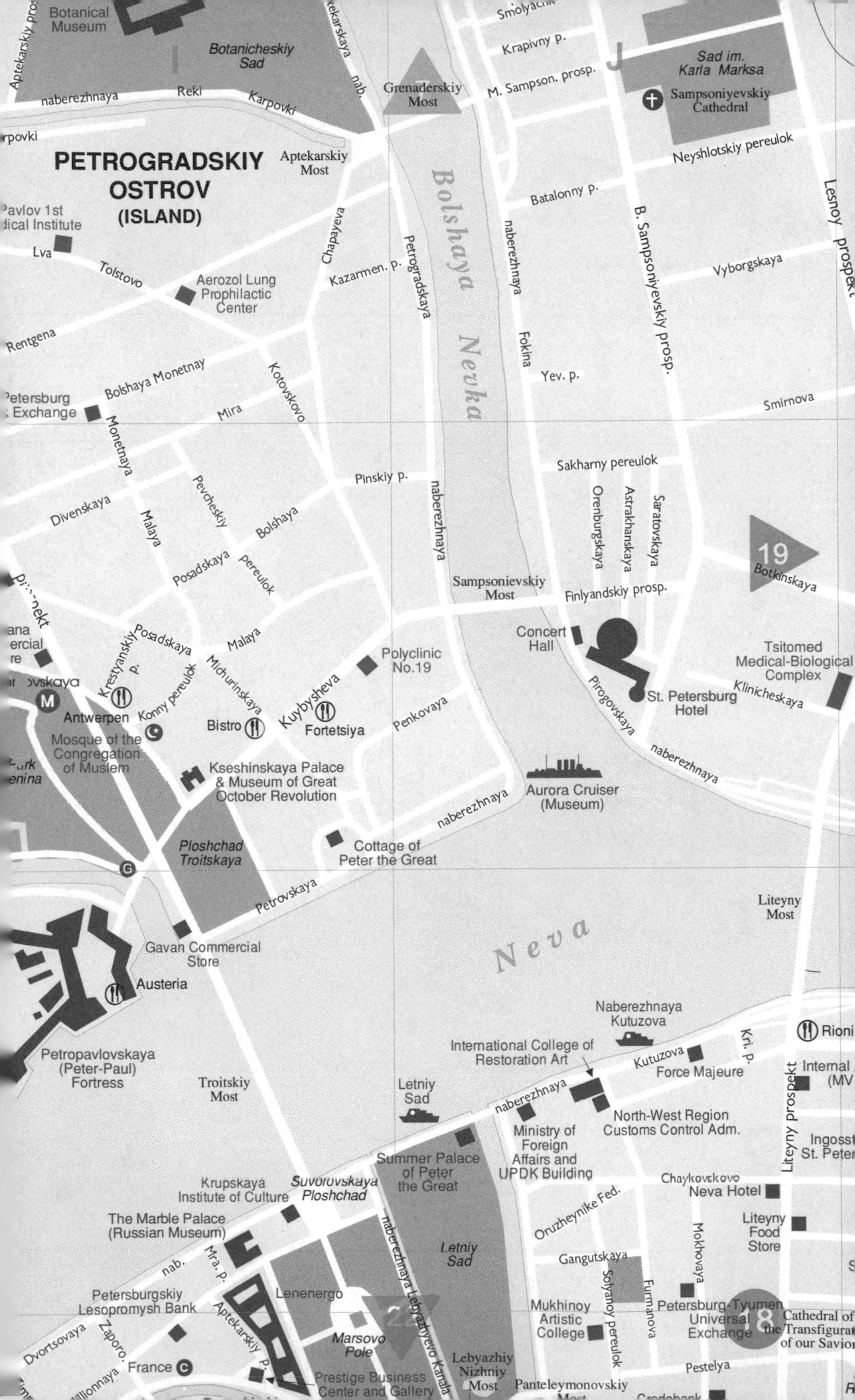

Botanical Museum
Botanicheskiy Sad
naberezhnaya
Reki
Karpovki
Grenaderskiy Most
M. Sampson. prosp.
Krapivny p.
Sad im. Karla Marksa
Sampsoniyevskiy Cathedral
PETROGRADSKIY OSTROV (ISLAND)
Aptekarskiy Most
Bolshaya Nevka
Neyshlotskiy pereulok
Batalonny p.
Lesnoy prospekt
B. Sampsoniyevskiy prosp.
Vyborgskaya
Lva
Tolstovo
Aerozol Lung Prophilactic Center
Chapayeva
Kazarmen. p.
Petrogradskaya
naberezhnaya
Fokina
Rentgena
Bolshaya Monetnay
Kotovskovo
Yev. p.
Smirnova
Mira
Monetnaya
Pevcheskiy pereulok
Pinskiy p.
Sakharny pereulok
Orenburgskaya
Astrakhanskaya
Saratovskaya
Divenskaya
Malaya
Bolshaya
Posadskaya
19
Botkinskaya
Sampsonievskiy Most
Finlyandskiy prosp.
Concert Hall
Posadskaya
Malaya
Krestyanskiy p.
Michurinskaya
Konny pereulok
Polyclinic No.19
Tsitomed Medical-Biological Complex
Klinicheskaya
St. Petersburg Hotel
Pirogovskaya
Kuybysheva
Fortetsiya
Penkovaya
Bistro
Antwerpen
Mosque of the Congregation of Muslem
Kseshinskaya Palace & Museum of Great October Revolution
naberezhnaya
Aurora Cruiser (Museum)
Ploshchad Troitskaya
Cottage of Peter the Great
Petrovskaya
Liteyny Most
Neva
Gavan Commercial Store
Austeria
Naberezhnaya Kutuzova
Rioni
Petropavlovskaya (Peter-Paul) Fortress
International College of Restoration Art
Kutuzova
Kri. p.
Force Majeure
Troitskiy Most
Letniy Sad
naberezhnaya
North-West Region Customs Control Adm.
Liteyny prospekt
Ministry of Foreign Affairs and UPDK Building
Summer Palace of Peter the Great
Krupskaya Institute of Culture
Suvorovskaya Ploshchad
Chaykovskovo
Neva Hotel
Oruzheynike Fed.
Liteyny Food Store
The Marble Palace (Russian Museum)
Letniy Sad
Gangutskaya
nab.
Mra. p.
Mokhovaya
Lenenergo
naberezhnaya Lebyazhyevo Kanala
Solyanoy pereulok
Furmanova
Petersburgskiy Lesopromysh Bank
Aptekarskiy p.
22
Mukhinoy Artistic College
Petersburg-Tyumen Universal Exchange
18
Dvortsovaya
Zaporo.
Marsovo Pole
Lebyazhiy Nizhniy Most
Pestelya
France
Prestige Business Center and Gallery
Panteleymonovskiy

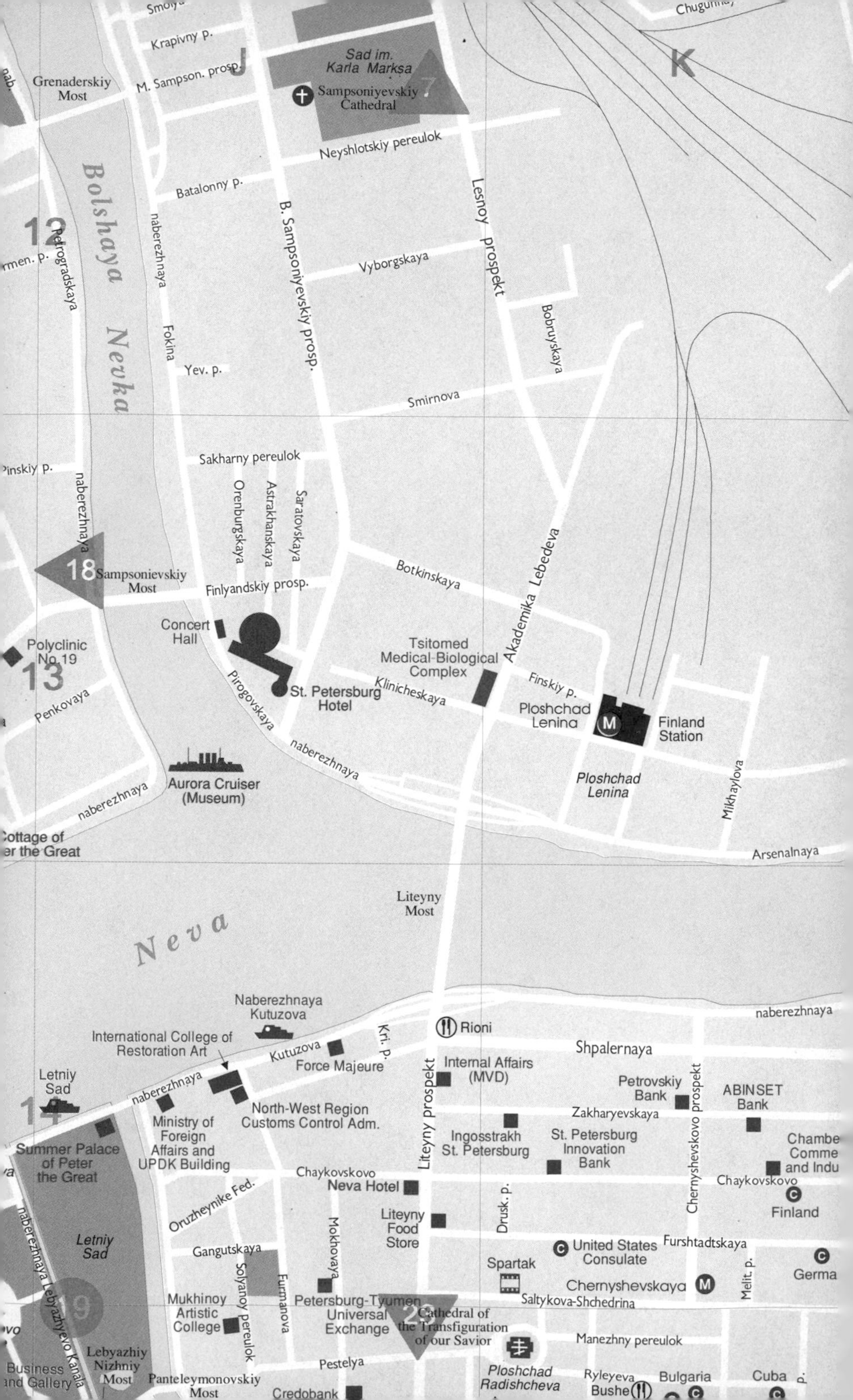

Krapivny p.
J
K
Grenaderskiy Most
M. Sampson. prosp.
Sad im. Karla Marksa
Sampsoniyevskiy Cathedral
7
Neyshlotskiy pereulok
Batalonny p.
Bolshaya Nevka
12
Petrogradskaya
naberezhnaya
B. Sampsoniyevskiy prosp.
Lesnoy prospekt
Vyborgskaya
Bobruyskaya
Fokina
Yev. p.
Smirnova
Sakharny pereulok
Orenburgskaya
Astrakhanskaya
Saratovskaya
naberezhnaya
18
Sampsonievskiy Most
Finlyandskiy prosp.
Botkinskaya
Akademika Lebedeva
Concert Hall
Polyclinic No.19
13
Tsitomed Medical-Biological Complex
Klinicheskaya
Finskiy p.
St. Petersburg Hotel
Pirogovskaya
Ploshchad Lenina
Finland Station
Penkovaya
naberezhnaya
Ploshchad Lenina
Mikhaylova
Aurora Cruiser (Museum)
naberezhnaya
Arsenalnaya
Liteyny Most
Neva
Naberezhnaya Kutuzova
naberezhnaya
International College of Restoration Art
Kutuzova
Kri. p.
Rioni
Shpalernaya
Force Majeure
Internal Affairs (MVD)
Letniy Sad
naberezhnaya
14
Petrovskiy Bank
ABINSET Bank
North-West Region Customs Control Adm.
Zakharyevskaya
Ministry of Foreign Affairs and UPDK Building
Summer Palace of Peter the Great
Ingosstrakh St. Petersburg
St. Petersburg Innovation Bank
Chernyshevskovo prospekt
Chaykovskovo
Neva Hotel
Liteyny prospekt
Chaykovskovo
Finland
Oruzheynike Fed.
Liteyny Food Store
Drusk. p.
Mokhovaya
Letniy Sad
Gangutskaya
United States Consulate
Furshtadtskaya
Spartak
Melit. p.
Germa
naberezhnaya Lebyazhyevo Kanala
19
Solyanoy pereulok
Furmanova
Chernyshevskaya
Mukhinoy Artistic College
Petersburg-Tyumen Universal Exchange
Saltykova-Shchedrina
23
Cathedral of the Transfiguration of our Savior
Manezhny pereulok
Lebyazhiy Nizhniy Most
Pestelya
Ploshchad Radishcheva
Ryleyeva
Bulgaria
Cuba
Business and Gallery
Panteleymonovskiy Most
Credobank
Bushe

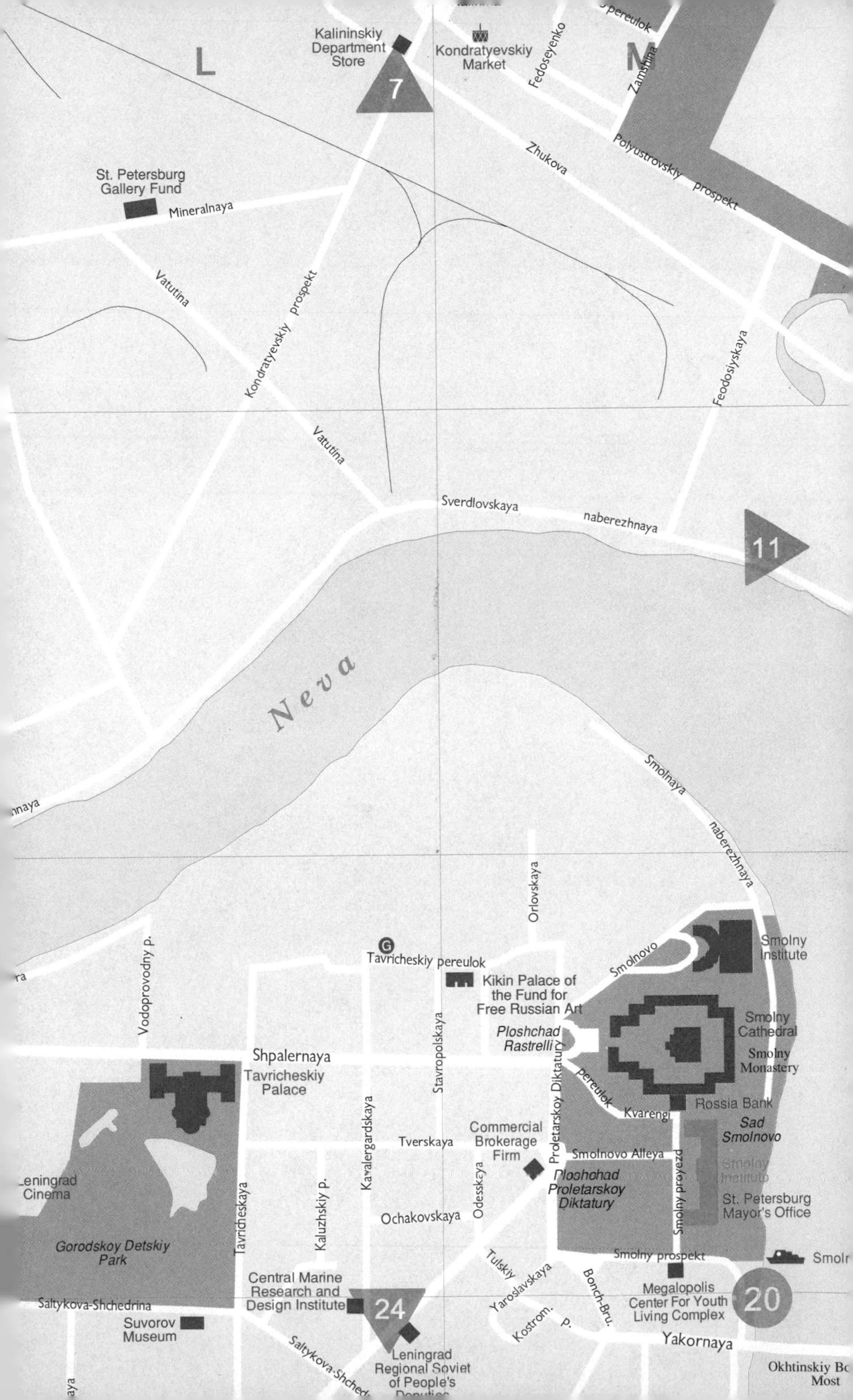

L
M
Kalininskiy Department Store
Kondratyevskiy Market
7
Fedoseyenko
Zamshina
Polyustrovskiy prospekt
Zhukova
St. Petersburg Gallery Fund
Mineralnaya
Vatutina
Kondratyevskiy prospekt
Feodosiyskaya
Vatutina
Sverdlovskaya naberezhnaya
11
Neva
Smolnaya naberezhnaya
Orlovskaya
Vodoprovodny p.
Tavricheskiy pereulok
Kikin Palace of the Fund for Free Russian Art
Smolnovo
Smolny Institute
Smolny Cathedral
Smolny Monastery
Ploshchad Rastrelli
Shpalernaya
Tavricheskiy Palace
Stavropolskaya
Proletarskoy Diktatury pereulok
Kvarengi
Rossia Bank
Sad Smolnovo
Kavalergardskaya
Tverskaya
Commercial Brokerage Firm
Smolnovo Alleya
Smolny Institute
St. Petersburg Mayor's Office
Leningrad Cinema
Ploshchad Proletarskoy Diktatury
Smolny proyezd
Tavricheskaya
Kaluzhskiy p.
Ochakovskaya
Odesskaya
Gorodskoy Detskiy Park
Smolny prospekt
Tulskiy
Yaroslavskaya
Bonch-Bru.
Central Marine Research and Design Institute
Megalopolis Center For Youth Living Complex
20
Saltykova-Shchedrina
24
Suvorov Museum
Kostrom. p.
Yakornaya
Saltykova-Shched.
Leningrad Regional Soviet of People's Deputies
Okhtinskiy Most

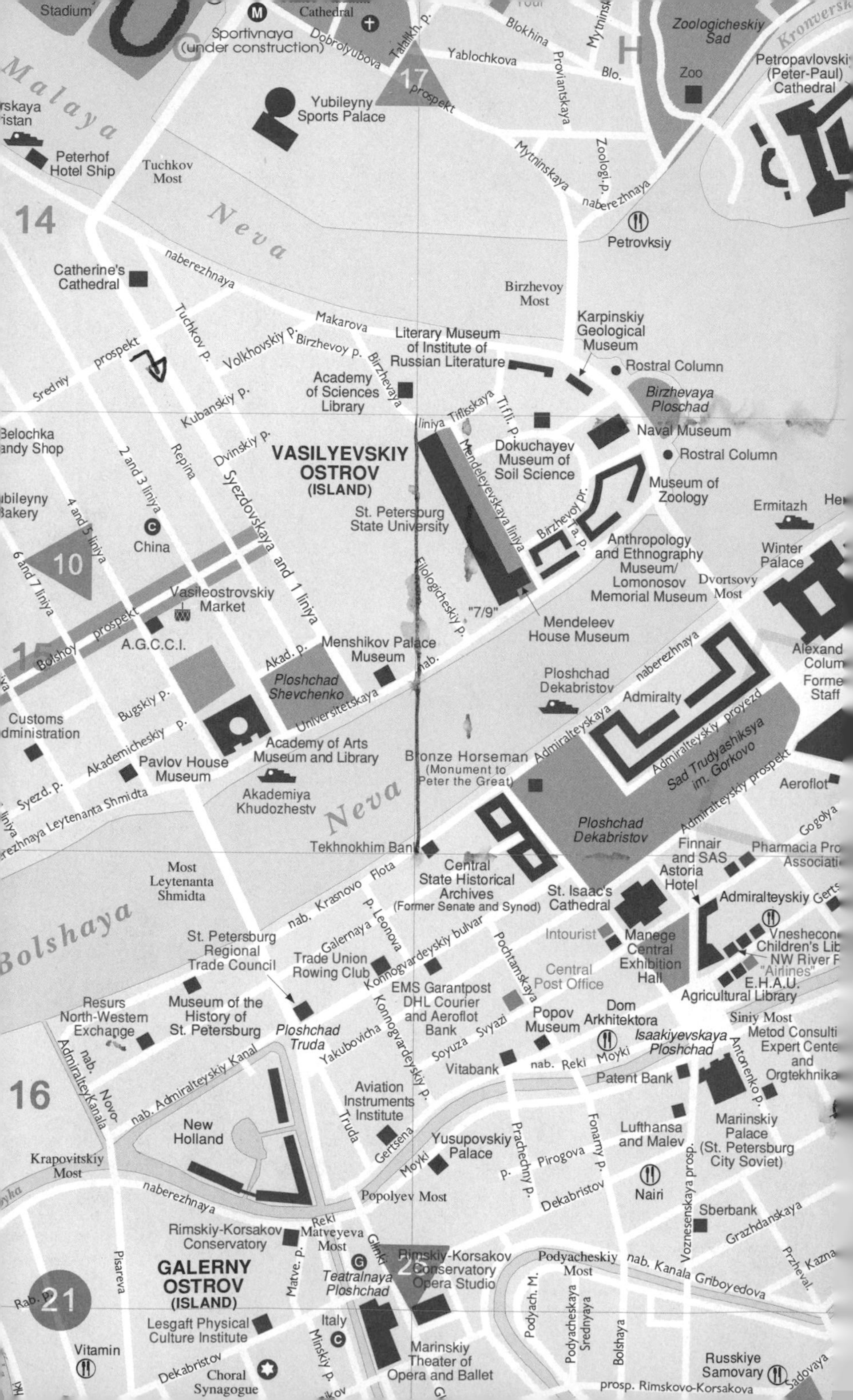

Stadium
Cathedral
Sportivnaya
(under construction)
Dobrolyubova
Talalikh. p.
17
prospekt
Blokhina
Yablochkova
Proviantskaya
Mytninskaya
Zoologicheskiy
Sad
Zoo
Petropavlovskiy
(Peter-Paul)
Cathedral
Kronverska
Malaya
Yubileyny
Sports Palace
Peterhof
Hotel Ship
Tuchkov
Most
14
Neva
Mytninskaya
Zoologi. p.
naberezhnaya
Petrovksiy
Catherine's
Cathedral
naberezhnaya
Birzhevoy
Most
Karpinskiy
Geological
Museum
Makarova
Literary Museum
of Institute of
Russian Literature
Rostral Column
Tuchkov p.
Volkhovskiy p.
Birzhevoy p.
Birzhevaya
Sredniy
prospekt
Academy
of Sciences
Library
Birzhevaya
Ploschad
Kubanskiy p.
liniya
Tiflisskaya
Tifli. p.
Belochka
Candy Shop
Naval Museum
Dvinskiy p.
VASILYEVSKIY
OSTROV
(ISLAND)
Dokuchayev
Museum of
Soil Science
Rostral Column
2 and 3 liniya
Repina
Syezdovskaya and 1 liniya
Mendeleyevskaya liniya
Museum of
Zoology
Yubileyny
Bakery
4 and 5 liniya
St. Petersburg
State University
Birzhevoy pr.
Ermitazh
China
Anthropology
and Ethnography
Museum/
Lomonosov
Memorial Museum
Winter
Palace
10
6 and 7 liniya
Filologicheskiy p.
Dvortsovy
Most
Vasileostrovskiy
Market
"7/9"
Mendeleev
House Museum
Bolshoy
prospekt
A.G.C.C.I.
Akad. p.
Menshikov Palace
Museum
naberezhnaya
Alexander
Column
Ploshchad
Shevchenko
Universitetskaya
Ploshchad
Dekabristov
Admiralty
Former
Staff
Customs
Administration
Bugskiy p.
Admiralteyskaya
Admiralteyskiy proyezd
Akademicheskiy p.
Academy of Arts
Museum and Library
Bronze Horseman
(Monument to
Peter the Great)
Sad Trudyashiksya
im. Gorkovo
Pavlov House
Museum
Aeroflot
Syezd. p.
Akademiya
Khudozhestv
Admiralteyskiy prospekt
naberezhnaya Leytenanta Shmidta
Neva
Ploshchad
Dekabristov
Gogolya
Finnair
and SAS
Pharmacia
Association
Tekhnokhim Bank
Most
Leytenanta
Shmidta
Central
State Historical
Archives
(Former Senate and Synod)
Astoria
Hotel
nab. Krasnovo Flota
St. Isaac's
Cathedral
Admiralteyskiy
Bolshaya
p. Leonova
Konnogvardeyskiy bulvar
Intourist
Manege
Central
Exhibition
Hall
Vneshecon
Children's Lib
NW River
"Airlines"
St. Petersburg
Regional
Trade Council
Galernaya
Trade Union
Rowing Club
Pochtamskaya
Central
Post Office
E.H.A.U.
Agricultural Library
EMS Garantpost
DHL Courier
and Aeroflot
Bank
Resurs
North-Western
Exchange
Museum of the
History of
St. Petersburg
Ploshchad
Truda
Konnogvardeyskiy p.
Popov
Museum
Dom
Arkhitektora
Siniy Most
Metod Consulti
Expert Cente
and
Orgtekhnika
Yakubovicha
Soyuza
Svyazi
Isaakiyevskaya
Ploshchad
nab. Admiralteyskiy Kanala
Novo-
nab. Admiralteyskiy Kanal
Vitabank
nab. Reki Moyki
Patent Bank
Antonenko p.
16
Aviation
Instruments
Institute
Truda
New
Holland
Gertsena
Yusupovskiy
Palace
Prachechny p.
Fonarny p.
Lufthansa
and Malev
Mariinskiy
Palace
(St. Petersburg
City Soviet)
Krapovitskiy
Most
Moyki
p. Pirogova
Nairi
Voznesenskaya prosp.
naberezhnaya
Popolyev Most
Dekabristov
Sberbank
Rimskiy-Korsakov
Conservatory
Reki
Matveyeva
Most
Grazhdanskaya
Pisareva
Glinki
Rimskiy-Korsakov
Conservatory
Opera Studio
Podyacheskiy
Most
nab. Kanala Griboyedova
Przheval.
Kazna
GALERNY
OSTROV
(ISLAND)
Matve. p.
Teatralnaya
Ploshchad
26
Podyach. M.
Rab. p.
21
Lesgaft Physical
Culture Institute
Italy
Podyacheskaya
Srednyaya
Bolshaya
Minskiy p.
Marinskiy
Theater of
Opera and Ballet
Vitamin
Dekabristov
Choral
Synagogue
Russkiye
Samovary
Sadovaya
prosp. Rimskovo-Korsakova

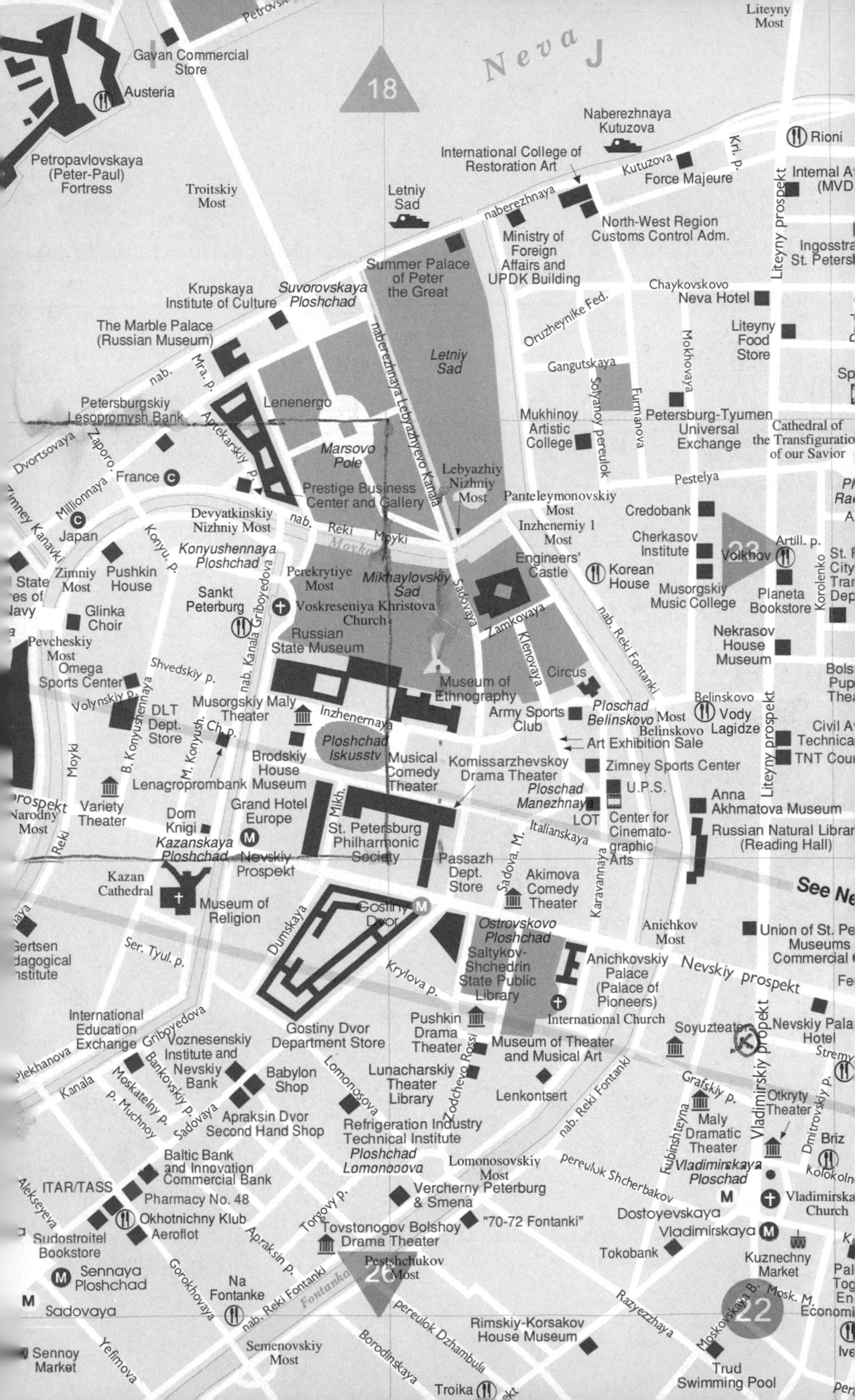

Neva
18
Gavan Commercial Store
Austeria
Petropavlovskaya (Peter-Paul) Fortress
Troitskiy Most
Letniy Sad
Naberezhnaya Kutuzova
International College of Restoration Art
Kutuzova
Force Majeure
Rioni
Internal Af (MVD
North-West Region Customs Control Adm.
Ministry of Foreign Affairs and UPDK Building
Summer Palace of Peter the Great
Ingosstra St. Petersb
Krupskaya Institute of Culture
Suvorovskaya Ploshchad
Chaykovskovo
Neva Hotel
Liteyny prospekt
Liteyny Food Store
The Marble Palace (Russian Museum)
Oruzheynike Fed.
Letniy Sad
Gangutskaya
Lenenergo
Petersburgskiy Lesopromysh Bank
Mukhinoy Artistic College
Petersburg-Tyumen Universal Exchange
Cathedral of the Transfiguration of our Savior
Marsovo Pole
Lebyazhiy Nizhniy Most
Pestelya
France
Prestige Business Center and Gallery
Panteleymonovskiy Most
Credobank
Japan
Devyatkinskiy Nizhniy Most
Inzhenerniy 1 Most
Cherkasov Institute
Volkhov
Konyushennaya Ploshchad
Engineers' Castle
Korean House
Planeta Bookstore
Zimniy Most
Pushkin House
Perekrytiye Most
Mikhaylovskiy Sad
Musorgskiy Music College
Sankt Peterburg
Voskreseniya Khristova Church
Glinka Choir
Russian State Museum
Nekrasov House Museum
Pevcheskiy Most
Omega Sports Center
Circus
Museum of Ethnography
Ploschad Belinskovo
Belinskovo Most
Vody Lagidze
DLT Dept. Store
Musorgskiy Maly Theater
Army Sports Club
Civil A Technica
TNT Cou
Ploschad Iskusstv
Art Exhibition Sale
Brodskiy House Museum
Musical Comedy Theater
Komissarzhevskoy Drama Theater
Zimney Sports Center
Lenagroprombank
U.P.S.
Variety Theater
Ploschad Manezhnaya
Anna Akhmatova Museum
Narodny Most
Dom Knigi
Grand Hotel Europe
St. Petersburg Philharmonic Society
LOT
Center for Cinematographic Arts
Russian Natural Library (Reading Hall)
Kazanskaya Ploshchad
Nevskiy Prospekt
Passazh Dept. Store
Akimova Comedy Theater
Kazan Cathedral
Museum of Religion
Gostiny Dvor
See Ne
Ostrovskovo Ploshchad
Anichkov Most
Union of St. Pe Museums Commercial
Gertsen Pedagogical Institute
Saltykov-Shchedrin State Public Library
Anichkovskiy Palace (Palace of Pioneers)
Nevskiy prospekt
International Education Exchange
Pushkin Drama Theater
International Church
Gostiny Dvor Department Store
Museum of Theater and Musical Art
Soyuzteater
Nevskiy Palace Hotel
Voznesenskiy Institute and Nevskiy Bank
Babylon Shop
Lunacharskiy Theater Library
Lenkontsert
Vladimirskiy prospekt
Otkryty Theater
Apraksin Dvor Second Hand Shop
Refrigeration Industry Technical Institute
Maly Dramatic Theater
Briz
Ploshchad Lomonosova
Vladimirskaya Ploschad
Baltic Bank and Innovation Commercial Bank
Lomonosovskiy Most
ITAR/TASS
Pharmacy No. 48
Vercherny Peterburg & Smena
Vladimirskaya Church
Okhotnichny Klub
Aeroflot
"70-72 Fontanki"
Dostoyevskaya
Sudostroitel Bookstore
Tovstonogov Bolshoy Drama Theater
Vladimirskaya
Tokobank
Kuznechny Market
Sennaya Ploshchad
Pestshchukov Most
26
Na Fontanke
22
Sadovaya
Rimskiy-Korsakov House Museum
Sennoy Market
Semenovskiy Most
Trud Swimming Pool
Troika

Liteyny
Most
Neva
J
K
19
Naberezhnaya
Kutuzova
International College of
Restoration Art
Rioni
Kutuzova
Kri. p.
Shpalernaya
naberezhnaya
Letniy
Sad
14
naberezhnaya
Force Majeure
Internal Affairs
(MVD)
Liteyny prospekt
Petrovskiy
Bank
ABINSET
Bank
Chernyshevskovo prospekt
Zakharyevskaya
Ministry of
Foreign
Affairs and
UPDK Building
North-West Region
Customs Control Adm.
Ingosstrakh
St. Petersburg
St. Petersburg
Innovation
Bank
Chamber
Commer
and Indus
Summer Palace
of Peter
the Great
Chaykovskovo
Chaykovskovo
Neva Hotel
Oruzheynike Fed.
Liteyny
Food
Store
Drusk. p.
Finland
naberezhnaya Lebyazhyevo Kanala
Letniy
Sad
Gangutskaya
Mokhovaya
Furshtadtskaya
United States
Consulate
Spartak
Solyanoy pereulok
Furmanova
Chernyshevskaya
Melit. p.
German
Saltykova-Shchedrina
Mukhinoy
Artistic
College
Petersburg-Tyumen
Universal
Exchange
Cathedral of
the Transfiguration
of our Savior
Manezhny pereulok
Lebyazhiy
Nizhniy
Most
Pestelya
Ploshchad
Radishcheva
Ryleyeva
Bushe
Bulgaria
Cuba
e Business
and Gallery
Panteleymonovskiy
Most
Credobank
Artilleriyskaya
U.S.
General Residence
Grodnenskiy p.
Moyki
Inzhenerniy 1
Most
Cherkasov
Institute
Artill. p.
Radishcheva
22
Engineers'
Castle
Korean
House
Volkhov
St. Petersburg
City Council
Transport
Depot
Saperny
pereulok
Mikhaylovskiy
Sad
Sadovaya
Musorgskiy
Music College
Planeta
Bookstore
Korolenko
VIZA Business
Mitav. p.
Northern
Trade
Bank
Zamkovaya
nab. Reki Fontanki
Baskov pereulok
Klenovaya
Nekrasov
House
Museum
Alkonic-Lakomka
Maltse
Mar
15
Nekrasova
Circus
Bolshoy
Puppet
Theater
Chekhova
Mayakovskovo
Museum of
Ethnography
Belinskovo
Vody
Lagidze
Choreographic
Miniatures
State Ballet
Vosstaniya
Army Sports
Club
Ploschad
Belinskovo
Most
Belinskovo
Ozernoy p.
Civil Aviation
Technical College
Art Exhibition Sale
Kovenskiy p.
Musical
Comedy
Theater
Komissarzhevskoy
Drama Theater
Zimney Sports Center
TNT Courier
Church of
Our Lady
of Lourdes
St. Petersburg
Information
Center
Sold. p.
Radishcheva
Ploschad
Manezhnaya
U.P.S.
Anna
Akhmatova Museum
Greci
Plos
LOT
Center for
Cinemato-
graphic
Arts
Zhukovskovo
Petersburg
ilharmonic
Society
Italianskaya
Russian Natural Library
(Reading Hall)
Ligovskiy prospekt
Okty
Con
Passazh
Dept.
Store
Sadova. M.
Akimova
Comedy
Theater
Karavannaya
See Nevskiy Prospekt Map for Detail
Ulyany
Gromovoy
Gostiny
Dvor
Ostrovskovo
Ploshchad
Anichkov
Most
Union of St. Petersburg
Museums and
Commercial Center
Saltykov-
Shchedrin
State Public
Library
Anichkovskiy
Palace
(Palace of
Pioneers)
Nevskiy prospekt
Federal Express
Oktyabrskaya Hotel
Krylova p.
Ploshchad
Vosstaniya
Orlovskiy p.
Pushkin
Drama
Theater
International Church
Soyuzteater
Nevskiy Palace
Hotel
Mayakovskaya
Sovetskaya
Store
Museum of Theater
and Musical Art
Stremyannaya
Ploshchad
Vosstaniya
Lunacharskiy
Theater
Library
Zodchevo Rossi
Elf Cafe
Lenkontsert
nab. Reki Fontanki
Grafskiy p.
Vladimirskiy prospekt
Otkryty
Theater
Dmitrovskiy p.
p. Povarskoy
Marata
16
Maly
Dramatic
Theater
Moscow
Station
efrigeration Industry
echnical Institute
Rubinshteyna
Briz
Hungary
Ploshchad
omonosova
Lomonosovskiy
Most
pereulok Shcherbakov
Vladimirskaya
Ploschad
Kolokolnaya
Museum of
the Arctic
and
Antarctic
Ligovskiy p.
Vercherny Peterburg
& Smena
Vladimirskaya
Church
Pushkinskaya
tonogov Bolshoy
rama Theater
"70-72 Fontanki"
Dostoyevskaya
Vladimirskaya
Tokobank
Kuznechny pereulok
Pestshchukov
Most
Kuznechny
Market
Palmiro
Togliatti
Eng. &
Economic Institute
Lutheran
Church
Dostoevskiy
House Museum
23
Razyezzhaya
Moskovskaya
Mosk. M.
27
Kolomenskaya
Rimskiy-Korsakov
House Museum
pereulok Dzhambula
Iveria Cafe
Borodinskaya
Trud
Swimming Pool
Troika

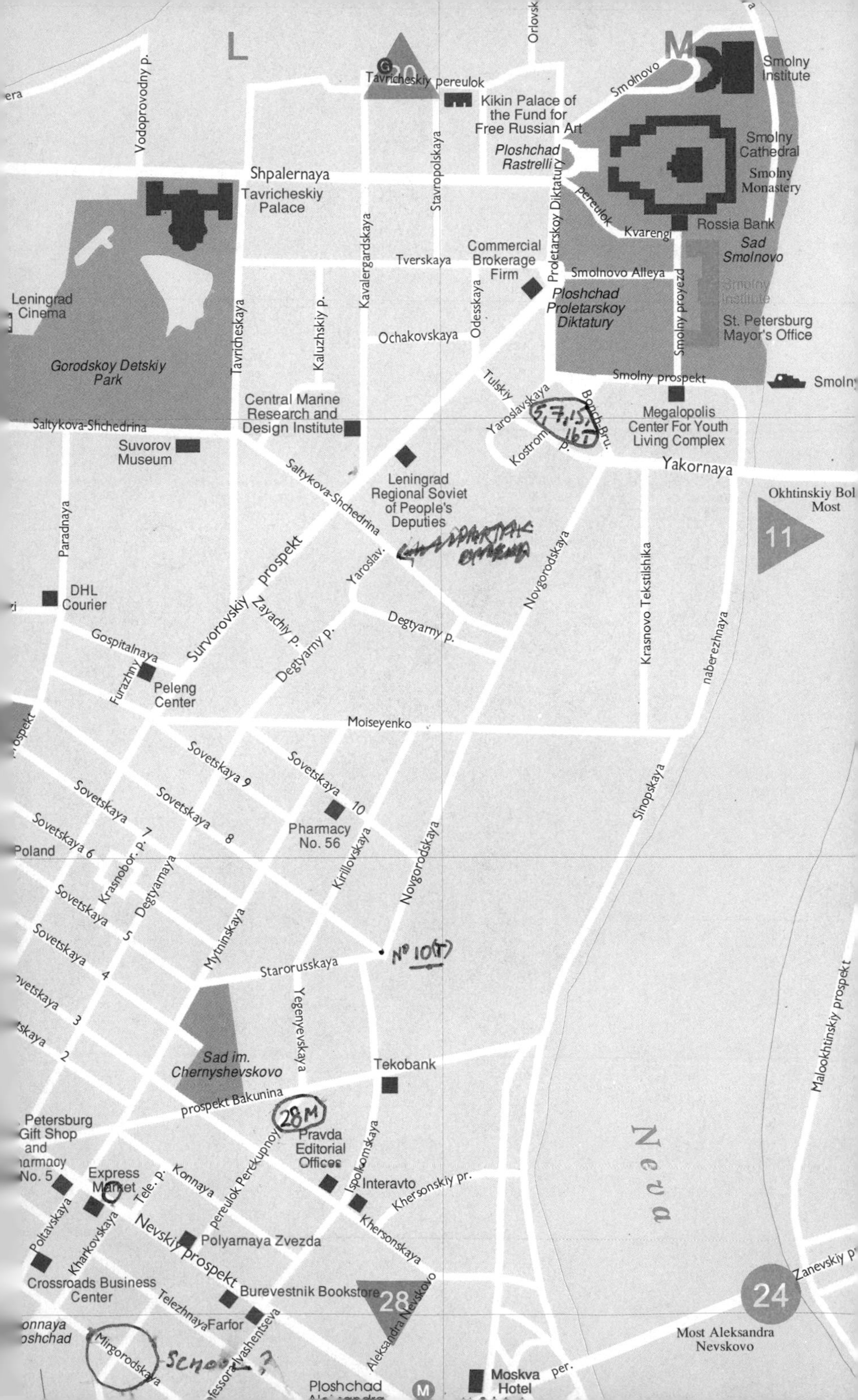
L
M
20
Tavricheskiy pereulok
Kikin Palace of the Fund for Free Russian Art
Smolnovo
Smolny Institute
Smolny Cathedral
Smolny Monastery
Rossia Bank
Sad Smolnovo
St. Petersburg Mayor's Office
Orlovsk
Vodoprovodny p.
Shpalernaya
Tavricheskiy Palace
Stavropolskaya
Ploshchad Rastrelli
Proletarskoy Diktatury
pereulok
Kvarengi
Leningrad Cinema
Gorodskoy Detskiy Park
Tavricheskaya
Kaluzhskiy p.
Kavalergardskaya
Tverskaya
Commercial Brokerage Firm
Odesskaya
Ochakovskaya
Smolnovo Alleya
Ploshchad Proletarskoy Diktatury
Smolny proyezd
Smolny prospekt
Smolny
Tulskiy
Yaroslavskaya
Bonch-Bru. p.
Kostrom
Megalopolis Center For Youth Living Complex
Yakornaya
Saltykova-Shchedrina
Central Marine Research and Design Institute
Suvorov Museum
Leningrad Regional Soviet of People's Deputies
Okhtinskiy Bol Most
11
Paradnaya
Surovorovskiy prospekt
Yaroslav.
Novgorodskaya
Krasnovo Tekstilshika
naberezhnaya
DHL Courier
Zayachiy p.
Degtyarny p.
Gospitalnaya
Furazhny
Peleng Center
Moiseyenko
Sovetskaya 9
Sovetskaya 10
Sovetskaya 7
Sovetskaya 8
Sovetskaya 6
Sovetskaya 5
Sovetskaya 4
Sovetskaya 3
Sovetskaya 2
Pharmacy No. 56
Kirillovskaya
Sinopskaya
Poland
Krasnobor. p.
Degtyarnaya
Mytninskaya
Starorusskaya
Yegenyevskaya
Malookhtinskiy prospekt
Sad im. Chernyshevskovo
Tekobank
prospekt Bakunina
Neva
Petersburg Gift Shop and Pharmacy No. 5
Express Market
Tele. p.
Konnaya
pereulok Perekupnoy
Pravda Editorial Offices
Ispolkomskaya
Interavto
Khersonskiy pr.
Khersonskaya
Poltavskaya
Kharkovskaya
Nevskiy prospekt
Polyarnaya Zvezda
Crossroads Business Center
Burevestnik Bookstore
28
Aleksandra Nevskovo
Zanevskiy pr.
24
Most Aleksandra Nevskovo
Telezhnaya
Farfor
Mirgorodskaya
Professora Ivashentseva
Ploshchad
Moskva Hotel
per.

Pavlov House Museum
Museum and Library
Bronze Horseman
(Monument to Peter the Great)
Akademiya Khudozhestv
Neva
Syezd. p.
nab. Leytenanta Shmidta
Aeroflot
Sad Trudy im. Gorkogo
Admiralteyskiy prospekt
Ploshchad Dekabristov
Gogolya
Tekhnokhim Bank
21
Central State Historical Archives
(Former Senate and Synod)
Finnair and SAS
Pharmacia Produ
Association
Astoria Hotel
Most Leytenanta Shmidta
nab. Krasnovo Flota
St. Isaac's Cathedral
Admiralteyskiy
Gertsena
Bolshaya
p. Leonova
Galernaya
Konnogvardeyskiy bulvar
Pochtamskaya
Intourist
Manege Central Exhibition Hall
Vnesheconom
Children's Libra
NW River Flee
"Airlines"
E.H.A.U.
Agricultural Library
St. Petersburg Regional Trade Council
Trade Union Rowing Club
EMS Garantpost
DHL Courier
and Aeroflot Bank
Central Post Office
Resurs North-Western Exchange
Museum of the History of St. Petersburg
Ploshchad Truda
Yakubovicha
Konnogvardeyskiy p.
Soyuza Svyazi
Popov Museum
Dom Arkhitektora
Isaakiyevskaya Ploshchad
Siniy Most
Metod Consulting-Expert Center and Orgtekhnika
16
nab. Admiralteyskiy Kanala
Novo-Admiralteyskiy Kanal
nab. Admiralteyskiy Kanal
Vitabank
nab. Reki Moyki
Patent Bank
Antonenko p.
Aviation Instruments Institute
Truda
Gertsena
New Holland
Yusupovskiy Palace
Prachechny p.
p. Pirogova
Fonarny p.
Lufthansa and Malev
Mariinskiy Palace
(St. Petersburg City Soviet)
Voznesenskaya prosp.
Krapovitskiy Most
naberezhnaya
Moyki
Popolyev Most
Dekabristov
Nairi
Sberbank
Grazhdanskaya
Reki
Rimskiy-Korsakov Conservatory
Matveyeva Most
Matve. p.
Glinki
Rimskiy-Korsakov Conservatory Opera Studio
Podyacheskiy Most
nab. Kanala Griboyedova
Przheval.
Kaznach.
10
Pisareva
GALERNY OSTROV
(ISLAND)
Teatralnaya Ploshchad
Podyach. M.
Podyacheskaya Srednyaya
Bolshaya
Rab. p.
Lesgaft Physical Culture Institute
Italy
Minskiy p.
Marinskiy Theater of Opera and Ballet
Vitamin
Dekabristov
Choral Synagogue
Russkiye Samovary
Sadovaya
prosp. Rimskovo-Korsakova
Pechatnikov
Glinki
Blok House Museum
nab. Reki Pryazhki
Soyuza
Lermontovskiy
Ploshchad Nikolskaya
Railway Museum
Kashin Most
St. Nicholas and the Epiphany Cathedral
Belye Nochi
Podyacheskaya
Yusupovskiy Sad
Drovyanoy
prospekt Maklina
Masterskaya
17
nab. Kanala
Ploshchad Kulibina
Rimskovo - Korsakova
Kanal
Griboyedova
Novo-Nikolskiy Most
Myasnikova
p. Boytsova
Volodi Yermaka
p.
Aparchiy Most
Griboyedova
Pastoro.
Pikalov Most
Kryukova
Staro-Nikolskiy Most
Shchep. p.
Fontanki
Kanala
prospekt
Rekord
Kustar. p.
Reki
prospekt
Kanonerskaya
Izmaylovskiy Most
naberezhnaya
Sadovaya
Makarenko
Interior Stu Theater
naberezhnaya
Kolomna
Ploshchad Turgeneva
Labutina
p. Klimov
Pryadilny p.
Park Kultury i Otdykha Izmaylovskiy
Yegipetskiy Most
Troitskiy Cathedral
Troitskaya Ploshchad
Kalinkin Most
Fontanka
Moskvinoy
prospekt
Krasnoarmeyskaya
naberezhnaya
Reki
Fontanki
Helen Hotel
Dub.
Beriozka
Krasnoarmeyskaya 13
Yakobshtadtskiy pereulok
Krasnoarmeyskaya
Sovetskiy pereulok
Derptskiy pereulok
Krasnoarmeyskaya 8
Krasnoarmeyskaya
Tsiolkovskovo
18
Rizhskiy
prospekt
Sovetskaya Hotel
Krasnoarmeyskaya 9
St. Petersburg Association of Industries
Krasnoarmeyskaya
Ladygina p.
Revelskiy p.
Krasnoarmeyskaya 10
Krasnoarmeyskaya
Khachapuri
Krasnoarmeyskaya
Kurlyandskaya
Drovyanaya
Lermontovskiy prospekt
Krasnoarmeyskaya 11
Krasnoarmeyskaya 12
Krasnoarmeyskaya
Izmaylovskiy prospekt
Strela Food Store
Yegorova
25
10
Obvodny
Kanal
naberezhnaya
Obvodnovo
Kanala

Comedy Theater
Drama Theater
Zimney Sports Center
House
Lenagroprombank Museum
Variety Theater
Dom Knigi
Grand Hotel Europe
St. Petersburg Philharmonic Society
Ploschad Manezhnaya
U.P.S.
LOT
Center for Cinematographic Arts
Anna Akhmatova Museum
Russian National Library (Reading Hall)
Italianskaya
Kazanskaya Ploshchad
Nevskiy Prospekt
Kazan Cathedral
Museum of Religion
Passazh Dept. Store
Akimova Comedy Theater
Sadova. M.
Karavannaya
See Ne
Gostiny Dvor
Ostrovskovo Ploshchad
Saltykov-Shchedrin State Public Library
Anichkov Most
Union of St. Pet Museums a Commercial C
Anichkovskiy Palace (Palace of Pioneers)
Nevskiy prospekt
Fed
Gertsen Pedagogical Institute
Ser. Tyul. p.
Dumskaya
Krylova p.
International Church
International Education Exchange
Griboyedova
Voznesenskiy Institute and Nevskiy Bank
Gostiny Dvor Department Store
Pushkin Drama Theater
Museum of Theater and Musical Art
Soyuzteater
Vladimirskiy propekt
Nevskiy Palace Hotel
Stremyan
Plekhanova
Kanala
Bankovskiy p.
Moskatelny p.
p. Muchnoy
Babylon Shop
Lomonosova
Lunacharskiy Theater Library
Zodchevo Rossi
Lenkontsert
nab. Reki Fontanki
Grafskiy p.
Otkryty Theater
Sadovaya
Apraksin Dvor Second Hand Shop
Refrigeration Industry Technical Institute
Rubinshteyna
Maly Dramatic Theater
Dmitrovskiy p.
Briz
Ploshchad Lomonosova
Baltic Bank and Innovation-Commercial Bank
Lomonosovskiy Most
pereulok Shcherbakov
Vladimirskaya Ploschad
Kolokolnaya
ITAR/TASS
Alekseyeva
Pharmacy No. 48
Vercherny Peterburg & Smena
Vladimirskaya Church
Okhotnichny Klub
Aeroflot
Torgovy p.
"70-72 Fontanki"
Dostoyevskaya
Sudostroitel Bookstore
Apraksin p.
Tovstonogov Bolshoy Drama Theater
Vladimirskaya
Kuz
Tokobank
Kuznechny Market
Gorokhovaya
Pestshchukov Most
Sennaya Ploshchad
Na Fontanke
Fontanka
Palm Togli Eng
Mosk. M.
Sadovaya
Razyezzhaya
Moskovskaya B.
Economic
pereulok Dzhambula
Rimskiy-Korsakov House Museum
Iver
Sennoy Market
Yefimova
Semenovskiy Most
Borodinskaya
Trud Swimming Pool
pereu
Troika
Zagorodny prospekt
nab. Reki Fontanki
Dostoyevskovo
Dialog Invest Group
Cinema Engineers Institute
Sotsialisticheskaya
Pravdy
nab. Vedenskovo Kanala
pereulok Ilicha
Obukhovskiy Most
Museum of Military Medicine
Lazaretny p.
Astoria-Service
Pionerskaya Ploshchad
Zveningorodskaya
Marata
Volokolam. p.
Vitebskaya Ploshchad
Pushkinskaya
Borovaya
Damian Drugstore
Polyclinic No. 2
Children's Theater
Grigoryeva
Vitebsk Station
Lokomotiv Swimming Pool
Konstantina Zaslonova
Pechatnika
Ryazan
Technological Institute
Podyezdnoy pereulok
Medte
Petrovskiy Bank
nab. Vedenskovo
Voronezhskaya
kaya
Minor-Neva Consulting Co.
Tyushina
Tekhnologicheskiy Institut
Obvodnovo
Institute
Medtekhnika
Kanala
naberezhnaya
naberezhnaya
Obvodn
Vostpchnye Sladosti Candy Shop
Klinskiy prospekt
Pizza Express
Kanala
Gorodskoy Tsentr Perevodov
Serpukhovskaya
Podolskaya
Vereyskaya
Mozhayskaya
Ruzovskaya
Baptist Gospel House
prosp.
Bataysky p.
Doynikova p.
Bronnitskaya
Ruzovskiy Most
Moskovskiy prospekt
Malodetskoselskiy
Rybinskaya
Borovaya
Voronezhskaya
Ligovskiy prospekt
Kurskaya
Assko
Sovintervtoservice
11
26
Masly any per
Yuzhnaya Hotel
Priluksakya

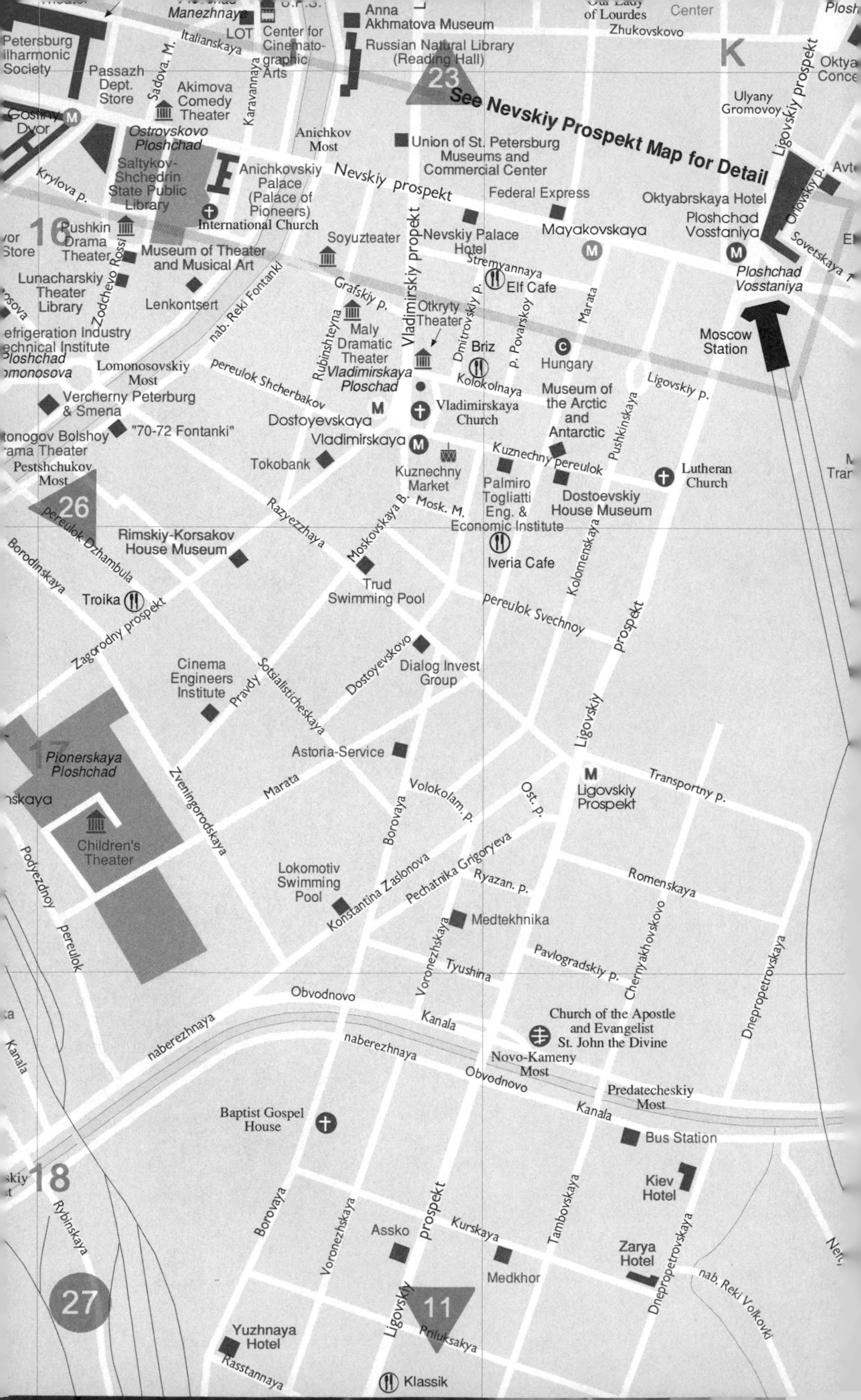

Manezhnaya
LOT
Center for Cinematographic Arts
Anna Akhmatova Museum
Russian Natural Library (Reading Hall)
of Lourdes
Center
Zhukovskovo
K
Plosh
Petersburg ilharmonic Society
Italianskaya
Sadova. M.
Karavannaya
Passazh Dept. Store
Akimova Comedy Theater
23
See Nevskiy Prospekt Map for Detail
Ligovskiy prospekt
Oktya Conce
Ulyany Gromovoy
Gostiny Dvor
Ostrovskovo Ploshchad
Anichkov Most
Union of St. Petersburg Museums and Commercial Center
Saltykov-Shchedrin State Public Library
Anichkovskiy Palace (Palace of Pioneers)
Nevskiy prospekt
Federal Express
Oktyabrskaya Hotel
Avt
Krylova p.
International Church
Orlovskiy p.
16
Pushkin Drama Theater
Soyuzteater
Vladimirskiy prospekt
Nevskiy Palace Hotel
Mayakovskaya
Ploshchad Vosstaniya
Store
Museum of Theater and Musical Art
Stremyannaya
Sovetskaya
Zodchevo Rossi
Lunacharskiy Theater Library
Lenkontsert
nab. Reki Fontanki
Grafskiy p.
Elf Cafe
Marata
Ploshchad Vosstaniya
Otkryty Theater
Dmitrovskiy p.
p. Povarskoy
efrigeration Industry echnical Institute
Ploshchad omonosova
Rubinshteyna
Maly Dramatic Theater
Briz
Hungary
Moscow Station
Lomonosovskiy Most
pereulok Shcherbakov
Vladimirskaya Ploschad
Kolokolnaya
Museum of the Arctic and Antarctic
Ligovskiy p.
Vercherny Peterburg & Smena
Pushkinskaya
Dostoyevskaya
Vladimirskaya Church
"70-72 Fontanki"
tonogov Bolshoy rama Theater
Vladimirskaya
Kuznechny pereulok
Tokobank
Kuznechny Market
Palmiro Togliatti Eng. & Economic Institute
Lutheran Church
Pestshchukov Most
Dostoevskiy House Museum
26
Mosk. M.
Razyezzhaya
Moskovskaya B.
pereulok Dzhambula
Borodinskaya
Rimskiy-Korsakov House Museum
Iveria Cafe
Kolomenskaya
Trud Swimming Pool
Troika
pereulok Svechnoy
prospekt
Zagorodny prospekt
Dostoyevskovo
Dialog Invest Group
Cinema Engineers Institute
Sotsialisticheskaya
Pravdy
Ligovskiy
Astoria-Service
17
Pionerskaya Ploshchad
Zveningorodskaya
Marata
Ligovskiy Prospekt
Transportny p.
nskaya
Volokolam. p.
Ost. p.
Borovaya
Children's Theater
Romenskaya
Podyezdnoy
Lokomotiv Swimming Pool
Pechatnika Grigoryeva
Ryazan. p.
Konstantina Zaslonova
Chernyakhovskovo
Medtekhnika
Voronezhskaya
pereulok
Pavlogradskiy p.
Tyushina
Dnepropetrovskaya
Obvodnovo
Kanala
naberezhnaya
Church of the Apostle and Evangelist St. John the Divine
Kanala
naberezhnaya
Novo-Kameny Most
Obvodnovo
Predatecheskiy Most
Kanala
Baptist Gospel House
Bus Station
18
Kiev Hotel
Rybinskaya
Borovaya
Voronezhskaya
prospekt
Kurskaya
Tambovskaya
Dnepropetrovskaya
Assko
Zarya Hotel
Medkhor
nab. Reki Volkovki
27
11
Ligovskiy
Priluksakya
Yuzhnaya Hotel
Rasstannaya
Klassik

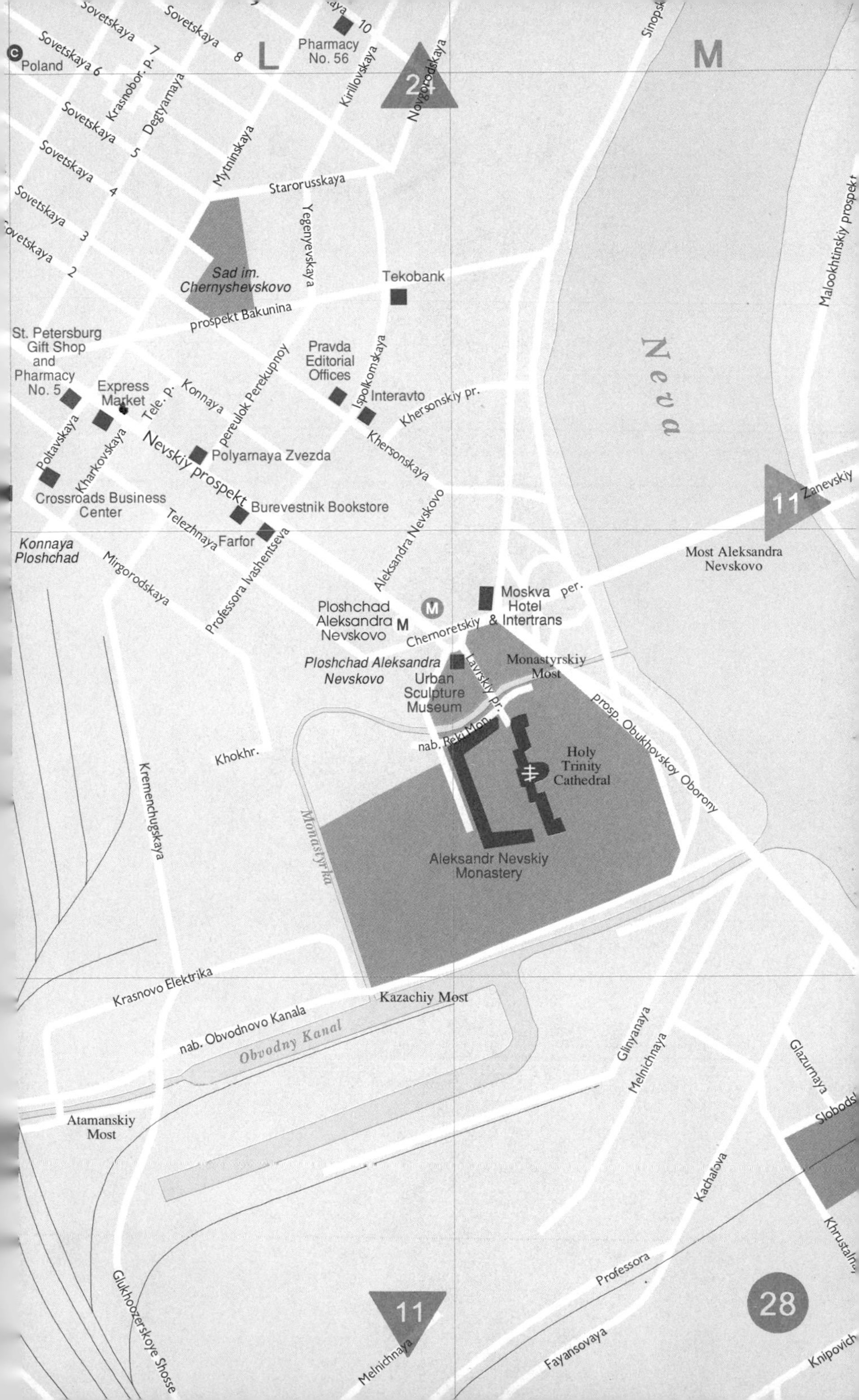

L
M
24
11
11
28
Poland
Pharmacy No. 56
Sovetskaya 6
Sovetskaya 7
Sovetskaya 8
Sovetskaya 5
Sovetskaya 4
Sovetskaya 3
Sovetskaya 2
Krasnobor. P.
Degtyarnaya
Mytninskaya
Kirillovskaya
Novgorodskaya
Starorusskaya
Yegenyevskaya
Sad im. Chernyshevskovo
Tekobank
prospekt Bakunina
St. Petersburg Gift Shop and Pharmacy No. 5
Express Market
Tele. P.
Konnaya
pereulok Perekupnoy
Pravda Editorial Offices
Ispolkomskaya
Interavto
Khersonskiy pr.
Khersonskaya
Poltavskaya
Kharkovskaya
Nevskiy prospekt
Polyarnaya Zvezda
Crossroads Business Center
Burevestnik Bookstore
Telezhnaya
Farfor
Konnaya Ploshchad
Mirgorodskaya
Professora Ivashentseva
Aleksandra Nevskovo
Neva
Zanevskiy
Most Aleksandra Nevskovo
Sinopsk
Malookhtinskiy prospekt
Moskva Hotel & Intertrans
per.
Ploshchad Aleksandra Nevskovo
Chernoretskiy
Ploshchad Aleksandra Nevskovo
Urban Sculpture Museum
Lavrskiy pr.
Monastyrskiy Most
prosp. Obukhovskoy Oborony
nab. Reki Mon.
Holy Trinity Cathedral
Aleksandr Nevskiy Monastery
Monastyrka
Khokhr.
Kremenchugskaya
Krasnovo Elektrika
Kazachiy Most
nab. Obvodnovo Kanala
Obvodny Kanal
Atamanskiy Most
Glinyanaya
Melnichnaya
Glazurnaya
Slobods
Kachalova
Khrustaln
Professora
Fayansovaya
Knipovich
Glukhoozerskoye Shosse
Melnichnaya

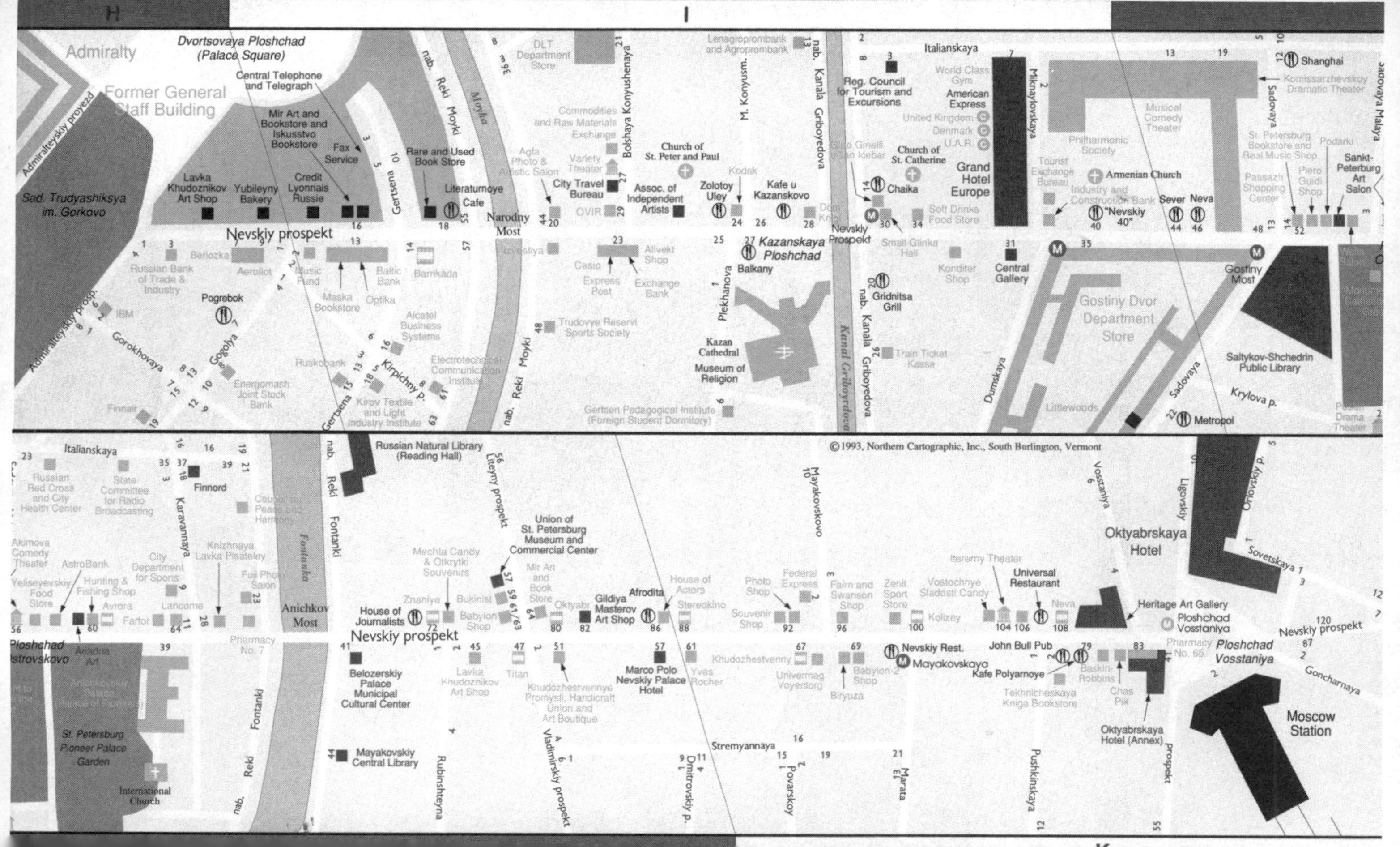
H
I
K
Admiralty
Dvortsovaya Ploshchad (Palace Square)
Former General Staff Building
Admiralteyskiy proyezd
Sad. Trudyashiksya im. Gorkovo
Central Telephone and Telegraph
Mir Art and Bookstore and Iskusstvo Bookstore
Fax Service
Lavka Khudoznikov Art Shop
Yubileyny Bakery
Credit Lyonnais Russie
Rare and Used Book Store
Literaturnoye Cafe
nab. Reki Moyki
Moyka
Gertsena
Nevskiy prospekt
Russian Bank of Trade & Industry
Beriozka
Aeroflot
Music Fund
Baltic Bank
Barrikada
Maska Bookstore
Optika
Pogrebok
IBM
Gorokhovaya
Gogolya
Alcatel Business Systems
Ruskobank
Kirpichny p.
Electrotechnical Communication Institute
Energomash Joint Stock Bank
Kirov Textile and Light Industry Institute
Finnair
Narodny Most
DLT Department Store
Commodities and Raw Materials Exchange
Agfa Photo & Artistic Salon
Variety Theater
City Travel Bureau
OVIR
Izvestiya
Bolshaya Konyushenaya
Church of St. Peter and Paul
Assoc. of Independent Artists
Casio
Express Post
Alivekt Shop
Exchange Bank
Trudovye Reservi Sports Society
Gertsen Pedagogical Institute (Foreign Student Dormitory)
Lenagroprombank and Agroprombank
M. Konyusm.
Zolotoy Uley
Kodak
Kafe u Kazanskovo
Dom Knigi
Kazanskaya Ploshchad
Balkany
Plekhanova
Kazan Cathedral
Museum of Religion
nab. Kanala Griboyedova
Kanal Griboyedova
Reg. Council for Tourism and Excursions
Italianskaya
World Class Gym
American Express
United Kingdom
Denmark
U.A.R.
Gilio Ginelli Italian Icebar
Church of St. Catherine
Chaika
Nevskiy Prospekt
Small Glinka Hall
Soft Drinks Food Store
Grand Hotel Europe
Kondifer Shop
Gridnitsa Grill
Train Ticket Kassa
Central Gallery
Dumskaya
Miknaylovskaya
Philharmonic Society
Tourist Exchange Bureau
Armenian Church
Industry and Construction Bank
"Nevskiy 40"
Sever
Neva
Musical Comedy Theater
Gostiny Dvor Department Store
Littlewoods
Gostiny Most
Sadovaya
Metropol
Saltykov-Shchedrin Public Library
Krylova p.
Shanghai
Komissarzhevskoy Dramatic Theater
St. Petersburg Bookstore and Real Music Shop
Passazh Shopping Center
Podarki
Piero Guidi Shop
Sankt-Peterburg Art Salon
Sadovaya Malaya
Pushkin Drama Theater
© 1993, Northern Cartographic, Inc., South Burlington, Vermont
Italianskaya
Russian Red Cross and City Health Center
State Committee for Radio Broadcasting
Finnord
Karavannaya
Council for Peace and Harmony
Akimova Comedy Theater
AstroBank
Yeliseyevskiy Food Store
Hunting & Fishing Shop
Avrora
City Department for Sports
Farfor
Lancome
Knizhnaya Lavka Pisateley
Fuji Photo Salon
Pharmacy No. 7
Ploshchad Ostrovskovo
Aniadna Art
Anichkovskiy Palace (Palace of Pioneers)
St. Petersburg Pioneer Palace Garden
International Church
nab. Reki Fontanki
Fontanka
Anichkov Most
Russian Natural Library (Reading Hall)
Liteyny prospekt
House of Journalists
Znaniya
Mechta Candy & Otkrytki Souvenirs
Bukinist
Babylon Shop
Union of St. Petersburg Museum and Commercial Center
Mir Art and Book Store
Oktyabr
Gildiya Masterov Art Shop
Afrodita
House of Actors
Stereokino
Belozerskiy Palace Municipal Cultural Center
Lavka Khudoznikov Art Shop
Titan
Khudozhestvennye Promysli, Handicraft Union and Art Boutique
Marco Polo Nevskiy Palace Hotel
Yves Rocher
Mayakovskiy Central Library
Rubinshteyna
Vladimirskiy prospekt
Dmitrovskiy p.
Mayakovskovo
Photo Shop
Federal Express
Souvenir Shop
Fairn and Swanson Shop
Zenit Sport Store
Khudozhestvenny
Univermag Voyentorg
Biryuza
Babylon-2 Shop
Stremyannaya
Povarskoy
Marata
Vostochnye Sladosti Candy
Kolizey
Itereny Theater
Universal Restaurant
Neva
Nevskiy Rest.
Mayakovskaya
John Bull Pub
Kafe Polyarnoye
Tekhnicheskaya Kniga Bookstore
Baskin-Robbins
Chas Pik
Pushkinskaya
Vosstaniya
Oktyabrskaya Hotel
Ligovskiy
Orlovskiy p.
Sovetskaya
Heritage Art Gallery
Ploshchad Vosstaniya
Pharmacy No. 65
Ploshchad Vosstaniya
Oktyabrskaya Hotel (Annex)
prospekt
Nevskiy prospekt
Goncharnaya
Moscow Station

St. Petersburg City Street Map Index

ABBREVIATIONS AND GLOSSARY

B., Bolshoy, -aya, -oye: big, great
bul., bulvar: boulevard
estakada: overpass
kanal: canal
M. Maly, -aya, -oye: small, little
liniya: line
most: bridge
nab. naberezhnaya: embankment
Nizhniy, -yaya, -oye: lower
Novy, -aya, -oye: new
ostrov: island
P.S.: Petrodradskaya storona
p., per., pereulok: side street
pl,. ploshchad: square
pos., poselok: village
proliv: sound
pr., proyezd: passage
prosek: lane
prosp., prospekt: avenue
reka, reki: river
sh., shosse: highway
Sr., Sredniy, -yaya, -oye: middle
St,. Stary, -aya, -oye: old
tupik: blind alley
ul., ulitsa: street, avenue
V.O.: Vasilyevskiy ostrov
V., Verkhniy, -yaya, -oye: upper
val: rampart, embankment

This map utilizes the most current "official" names of streets, squares and metro stations, as designated by the St. Petersburg government and in force in early 1994. This index lists both the previous and current street names, with appropriate cross-referencing. The maps label all features with *current names only*. In fact, many street names may have been officially changed, while the newly designated name is not yet in common use.

The index includes the Russian generic terms (abbreviated, see table at left) for all the streets listed. Please note that the generic "ulitsa" (street) has been omitted from the street names on the map.

FINDING STREETS

This index lists streets alphabetically by the "main word" in the street's name, rather than by the way in which the street name is commonly written (i.e. in the Yellow and White Pages) or spoken. Thus, "ulitsa Marata" or "ulitsa Gogolya" would be found in the index under "Marata ul." or "Gogolya ul.", respectively. "Naberezhnaya Kanala Griboyedova" is under "Griboyedova Kanal nab." Under this system, the reader need not know whether the street is a prospekt, shosse or ulitsa to find it in the index and on the map.

© 1994, Russian Information Services, Inc.

All rights reserved, no reproduction is permitted, by any means, electronic or mechanical, without the expressed written permission of Russian Information Services, Inc. This map was designed and produced by Northern Cartographic, of Burlington, VT.

STREETS

BRIDGES

For a list of summer bridge-raising schedules, see page 86, in the Yellow Pages.

LOCALITIES

METRO STATIONS

RIVERS & ISLANDS

River/Island	Coord.	Pg.
Kamenny Ostrov	G10	6
Kanal Griboyedova	I16	22
Kanonerskiy Ostrov	C19	9
Karpovka (river)	G12	17
Krestovka (river)	F11	6
Krestovskiy Ostrov	D11	5
Kronverskiy Proliv	H14	21
Kryukov Kanal	H17	25
M. Neva (river)	F13	10
M. Nevka (river)	G11	6
Monastyrka (river)	L17	28
Morskoy Kanal	C19	9
Moyka (river)	I15	22
Neva (river)	O19	12
Obvodny Kanal	L18	28
Olkhovka (river)	E19	9
Ostrov Dekabristov	D13	9
Petrogradskiy Ostrov	H13	17
Petrovskiy Ostrov	F13	10
Pryazhka (river)	G17	25
Rezvy B. Ostrov	D19	9
Rezvy M. Ostrov	E19	9
Smolenka (river)	F14	10
Sr. Nevka (river)	E11	5
Vasilyevskiy Ostrov	E15	9
Volkovka (river)	K19	11
Yekateringofka (river)	E19	9
Yelagin Ostrov	E11	5
Zhdanovka (river)	F13	10

SQUARES

Square	Coord.	Pg.
Aleksandra Nevskovo, pl.	M17	28
Belinskovo, pl.	J15	22
Chernyshevskovo, pl.	I23	14
Dachnoye pl.	F26	14
Dekabristov, pl.	H15	21
Dvortsovaya pl.	I15	22
Grecheskaya pl.	K15	23
Isaakiyevskaya pl.	H16	21
Iskusstv, pl.	I15	22
Kalinina, pl.	M12	20
Kazanskaya pl.	I15	22
Kirovskaya pl.	F20	14
Kommunarov, pl., see Nikolskaya pl.	H17	25
Komsomolskaya pl.	E22	13
Konnaya pl.	L17	28
Konyushennaya pl.	I15	22
Krasnogvardeyskaya pl.	N14	11
Kulibina, pl.	G17	25
Lenina, pl.	K13	19
Lomonosova, pl.	J16	22
Lva Tolstovo, pl.	H12	17
Manezhnaya pl.	J15	22
Mira, pl., see Sennaya pl.	I16	22
Morskoy Slavy, pl.	D16	9
Moskovskaya pl.	I25	14
Moskovskiye Vorota pl.	I20	14
Muzhestva, pl.	K8	7
Nikolskaya pl.	H17	25
Ostrovskovo, pl.	J16	22
Petrovskaya pl.	E13	9
Pionerskaya pl.	J17	26
Pobedy, pl.	I26	14
Proletarskoy Diktatury, pl.	M14	24
Pushkinskaya pl.	H14	21
Radishcheva, pl.	K15	23
Rastrelli, pl.	M14	24
Repina, pl.	G17	25
Revolyutsii, pl., see Troitskaya pl.	I13	18
Sennaya pl.	I16	22
Shevchenko, pl.	G15	21
Stachek pl.	F19	10
Suvorovskaya pl.	I14	22
Svetlanovskaya pl.	I8	6
Sytninskaya pl.	H13	17
Teatralnaya pl.	G16	21
Tekhnologicheskaya pl.	I17	26
Troitskaya pl.	I13	18
Truda, pl.	G16	21
Turgeneva, pl.	G17	25
Vitebskaya pl.	I17	26
Vladmirskaya pl.	J16	22
Vosstaniya pl.	K16	23

TRANSPORT

Station	Coord.	Pg.
Baltic Train Station	H19	10
Finland Train Station	K13	19
Maritime Passenger Terminal	D17	9
Moscow Train Station	K16	23
Vitebsk Train Station	I17	26
Warsaw Train Station	H19	10

Nobody Covers Russia Better

Business & Travel Guides

Russia Survival Guide
The essential guide to doing business in the new Russia, now in its 4th edition. (March 1994, $18.50)

Where in Moscow
Essential directories and color city street map, now in its third edition. (March 1994, $13.50)

Where in St. Petersburg
Essential directories and color city street map, updated and now in its 2nd edition. (March 1994, $13.50)

Language

Business Russian
The practical Russian you need to know for doing business in Russia. (May 1993, $16)

Maps

New Moscow City Map & Guide
A meticulously-accurate color map of the capital city. (March 1994, $6.95)

New St. Petersburg City Map & Guide
The first new Western city map of St. Petersburg in decades. (April 1993, $6.95)

Travel Information

Russian Travel Monthly
What to read to keep up-to-date on the latest business and independent travel news. (Monthly, $36/yr.)

Reference Information

Russian News Abstracts
Indexed abstracts of over 1900 key articles from the Russian press during 1993 (1992 volume also avail.). (April 1994, $48)

Legal Information

Business Legal Materials: Russia
A monthly listing of current Russian legal acts related to trade and investment. (Monthly, $225/yr)

Russian Business Legal Materials: 1992
A comprehensive, indexed listing of over 800 Russian laws related to foreign trade with, and investment in, Russia. (February 1994, $68)

Access Russia Catalogue

Be sure to also ask for a copy of ***Access Russia,*** our catalogue of over 130 publications on Russia by over 40 US and European publishers.

For more information,
or to place an order, contact:

Russian Information Services, Inc.

89 Main St., Box 2
Montpelier, VT 05602
ph. (802) 223-4955
fax (802) 223-6105

B. Kondratyevskiy per. 4
Moscow, Russia
ph./fax (095) 254-9275